The Wonderful World of Country Music

The Wonderful World of Country Music

by Jeannie Sakol

A GD/PERIGEE BOOK

The publishers gratefully acknowledge permission to reprint material from the following:

From *Bluegrass* by Bob Artis, copyright © 1975 by Bob Artis. Reprinted courtesy of Hawthorn Books, Inc.

From "Songs of Outlaw Country" by Pete Axthelm, published in *Newsweek* magazine March 12, 1976. Copyright © 1976 by Pete Axthelm. Reprinted by permission of the Sterling Lord Agency, Inc.

From "Oedipus Rocks" by John Eskow, published in *New Times* magazine May 29, 1978. Copyright © 1978 by John Eskow. Reprinted by permission of the author and publisher.

Perigee Books
are published by
The Putnam Publishing Group
200 Madison Avenue
New York, New York 10016

Library of Congress catalog card number: 78-58113
ISBN 0-399-50819-8
First Perigee Printing, 1983
Three previous Grosset & Dunlap printings
Printed in the United States of America
1 2 3 4 5 6 7 8 9

Acknowledgments

The word "thanks" is totally inadequate to express the gratitude, affection, and overall good feelings I have for all the wonderful people who gave me aid, comfort, and their precious time in putting this book together. Working with all of you has been an experience I shall treasure always.

Thank you: Jo Walker, Executive Director, Country Music Association, for your encouragement and help and to your superb staff including Ann Booth, Toby Cannon, and Marcia Gepner; Danny Hatcher and Diana Johnson, Country Music Foundation and Hall of Fame; Betty Arnold, Monument Records; Dot Boyd, RCA Records; Kelly Delaney, MCA Records; Kay Dickerson, Jim Halsey, Inc.; Carolyn Gilmer, United Artists Records; Laura Loncteaux, Asylum/Elektra; Kathy McClintock, The Oak Ridge Boys; Marianne McCready, CBS Records; Maureen O'Connor, Capitol Records; Janet Rickman, Mercury Records; Bonnie Rasmussen, Warner Brothers/Reprise Records; Suzanne Weller, Warner Brothers/Reprise Records; Fran Boyd, the Academy of Country Music; Irish Bahan, WSM, Nashville; Dan Beck and Don Cusic of Southern Sky; Bill Bentley, KLRN TV, Austin, Texas; John Dotson, CBS Records; Joan Guertin, Universal Management; James E. Gray, Custom Productions; Jack Hurst, *Chicago Tribune;* Jerry Juroe, Universal Pictures; Brenda Kim, Monument Records; Dean May, Acuff-Rose; David Merrick, producer of *Semi-Tough;* Danny O'Neill, WNYC TV, NYC; Betty Oliver, KLRN TV, Austin, Texas; Dolores Smiley, William Morris Agency; Ellen Stolzman, CBS Records; Jerry Strobel, Grand Ole Opry; Steve Tisch, producer *Outlaw Blues;* Paul Wells, John Edwards Memorial Foundation.

Also: Lee Arnold and Dale Pon, WHN, NYC; Loreen Joy Arbus, ABC TV; Ronnie Bennett, ABC TV; Laurel Fry, Phyllis Grygalin, *People* magazine; Harlann Lebo, The White House, Washington, D.C.; Hugh O'Lunney; Mort Persky, *Playboy;* Louise Scruggs; John Sturdivant, Tree Publishing.

Special thanks to: Pete Axthelm for his tribute to Willie Nelson and to Barbara Walters for her interview with Dolly Parton.

And to Lanning Aldrich for his helpful suggestions; Gerald Ament for always being available; Michael Kosser, for a lot of things, including taking me to the Elliston Place Cafe for down-home cooking; Madeleine Morel and Diane Oliver, for help above and beyond the call of friendship; the folks at the Spence Manor Hotel, Music City, Nashville, for putting me up and putting up with me.

And finally, Grosset & Dunlap for perceiving the broad universal appeal of country music; John Golden, my editor, for his patience and brilliance in working with me on the manuscript; Diana Price for understanding my problems.

And Stephanie Bennett, my partner in Delilah Communications, and chief hand-holder, crying towel, and friend.

Introduction

I got to country by way of folk: John Jacob Niles's "The Golden Vanity," Burl Ives's "The Wayfaring Stranger," Pete Seeger's "Frontier Ballads," then moving along to Woody Guthrie's songs of the Great Depression and union struggles, Josh White with his shirt slashed to the waist groaning "Outskirts of Town" and Susan Reed, Harry Belafonte, The Weavers—all of them leading to my discovery of Flatt and Scruggs and Bill Monroe, then Johnny Cash and The Carter Family and all the permutations forwards, sideways, and backwards that come about when interest and passions are stirred.

Growing up in New York City, I didn't know the word "hillbilly" was pejorative. My childhood boy friend, Buddy Meyers, and I were crazy about Homer and Jethro ("Somewhere Over the Rainbow—Ho!") and considered them and Minnie Pearl as hilarious as our major culture heroes, S.J. Perelman and Henry "Here's" Morgan. Buddy's imitation of Bob Wills's "San Antonio Rose" was punctuated with an "Ah—ah-haaaa" that echoed through our Riverside Drive playground. It was someuiing I could never get my voice to do then—or later when I tried to yodel along with Roy· Acuff's "Freight Train Blues" and Tennessee Ernie's "Rockabye, I'm Gonna Be a Daddy, Now."

About 1961, I discovered bluegrass. Flatt and Scruggs were giving a concert at the Ethical Culture Society in New York. I had never seen or heard anything like it till then—and still in my possession is the Carnegie Hall program for December 8, 1962, their first concert there that sold out and was repeated a week later. About that time, too, the popular folk place in town was Gerde's Folk City in Greenwich Village, with artists like Doc Watson singing "Bury Me Beneath the Willows" and playing Carter Family tunes on the autoharp.

In the most basic sense, I am an audience, doomed by a gross voice and the manual skills of a turtle to do little more than listen. Two years of recorder lessons have resulted in one nervous chorus of "Go Tell Aunt Rhody," made even more hazardous by a terrible compulsion to laugh.

Where, some may ask, does folk leave off and country start? I, for one, don't particularly know or especially worry about that question. The music and lyrics themselves are what count, whatever the label. For me, the enjoyment is intense. My response is a sight-and-sound kaleidoscope of all my senses. I am crazy with desire for Dink who moved his body like a cannonball, furious with Barbry Allen for scorning Sweet William, gleeful with erotic expectation as Meri Wilson reveals her plugged-in experience with the telephone man. I dream "The Wreck on the·Highway" and of a parched Leadbelly calling to Sylvie for a drink of water.

I feel deprived at not having known Dylan *or* Mary Travers when they were playing the Village coffee houses, though I have seen Sonny Terry and Brownie McGhee in numerous New York gigs. I've traveled far to see the New Lost City Ramblers, and I have special warms for Ramblin' Jack Elliott.

I love Roy Clark, Glen Campbell, and The Oak Ridge Boys, and June's responses to Johnny Cash in their duet, "Jackson." I love every version I've ever heard of "The House of the Rising Sun"—and once played Woody Guthrie's and Bob Dylan's simultaneously and nearly died of aural arrest.

I'd love to find a singer named Larry Mohr who appears on an Odetta LP singing "Pay Day" and to shake hands with Darryl Duke for directing a

Minnie Pearl

film of the same name, starring Rip Torn, which gives the most accurate, dramatic, and poignant view of the country singer's life of any movie I've ever seen.

I could stretch a billboard from here to Nashville to list the artists and songs I love. Kris Kristofferson. Willie Nelson. Jimmy Buffett. Dolly Parton. Loretta Lynn. Elvis. Johnny Paycheck. The Kendalls. Kenny Rogers. Dottie. Emmylou. Crystal. Linda.

I mourn Janis Joplin. I may not be the queen of the Silver Dollar, but often I seek the late-night benediction of the "y'all come back saloon" and do pause and consider the longing and losses of my life Sunday morning come down.

My own brown eyes "pore pore" pitifully blue, I too, am ready for the times to get better.

Jeannie Sakol
New York City

Willie Nelson

© 1976 Melinda Wickman

Academy of Country Music

The Academy was founded in 1964 by Eddie Miller, Tommy Wiggins, and Mickey and Christ Christiansen in Los Angeles. Their aim: to promote country music. Their activities include concerts, radio and TV shows, showcase productions for upcoming performers, and the Annual Academy of Country Music Awards to performers, musicians, and composers.

The 1977 award show, "I Am Country Music," hosted by Kenny Rogers, Donna Fargo, and Barbara Mandrell at the Shrine Auditorium, was televised nationally, May 23, 1977, on ABC TV.

Award Winners for 1965
Man of the Year......................................Roger Miller
Top Male Vocalist...................................Buck Owens
Top Female Vocalist..............................Bonnie Owens
Best Song Writer.....................................Roger Miller
Best Bandleader or Band.........................Buck Owens
Best Vocal Group.........Bonnie Owens/Merle Haggard
Best TV Personality.....................................Billy Mize
Best Radio Personality...............................Biff Collie
Best Producer/A&R Man..........................Ken Nelson
Best Talent Management....................Jack McFadden
Best Music Publisher..............................Central Songs
Best Music Publication..................Billboard Magazine
Best Nightclub.....................................The Palomino
Most Promising Male Vocalist..............Merle Haggard
Most Promising Female Vocalist..............Kaye Adams
Best Steel Guitar...Red Rhodes
Best Fiddle..Billy Armstrong
Best Lead Guitar...Phil Baugh
Best Bass..Bob Morris
Best Piano..Billy Liebert
Best Drums..Muddy Berry

Award Winners for 1966
Man of the Year......................................Dean Martin
Top Male Vocalist...............................Merle Haggard
Top Female Vocalist.............................Bonnie Guitar
Song of the Year............................"Apartment No. 9"
          (Bobby Austin/Fuzzy Owens/Johnny Paycheck)
Best Bandleader......................Buck Owens Buckaroos
Best Vocal Group.........Bonnie Owens/Merle Haggard
Best TV Personality.....................................Billy Mize
Best Radio Personality...............................Biff Collie/
                                                Bob Kingsley (Tie)
Best Producer/A&R Man..........................Ken Nelson
Best Talent Management....................Jack McFadden
Best Music Publisher..............................Central Songs
Best Country Nightclub..........................The Palomino

Most Promising Vocal Group....................Bob Morris/
                                                    Faye Hardin
Most Promising Male Vocalist......................Billy Mize
Most Promising Female Vocalist............Cathie Taylor
Best Steel Guitar....................................Tom Brumley/
                                            Ralph Mooney (Tie)
Best Fiddle..Billy Armstrong
Best Lead Guitar....................................Jimmy Bryant
Best Bass..Bob Morris
Best Piano..Billy Liebert
Best Drums..Jerry Wiggins

Award Winners for 1967
Man of the Year......................................Joey Bishop
Top Male Vocalist...............................Glen Campbell
Top Female Vocalist............................Lynn Anderson
Song of the Year....."It's Such a Pretty World Today"
Best Album...........*Gentle on My Mind*/Glen Campbell
Best Bandleader/Band.............Buck Owens/Buckaroos
Best Vocal Group.........................Sons of the Pioneers
Best Duet......................Merle Haggard/Bonnie Owens
Best TV Personality.....................................Billy Mize
Best Radio Personality.............................Bob Kingsley
Best Producer/A&R Man..........................Al DeLory
Best Music Publisher.............................Freeway Music
Most Popular Country Nightclub.......... The Palomino
Most Promising Male Vocalist..................Jerry Inman
Most Promising Female Vocalist..........Bobbie Gentry
Best Steel Guitar...Red Rhodes
Best Lead Guitar....................................Jimmy Bryant
Best Piano...Earl Ball
Best Bass...Red Wooten
Best Fiddle..Billy Armstrong
Best Drums..Pee Wee Adams

Woody Guthrie

Award Winners for 1968

Country Music Man of the Year...........Tom Smothers
Directors' Award..................................Nudie
Pioneer Award.........................."Uncle Art" Satherly
Most Promising Female.........................Cheryl Poole
Most Promising Male............................Ray Sanders
Top Female Vocalist.............................Cathie Taylor
Top Male Vocalist................................Glen Campbell
Album of the Year...............................*Glen Campbell and Bobbie Gentry*
Single Record of the Year (Award to Artist)................
"Little Green Apples"/Roger Miller
Song of the Year (Award to Composer)....................
"Wichita Lineman"/Jim Webb
Top Vocal Group..................Johnny & Jonie Mosby
Band of the Year (Club)........Billy Mize's Tennesseans
Band of the Year (Touring)......................Buckaroos
Radio Personality (Regional)..................Tex Williams
Radio Personality (Los Angeles)...............Larry Scott
TV Personality......................................Glen Campbell
Country Nightclub (Regional)............Golden Nugget
Country Nightclub (Metropolitan)................Palomino
Steel Guitar..Red Rhodes
Piano...Earl Ball
Lead Guitar.......................................Jimmy Bryant
Fiddle..Billy Armstrong
Drums...Jerry Wiggins
Bass...Red Wooten

Award Winners for 1969

Man of the Year.............................John Aylesworth/
Frank Peppiatt (Tie)
Pioneer Award...................................Bob Wills
Jim Reeves Memorial Award.....................Joe Allison
Man of the Decade.........................Marty Robbins
Specialty Instrument...........................John Hartford
Rhythm Guitar....................................Jerry Inman
Comedy Act..Roy Clark
Most Promising Male Vocalist..............Freddy Weller
Most Promising Female Vocalist............Donna Fargo
Top Female Vocalist.........................Tammy Wynette
Top Male Vocalist..........................Merle Haggard
Album of the Year........................*Okie from Muskogee*
Single Record of the Year......."Okie from Muskogee"
Song of the Year....................."Okie from Muskogee"
Top Vocal Group....................................Kimberlys
Band of the Year..............Merle Haggard's Strangers
Disc Jockey.......................................Dick Haynes
TV Personality....................................Johnny Cash
Nightclub.......................................Palomino Club
Steel Guitar....................................Buddy Emmons
Piano...Floyd Cramer
Lead Guitar...Al Bruno
Fiddle..Billy Armstrong
Drums...Jerry Wiggins
Bass...Billy Graham

Award Winners for 1970

Man of the Year..Hugh Cherry
Jim Reeves Memorial Award........................Bill Boyd
Pioneer Award............Tex Ritter/Patsy Montana (Tie)
Entertainer of the Year.........................Merle Haggard
Top Male Vocalist.................................Merle Haggard
Top Female Vocalist.............................Lynn Anderson
Album of the Year.......................*For the Good Times*
Single Record of the Year........"For the Good Times"
Song of the Year....................."For the Good Times"
Top Vocal Group.......................................Kimberlys
Most Promising Male Vocalist...................Buddy Alan
Most Promising Female Vocalist............Sammi Smith
Country Nightclub...............................Palomino Club
TV Personality.......................................Johnny Cash
News Publication..Billboard
Radio Station......................KLAC, Los Angeles
Disc Jockey..........................Corky Mayberry (KBBQ)
Comedy Act..Roy Clark
Band of the Year
(Non-Touring)......................The Tony Booth Band
Band of the Year (Touring)....................The Strangers
Steel Guitar...J. D. Maness
Piano...Floyd Cramer
Lead Guitar...Al Bruno
Fiddle..Billy Armstrong
Drums...Archie Francis
Bass..........................Billy Graham/Doyle Holly (Tie)

Glen Campbell

Award Winners for 1971

Man of the Year.......................................Walter Knott
Jim Reeves Memorial Award.....................Roy Rogers
Pioneer Award...Bob Nolan/
    Stuart Hamlin/Tex Williams (Tie)
Entertainer of the Year.............................Freddie Hart
Top Male Vocalist.....................................Freddie Hart
Top Female Vocalist.................................Loretta Lynn
Album of the Year..*Easy Lovin'*
Single Record of the Year.................."Easy Lovin' "/
    Freddie Hart
Song of the Year....................................."Easy Lovin'"
Top Vocal Group...........Conway Twitty/Loretta Lynn
Most Promising Male Vocalist...................Tony Booth
Most Promising Female Vocalist......Barbara Mandrell
Country Nightclub...............................Palomino Club,
    North Hollywood, California
TV Personality....................................Glen Campbell
Radio Station................................KLAC, Los Angeles
Disc Jockey....................................Larry Scott (KLAC)
Comedy Act...Roy Clark
Band of the Year (Non-Touring)......Tony Booth Band
Band of the Year (Touring)............................Strangers
Steel Guitar..J. D. Maness
Piano...Floyd Cramer
Lead Guitar...Al Bruno
Fiddle...Billy Armstrong
Drums...Jerry Wiggins
Bass...Larry Booth

Award Winners for 1972

Man of the Year.................................Lawrence Welk
Jim Reeves Memorial Award.............Thurston Moore
Pioneer Award.............Cliffie Stone/Gene Autry (Tie)
Entertainer of the Year................................Roy Clark
Top Male Vocalist...............................Merle Haggard
Top Female Vocalist...............................Donna Fargo
Album of the Year........................*Happiest Girl/USA*
Single Record of the Year........"Happiest Girl/USA"/
    Donna Fargo
Song of the Year......................."Happiest Girl/USA"
Top Vocal Group.............................Statler Brothers
Most Promising Male Vocalist.........Johnny Rodriguez
Most Promising Female Vocalist...........Tanya Tucker
Country Nightclub...............................Palomino Club,
    North Hollywood, California
TV Personality...Roy Clark
Radio Station................................KLAC, Los Angeles
Disc Jockey....................................Larry Scott (KLAC)
Band of the Year
(Non-Touring)................................Tony Booth Band
Band of the Year (Touring)............................Strangers
Steel Guitar..Buddy Emmons
Piano...Floyd Cramer
Lead Guitar...Al Bruno
Fiddle...Billy Armstrong
Drums...Jerry Wiggins
Bass...Larry Garner (Booth)

Warner Bros. Records/Curb Records

Debby Boone

Award Winners for 1973

Song of the Year..................."Behind Closed Doors"/
    Kenny O'Dell
Entertainer of the Year................................Roy Clark
Single of the Year.................."Behind Closed Doors"/
    Charlie Rich
Top Female Vocalist of the Year............Loretta Lynn
Top Male Vocalist of the Year.................Charlie Rich
Album of the Year.....................*Behind Closed Doors*/
    Charlie Rich
Most Promising Female Vocalist.............................
    Olivia Newton-John
Most Promising Male Vocalist............Dorsey Burnette
Top Vocal Duet or Group of the Year....................
    Brush Arbor
Country Night Club............................. The Palomino,
    North Hollywood, California
Band of the Year (Non-Touring)......Sound Company/
    Ronnie Truhett
Band of the Year (Touring).....................Brush Arbor
Steel Guitar..Red Rhodes
Piano...Floyd Cramer
Lead Guitar...Al Bruno
Fiddle...Billy Armstrong
Drums...Jerry Wiggins
Bass...Larry Booth
Jim Reeves Memorial Award.................Sam Louvello
Pioneer Award..Hank Williams
Disc Jockey of the Year Award.................Craig Scott/
    WJJD, Chicago
Radio Station of the Year............KLAC, Los Angeles

Award Winners for 1974

Bass Guitar..Billy Graham
Drums...Jerry Wiggins
Fiddle...Billy Armstrong
Lead Guitar...Al Bruno
Piano...Floyd Cramer
Steel Guitar...J. D. Maness
Country Disc Jockey of the Year...............Larry Scott
Country Radio Station of the Year...................KLAC
Band of the Year (Touring)..........................Strangers
Band of the Year
(Non-Touring)........................The Palomino Riders
Country Night Club of the Year.........Palomino Club
Most Promising Female Vocalist..........Linda Ronstadt
Most Promising Male Vocalist................Mickey Gilley
Top Vocal Group of the Year................Loretta Lynn/
Conway Twitty

Roy Clark

Album of the Year..........................*Back Home Again*/
John Denver
Male Vocalist of the Year.....................Merle Haggard
Female Vocalist of the Year....................Loretta Lynn
Single of the Year.......“Country Bumpkin”/Cal Smith
Entertainer of the Year...............................Mac Davis
Song of the Year......“Country Bumpkin”/Don Wayne
Jim Reeves Memorial Award..................Merv Griffin
Pioneer Award.....................................Merle Travis/
Tennessee Ernie Ford/Johnny Bond (Tie)

Award Winners for 1975

Bass..Billy Graham
Drums...Archie Francis
Fiddle..Billie Armstrong
Lead Guitar...Russ Hansen
Piano..Jerry Lee Lewis
Steel Guitar..J. D. Maness
Rhythm Guitar..Jerry Inman
Country Radio Station of the Year...................KLAC,
Los Angeles, California
Country Disc Jockey of the Year.............Billy Parker/
KVOO, Tulsa, Oklahoma
Country Music Night Club of the Year.......Palomino/
North Hollywood, California
Band of the Year (Touring).........................Strangers/
Merle Haggard
Band of the Year (Non-Touring)......Palomino Riders/
Jerry Inman
Most Promising Female Vocalist.............Crystal Gayle
Most Promising Male Vocalist..............Freddy Fender
Top Vocal Group...........Conway Twitty/Loretta Lynn
Album of the Year..*Feelings*/
Loretta Lynn/Conway Twitty
Male Vocalist of the Year.....................Conway Twitty
Female Vocalist of the Year....................Loretta Lynn
Single Record of the Year...... “Rhinestone Cowboy”/
Glen Campbell
Entertainer of the Year...........................Loretta Lynn
Song of the Year................... “Rhinestone Cowboy”/
Glen Campbell
Jim Reeves Memorial Award....................Dinah Shore
Pioneer Award...Roy Rogers

Award Winners for 1976

Bass..Curtis Stone
Fiddle..Billy Armstrong
Drums...Archie Francis
Lead Guitar.......................................Danny Michaels
Piano..Hargus “Pig” Robbins
Steel Guitar...J. D. Maness
Rhythm Guitar..Jerry Inman
Radio Station...............................KLAC, Los Angeles
Disc Jockey.......Charlie Douglas, WWL, New Orleans
Night Club......................Palomino, North Hollywood
Band of the Year (Touring)..............Red Rose Express
Band of the Year (Non-Touring)...........Possum Holler
Most Promising Female Vocalist..........Billie Jo Spears
Most Promising Male Vocalist..................Moe Bandy
Top Vocal Group...........Conway Twitty/Loretta Lynn
Album of the Year.........................*Gilley's Smoking*/
Mickey Gilley
Male Vocalist of the Year......................Mickey Gilley
Female Vocalist of the Year....................Crystal Gayle
Single Record of the Year..........“Bring It On Home”/
Mickey Gilley
Entertainer of the Year...........................Mickey Gilley
Song of the Year.........................“Don't the Girls Get
Prettier at Closing Time”/Mickey Gilley

ABC Dot/The Jim Halsey Co., Inc.

Jim Reeves Memorial Award......................Roy Clark
Pioneer Award...Owen Bradley

Award Winners for 1977

Bass...Larry Booth
Fiddle..Billy Armstrong
Drums....................Archie Francis/George Manz (Tie)
Guitar..Roy Clark
Keyboard.................................Hargus "Pig" Robbins
Steel Guitar...Buddy Emmons
Specialty Instrument..........Charlie McCoy, Harmonica
Radio Station of the Year.............KGBS, Los Angeles
Disc Jockey of the Year...........................Bill Parker/
KVOO, Tulsa, Oklahoma
Country Night Club of the Year.................Palomino/
North Hollywood
Band of the Year (Touring).........Asleep at the Wheel/
Sons of the Pioneers

Dolly Parton and Porter Wagoner

Band of the Year (Non-Touring)........Palomino Riders
Top New Female Vocalist.......................Debby Boone
Top New Male Vocalist...........................Eddie Rabbitt
Top Vocal Group..............................Statler Brothers
Album of the Year....................................*Kenny Rogers*
Top Male Vocalist of the Year...............Kenny Rogers
Top Female Vocalist of the Year...........Crystal Gayle
Single Record of the Year......"Lucille"/Kenny Rogers
Entertainer of the Year............................Dolly Parton
Song of the Year.................."Lucille" (Kenny Rogers)
Career Achievement...........................Johnny Paycheck
Jim Reeves Memorial Award.......................Jim Halsey
Pioneer Award.......................The Sons of the Pioneers

MCA Records/United Talent, Inc.

Kenny Rogers

Loretta Lynn and Conway Twitty

Acuff, Roy Claxton

Born: September 15, 1903, May-
nardville, Tennessee
Married: Mildred Louise Douglas
Children: s. Roy Neill, Jr.

Roy Acuff was the first living artist
elected to the Country Music Hall of
Fame (1962). He cofounded the
Acuff-Rose Publishing Company,
the first music publishers devoted
exclusively to country music.

I wore out my first copy of *Great
Speckled Bird and Other Favorites,*
couldn't get enough of "Wreck on
the Highway," "Fireball Mail,"
"Low and Lonely," and especially,
"Freight Train Blues," which fills
me with longing for a time and place
I have never known and can only
know through Roy.

While the phrase "living legend"
would embarass him, that's what he
is, his lifetime a history of country
music in America. Growing up in
the beautiful Smoky Mountains, his
father at various times a postmaster,
farmer, Baptist minister, and lawyer, young Roy played the Jew's
harp and harmonica and made fiddles out of cornstalks (cleaning out
the pulp, leaving strips for strings,
and playing with a stick!). Later his
father taught him to play a real fiddle but not as a means of livelihood.

Roy wanted to be a professional
baseball player. At sixteen he was
the star athlete at Central High
School in Fountain City, a suburb
of Knoxville to which the family had
moved. He also acted in everything
from Shakespeare to minstrel
shows, but it was at sports that he
truly excelled. He earned a record
thirteen athletic letters, although he
weighed a mere 130 pounds and was
nicknamed "Rabbit." Small but
cocky, he played semipro ball until
the hot July day in 1929 when he collapsed in the outfield from sun-
stroke. During his two-year re-
cuperation, he improved his fiddle
playing and began to sing. Instead
of throwing a baseball, he took up
his later famous sport—the Yo-yo.

It wasn't till 1932 that his music
career actually began when a friend

Hickory Records, Inc. Acuff-Rose Artists, Corp.

asked him to join a traveling medicine show. After this came Roy's
own band, Roy Acuff and His Crazy
Tennesseans, who could be heard on
Knoxville radio stations WROL and
WNOX. In 1936, they recorded
"Great Speckled Bird" for Columbia. In 1938, they made their debut
on Grand Ole Opry, changing the
group's name to the Smoky Mountain Boys. Unlike many country
groups, Roy's did not wear cowboy
clothes but dressed like country people instead. Pete Kirby, known as
Bashful Brother Oswald, in bib
overalls, played dobro, guitar, and
banjo and sang tenor. Other members included Rachel Veach and her
five-string banjo, Jimmie Riddle on
harmonica, piano, and accordion,
and Jackie Phelps who later joined
"Hee Haw" on TV.

Acuff is the acknowledged king of
country music, and his records have
sold into the hundred millions. He
has toured the world, performing at
military bases and doing concerts.
In 1943, he and Fred Rose formed
the first—and now the world's largest—country music publishing
house, expanding in the 1950s to include Hickory Records. His other
interests include Dunbar Cave,
Clarksville, Tennessee, a tourist at-
traction with cave tours, peacocks,

swimming and golf. A hobby exhibit
in Nashville displays his collections
of old musical instruments, phono-
graphs, miniature whiskey bottles,
dolls, early song books, and other
memorabilia, including the original
fiddle played by Uncle Jimmy
Thompson on the first Opry broadcast in 1925.

His brief fling in politics began
with an insult. In October 1943, the
Opry went coast to coast. Tennessee
governor Prentice Cooper refused to
attend the celebration at Ryman
Auditorium, saying Roy Acuff was
bringing disgrace to Tennessee by
making it the Hillbilly capitol of the
world. Some reporters, who thought
Acuff would make a better governor, collected qualifying signa-
tures. Not knowing if he were a Re-
publican or Democrat, they filed
with both. After toying with the

idea, Roy withdrew, only to run again in 1948 when he drew enormous crowds but insufficient votes to win.

According to his best-known biographer, Elizabeth Schlappi, Roy's secret phobias include automatic elevators, cats, and sleeping alone or in the dark. He loves thunderstorms and has a small white looped rope tied on his ukelele "to catch snakes with." Of lasting pleasure to him is the battle cry of a Japanese banzai soldier during an attack on the U.S. Marines in the Pacific during World War II: "To hell with President Roosevelt, to hell with Babe Ruth, to hell with Roy Acuff!" As Schlappi concludes, this was fast company for a Smoky Mountain boy but, "Roy Acuff deserves the company."

Roy's films include: *Grand Ole Opry* (1940); *Hi, Neighbor* (1942); *O, My Darling Clementine* (1943); *Cowboy Canteen* (1944); *Sing, Neighbor Sing* (1944); *Night Train to Memphis* (1946); *Smoky Mountain Melody* (1947); *Home in San Antone* (1949).

Agencies Booking Country Acts

Acuff-Rose Artist Corp.
2510 Franklin Rd.
Nashville, TN 37402
(615) 297-5366

Allied Artists of America
4209 E. Lancaster
Ft. Worth, TX 76103
(817) 534-1363

Allstar Artist Agency
Box 9411
North Hollywood, CA 91609
(213) 335-9379

Americana Corp.
Box 47
Woodland Hills, CA 91364
(213) 347-1976

Andrews Enterprises
PO Box 175
Mt. Morris, MI 48458
(313) 787-8186
Contact: Joan Andrews

ARCO Enterprises
1516 16th Ave.
Nashville, TN 37212
(615) 298-5471
Contact: X. Cosse

Artist Management Bureau
8533 Sunset Blvd.
Los Angeles, California
(213) 652-4200

Ashley-Famous Agency
9255 Sunset Blvd.
Los Angeles, CA 90069

Atlas Artist Bureau
119 Two Mile Pike
Goodlettsville, TN 37072
(615) 859-1343
Contact: Haze Jones

Attarack-Heller Corp.
9220 Sunset Blvd.
Hollywood, CA 90069

Ray Baker
PO Box 162
Madison, Tennessee
(615) 865-1445

Bojac Management
PO Box 1533
Nashville, TN 37202

Brite-Star Promotions
728 16th Ave.
Nashville, TN 37203
(615) 244-4064
Contact: Wally Carter

Jack Brumley Talent
3925 S. Chester Ave.
Bakersfield, California

Chalet Record Co., Inc.
108 Thompson La.
Nashville, TN 37211

Chartwell Artists, Ltd.
2720 Wilshire Blvd.
Beverly Hills, CA 90212

Cherokee Agency
894 N. Garey
Suite 110
Pomona, California
(714) 629-0610
Contact: Frank Jey

Country Talent Agency
806 16th Ave. S.
Nashville, TN 37203
(615) 256-4170

Creative Management Associates, Inc.
600 Madison Ave.
New York, NY 10022
(212) 935-4000

Billy Deaton Productions
1314 Pine St.
Nashville, TN 37203
(615) 244-4259

Drake Talent Agency
809 18th Ave. S.
Nashville, TN 37203
(615) 327-3211

Lester Flatt Artist Service
New Schackle Island Rd.
Hendersonville, Tennessee
(615) 824-0142

Tillman Franks Enterprises
604 Commercial Bldg.
Shreveport, Louisiana
(318) 423-5886
Contact: Tillman Franks

Sam Gibbs Agency
2709 Armory Rd.
Wichita Falls, TX 76302
(817) 767-1457
Contact: Sam Gibbs

Jim Halsey Co., Inc.
6922 Hollywood Blvd.
Hollywood, CA 90028
(213) 462-2378
Contact: Jim Halsey

Dick Heard Artist
Management
813 18th Ave. S.
Nashville, TN 37208
(615) 327-0022
Contact: Dick Heard

Horseshoe Productions
3008 117th St.
Hammond, IN 46323
(219) 845-8053
Contact: Webb Foley

J & J Talent Service
PO Box 574
Winchester, VA 22601
(703) 662-3520
Contact: Jim McCoy

Jet Set Enterprises
4167 San Jose Blvd.
Jacksonville, FL 32207
(904) 398-3786
Contact: Sidney Drashin

Jack D. Johnson Talent
PO Box 40484
Nashville, TN 37204
(615) 383-6564
Contact: Jack D. Johnson

Key Talent Agency
1531 Demonbreun St.
Nashville, TN 37203
(615) 242-2461
Contact: E. Jimmy Key

Shorty Lavender
Talent, Inc.
722 17th Ave. S.
Nashville, TN 37203
(615) 244-5265
Contact: Shorty Lavender

Buddy Lee Attractions
806 16th Ave. S.
Nashville, TN 37203
(615) 244-4336

Don Light Talent, Inc.
816 19th Ave. S.
Nashville, TN 37203
(615) 327-4785
Contact: Don Light

Hubert Long International
1513 Hawkins St.
Nashville, TN 37203
(615) 244-9550
Contact: Hubert Long

Bill Lowery Talent, Inc.
1224 Fernwood Circle N.E.
Atlanta, Georgia
Contact: Bill Lowery

Les Malachuk Promotions
194 Hunting Creek Rd.
Canonsburg, PA 15317
(412) 745-2455
Contact: Les Malachuk

Metro Country Talent
PO Box 567
Hendersonville, Tennessee

Moeller Talent
2106 Crestmore Rd.
Nashville, TN 37215
(615) 383-6666
Contact: Lucky Moeller

Montgomery Booking
Agency
8914 Georgian Dr.
Austin, TX 78753
(512) 836-3201
Contact: Ray Montgomery

William Morris Agency
1150 Avenue of the
Americas
New York, NY 10019
(212) 586-5100

National Artists
Attractions
6 Danny Thomas Blvd.
Memphis, TN 38103
(901) 525-8341
Contact: Ray Brown

Neal Agency, Ltd.
2325 Crestmoor Ave.
Nashville, TN 37215
(615) 385-0310
Contact: Bob Neal

OMAC Artist Corp.
403 Chester Ave.
Bakersfield, CA 93301
(805) 327-7201

One-Niters, Inc.
111 Lyle Ave.
Nashville, TN 37203
(615) 244-1145
Contact: Billy Smith

Pipeline Enterprises
425 W. Pipeline Rd.
Hurst, TX 76053
(817) 282-1701
Contact: Budde Harbal
Tom Schneider

Gerard Purcell &
Associates
150 E. 52nd St.
New York, NY 10022

Marty Robbins Enterprises
713 18th Ave. S.
Nashville, TN 37203
(615) 327-4940

Jack Roberts Agency
10222 N.E. First St.
Bellvue, WA 98004
(206) 455-2600
Contact: Jack Roberts

Scruggs Talent Agency
201 Donna Dr.
Madison TN 37115
(615) 868-2254
Contact: Louise Scruggs

Sea Cruise Productions
PO Box 6329
New Orlenas, LA 70114
(504) 367-0415
Contact: Ken Keene

Skylight Talent, Inc.
1008 17th Ave. S.
Nashville, TN 37215
(615) 244-6116

Sound Incorporated Agency
203 Courtland Ave.
Baltimore, MD 21204
(301) 828-1303
Contact: Richard Fay

Cliff Steele Management
PO Box 246
1480 Quince Ave.
Atwater, CA 95301
(209) 358-3525
Contact: Cliff Steele

Sumar Talent Agency
912 17th Ave. S.
Nashville, TN 37203
(615) 329-4272
Contact: Joe Taylor

Top Billing, Inc.
110 21st Ave. S.
Nashville, TN 37203
(615) 327-1041
Contact: Tandy Rice

Town & Country
Enterprises Agency
242 Lakeshore Dr.
New Toronto, Ontario
Canada
(416) 252-3145

Variety Attractions, Inc.
Box 2276
Zanesville, Ohio
Contact: Jim Wagner

Shane Wilder Talent
PO Drawer M
Palm Springs, CA 92262
Contact: Jim Wagner

Wil-Helm Agency
801 16th Ave. S.
Nashville, TN 37203
(615) 244-1403
Contact: Larry Hart

Williams & Price
8831 Sunset Blvd.
Hollywood, CA 90069
Contact: Don Williams

Skip Williams Agency
5332 Plaze Rd.
Peoria, IL 61604
(309) 685-5975
Contact: Skip Williams

Wright Talent Agency
Box 516
Goodlettsville, Tennessee
(615) 859-2446
Contact: Joe Wright

Alan, Buddy

Born: May 22, 1948, Tempe, Arizona
Married: Jane
Children: s. Paul, Douglas

Buddy Alan is the son of superstar Buck Owens and the beautiful Bonnie, now Mrs. Merle Haggard. In his own right, Buddy Alan is a respected solo performer, session guitarist, and writer. Among his best records are duets with Don Rich, "Cowboy Convention," and "I'm on the Road to Memphis." He purposely avoided cashing in on father's fame, yet if you listen carefully you'll hear the talent he has inherited and worked at to develop.

Allen, Rex, Sr.

Born: December 31, 1924, Wilcox, Arizona
Married: Bonita Lindner
Children: s. Rex, Jr., Curtis, Mark; d. Bonita

Beginning as an authentic rodeo cowboy who became a singing cowboy star on WLS "National Barn Dance" radio show in Chicago during the forties, Allen moved on to his own TV show in 1950, "The Rex Allen Show," and then to movies for Republic Pictures and Walt Disney Productions. He was elected to the Cowboy Hall of Fame in 1968, and he is a songwriter as well as a singer, with some two hundred songs published. Hit recordings include: "Crying in the Chapel" (1953) and "Don't Go Near the Indians" (1962).

Allen, Rex, Jr.

Birthday: August 23

Since he joined with Warner Brothers in 1974, he's logged such hits as "Can You Hear Those Pioneers," "Play Me No Sad Songs," and "Another Good-bye Song" while also managing to bring his spirited baritone to one of the most successful TV commercials of the decade, "Me and My R.C." Ef-

Rex Allen, Jr.

fective with traditional standards like "Streets of Laredo" and "San Antonio Rose," he brings special contemporary meaning to "Cryin' in the Rain," "I Can See Clearly Now," and his own composition, "I Gotta Remember to Forget You." Among his albums are *Rex,* which includes "Two Less Lonely People," "Let Me Love You Once Before You Go," and "Don't Say Goodbye." By the summer of 1978, this younger Rex Allen had firmly established himself on top of the charts with such hits as "No, No, No, (I'd Rather Be Free)."

American Fiddlers News

This publication is a fifty-page quarterly devoted to "preserving and promoting the art and skill of old-time fiddling and its related arts and skills." It covers everything played on the fiddle/violin anywhere in the world. It has reviews of records, books, and music, and information on repairs, contests, bluegrass, Western hoedown, and so forth. Classified ads. International information exchange.

Annual Membership dues: $5. For information, write: American Fiddlers, 6141 Morrill Avenue, Lincoln, NB 68507.

Anderson, Bill

Born: November 1, 1937, Columbia, South Carolina
Married: Bette (div.), Becky
Children: d. Terri Lee, Jennifer; s. James William IV

Bill Anderson learned to play the guitar at twelve and organized a country band in high school. His first professional appearances were on Atlanta, Georgia, radio and TV. While he was earning his bachelor's degree in journalism at the Univ. of Georgia, Bill was a DJ at WGAU, Athens, and WJJC in Commerce. He joined the Opry in June 1961. A prolific songwriter of nearly one thousand songs, his first big hit was

"City Lights" in 1958. In 1960, the nation's DJs named him among the top five country and western songwriters and top three performers. Superstardom in the sixties catapulted him into the realms of palatial homes, Cadillacs, a bus with a telephone, and business interests from real estate to men's fashions. One of his favorite stories dates from March 1961 at the Chestnut Inn in Kansas City, Missouri. Bill's "Walk Out Backwards" was number one in Kansas City and he was requested to sing it continually. After one session a man grinned boozily and said, "You sure sing that good." Bill said, "Thank you." Encouraged, the man added, "You sing a lot better than that guy on the record."

Forty Acre Farms and *Las Vegas Hillbillies* were two films in which he appeared.

Lynn Anderson

Anderson, Liz

Born: March 13, 1930, Roseau, Minnesota
Married: Casey Anderson
Children: d. Lynn

Liz was a songwriter first and then a performer. Some of her most famous compositions are Merle Haggard's first hit, "All My Friends Are Going to Be Strangers," Conway Twitty's, "Guess My Eyes Were Bigger Than My Heart," "Ride, Ride, Ride," and "Big Girls Don't Cry."

Anderson, Lynn

Born: September 26, 1947, Grand Forks, North Dakota
Married: Glenn Sutton (div.), Harold Stream
Children: d. Lisa Lynn

Beauty, talent, sweetness, dedication, and an instinct for being in the right place at the right time add up to the incredible Lynn. Daughter of Liz Anderson (a successful songwriter) and Casey Anderson (a successful music publisher), she went to Nashville with her mother in 1967 "just for the ride," signed up with Chart Records, fell in love with and married Epic Records biggie Glenn Sutton and had her first hit, "Promises, Promises" in 1968. Soon switching over to Columbia Records, she became a regular on "The Lawrence Welk Show" and won a Grammy in 1971 for Best Female Country Vocal Performance. She made country music history with "I Never Promised You a Rose Garden," which earned a RIAA certified gold record for both the single and the LP. Among her chart-toppers are "You're My Man," "Top of the World," "Cry," and "He Turns It into Love Again." In late 1978, her "Last Love of My Life" made the Cash Box charts. Lynn's gorgeous blonde hair and perfect features add to the impact of her talents on such TV shows as "Tonight," "Merv Griffin," "Mike Douglas," and "Hee Haw." As if all this and her family were not enough, Lynn is an accomplished equestrienne, with hundreds of trophies and ribbons in quarter horse competitions, both local and international. Very much the concerned citizen, she is Youth Advisor for the Tennessee Quarter Horse Association and gives considerable time to raising funds for Easter Seals, Christmas Seals, and Cerebral Palsy. Maybe nobody ever promised her a rose garden, but she has earned it as well as a stately Nashville mansion, a swimming pool, and a happy family life.

Arnold, Eddy

Born: May 15, 1918, Henderson, Tennessee
Married: Sally Gayhart
Children: s. Richard E. (Dickie); d. Jo Ann

The most frequent word you hear about Eddy Arnold is *perfectionist.* Known as the Tennessee Plowboy, he is nevertheless the epitome of sleek sophistication, with his well-tailored appearance and smooth style even when singing something as rural as "Cattle Call," one of the thirteen number-one hits in a career that has seen an incredible 70 million records sold. In 1966 he was elected to the Country Music Hall of Fame; in 1967 he was named Entertainer of the Year by the Country Music Association. An SRO topliner at state fairs and summer theaters, he also breaks attendance records for concerts in places as disparate as Pittsburgh and Seattle and is a regular among the long-haired fans of symphony orchestras in Atlanta, Dallas, Denver, Hartford, Memphis, Phoenix, etc. He drew 46,583 fans at Houston's Astrodome. Add to this New York's august Carnegie Hall, L.A.'s Coconut Grove, every major TV network variety show in the U.S. and Europe, sitting in for Johnny Carson, cohosting with Mike Douglas, hosting more then forty of his own TV specials—and you get some small idea of his versatility and impact. Among his biggest songs are "Bouquet of Roses," "That's How Much I Love You," "Anytime," "Make the World Go Away," and my favorite, "What's He Doing in My World?" It's fascinating that this sharecropper's son learned to play the harmonica and guitar while working in the fields with his brothers. Early appearances on WMPS in Memphis led to small club dates in St. Louis and finally to an RCA Records contract in 1944.

Eddy Arnold

In addition to performing, he is an astute businessman; his interests include real estate, land development, music publishing, and food franchising. Past president and honorary governor of the Nashville Chapter of the National Academy of Recording Arts and Sciences, he spends whatever spare time he can enjoying boating, fishing, and golfing. In describing himself, he says, "I'm a Heinz 57 Variety singer—I sing many different kinds of songs which mean something different to many different kinds of people." One of the first to bridge the gap between down-home and urban tastes, he is proud to be credited with this attitude but firmly shares the spotlight with Tennessee Ernie Ford, citing his classic "Sixteen Tons" as an example. "I want to see country music find its own dignity and not just be the kind of music found in beer joints and dives," says Arnold.

Ashworth, Ernie

Born: December 15, 1928, Huntsville, Alabama
Married: Bettye
Children: s. Mike, Mark, Paul; d. Rebecca

Ernie Ashworth joined Grand Ole Opry in 1964, known for "Talk Back Tremblin' Lips" on Hickory Records. He won Most Promising Country and Western Artist awards from both *Billboard* and *Cash Box* in 1963 and from *Record World* in 1964. Writer or cowriter of over four hundred songs, he also recorded "Each Moment" and "You Can't Pick a Rose in December."

Association of Country Entertainers

This is a nonprofit organization (1300 Division Street, Nashville, TN 37203, (615) 256-0201); membership is composed entirely of established country music artists and entertainment celebrities who derive their living as country performers.

Purposes of the association include the improvement of country entertainers' working conditions, career opportunities, and to help deserving performers in time of crisis or emergency.

Country music fans are invited to participate in programs of the Association through the ACE Boosters organization. The Boosters are fans and other interested persons who do not qualify for membership in ACE as established entertainers. Although ACE is a professional organization, with strict membership requirements, its Boosters organization is open to anyone wanting to participate.

Atkins, Chet

Born: June 20, 1924, Luttrell, Tennessee
Married: Leona Johnson
Children: d. Merle

Starting life as Chester Burton Atkins on a fifty-acre farm in the Clinch Mountains, he grew up in rural poverty. His father, James, was an old-time fiddler who also had formal music training. His early life was dominated by an old wind-up phonograph, Jimmie Rodgers records, and an asthmatic condition. At 18, he was a fiddler on WNOX, Knoxville, and toured with Archie Campbell and Bill Carlisle. Later, he auditioned—unsuccessfully—for a job with Roy Acuff's Smoky Mountain Boys; he didn't get the job and instead went to WLW, Cleveland, where he met and married the local vocalist, Leona Johnson. In 1946, he joined Red Foley at the Grand Ole Opry, making Nashville his permanent home in 1950, the year of his success with "Galloping Guitar." With over thirty RCA albums and many singles to his name, he is acknowledged to be a leading force in the development of Nashville as a primary music center. When RCA built a sophisticated recording complex there in 1957, Chet master-

RCA Records and Tapes

minded the operation and in 1968 became division vice president and a leader in the phenomenon known as the Nashville Sound. As *Record World* at the time noted, "No individual has been more responsible than Chet Atkins."

As a performer he has appeared with various symphony orchestras, at the historic Newport Jazz Festival of 1960, for President Kennedy at the White House, and with the Boston Pops, drawing from a repertoire ranging from Bach to Spanish classics, pop, rock, and country. Chosen Outstanding Instrumentalist for thirteen consecutive years by *Cash Box,* he has won the *Playboy* poll as Best Guitarist four times, a Grammy for Best Contemporary Instrumental Performance of 1967 (for "Chet Atkins Picks the Best"), the Best Country Instrumental Perfor-

mance in 1971 (for "Snowbird"), and in 1973 was elected to the Country Music Hall of Fame. For guitar freaks, two important classics are the "Atkins-Travis Traveling Show" he made with his best friend Merle Travis in 1974 and "Chester and Lester" with Les Paul in 1976.

Perhaps one of the most noteworthy historic facts of Chet Atkins's career was the time in late 1955 when RCA's Steve Sholes asked his assistance in recording a newly signed performer—Elvis Presley. The record was "Heartbreak Hotel," the success of which led to the new RCA studios in Nashville, with Atkins in charge. Among other performers to whom he gave A & R guidance were Jerry Reed, Hank Snow, Floyd Cramer, Perry Como, and Curley Putman. The famous Chet Atkins style of guitar tech-

nique depends on rhythmic bass notes sounded with the thumb of the right hand with the melody picked out by three fingers while sounding the strings with the fingernails and a thin thumbpick. His classical guitar heroes are Andres Segovia, Julian Bream, and John Williams, though he pays respectful tribute to Merle Travis and Django Rheinhardt.

Chet Atkins Note for Note

This collection contains nine guitar solos transcribed exactly as played by the great instrumentalist. Includes chord diagrams, instructional text, playing and performance hints. 72 pages. Illustrated.

Send $4.95 to Music Sales Corporation, 33 West 60 Street, New York, NY 10023 (or call, toll free, 800-223-7326).

Austin City Limits

During the early unsettled seventies, the popular music industry began turning to the past, reviving artists, remaking old hits, and exploring underdeveloped musical styles for new possibilities. It is no wonder, then, that heads have turned to look at the music scene of the Southwest, focused in Austin, Texas.

There has always been a wealth of regional sounds in the Southwest, but now they flourish in conjunction with contemporary country music, the most popular sound emerging from Austin. It has been variously tagged as progressive country, cross-country, redneck rock, cosmic country, underground country, and so on. In general, it is a style that digs back into a variety of traditional country music roots and, at the same time, moves forward into contemporary interpretations. Instrumentation is usually simple and direct, yet innovative, and the lyrics are relevant to life-styles and attitudes of the 1970s. It is an honest and forthright approach that brings out the potential of an underdeveloped country and western idiom. But, perhaps more importantly, the Austin progressive country scene provides a vigorous and thriving musical environment, nurturing not only itself, but other musical forms ranging from traditional/ regional to contemporary jazz.

Austin music supports a very lively scene of more than two hundred bars and clubs; only eight are discos, while more than eighty offer live music. It is indeed remarkable that such an intense musical scene has grown so quickly in the city.

Austin, a pleasant medium-sized city of 300,000, is in many ways a veritable oasis. Culturally, music flourishes there because of an anticommercial attitude, a local pride of community, and a strong sense of regionalism. Where else but in such a metaphorical oasis could the myth survive that the "magic" sounds of Austin's contemporary country music have the power to transform rednecks into "cosmic cowboys" and hippies into "redneck rockers"?

Michael Murphey

The Texas Playboys

Ernest Tubb

Steve Goodman

Johnny Rodriguez

The musical environment of the Southwest hasn't always been so hospitable. Although the area has continuously produced outstanding musicians, representing virtually every musical style (blues, rhythm and blues, rock and roll, swing, jazz, zydeco, conjunto as well as country and western), in the past many have felt the need to move to other parts of the country to pursue musical careers. Today many Texans are returning, and many Texans-at-heart have joined in to revitalize and develop the music of the Southwest.

The turnaround began in 1972 when the talented singer/composer Willie Nelson gave up on a traditional Nashville country music establishment and accepted the hospitality and appreciation of Texas and Austin audiences. Although he's not the originator of the "scene," Willie became the catalyst and gave it validity, introducing the area to other "outlaws" from the Nashville sound, while simultaneously supporting the efforts of regional artists to develop the potential of country music.

Willie became a sort of cult hero, attracting seventy thousand fans to his Third Annual Fourth of July Picnic in 1975. His informality of dress and sincere smile have bridged cultural as well as generation gaps and have helped set a mood for the growth of a wide range of music in Austin's thriving, yet relaxed, musical environment. With the help of Willie, "family," and friends, Austin has become the center of the fastest-growing musical movement in the country.

Gove Scrivenor

"Austin City Limits"

This TV series was produced for PBS by KLRN TV, Austin, Texas. Begun in 1975 to chronicle the rise of the "Austin" sound, also known as outlaw, redneck rock, progressive, cosmic, and even underground country, the

PBS

Chet Atkins

sound is really a blend of many styles—blues, rock 'n' roll, swing, folk, country, bluegrass, and traditional. Seen on some 124 TV stations coast to coast in 1978, "Austin City Limits" presented live-audience concerts by such performers as the following.

Michael Murphey—composer and performer of "Wildfire," "Carolina in the Pines," "Paradise Tonight," "Song Dog," and "Nothing's Your Own"—was born in Dallas and studied Greek in preparation for joining the ministry. But instead, he moved to California, married, had a son, wrote four hundred songs for such stars as Roger Miller, Bobbie Gentry, and Flatt and Scruggs, and found a home at last in Colorado.

John Prine grew up in Chicago and worked for the post office until Kris Kristofferson heard him play at a local club, the Fifth Peg, in 1970. His first LP, *John Prine* came out in 1971. One of the best examples of his unique way of mixing tragedy, comedy and foolishness is "Bottomless Lake."

John Hartford has been described as a "sophisticated man, dry humorist, author, poet . . . who can really pick a banjo, play a hypnotic fiddle, and make magic with a six-string guitar." Born in New York City, and reared in St. Louis, his musical roots are bluegrass, his childhood idol, Earl Scruggs. He was the composer of "Gentle on My Mind," which made Glen Campbell a superstar and won Hartford three Grammys.

The Dillards have been together since 1962, but Rodney is the only "real" Dillard (his brother Doug joined the Byrds in 1967), the others being Dean Webbon, mandolin; Billy Ray Lathum, banjo; Paul Alvin York, drums; Jeff Gilkinson, bass.

Jesse Winchester, Memphis born, lives in Canada with his wife and three children. He's the composer of "Nothing but a Breeze," "Yankee Lady," and "Mississippi." Appearing with him are David Lewis, drums; Michael Francis, guitar; Ron Dann, guitar and dobro.

Mother of Pearl, organized in 1975, has become one of Texas's most captivating groups, the nucleus coming from Plum Nelly, an Austin rock band. And Jerrie Jo Jones is being hailed as the next Janis Joplin. She and Don Fisher formed the group that includes Ernie Gammage, Johnny Richardson, and Layton DePenning.

Chet Atkins and Merle Travis. Chet named his daughter after Merle Travis, the man he credits with being the largest single influence in his musical development as a guitarist. Creator of the "Nashville Sound," Atkins has discovered such talents as Connie Smith, Dottie West,

Charley Pride, Roger Miller, and Roy Orbison; Travis, born in the coal mining community of Rosewood, Kentucky, wrote "Sixteen Tons," "Nine Pound Hammer," "Smoke, Smoke, Smoke that Cigarette," "Dark As a Dungeon," and "I Am a Pilgrim."

Johnny Rodriguez and Linda Hargrove. She wrote "Just Get Up and Close the Door" for him, and it zoomed to number one on the charts. Lynn Anderson and Olivia Newton-John have also recorded her songs. As a performer, she is known for "Blue Jean Country Queen," "Music Is Your Mistress," and "All Alone in Austin." Rodriguez had the surprise of his life while taping "Austin City Limits": Willie Nelson wandered onstage to join him for a historic impromptu of "Come on in, Stay a Little Longer."

Tracy Nelson and Willie Nelson are not related except by music and a joint appearance on "Austin City Limits," where Tracy sings her 1974 Grammy Award, "After the Fire Is Gone," which she recorded with Willie. Her big voice first emerged as a folk singer in 1967, and her fame grew as she toured and recorded with Mother Earth. Born during the Depression, in Texas, Willie

Merle Travis

Linda Hargrove

John Hartford (center) and The Dillards

The Texas Playboys was founded by the late Bob Wills in the mid-thirties, directed now by Leon McAuliffe, who originally joined the band in 1935. Among their classics are "San Antonio Rose," "Faded Love," and "Take Me Back to Tulsa."

Ernest Tubb and the Texas Troubadours were one of the originators of the honky-tonky sound, and Tubb was among the first singers to incorporate western swing into the traditional Grand Ole Opry Nashville sound. His "Walking the Floor over You" has sold three million copies. Continuing favorites include "Take Me Back and Love Me One More Time" and "It Don't Hurt Anymore."

Nelson's first job at age ten was playing rhythm guitar with a Bohemian polka band. After his house in Nashville burned down, Willie settled down outside Austin and became one of the creators of the Austin Sound.

Doc Watson was born in Stoney Fork, North Carolina, in 1923. His daddy made him a banjo out of a hickory sapling when he was three; but he moved up to guitar and was soon playing square dances, gaining wide attention during the "folk boom" of the sixties. Among his country classics are "Rain Crow Bill" and "Will the Circle Be Unbroken?"

Gove Scrivenor plays bottleneck-style guitar with a rich, expressive voice, and his one-man band consisting of harmonica, autoharp, and "foot" provide the percussion. Among his selections are: "Poor Howard" and "Change Partners."

Steve Goodman was discovered by Kris Kristofferson who heard him performing in Chicago's "Old Town," and subsequently told friends he had heard "the greatest pickin' songwriter in the world." (But then it was Goodman who two years later took Kris to hear John Prine!) Goodman's the composer of "You Never Called Me By My Name" and "City of New Orleans." His LP *Say It in Private* includes: "Men Who Love Women," "The Twentieth Century Is Almost Over," and "Video Tape."

John Prine

27

Bandy, Moe

Born: February 12, 1944, Meridian, Mississippi

He sings pure hardcore honky-tonk, the kind of music that empties beer glasses and caused one critic to call him the Jesus Christ of country music. A former sheet-metal worker, Bandy says, "I'm a cornbread country boy. I could sing 'Jingle Bells' and it would come out country." His big CBS hit, *Soft Lights and Hard Country Music,* includes "Pa-

Columbia

per Chains" and "That's What Makes the Jukebox Play," with backing by such top Nashville musicians as Charlie McCoy, Hargus "Pig" Robbins, Johnny Gimble, Reggie Young, Kenny Malone, and Tommy Allsup. Moe's grandfather worked the railroads with Jimmie Rodgers, whose records were the first young Moe heard. In 1950, the Bandy family moved to San Antonio, Texas, where Moe's father started a local band, the Mission City Cowboys, and gave Moe a guitar. In high school, he rode wild

bulls in rodeos until a series of broken bones "steered" him to concentrate solely on music. After high school, he became a sheet-metal worker by day and country-music singer at night until 1964 when Satin Records released "Lonely Lady" in San Antonio and he began performing on a local TV show, "Country Corner."

More years of writing and trying took him to 1973 when "I Just Started Hatin' Cheatin' Songs Today" put him in the top five of the national charts. Following this came "Honky-Tonk Amnesia," "It Was Always so Easy to Find an Unhappy Woman," "Doesn't Anyone Make Love at Home Anymore?" and "Bandy the Rodeo Clown." In 1975, producer Ray Baker brought Moe to CBS with "Hank Williams You Wrote My Life" and continued with such consistent top-ten hits as "The Biggest Airport in the World," "I'm Sorry for You My Friend," "Here I Am Drunk Again," and "Two Lonely People," a 1978 Top Twenty single and hit LP *Love Is What Life's All About.*

Banjo

History of the 5-String Banjo
by Louise Scruggs
(from a paper read at the Annual Meeting of the Tennessee Folklore Society, November 12, 1960.)

No sound is more deeply rooted in American history than the thrilling ring of the banjo. Our national instrument almost a hundred years ago, it was played by many thousands of people. And yet, by 1940, the instrument and the secrets of playing it had nearly died out. Modern Americans had almost forgotten the friendly country ring of that fifth string until a group of young enthusiasts refused to let it die and once again began strumming on the ol' banjo.

Today. . .the old-time banjo, and the wonderful music once played on it, are enjoying a new vogue. This American folk art was saved principally through the unreconstructed stubbornness of certain musicians in the Appalachian Mountains and the Carolinas, who simply paid no attention when they were told the banjo was dead.

The banjo has a romantic history to match its sparkling sound. The ancient ancestor of the banjo, an instrument called the rebec, originated in Arabia a thousand years ago and can still be purchased today in the larger marts of the Middle East. It consists of a skin head stretched over a gourd or hollow body, with a neck holding three gut strings.

The rebec was probably carried both east and west with the spread of Islam. Negro slaves brought it to the United States from North and West Africa. In his *Notes on the State of Virginia,* published in 1785, Thomas Jefferson says the "banjar" was the principal musical instrument of the American Negroes.

By this time the banjo had developed into a four-string instrument. But the true American banjo was not invented until about 1830 when a banjo enthusiast named Joe Sweeney made a small but revolutionary modification. He added a fifth string, higher in pitch than any of the others, right next to the lowest-pitched string, and secured by a peg mounted halfway up the neck.

This odd instrument, with four pegs at the top of the neck and one peg sticking out on the side, captured the heart of America. The five-string banjo is therefore sometimes called America's most original and distinctive musical invention.

Joe Sweeney, the inventor of the five-string banjo, was born in Appomattox, Virginia, in 1810. He died at home in 1860. At an early age,

Sweeney organized his own Appomattox band. He composed many songs based on the melodies created by the slaves he knew and loved. Billed as the "Banjo King," he made a hit on the New York stage after a wagon tour through the South and Pennsylvania. His fame carried him to England where he appeared before Queen Victoria at a command performance. Research has disclosed that what is believed to be "America's first banjo" is now in the possession of the Los Angeles County Museum in California.

The fifth string is the "blend" in the banjo. It is plucked by the thumb in various intricate and ingenious ways, while the other fingers are busy on the other four strings. No other instrument in the world is strung like the American five-string banjo, and entirely new playing methods were invented unique to this instrument.

Thousands of nameless Americans developed these playing methods during long evenings in log cabins, sod shanties, river steamboats, and gold-mining boom towns. The banjo went west in covered wagons and was enjoyed by both whites and Negroes throughout the nation. No two people had exactly the same method for working in that fifth string. For that matter, many people used four or five different tunings and changed both the tunings and the style to play different songs.

Little music has ever been written for the banjo. Instead, a tremendous amount of lore developed, passed on from player to player. The old folks taught the young ones, and good players swapped style secrets. In a nation of rugged individualists, the banjo was an appropriately individualistic instrument!

Banjoists played "old-time songs" —what we now call folk music. The popularity of the banjo was important in perpetuating and preserving many old folk songs that would otherwise have been forgotten. In addition, a special body of banjo music began to develop—and this, too, is

Uncle Dave Macon and Dorris Macon

now part of America's folk-music heritage. For the most part, the authors of this music are virtually unknown, as are the inventors of the principal playing styles.

Throughout the nineteenth century, the banjo held its place in America's affections. But around the turn of the century a decline set in.

The advent of jazz was an important factor in this decline. Jazz musicians altered the banjo and the method of playing it in order to adapt it to the new jazz combos. Joe Sweeney's fifth string was dropped off, completely killing the distinctiveness of the instrument. The neck was shortened, the head was enlarged, and heavier strings were used. The resulting four-string or "tenor" banjo was installed in jazz bands as a noisemaker. The old finger-picking styles were abandoned along with the fifth string; a pick was used, and the instrument was expected to produce enough

noise to be heard through a brass section. In some cases, the change went even further. The instrument was reduced to mandolin size and was strung with eight strings, like a mandolin.

Such instruments, of course, did not sound even remotely like the brilliant old-time banjo. These innovations apparently signaled the death knell of the five-string banjo. Only a few bands and a few natives of the more remote recesses of the South kept the old tradition going.

In the 1920s, when commercial recording companies put out their earliest folk discs, some of the remaining old-time banjo players were recorded. These records, once looked on as "beneath the notice of cultured people," are now among our most important sources of American folk music. Before country or folk music became highly commercial, these performers played true folk songs. The master discs were destroyed long ago, so the

Fretless banjos

records that survived are now rare, precious, and very costly collectors' items.

By 1930, even the four-string banjo was fading out. It was no longer used in jazz or popular music bands. As for the five-string instrument, fewer and fewer people remembered how to play it. America was on the verge of losing one of its most remarkable folk arts.

During these lean years, a few performers stuck stubbornly by their five-string banjos—certain players in old-time square-dance bands in the Southern mountains, and a few performers on country music radio shows such as the famous "Grand Ole Opry." Among the most famous of this era was Uncle Dave Macon, from Readyville, Tennessee. "Uncle Dave," as he was affectionately known, was a rotund minstrel with gold teeth and gold watch chain, whose uninhibited per-

formances on the five-string banjo were one of the Grand Ole Opry's best-loved attractions.

However, by 1940, even the country-music bands were dropping the five-string banjo, and apparently the end was in sight. The instrument was no longer even made. But by this time a few young purists and folklorists had discovered the five-string banjo and recognized it as one of our most remarkable contributions to the world's music. Several of them even went into the remote areas in the South and learned some of the playing styles and secrets from the few surviving players. These young folk musicians made some records with the five-string banjo. Almost as if by magic, the lost art was saved as it was on the brink of extinction. Soon after World War II a few bands, perhaps influenced by the growing interest of folklorists, began to use the five-string banjo again.

Earl Scruggs, who is now one of the leaders of the Flatt and Scruggs show on the Grand Ole Opry, had developed a sparkling new playing style that was soon being imitated throughout the nation. Earl introduced what is now known as Scruggs-Style Picking on the Grand Ole Opry in 1945. Earl's father, who was also a banjo player, was his greatest inspiration to master playing the banjo. Earl first began playing tunes on the banjo when he was five years old. Instead of the style he now uses, he could play with one finger and thumb. At the age of ten he developed a three-fingered style, or that using two fingers and thumb, which later was to give him national acclaim. After his appearance on the Grand Ole Opry, his style spread rapidly, caught on like a craze, and he is now receiving more national acclaim than any other artist in the folk music field. (In 1952, Earl invented a tuning device that made the banjo even more versatile. The tuners are two extra pegs mounted on the peghead that enable the player to change the pitch while playing.)

In the *New York Times* (1959), Robert Shelton wrote, "Earl Scruggs bears about the same relationship to the banjo that Paganini does to the violin." In a later *Times'* article, Shelton spoke of those superhuman qualities that have produced artists like Andres Segovia, Django Reinhardt, Charlie Byrd, and Earl Scruggs. . . .

Newsweek magazine has written that "the new aficionados discuss the merits of Earl Scruggs's three-fingered banjo playing as rabidly as jazzmen debate the far-out trumpet playing of Miles Davis."

Folk musicians have built up a following whose dedication begins to rival that of the most fervent jazz buffs. Indoor concerts are being held across the nation. It is not unusual to see artists play to filled halls holding one thousand to four thousand people. Furthermore, the bulk of the attendance comes from colleges and large urban centers.

Earl Scruggs is credited with

creating this veritable banjo epidemic and is responsible for the upsurge of interest in folk music. The Vega Company in Boston, Massachusetts, is now manufacturing twelve different styles of banjos. Two of these models were designed by Scruggs. *Time* magazine reports also that banjo sales increased over three hundred percent in two years (1958 and 1959).

And, perhaps most important of all, the scraps and fragments of the old-style playing of the old songs, and the pure, authentic sound of the old mountain banjo, have been preserved forever on long-playing records. Several recording companies have sent teams with tape recorders into the remote recesses of the South and have issued commercial long-playing records of some of the old-timers who are still living. Such an album has been issued by Folkways Records and titled *American Banjo: Songs and Tunes in Scruggs Style.*

Another of the popular old-time banjo styles is called beating, frailing, or thumbing the banjo. The basic strum consists of a combination of both picking individual strings and strumming whole chords. Such performers on the Grand Ole Opry who use this style are Grandpa Jones, Stringbean, and Oswald.

It is a thrilling and moving experience to hear the older versions of folk music. Today the whole nation is aware of the great mass of lore provided by the various peoples of this country. In the Library of Congress in Washington, D.C., there is stored a huge collection of phonograph records of folk songs and ballads. Preserved in record form, these songs can be heard by lovers of folklore long after the artists who sing them are gone.

American universities have sent their folklore scholars into the neighborhoods where groups with certain national characteristics live, in order to understand more fully their folklore. Those reports help us to understand all the people who make up America. Knowledge of a nation's folklore is knowledge of the creative workings of the minds of its folk. It is a key to a nation's value, a highway that leads into the heart of its people.

America owes much to these folklorists and to the grand old players of the five-string banjo who held staunch against the tide, who preserved a precious and wonderful American heritage when nobody else cared.

Banjo Newsletter

A monthly magazine that specializes in the history and playing aspects of the five-string banjo. Interviews with musicians and craftsmen; tablature of tunes for bluegrass/old-time /classic/jazz. Product evaluations and reviews of instructional material. Indexed at end of volume (October issue). In its fifth year with 5,700 subscribers worldwide. Monthly columns on Back-Up, Classic Banjo, Beginners Corner, Scruggs Style, Five-String Breakdown, Exploring the Fingerboard. It's $8 a year (U.S.); $9 a year (Canada); $11 a year (Foreign Surface); $27 a year (Foreign Air). *Banjo Newsletter,* 1310 Hawkins Ln., Annapolis, MD 21401. Editor/Publisher: Hub Nitchie.

Bare, Bobby

Born: April 7, 1935, Ironton, Ohio
Married: Jeannie
Children: s. Bobby, Jr.; d. Cari Jean, Sharon

Bobby Bare's first hit, "Detroit City," won the 1963 Grammy for Best Country and Western. Since then, he's hit the charts with "Miller's Cave," "Streets of Baltimore," "How I Got to Memphis," "Come Sundown," "Don't Tell Me How the Story Ends," and in late 1978, "Sleep Tight, Goodnight." LPs include *Lullabies, Legends, and Lies* and *Singing in the Kitchen,* which included the whole Bare family. A sad postscript was the death of his daughter, Cari, age fifteen, in 1976.

Bess, Tootsie (Hattie Louise)

Born: 1914, Hohenwald, Tennessee
Died: February 18, 1978, Nashville, Tennessee
Married: Big Jeff Bess

She was the legendary proprietor of Tootsie's Orchid Lounge on Lower Broadway in Nashville, located just a few steps from the backdoor of the Ryman Auditorium, home of the Grand Ole Opry until it moved to Opryland. Tootsie's is where Nashville newcomers would congregate to get acquainted, sing the songs they'd written, and try to make one beer last for hours. A tiny, spirited woman, described by writer Paul Hemphill as "jabbing the slow drinkers with a diamond-headed three-inch hatpin presented to her by Charley Pride," she was known as a soft touch for anyone sincerely struggling to make a career in country music.

R. W. Blackwood

Blackwood, R. W.

Born: Memphis, Tennessee,
Birthday: November 27
Married: Donna
Children: s. Robbie; d. Andrea

He grew up in the First Assembly of God Church along with another Memphis worshipper, Elvis Presley.

R. W. Blackwood and the Blackwood Singers and Rhythm Band

He and The Blackwood Singers and the Rhythm Band are a troupe of eight, including his wife and children, a rhythm quartet, and Judd, a country comic. Hits include: "Turn Your Radio On," "Sunday After-noon Boat Ride," "Daddy Sang Bass," "Put Your Hand in the Hand."

Bluegrass

Mountains and Music*
The Roots

The fiddle is again in vogue in pop-country circles. It never left bluegrass. Neither did the mandolin or five-string banjo. Bluegrass smoothed the squeaks out of the fiddle and brought the banjo out of the nineteenth century. It isn't "old-time" anymore, but if the music brought from the British Isles by the first white settlers has a modern heir, it's bluegrass and not modern "country music."

Music has been in the hills as long as people have been there. Some of the songs sung today as part of the standard bluegrass song bag could have been heard over two centuries ago, drifting through the mountains from the backs of creaking, ox-drawn wagons, out of cabin windows and log church houses. Many of them were rediscovered as folk songs several years ago, but most of the older bluegrass artists learned them from their parents, who learned them from their parents, and so on back through the dim and misty past of the dark, mossy hollows of central Appalachia.

The accents were once tinged with British and Scotch-Irish inflection, but eventually the slow life of the remote southern highlands melted speech into a drawl resembling that of their neighbors of the southern flatlands. Their traditions and music evolved into a personality and sound as uniquely mountain as it had once been British.

Life in Appalachia is hard even today, and we can imagine what it must have been like a century or two ago. Living often meant squeezing a bare-survival crop of corn from a mountaintop or valley-bottom dirt farm and keeping a few scrawny milk cows. There was some trapping, and logging provided work until most of the trees were gone and the mills shut down. Then, early in the twentieth century, the coal companies came, gouging and scarring the hills and ridges to feed the progress that was settling everywhere but in the mountains. Mining brought jobs and a new set of hazards: labor riots, cave-ins, and a disease called black lung.

*From *Bluegrass* by Bob Artis. Copyright © 1975 by Bob Artis. Reprinted courtesy of Hawthorn Books, Inc.

My own grandfather, Frank Dunn, was a coal miner from a little place called Coal Hill, Arkansas. He earned a good wage before World War I by going into new shafts, carbide lamp and kerosene lantern ablaze, checking for leaking gas. If gas was present, the flame of his lantern would ignite it and probably burn him to death. My grandmother, who was from Russellville, dreamed one night that he was carried home on a stretcher, badly burned. She was awakened by a knock at the door. It was one of his fellow miners; the nightmare had come true. A similar story is told in a bluegrass song, a tune from the older traditions called "Dream of the Miner's Child." Carter Stanley, one of the Stanley Brothers, sang the song. He, too, was once a coal miner.

Music was as much a part of life in the New World as it had been in the old. There were the old Protestant hymns and the ballads, and there was the highly ornamented fiddle music that the people danced to at weddings and corn-huskings. It was playful music, and the fiddle tunes, like the ballads and the hymns, were passed from father to son in an endless handing down of the musical traditions. Many of the old fiddle tunes—songs like "Devil's Dream" and "Billy in the Low Ground"—are also still a vital part of today's bluegrass.

The tradition of the fiddler still lives in most rural areas, in the mountains and elsewhere. It takes years to become a good fiddler; not everyone can cut it, and a good fiddler is something special. Technique as well as tradition have to be well within the fiddler's grasp, and those fifteen- and twenty-minute cake walks at the end of a night's square dancing are as physically demanding as pitching an inning of major-league baseball. While most square-dance callers today prefer to play records— they're consistent and cheaper than paying live musicians—an accomplished fiddler is still in demand and is becoming too scarce to suit a lot of people.

If there was a primary folk instrument, it was the fiddle. There were dulcimers, too, both the multi-stringed type based on the Hungarian cymbalon and the elongated northern European type popularized by Jean Ritchie. The dulcimers weren't widely used though; they could be popular in one hollow but virtually unknown in the surrounding area. The fiddle seemed more versatile and structurally durable, and thus easier to carry from place to place. It was the fiddle of the classic Italian shape and design that survived the changes of time in the mountains, as it did elsewhere.

Something new was added in the middle of the nineteenth century—the banjo. In the 1840s someone took the crude version, with its varying number of strings, standardized it, made it manufacturable, and arrived at a set number of strings. For the next half-century all banjos had five strings; four running the length of the instrument and a short, high-pitched fifth string running only halfway up the neck. A white minstrel named Joe Sweeney took credit for the "invention," and it became something of a musical rage. The Civil War drew many young men out of the mountains to the battlefields of the South, and they brought the concept of the banjo back home with them. By the turn of the century the banjo was being widely manufactured and sold through the mail order houses, and it was becoming so common in the hills that a country band was thought of in terms of the fiddle and banjo.

Like the mountain fiddlers, the mountain banjo pickers developed their own personal and regional styles. There was not even any set way of tuning a banjo, let alone playing one, and many used the minstrel styles, while others experimented with the possibilities. A three-finger style is often associated with the Carolinas, while some Kentuckians used just the thumb and first finger. But most used a sort of controlled down-strum that has come to us as "frailing" or "clawhammer" style, much like that played rather raucously by country comedian Louis "Grandpa" Jones. Whatever style was used, the people of the rural South found the five-string banjo almost as good as the fiddle for accompanying their ballads.

The mail order houses, with their thick, goods-laden catalogs, were a boon to the country people, who bought many of their manufactured goods through the mail, as well as seeds for planting and the patent medicines guaranteed to cure croup, quinsy, swelled breasts, gout, cold hands, and dandruff. The catalog showed them what was going on in the world of fad and fashion, music and the arts. Part of the fashion trend of 1900 was toward things Latin, as immigrants from southern Europe poured into the big American cities. Mandolin ensembles were making the concert rounds, and cheap prints of the *Battleship Maine* and *The Charge Up San Juan Hill* graced almost every wall. And two new instruments appeared in the catalogs: the guitar and the mandolin.

Progress was the key word as the new century bounded in. Changes were everywhere. Thousands poured into the mountains, digging coal, laying track, milling lumber. New railroads wound through the Blue Ridge and the Great Smokies, and electricity lit the streets of Galax, Virginia, and Hazard, Kentucky. New ideas were breaking the seal of a century of isolation and new gadgets were finding a welcome place in even the most remote dwelling.

Before technology began its fateful hike into the mountains, most music was confined to the hearth and home. After the day's work was done, the more musically inclined would sit around the fire or outside on the porch and sing. An old crone who was the mother of fifteen and called "aunt" by everyone for miles around would know several croaking verses of the song about "Fair Ellender," and the blind man rumored to be her son would play the fiddle while she sang, his keen ears following the chilling inflections of her voice. Back and forth the songs would go, each family member taking a turn. An old man, the brother of the old woman, would sing a song in the same style about Jonah being swallowed by the fish on his way to warn the citizens of

Nineveh of God's wrath at their wickedness. There seemed to be almost no melody or chords, just a continuing wail, high and mournful, until the storyline reached its end.

Then the old man would play one on his fiddle, just music, mumbling something now and again about "Shake that little foot, Sally Ann," and everyone would rock a little faster in their chairs and tap their feet. The younger kids would dance barefoot in the dust in front of the porch until they were told that the dust was getting a little too thick up where the grown-ups were. Things would get going, and someone would tell one of the kids to run up the creek bed and get the neighbors; tell the old man up there to bring his banjo.

That was their music; homemade and for the home. The fiddler inherited his instrument and songs from his father, the old woman got her songs from her mother, and no one remembered where it all started. There could have been several musicians just a few miles away, but if the folks at this particular cabin had heard of them, they had probably never seen them. Their limited style, whatever it was, consisted entirely of what they inherited from those who came before them along with the very little they added to it themselves.

The phonograph changed things. It was a revelation; now they had something to listen to and learn from, something from which to draw new ideas, a whole world of music for just a few cents a disc. Now an evening's entertainment might well mean sitting around listening to the old wind-up Victrola.

Next came the radio. Mass communication saw no greater boon than the little box that talked. There were several hundred commercial radio stations broadcasting by the early 1920s, many of them in the South. A lot of the programming was done live in those days (almost all of it, in fact), and the radio stations didn't have to look far to find good local talent. Country music had been home music before, strictly an amateur enterprise, but now the rural fiddlers and balladeers had a chance to take their music to a larger audience, and perhaps even turn professional.

It was just a matter of time before someone put the pieces together—the phonograph and the extensive radio play of country music—and decided that there might just be a market, however regional, for recordings of the rustic mountain sounds. As it happened, a recording company sales representative in Atlanta saw a flickering newsreel of a Georgia fiddlers' convention and was impressed not only by the size of the crowd but also by the audience's response to one of the fiddlers, a mountain man named "Fiddlin" John Carson. The Okeh Recording Company dispatched Ralph Peer to investigate.

The man Peer met in Atlanta in the spring of 1923 was as rough and crude as the moonshine he often bragged about making. Peer found Carson's oldtime fiddling, untrained mountain voice, and generally uncouth ways a little distasteful at first and reportedly had trouble convincing his company that the fiddler could sell records. But they released the material, and much to everyone's surprise, it sold well in the mountains.

A whole new field of music was opening up, and each year brought new discoveries and popular performers. There was healthy competition among the major recording companies to find good native talent whose music they could record, promote, and sell to the Southern regional market. The big companies began organizing and equipping field recording expeditions and sending them south.

The way in which talent was located involved a beautifully simple and direct approach. People like Ralph Peer and Columbia's Frank Walker would simply go into an area and run an ad in the local newspaper. Down they would come from the mountains, one by one: the bands, fiddlers, and balladeers. They would be auditioned, sorted and selected, rehearsed and recorded. The luckiest would get their work pressed into wax and put into commerical circulation throughout the South. Stars were being born, and bands like Gid Tanner and the Skillet Lickers (from northern Georgia) and Charlie Poole's North Carolina Ramblers were becoming as well known in the Southern mountains as Paul Whiteman and Ted Lewis were in the North.

To the folk purists the years between 1925 and 1935 were the Golden Years of country music. Much of what was being recorded for commercial release was authentic folk music, music that had been developing in its own environment for generations. The early country recordings, when viewed as a single body, certainly rank as one of the most extensive blocks of traditional folk music ever collected.

Things sped along as the market grew. Okeh and Victor were among the first labels in the breach with their recordings of the solitary fiddlers John Carson and Eck Robertson. Vocalion was recording Uncle Dave Macon, a jocular, rustic banjo player who was the first star of the Grand Ole Opry. Gennett and Brunswick jumped into the field, and so did Victor, the biggest label of the day. Victor did a lot to break the ice jam of inner-office prejudice against the rural sound when it gave country music its first national hit, the song "Wreck of the Old 97," performed by Vernon Dalhart (Marion Try Slaughter), a popular singer from Texas. Based on the Henry Whitter version of the same song, the Victor recording still ranks among the biggest-selling country hits, even though it was recorded back in 1924. Victor couldn't argue with the cash returns from "Old 97," and Ralph Peer was soon on their payroll.

Ralph Peer made one of his trips to Tennessee in the summer of 1927 to do some of the recording that by then had become routine. He ran his ad in the Tennessee-Virginia border town of Bristol. One of the acts to audition was a sickly-looking Mississippian named Jimmie Rodgers. Another was a family named Carter.

Alvin P. Carter was a salesman on his rounds in Virginia when he met a pretty girl named Sara Dougherty. Legend states that she was playing the guitar and singing

Maybelle, A.P., and Sara Carter

Henry C. Gilliland

the old train-wreck tune "Engine 143" when he first saw her. They married and began to sing together. Sara was often visited by her cousin Maybelle Addington, who eventually married A.P. Carter's brother. A. P., Sara, and Maybelle sang while Sara strummed on autoharp and Maybelle played a distinctive lead guitar. They caught on in their local area and were persuaded into going to Bristol to audition for the man who made the records.

Their simple, home-style harmonies and enormous repertoire of great old songs caught the ear of the South like none before them. Carter's rich bass voice blended with his wife's moving and soulful lead, joined on the choruses by the sweet, tenor-range voice of Maybelle. Their sound was smoother and more professional than that of any of the groups before them, but it still had that warmth-of-the-hearth sound that struck a responsive chord in the hearts of the country people. They re-

corded hundreds of songs between 1927 and their final performance as a group in 1941: blues, cowboy songs, old murder ballads, gospel tunes, humorous numbers, love songs, and timeless folk ballads they collected and arranged to suit their uniquely warm trio style. Their vocal style laid much of the ground-work for bluegrass singing, which was just beginning to emerge.

As the music of the Carters was being broadcast from Texas to the Carolinas, they were shifting the country music emphasis from the oldtime, whoop-'em-up fiddle breakdowns to the actual singing of songs, and more importance was being placed on good singing and harmony arrangements. But paralleling their successful career was the skyrocketing star of Jimmie Rodgers, shifting the spotlight even farther away from the old fiddle bands to the concept of the country singing star.

Rodgers, "The Singing Brakeman," was probably more responsible than anyone for the "advancement" of early country music. The consumptive son of a Mississippi railroader, he grew up in freight yards all over the South and West. He learned his music from blacks and whites, cowboys and mountaineers, laborers and roustabouts, and the resulting personal style was something that went beyond region. He had a song for everyone, and everyone seemed to buy what he was selling.

He sang the "blue yodels" picked up from the black traditions. He sang the songs of bumming freight trains, of life on the western plains. When he died of tuberculosis in 1933, he had become the closest thing country music ever had to a "king."

The stock market had collapsed in the fall of 1929, and the Great Depression brought the age of the Southern field recording expeditions to an abrupt halt. The nation was shaken, and no one suffered more than the country people. They didn't even have the cash for the basic needs of everyday life, let alone the luxury of phonograph records.

If the recording industry was forced to take a few steps backward, then radio was elevated one or two notches during the years of economic panic. Phonograph records cost money, but after the initial price was paid for a radio set, all the music in the world could be had by simply turning a dial. Many stations were broadcasting country music, and the Saturday night airings of the "National Barndance" from WLS in Chicago and Nashville's "Grand Ole Opry" became the major events of the week for thousands of families across the East.

The "Opry" and "Barn Dance" were the biggest and best, but hundreds of smaller radio stations sent live country music out over the airways during the darkest days of the Depression.

Thousands today still remember the old "farm time" programs, whether they were broadcast at noon or at five o'clock in the morning. The band would come on strong with a singing jingle bidding the listeners welcome and putting in a strong plug for the sponsor's product. A smooth-voiced announcer would then cut in, obviously trying to speak with something other than a Southern accent, giving the listeners a formal "good morning" and introducing the bandleader. The leader, if he was a good one, generally knew his audience wanted to hear the real down-home stuff. There would be a couple of fast fiddle tunes, an old ballad or two, and a funny song from the band's resident comedian. Then the announcer would cut back in with a word from the sponsor and maybe a word or two about where the "friends and neighbors" out in radio land could see the boys in person, at this or that country schoolhouse or miners' hall. There might be a plug about how the "friends and neighbors" could contact the band if they wanted to book them for their schoolhouse show, giving the musicians prospects of one or two more jobs. Then would come a little more music and a sign-off—all in just fifteen minutes of air time. Shows of almost identical content would run all day and into the evening, with each band getting the same plug for their personal ap-

The Blue Ridge Cornshuckers

pearances. The best bands drew the crowds and consequently stayed in business while keeping themselves and their families fed and clothed.

The "Grand Ole Opry," at Nashville's radio station WSM, soon established itself as the country's leading showcase for traditional music. Chicago's "National Barn Dance" was probably more important in spreading country music to the audiences of the North and Midwest.

Country music continued to grow through the radio years, and the major country variety programs brought the best of the bands to the widest audience. These acts were copied and imitated by thousands of amateurs who were still back in the hills, clustered around their old Atwater-Kents.

There had been duet and trio singing in the hills before the 1930s, of course: Sara and Maybelle Carter were one of the best, even though A. P.'s bass voice often was prominent below them. But the male duets were really catching on, and one of the best of the early ones was the Delmore Brothers, Alton and Rabon. They were from Alabama, and their style was relaxed and smooth, their approach polished almost to the point of slickness. Today, listening to their records of the 1930s, they seem astoundingly modern and commercial for

their time. Their harmony was soft and light, and it was "good" harmony: They didn't sing in unison as even some of the later bands did.

The Delmore Brothers had used the unique combination of two guitars, but the standard instrumentation of the acts that followed them was almost always the guitar and the mandolin. The Callahan Brothers were successful with this combination, as were Mac and Bob, the two blind musicians at WLS. Then came Karl and Harty, also at the Chicago station, the Blue Sky Boys, and the Monroe Brothers.

The duet formula was as simple as it was effective. The guitar player provided basic rhythm chords and usually sang the lower part, the melody line. The mandolin player (traditionally the guitarist's brother) would play whatever little instrumental work there was to do while singing the higher harmony, up in the tenor range. Most of the duets were ballad singers, in either the mountain or sentimental "parlor" tradition, and the best of them produced some of the most hauntingly beautiful vocal work the country people had ever heard.

The Blue Sky Boys were not asked to record until 1936, but they probably couldn't have recorded before then even if they had been asked. They were just kids (sixteen and eighteen years old) from Hickory, North

Carolina, when they first stepped up to a Victor microphone. Their family name was Bolick, oddly Eastern European-sounding for mountain people. Bill was the older and played the mandolin, while younger brother Earl played the guitar and sang lead. It's odd, too, that they were pushed into the guitar-mandolin mold. They had always carried a fiddler (usually Homer "Pappy" Sherrill), and Bill was as inclined to play the guitar as the mandolin, but the Monroe Brothers were setting the woods on fire in the Carolinas then—without a fiddler— so Bill and Earl Bolick were asked to drop the fiddle and forced into copying someone they had scarcely heard. The result was totally unlike the Monroe Brothers, and the Blue Sky Boys were the absolute, consummate perfection of the vocal duet.

Mandolinist Bill Bolick says that when he and Earl decided to become a duet, they wanted to be the best. The Delmores had done it right, but the others were sloppy, not caring that both singers were often singing the same part. The Blue Sky Boys developed a blend that was technically superb. They hit each note in perfect harmony, never crossing over and getting the same tone from both their voices. When they performed the old traditional ballad "Mary of the Wild Moor," they sang each word as if it meant something; and when they came to the line " 'Twas on a cold winter's night," the word *night* was rested on and blended with an uncanny dual inflection.

The first Victor Bluebird recordings by the Blue Sky Boys appeared in the Victor catalog in 1936, the same year that Victor made the first recordings of another great duet, the Monroe Brothers from western Kentucky.

Today a handpainted sign on Bill Monroe's battered mandolin case reads "ORIGINAL BLUEGRASS MUSIC SINCE 1927." That's when he and his brothers started playing together. Some date the birth of bluegrass as 1939, when Bill worked up his classic arrangement of the "New Muleskinner Blues," the first song in his characteristic "bluegrass time." Others date it as 1946, when Bill and his Blue Grass Boys recorded "Will You Be Lovin' Another Man?" with Earl Scruggs on the banjo. There are still others, and a lot of them, who date the birth of bluegrass from the 1936 Victor release of "What Would You Give in Exchange for Your Soul?" by Bill and Charlie Monroe.

This popular gospel tune was not in a bluegrass style as we know it today. It was just a duet with some tasteful mandolin backup, but it was a tremendously popular recording in the Carolinas, enhancing the already enviable reputation the Monroes had established on some of the major country radio stations.

The Monroes could sing the high ranges. They had a quality to their music that later became known as drive, a pounding rhythm unable to contain itself as they raced through songs like "Roll in My Sweet Baby's Arms" and "New River Train." Even their slow numbers had a beat; tunes like "Song of Old Kentucky" and "I

Eck Robertson

Bluegrass Unlimited

The magazine that has everything you want to know about bluegrass, old-time, and traditional country music. Rare photographs. Bluegrass songbook. Profiles. Record and book reviews. Monthly calendar. Festivals and personal appearances. Reader inquiries. Talent Directory. Classifieds. Subscription: $8 a year. Write: Box 111, Broad Run, VA. 22041. (Ask for leaflet listing bluegrass patches and bumper stickers.)

Blue Jeans Museum

In 1850, a twenty-year-old immigrant to the California gold fields made some work pants out of tent canvas and sold them to the miners. His name was Levi Strauss; soon "them pants of Levi's" grew into an industry that has since produced over 900 million pairs of pants. If

Dreamed I Searched Heaven for You" were done in three-quarter time, but they moved along in a way that made listeners feel Bill and Charlie couldn't wait to get the song over with and get on to the next fast one. Charlie's thumb and finger pick walked all over the bass strings, supplying unexpected runs totally unlike the bland rhythm of Earl Bolick and the others, and his voice was rich with a unique western Kentucky warmth that would make him one of the most popular singers in the South for decades.

Bill Monroe was something really different. His tenor voice was good and high, even though it lacked the technical perfection of the Delmores and the Bolicks, and it danced around and over his older brother's full-bodied lead with joyous exuberance. He wasn't content to play the straight melody line as most of the old-time mandolin players did. He brought a real sense of musicianship to his work, playing wild, improvisational mandolin breaks all over the little eight-stringed instrument's short fingerboard. It seemed almost unbelievable that the Monroes and the Bolicks, using such a similar vocal and instrumental format, could have been so entirely different. The Blue Sky Boys used their guitar and mandolin to enhance what was essentially an old-time mountain ballad singing style. Bill and Charlie Monroe used their instruments and voices in a style that had all the excitement of the old-time fiddle bands at their best—their hell-for-leather instrumentation and the breakneck rapport that existed between Charlie's surging guitar runs and Bill's sprinting mandolin. It laid the real groundwork for the style that was later to be known as bluegrass.

Debby Boone

you're in San Francisco, you can visit this museum that contains Levi's from the 1870s, old sewing machines, memorabilia of the miners, cowboys, loggers, and railroad workers.

Write: Levi Strauss History Room, 2 Embarcadero Center, San Francisco, California.

Boone, Debby

Born: September 22, 1956, Hackensack, New Jersey

Daughter of Pat Boone, granddaughter of country-western star Red Foley, the third of four Boone sisters (Cherry, Lindy, and Laury are the others), she attended Bible School and is a graduate of Marymount High. At thirteen, she accompanied her parents to Japan, where she and her sisters sang, "What the World Needs Now Is

Pat Boone and family

Tony Korody/Sygma

Love," which also proved the music world needed them! With two sisters married and one in college, the time came for Debby to solo. First time out her "You Light Up My Life" zoomed straight to the top of the charts as a single and won several awards, including a 1977 Grammy. An LP of the same name features Debby's sisters singing with her on several of the cuts, including "Hasta Manana." Her second LP, *Midstream,* includes her singles "God knows," "When You're Loved," and "Oh, No, Not My Baby."

Brown, Jim Ed

Born: April 1, 1934, Sparkman, Arkansas
Married: Becky Perry
Children: s. Jim Ed, Jr. (Buster); d. Kimberly

Jim started out with two sisters, Maxine and Bonnie, to form the famed country singing group, The Browns, whose "Three Bells" topped the million mark. The group joined the Opry in 1963. Two hit singles followed: "Scarlet Ribbons" and "The Old Lamplighter." The Browns performed for the last time together at the Forty-second Anniversary Show of the Grand Ole Opry in October 1967. The two sisters retired to care for their families, and Jim Ed moved on to bigger success on his own with such RCA hit singles as "Pop-a-Top," "Bottle, Bottle," "Morning," "Angel's Sunday," and "Don Junior." In 1976, his duet LP with Helen Cornelius, *I Don't Want to Have to Marry You,* zoomed to number one. Their association has continued with such hits as "If The World Ran Out of Love Tonight" and *I'll Never Be Free.*

Bryant, Felice and Boudleaux

Felice

Born: August 7, 1925, Milwaukee, Wisconsin

Boudleaux

Born: February 13, 1920, Sellman, Georgia

Jim Ed Brown and family   J. Clark Thomas/People Weekly

Married: (in) 1945
Children: s. Dane, Del

They are a top songwriting team, and members of CMA, NARAS, and Songwriters Hall of Fame. Their early hits include the Everly Brothers' "Bye-Bye Love," "Bird Dog," and "Wake Up Little Susie." In 1970, they won a BMI award for "Raining in My Heart" and "All I Have to Do Is Dream" (which was also one of the ten-most-performed songs of that year!). Their biggest recent hit: "Rocky Top."

Buffett, Jimmy

Born: December 25, 1946, Mississippi
Married: Jane Slagsvole

The Bard of Margaritaville has homes in Aspen and Nashville and owns a thirty-three-foot ketch, *Euphoria,* which he sails out of Key West. Listing his occupation as "professional misfit," Buffett earned a degree in journalism from Auburn and the University of Southern Mississippi. He has said of himself, "I try not to let my education get in the way of my writing." His first recording session at Nashville in the late sixties ended in disaster when the master tapes were lost. "My career as a country artist was severely short-changed!" he recalls. By 1972, he had signed with ABC and recorded his first Dunhill album, *A White Sport Coat and a Pink Crustacean,* followed by *Livin' and Dyin' in 3/4 Time* and later *A1A,* an LP that includes "A Pirate Looks at 40" and "Life Is Just a Tire Swing." With his own back-up band, the Coral Reefers, he did *Havana Daydreamin',* which *Record World* called "an album with something to offend everyone without losing a friend or a beat." In 1976, *Changes in Latitudes, Changes in Attitudes* takes us on a semitropical cruise through Jimmy's world of sun, sailing, women, and booze, including the mournfully wry search for the lost shaker of salt in "Margaritaville," also released as a single in 1977. In 1974, he scored and acted in Frank Perry's film,

Rancho Deluxe. His second wife, Jane, born 1951, comes from Columbia, South Carolina, and is a former fashion model. Their wedding at Redstone Castle near Aspen cost $3,000 for the champagne alone. Jimmy's big mid-1978 album, and a gold seller ($3,000 dollars seems like nothing now!), is *Son of a Son of a Sailor.*

Butler, Carl and Pearl

Carl
Born: June 2, 1927, Knoxville, Tennessee

Pearl
Birthday: September 20
Children: d. Carla

The Butlers were voted Country Music's #1 New Singing Team in 1963. Carl was a performer since age twelve and a member of the Opry since 1958. Songwriter Carl's hits include "I Know What It Means to Be Lonesome" and "If Teardrops Were Pennies" a 1950s hit later recorded in 1973 by Porter Wagoner and Dolly Parton. Their Columbia hit "Don't Let Me Cross Over" inspired them to name their Franklin, Tennessee, farm Cross Over Acres.

ABC Records   Don Light Talent Inc.

Jimmy Buffett

United Artists Records

Larry Butler

Butler, Larry

Born: March 26, 1942, Pensacola, Florida.
Married: E. J. Cresswell
Children: d. Schanda Lee

A producer, songwriter, and performing pianist, Butler appeared at the age of six on the radio; by eleven, he was singing country and pop on TV; at thirteen, he had won a five-state competition in classical music. A producer for Capitol, CBS, and Columbia Records, he joined Johnny Cash as arranger, producer, studio manager, and concert pianist. Later forming his own company, he produced songs which as of 1977 hit the national charts for four straight years—and no end in sight. As a songwriter, his hits include "Another Somebody Done Somebody Wrong Song," "Just for You," "Bring Him Safely Home to Me," and "Lullaby of Love." His first LP is United Artists' *Larry Butler and Friends* with the cream of Nashville musicians and cameos by Crystal Gayle, Dottie West, and Billie Jo Spears.

Byrd, Senator Robert C.

The West Virginia Democrat is famous as a country fiddler in his home state. During 1977, his fame branched out. At a Washington Press Club dinner for members of Congress and President Carter, he removed his tuxedo jacket and played "Rye Whiskey" and "Cumberland Gap," with "Amazing Grace" as an encore dedicated to the President.

C

Campbell, Archie

Born: November 7, 1914, Bulls Gap, Tennessee
Married: Mary Lee Lewis
Children: s. Stephen Archie, Philip Edward Lee

A top star performer and comedy writer for "Hee Haw." Archie first appeared on radio and TV in Knoxville, then went on to the "Prince Albert Show" on the Opry and a recording contract with RCA Victor. His best-known comedy records are "Beeping Sleauty" and "Rindercella."

Campbell, Glen Travis

Born: April 22, 1936, Delight, Arkansas
Married: Billie Jean Nunley
Children: s. William Travis, Wesley Kane; d. Debra, Kelli

Glen Campbell

For his thirty-fourth album on Capitol Records (released during his fifteenth year with the label), he decided to do a double-disc live recording. *Glen Campbell Live at the Royal Festival Hall* contains not only a number of his biggest hits, but also some of Campbell's own favorite songs (some of which he has never before recorded).

The album was recorded during the spring of 1977 at two shows one night in London during a British concert tour. Those shows also were taped by BBC Television for broadcast in that country and eventual worldwide distribution. Campbell was backed by his regular band and by the seventy-five-piece Royal Philharmonic Orchestra (which he says "fulfilled a lifelong dream"). Campbell produced the album himself except for one song that was handled by Gary Klein.

The hits Campbell covers include "Rhinestone Cowboy" (done in an opening medley with Janis Ian's "Stars"), "Dreams of the Everyday Housewife," "Sunflower" and "Southern Nights." In addition, one side is comprised of five Jimmy Webb songs—"By the Time I Get to Phoenix," "Galveston," "Wichita Lineman," "MacArthur Park," and "This Is Sarah's Song" (the latter written for Campbell's wife). For those five songs, Webb (Campbell's close friend) came out to conduct the orchestra. Webb also wrote a new ballad arrangement

for "Galveston."

Campbell does a tribute to Elvis with a medley of "(Let Me Be Your) Teddy Bear" and "Loving You." Campbell performed with The Beach Boys for awhile during the mid-sixties, and on this album he does a four-song medley tribute to that group as well as their "God Only Knows."

Campbell also performs songs by Rod McKuen and Jacques Brel, Ralph McTell, Neil Sedaka, and Rogers and Hammerstein. To top it off, Campbell roars through some instrumentals—Mason Williams's "Classical Gas" and the "William Tell Overture"—and finishes off with "Amazing Grace" (complete with bagpipes played by Campbell).

Besides the hits and the little-known or new-found personal favorites that Campbell includes, the album also contains between-song patter and thus personal glimpses of this one-of-a-kind entertainer.

Glen Campbell's success and popularity are due not only to his top-quality and much-loved recordings, but because he has universal musical appeal. He's one of the few artists of our time who transcends strict categories and reaches straight to the soul of each listener. His popularity is immense and attested to by the wealth of awards and honors he has received all over the world.

Campbell has never lost his down-home, country boy,

easy-going ways that he developed while he was growing up six miles outside of Delight, Arkansas (population about 280 when he left, and not much more now).

Because of his roots, his singing and playing style has helped bridge the gap between country and pop music, but when labelers try to limit him with definitions, he is quick to retort, "I'm not a country singer, I'm a country boy who sings."

This country boy was the seventh son in a farm family of eight boys and four girls. His parents and older brothers and sisters all played the guitar and sang. He learned to play on the family guitar and was given a five-dollar Sears and Roebuck guitar when he was four years old. He learned some guitar technique from his uncle, and he listened to Django Reinhardt, Barney Kessel, and even some horn players trying to learn new licks since he didn't read music. He also practiced his singing in his local Church of Christ.

"I spent the early part of my life looking at the north end of a southbound mule and it didn't take long to figure out that a guitar was a lot lighter than a plow handle," says Campbell.

While in his teens, he left Arkansas in the early 1950s and lived in New Mexico and Houston, Texas. His first musical jobs were with his uncle, Dick Bills, and they toured the Southwest playing at what Campbell describes as "dancin' and fightin' clubs." Soon he formed his own band.

At twenty-two, Campbell moved to Los Angeles with $300 cash and a small trailer filled with his belongings. He soon cut some tunes, including the hit "Tequila," with a studio group called The Champs, which included

Capitol Records

Jimmy Seals and Dash Crofts. He also began working studio sessions with recording stars such as Frank Sinatra, Dean Martin, Bobby Darin, Rick Nelson, Elvis Presley, Nat King Cole, The Mamas and the Papas, The Association, Merle Haggard, and others. In 1965 he toured with The Beach Boys, filling in for a reclusive Brian Wilson.

After achieving a modest hit, "Turn Around, Look at Me," on a small label, Campbell signed with Capitol. His first Capitol album was *Big Bluegrass Special* by The Green River boys, featuring Glen Campbell (released in 1962). After several albums and singles as a solo artist (including a top-fifty hit in 1965 with "The Universal Soldier"), Campbell finally broke into the national consciousness in 1967 with "Gentle on My Mind," penned by his friend John Hartford. Campbell followed it up four months later with another smash hit, "By the Time I Get to Phoenix," which kept him high on both pop and country charts. In 1968, he had four hits, beginning the year with "Hey Little One" and ending it with the top-of-the-charts "Wichita Lineman." The next year he had four more chart hits, including "Galveston," and he also released a live album that went gold. At about the same time, he had three hit singles and a gold album with Bobbie Gentry. In 1970, Campbell again scored with four hits, including the top ten "It's Only Make Believe."

In May 1975, Glen Campbell once again surged to the forefront of the music world with the single "Rhinestone Cowboy," which was one of the biggest-selling records of the year and was the only single that year to go number one on pop, country, and easy-listening charts (an extremely rare feat). The best-selling album of the same name also contained the top-ten hit "Country Boy (You Got Your Feet in L.A.)." In April 1977, Campbell

Capitol

was number one on both the pop and country charts with the single "Southern Nights" from the album of the same name. That same album also contained the hit "Sunflower."

Over the years, Campbell also has recorded with other Capitol artists such as Anne Murray and Tennessee Ernie Ford.

During his career, Campbell has been asked at various times to give special performances for presidents of the United States and the Queen of England. He also has presided as the "king" of the Mardi Gras in New Orleans and has hosted various tennis tournaments. Campbell even hosts a golf tournament—The Glen Campbell Los Angeles Open, one of the most prestigious on the Professional Golf Association Circuit.

In addition, he has starred in movies such as *True Grit, Norwood,* and *Strange Homecoming* (the latter made for television). His television series, "The Glen Campbell Show," ran for four-and-a-half years. During his career, he has made countless appearances on a wide variety of television music, talk, and variety shows.

At the release of *Glen Campbell Live at the Royal Festival Hall,* he had four gold singles, twelve gold albums, five platinum albums and one double platinum album in the United States alone. His career on Capitol Records spans some thirty-four albums and forty-five singles.

In 1978, his hits included "Can You Fool."

Carlisle Brothers, Bill and Cliff

Bill
Born: December 19, 1908, Wakefield, Kentucky
Married: Leona
Children: s. Bill, Jr.; d. Sheila

Clifford R.
Born: March 6, 1904, Wakefield, Kentucky
Married: Henrietta
Children: s. Tom; d. Violet

The brothers made their first radio appearance in Louisville, Kentucky, in the twenties. Their first big record was on Bluebird, "Rattlesnake Daddy." Cliff, one of the first important dobro players, was also a yodeler and backed Jimmie Rodgers on several records. After several big radio shows ("Louisiana Hayride," "Ozark Jubilee," and "The Carlisle Family Barn Dance"), Cliff retired in 1947. Bill formed a new group, joined Grand Ole Opry in 1953, and has won close to seventy awards, including Most Programmed Country and Western Vocal Group for 1953-55, and Best Comedian of the Year in 1955. His "Too Old to Cut the Mustard," and "No Help Wanted" won Best Record of the Year in 1953 and 1954 respectively.

Carter Family

A.P. (Alvin Pleasant Delaney) Carter
Born: April 15, 1891, Maces Springs, Scott County, Virginia
Married: Sara Dougherty
Children: s. Joe; d. Janet

Sara Dougherty Carter
Born: July 21, 1899, Nickelsville, Virginia
Married: Alvin Pleasant Delaney
Children: s. Joe; d. Janet

Maybelle Addington Carter
Born: May 10, 1909
Died: October 23, 1978
Married: Ezra J. Carter
Children: d. Anita, June, Helen

The legend of the original Carter Family can be traced to the time when Alvin Pleasant Carter and his brother Ezra J. Carter crossed to the other side of Clinch Mountain and brought themselves back wives. Alvin Pleasant (generally known as A.P. or Doc) and Sara Dougherty were married in 1915 and Ezra and Maybelle Addington in March of '26. Both couples settled in Maces Springs, Virginia, and later on that same year formed a singing group composed of A.P., Sara, and her cousin, Maybelle. They were the in-

novators in keeping alive the traditional mountain songs which influenced our present day folk and country performers.

Maybelle did most of the arranging for the group and quite a bit of the songwriting, too. Her style of flat-picking the melody on the bass strings of the guitar was admired and envied by many great artists. The Carter Family had been performing nonprofessionally at church socials, family gatherings, and school functions for some time. This was the beginning of establishing a name for themselves that would be well known throughout the Virginia area and remembered for many years to come.

A talent scout for RCA-Victor, Ralph S. Peer (who later formed a prominent publishing firm called Peer-Southern International), ran an ad in a local newspaper soliciting talent to audition for records. Peer recorded the Carter Family in an old

warehouse in Bristol, Virginia–Tennessee, on August 1, 1927. Little did anyone realize that on this day history was taking place. Three days later, he recorded another legendary artist, Jimmie Rodgers. Today a nine-foot monument is erected on this site commemorating that historical event. "When you recorded a session in those days," said Maybelle, "you didn't get a second take because they had to scrape away several inches of wax, and it was simply unheard of."

Maybelle and her husband were blessed with three beautiful daughters. The first was Helen, then June, and last, Anita. All of her girls were born with an abundance of talent. They quickly learned about music from their mother—to sing harmony, pick the auto harp, and play guitar—except for June. At that particular time in her life she could not have cared less about music. She just wanted to be back in Maces Springs, walking through the woods, playing with her cousin, pickin' huckleberries, and most of all—tending to her crawdads.

June outgrew her dislike for music and discovered she was talented in a different way from her sisters. She was gifted with quick wit and humor, which added variety and com-

edy to their act. The Carters were performing at XERF, a radio station on the Mexican border across from Del Rio, Texas. It was during this time (1938–1941) that Sara and Maybelle's children performed with the trio.

Sara and A.P. were divorced in

1938 and she married Coy Bayes (A. P.'s first cousin) about a year later. Sara worked with the group until they retired in 1943. The original Carter Family recorded more than 250 songs while they were together. Their recordings have sold in excess of millions. The last Carter Family recording session was for Columbia Records on October 14, 1941, in Chicago, Illinois.

Maybelle continued to perform with her three daughters and moved to Nashville, Tennessee, in 1950, joining the Grand Ole Opry. They called themselves the Carter Sisters, out of deep respect for uncle A. P. until his death in 1960. The words Keep on the Sunny Side (also the trio's theme song) are engraved on a gold record on his tombstone. After his death, the old Carter Family was restored.

The Carters had the pleasure of working the road with two of the biggest stars in the business. Chet Atkins performed with their show for three years, and they worked with Elvis Presley until he started making movies.

June went out as a single act and joined the Johnny Cash road show, leaving Mother Maybelle, Helen, and Anita to carry on the name. In 1961, the trio started recording with Cash and became regulars on his TV show in 1966. Their rendition of the old mountain songs had taken them to more than fifteen different countries and famous places in the U.S. Wherever they have played, the International Hotel in Las Vegas, Hollywood Bowl, Madison Square Garden in New York, Carnegie Hall or on the campus of Notre Dame University, the Carters were widely accepted by all age groups. Their stage shows consist of the current country and pop songs plus a few old standards that are still added for tradition. Anita's daughter, Lori, and Helen's son, David, now appear with their road show, making three generations of Carters.

People associated with the music business respected and loved Maybelle Carter . . . so much, that they adopted her as their "mother." *Music City News* officially named Maybelle the Mother of Country Music in 1968. In 1978, an album titled *Will the Circle Be Unbroken* with the Nitty Gritty Dirt Band, a folk-rock group, was nominated for a Grammy award. A history of folk music and the Carter Family is in the Smithsonian Institute. In 1970, the original Carter Family was elected to the Country Music Hall of Fame in Nashville. For two consecutive years, the Country Music Association nominated Maybelle and the girls as the Small Group of the Year.

The Carters (truly the first family in country music) and that first recording on August 1, 1927, influenced and broadened the horizons of our backwoods rural communities—to a sound heard and enjoyed throughout the universe.

Carter, President Jimmy

The President is a life-long country music fan who has received such stars as Johnny and June Cash, Willie Nelson, and Emmylou Harris at the White House. Each October he has designated that month as Country Music Month, referring to country music "as universal as a sunset and as personal as a baby's smile. It is fitting that we acknowledge the importance of a form that reflects so much the lives and hopes of the people who make up our nation and pay tribute to the talented people who have contributed to its growing popularity."

The following is the text of the President's statement sent to the Country Music Association in Nashville:

THE WHITE HOUSE

WASHINGTON

Country Music Month
October 1978

As modern American society becomes more and more hectic and complex, there is a desire in all of us to return to the simple things of life.

This perhaps in part explains the growing popularity -- even in our busiest metropolitan areas -- of country music. And designated as "Country Music Month," October invites us all to return, at least vicariously, to the hills and the farms of America and to retrace the everyday emotions and experiences of country life.

Country music is part of the soul and conscience of our democracy. It unfolds the inherent goodness of our people and of our way of life. It captures our indomitable spirit and pulsates with the sorrows, joys and unfailing perseverance of ordinary men and women who sustain our national vitality and strength.

I welcome the opportunity to applaud the Country Music Association on its sponsorship of this annual observance, and I encourage more Americans to share in the enjoyment and cultural enrichment that country music can bring.

Jimmy Carter

President Carter and Emmylou Harris

The White House

One of her fondest memories goes back to the days when she wore an organdy dress and ruffled pantaloons for performances on stage. In the middle of a dance, she was ready to show off her bloomers when she realized she had forgotten to put them on.

"I forgot something. . .," she announced and retreated hastily backstage to remedy the situation.

(*See also* Old Time Roots.)

Carlene Carter

Warner/Reprise

Carter, June

Born: June 23, 1929, Maces Spring, Virginia

Married: Rip Nix (div.) Johnny Cash

Children: s. John Carter Cash; d. Rebecca Carlene, Rozanna Lee

The middle of three daughters of Maybelle and Ezra Carter, June grew up as part of the singing Carter Family who performed on radio stations in places as far apart as Del Rio, Texas; Charlotte, North Carolina; and Knoxville, Tennessee. She then joined the Opry in 1951. Branching out early, she recorded "Baby, It's Cold Outside" and "Music, Music" with the legendary Homer and Jethro. She has won three BMI awards for her songs, "Ring of Fire," "The Matador," and "Wall to Wall Love." She and her husband Johnny Cash jointly won CMA's Best Vocal Duo in 1969. (*See* Johnny Cash for other joint appearances and hit records.)

June Carter
CBS Records

Cash, Johnny (John R. Cash)

Born: February 26, 1932, Kingsland, Arkansas
Married: Vivian Liberto (div.); June Carter
Children: s. John Carter Cash; d. Roseanne, Kathy, Cindy, Tara

The Grit and Grace of Johnny Cash
by
Jeannie Sakol

Look at Johnny Cash.
Who stares back?
Tom Joad on the run.
Dink's man, long and tall, moving his body like a cannonball.
Walker Evans faces. "Let Us Now Praise Famous Men."
Mark Smeaton singing and dying for Anne Boleyn.
The highwayman riding, riding up to the old inn door.
Sweet William on his deathbed for love of Barb'r'y Allen.
Oral Roberts, praising God.
The yeoman archer storming Agincourt with good old Harry the Fifth.
One of Woody Guthrie's bunch. Hard rambler. Hard gambler. Good talker.
Dublin brawler.
Welsh miner.
Sidewalk preacher. Gotta get a hold in that rock don't you see?
Lochinvar out of the South.

Johnny Cash is the quintessential country boy. In his looks, his life-style, the old songs he sings, the new ones he writes, he reflects attitudes toward love, betrayal, loneliness, and sorrow that profoundly affect all of us, whatever our background.

His roots are strong and trace easily to their cultural sources. There are the Elizabethan ballads of cru-el fate and lovers wronged that traveled to Appalachia with the early settlers: There are the gospel hymns of old tent-meeting times, the plaintive wails of men as prey to drugs, booze, false friends, and bad women, and the cold-belly pain of hungering men and hankering women of the Great Depression.

He's thirty-eight years old and six feet two and rising with somber Jesus eyes in a scarred and runneled face, his voice hot molasses dripping gravel. Thick black hair hangs long and shaggy, like that of a tintype frontiersman. He moves with the curious grace of the big man, chest and shoulders powerful enough to pull a plow, the arms strong enough to clutch the rung of a boxcar going forty miles an hour through the wrong side of town, the long legs that drape with careless elegance against a fence rail or a passing wall. Like Dink's man, he's long and tall and moves his body like a cannonball.

Johnny Cash and June Carter

His black frock coats conjure up many images. Gambling man. Outlaw. Circuit rider. Wagon master on a Saturday night. Often, he knots a calico sweat rag at his throat. Logger, ranch hand, trucker, trainman. He has the most heartbreaking hands. Big hands, but supple and tapering, hands that say what it is to birth a calf, chop cotton, cup a harmonica tight to a tender mouth, and rip hell out of a $2,000 Martin guitar.

On television and in a hundred recorded songs, he touches emotional buttons, and we respond to what we know and things we half remember. All are there, sometimes expressed with dignity, sometimes with humor, and often larded with maudlin self-pity. He celebrates joy and woe in a ritualistic style. Old conventions are stringently observed.

The loneliness of the drifter, for instance. He's stayed around and played around this old town too long; there's a lonesome freight at 6:08, and it feels like he's going to travel on. Girls, mothers, homes, wait patiently

CBS Records

Fields Forever." Simon & Garfunkel's "Scarborough Fair," Dylan's "Lay Lady Lay," Glen Campbell's "If You Go Away," are all in the same family. The sentimentality is the same. . . .

Johnny Cash is a mixture of past and present. He is a knight-errant protector of those in need, a slayer of dragons for the victimized weak. He is the troubadour of the workingman, glorifying in song those who work with their muscles and sweat.

His concern for men in prison is heard in two harrowing LPs, taped at San Quentin and Folsom prison, where the hoots and shouts of the condemned greet his "Starkville City Jail," "Folsom Prison Blues," "I Got Stripes," and the riveting "25 Minutes to Go," which chronicles the last moments of a man being hanged. . . .

A film of the San Quentin visit mingled the Cash troupe's songs with close-up interviews of convicts and guards. While the viewer was taken into the gas chamber, the sincere voice of a guard explained the procedure was painless. He could tell, he said, because those executed did not clench their fists, a normal reaction, the guard said, if there was any pain at all.

"Mr. Congressman, why don't you understand?" Johnny Cash's voice cries out to the cheers of unrehabilitated men.

He has also sung for inmates at state prisons in Texas, Kansas, Tennessee, and Arkansas. At Arkansas's Cummins Prison Farm, he lectured a group of state legisla-

CBS Records

for this drifter, who seems to have no other talents but an itching heel and a keen ear for railroad whistles in the distance. Nice to sing about in the comfort of one's own immobile life, but you wouldn't want your daughter to marry one. . . .

Many speak in awed tongues of the current country-music phenomenon, as if it were something new. The country ethic of popular music has been with us for years. Bob Dylan's musical roots are in Woody Guthrie; as are those of Pete Seeger; the Weavers; Peter, Paul, and Mary, to name but a few.

Where did Woody Guthrie find his material? The same place that Burl Ives, Glen Campbell, Joan Baez, Bobbie Gentry, and others, past and present—from the small farms, the mining towns, the lifelong mourning of poor Southerners, white and black.

The Beatles' early work rocked to an unabashed Gospel-Nashville beat and later moved into the electronic Elizabethan of "Eleanor Rigby" and "Strawberry

tors in attendance: "There's a lot of things that need changin', Mr. Legislator Man!"

He said he was giving $5,000 and Arkansas Governor Winthrop Rockefeller was giving $10,000 for a prison chapel. State Prison Commissioner Robert Sarver gave him an honorary "life sentence," and three weeks later, the Arkansas legislature okayed the first appropriation for prison reform in the state's history.

To express his views on guns, Cash wrote, "Don't Take Your Guns to Town," a mother's plea to her hot-tempered son to leave his gun on the farm, where it belongs.

"Guns don't belong in towns," he says. "They belong in the open air, hunting rabbits. When I was a boy, my daddy would give me two shells. Those shells cost money. I had to come back with two rabbits. Once, I lined up two rabbits, one behind the other, and got them both with one shell.

"It's the breath of life to me to go out into the woods, breathe the fresh air. Man's instinct is to be close to nature. We haven't been out of the woods that long!"

Himself one-fourth Cherokee, he is among the vanguard of public figures seeking civil rights for Indians. . . . National Educational Television presented the film *The Trail of Tears,* with Cash as John Ross, the Cherokee nation chief, in the true story of the Cherokees who were driven from their homes to an Oklahoma reservation in 1838.

His record of "The Ballad of Ira Hayes" tells the story of a young Pima Indian who became a Marine hero at Iwo Jima in World War II and later died a neglected alcoholic.

Drug addiction is another personal crusade, and for good cause. Pep pills and tranquilizers nearly destroyed his life. From 1961 to 1967, he depended on them to keep him on a roller-coaster course of one-night stands and a foundering first marriage. He suffered severe psychological damage then; his career took a downward turn from missed concerts and bad performances. He was arrested twice—once in El Paso with a suitcase full of pep pills; another time in Georgia, when he was picked up wandering the streets in an amnesic funk.

In late 1967, with the help of friends and the devotion of June Carter, the singer who later became his wife, Johnny Cash kicked the pill habit.

When President Nixon requested him to sing "Welfare Cadillac," at a White House soiree one spring, Cash politely declined. Although he feels profound respect for the office of the President of the United States, he would not do a song that characterizes welfare recipients as gyp artists driving Cadillacs at the expense of dumbhead taxpayers.

To see Johnny and his wife, June, together is to know the fabled love of mountain ballads does exist. June is the strong and beautiful mountain woman, all fullness, breasts, hips, and the generous, open smile.

In ballad terms, she was a daughter of the legendary Carter Family, crown princess of the music aristocracy of the Southern hills, her uncle the cherished A. P. Carter; her mother the Maybelle whose haunting voice, guitar, and autoharp poured through every farmland radio of the late twenties and thirties.

When the Carter Family joined Johnny's touring show in 1961, he was the stripling prince, fighting for a kingdom of his own. Both Cash and June were married, he to a Texas girl, Vivian Liberto, whom he had met during his basic training in the Air Force in 1950.

Life on the road can be a soldering iron. June wrote one of their hit recordings, "Ring of Fire," in which love is described as "a burning thing, and it makes a fiery ring,/Bound by wild desires,/I fell into a Ring of Fire."

It would be unseemly to pretend knowledge of how the romance grew. Ballads never give details. Nor do those involved. That it did grow is evidenced by their marriage on March 1, 1968, and by an incandescent happiness that is a poetic rarity even to the most cynical.

The day I met June she was large with child and dewy-eyed in her hope of giving her husband a son. Both have daughters by their previous marriages, he four, she two. It would be his first son, from Biblical times a woman's proudest gift to her man.

"That little hamster is kicking me. I can't hardly wait. A boy would be the most precious thing I could do for John."

A few days later, John Carter Cash was born, named for both parents. One more verse in the ballad.

June wears her thick walnut hair shoulder length and hiked back with a dimestore elastic. Her nails gleam colorless polish. Her wedding band, the same as John's, is a modest gold, purchased in Jerusalem on their trek to the Holy Land, inscribed, "Me to my love and my love to me."

She calls her husband "John." "Johnny is like a little boy. John is strength and sincerity and honesty, and that's what my husband is."

She holds his watch while he rehearses. At the end of each take, he looks over. "Is that okay, honey?" She beams at him. "Real fine." To these New York ears, *"Rill fahn."* They stay in my head, soft, warm, non-grandstanding love.

When I see him alone and ask how he feels about women, the dark brow unbroods itself, the face flushed terra cotta, the smiling teeth that blind, his voice a hymn of praise with a Gospel beat.

"My *wife* is the ideal woman. Just as *perfect* as perfect can be. She doesn't *hide* her love. She doesn't *hide* her appreciation. She's a perfect woman because she knows how to treat her man like a *man.* She's my *woman.* She's my *friend.* My *companion.* She not only *loves* me, she *likes* me. She's a *great* woman, and part of being a great woman is *realizing* she's a great woman!"

Unisex made him smile.

"What's that?"

Women's Liberation.

"Aw, hell."

The White House

While financial success has brought the status delights of fast cars, "maternity" mink, a house for John's parents, and the mighty red tractor John has wanted since childhood, they cling to traditional home pleasures. At their lakeside house in a suburb of Nashville, June bakes bread every day, cornbread or hot biscuits to go with the country ham and fresh eggs at breakfast. John tills the vegetable garden every morning, soothing his mind with the rich, dark earth before driving to Nashville for rehearsals and tapings.

His favorite dish is runner beans and turnip greens cooked with a little bacon. Another is fried ham with red-eye gravy, which June makes by adding strong black coffee to the ham grease. "No flour," he cautions. "If it's got flour, it's called slingshot gravy."

Their backgrounds are similar but disparate. In contrast to the Carter Family's relative wealth and local celebrity, Johnny Cash was born dirt poor, February 26, 1932, in a three-room shack in Kingsland, Arkansas, the fourth of Ray and Carrie Cash's seven children. There was a Depression in the land. The soil was poor. Ray Cash rode boxcars to find work to feed his brood. In 1935, the Roosevelt Administration gave twenty acres of land, a house, a barn, and a mule to farmers willing to settle in the wilderness of northeastern Arkansas.

Ray Cash took the offer, and the family spent the first year working sunup to sundown to clear ten acres and plant cotton. Everyone, including his mother and the babies as soon as they could walk, chopped cotton,

fought snakes and wildcats, and stayed together.

Impoverished as they were, the Cash family found strength in religion and the sacred Baptist hymns. The first the singer recalls are "What Would You Change for Your Soul" and "Can the Circle Be Unbroken?" One of his hits, "Daddy Sang Bass," recalls those family sing-songs when Daddy Ray did sing bass, Carrie sang tenor, and the little ones chimed in.

At eighteen, he joined the Air Force and spent two years in Germany. There, he bought his first guitar and began to sing the back-home songs. On his discharge in 1954, he moved to Memphis with his first wife, Vivian Liberto, to try to crash the music business. Two young mechanics, Luther Perkins and Marshall Grant, had the same idea and changed their name from "The Tennessee Two" to "The Tennessee Three," to include him in.

After months of the fruitless hanging around that is the cliche of movies but so hurtfully true, Cash got an audition with Sun Records. They signed him on. His first release was two songs he wrote himself, "Hey Porter" and "Cry, Cry, Cry," instant hits and instantly followed by "I Walk the Line," which has since become his signature.

By any accounting system, he has made it. He's rich and respected for doing what he loves doing, no mean achievement. He's married to the woman he loved for many years, and she has given him his first son. He feels real good. He looks real fine.

Cash, Tommy

Born: April 5, 1940, Dyess, Arkansas
Married: Barbara Ann Wisenbaker (div.), Pamela Dyer
Children: s. Mark Alan; d. Paula Jean.

Yes, he's Johnny Cash's baby brother, and yes, he's a fine performer in his own right as well as a songwriter. His "Six White Horses" is a powerful and moving tribute to the murdered Kennedy brothers and Martin Luther King. He won a BMI for his composition of the Kitty Wells recording of "You Don't Hear."

Tommy Cash

Chavin, Nick, "Chinga"

Born: 1944, El Paso, Texas

Star of the outrageous Country Porn musical group, Chavin brings an element of sex to country music. He calls his performances—on a guitar that looks like a lipstick-red toilet seat—"a cross between Lenny Bruce and Jimmy Buffett." With a master's degree in creative writing and a Texas upbringing with such classmates as Kinky Friedman, Janis Joplin, and Lynda Bird Johnson, Chavin considers "Get It on the Run" and "4 A.M. Jump" as parody

Nick "Chinga" Chavin

James Armstrong
RCA Records and Tapes

rather than smut. *Billboard* called his LP "four-letter but funny." For information on where to get it, write: PO Box 548, New York, NY 10022.

Clark, Guy

Born: 1941, Rockport, Texas
Married: Susanna

A musician, composer, singer, Clark once worked at the Dopera Brothers factory in California, making dobros, and as a result can build a guitar from scratch. His songwriting style is described as an integration of solid Austin, Texas, foundation, and funky Nashville. A writer for Johnny Cash, Rita Coolidge, Tom Rush, The Earl Scruggs Revue, Jerry Jeff

Guy Clark

Walker, and more, his own first LP *Old No. 1* for RCA in 1975 introduced his talents as a gritty vocalist ("L.A. Freeway," "Desperados Waiting for the Train," "A Nickel for the Fiddler," "Texas—1947"). His next, "Texas Cookin'," features ten original Guy Clark songs with such friends as Emmylou Harris, Hoyt Axton, Waylon Jennings, Tracy Nelson—and Jerry Jeff Walker, of course.

Clark, Roy

Born: April 15, 1933, Meaherrin, Virginia
Married: Barbara

An incredibly versatile musician, he plays guitar, violin, banjo, piano, trumpet, trombone, and drums. Not content with playing, singing, and doing comedy routines, he also dances; proof of this came when he wore white tie and tails for a staircase routine on "The Donny and Marie Show," and when he also managed to keep up with Mitzi Gaynor on her 1977 TV special on CBS. A pilot, too, he flies his Mitsubishi prop jet to his 250 annual concerts, including New York's Carnegie Hall. But there's more: Roy's a radio broadcaster, photographer, boat captain, rancher, horse breeder, and president of his own line of low-calorie foods, Roy Clark's Dieter's Choice.

His career began when at age three he discovered his father's banjo. By sixteen, he won the national Country Music Banjo Championship (and won it again the following year). His first number-one record was "Yesterday When I Was Young" for Dot. He has nearly forty LPs to his credit. His cohosting of "Hee Haw" alone was seen by over 34 million viewers weekly. CMA named him Entertainer of the Year in 1973. One of his proudest achievements was appearing on Public Service TV with Arthur Fiedler and the ninety-piece Boston Pops Orchestra in 1977. Among his 1978 hits is the LP *Banjo Bandits*, made with Buck Trent.

Roy Clark

Clayton, Lee T.

Born: Russelville, Alabama

He gave "Outlaw" music its name when he wrote "Ladies Love Outlaws" in 1972 for Waylon Jennings (subsequently recorded by Jimmy Rabbitt, Tom Rush and The Everlys). His "If You Could Touch Her At All" is a classic of poetic melancholy and need; a hit single recorded by Willie Nelson and which he himself recorded in 1978 in his Capitol LP *Border Affair*. Among his other recorded songs are: Jerry Jeff Walker's "Won'cha Give Me One More Chance," Bonnie Koloc's "Silver Stallion" and Hoy Axton's "Whisper On A Velvet Night" on the *Outlaw Blues* soundtrack.

Clements, Vassar

Born: April, 1928

Known as the philosopher fiddler, he played at the Grand Ole Opry for the first time in 1949 with Bill Monroe and his Bluegrass Boys, cutting his first record with them the following year. It took twenty more years of hard traveling until 1969 when the Nitty Gritty Dirt Band gained him national exposure on the classic album, *Will The Circle Be Unbroken.* For the next four years, he performed with such artists as Dickie Betts, The Grateful Dead, Hot Tuna, Papa John Creach, and the Marshall Tucker Band. In 1973, he formed his own group, that plays a fusion of various types of American music—country, bluegrass, jazz, blues, and rock.

Cline, Patsy

Born: September 8, 1932, Winchester, Tennessee
Died: March 5, 1963, Camden, Tennessee

One of the first country pop stars, Patsy (real name, Virginia) burst on the national scene in 1957 as winner of the Arthur Godfrey *Talent Scouts,* singing "Walkin' After Midnight," which was then released by

Lee Clayton

Decca and became one of the year's biggest hits. Later, "I Fall to Pieces," "She Got You," "Imagine That," "Faded Love," and "Leavin' on Your Mind" were among her biggies until the March day she was returning home by plane from a benefit with Hawkshaw Hawkins, Randy Hughes, and Cowboy Copas —and all of them were killed. In 1973, she was el ected posthumously to the Country Music Hall of Fame.

Clower, Jerry

Born: September 28, 1926, Liberty, Mississippi
Married: Homerline Wells
Children: s. Ray; d. Amy, Sue, Katy

Homespun hilarity has made Jerry the country's top country comic with seven LPs that just keep selling year after year. His first, *Jerry Clower from Yazoo City, Mississippi, Talkin',* brought to the public what friends and business associates had been laughing about for years. As Field Services Director for the Mississippi Chemical Corporation, Jerry became the "Will Rogers" of the region, telling his stories of Amite County, youthful escapades of coon hunting, playing 'gator, and smothering French fries with molasses. His first LP led to national TV spots on the "Grand Ole Opry," "Mike Douglas," "David Frost," and other shows. A deacon of the First Baptist Church of Yazoo City, he has received numerous awards for service to mankind from the 4-H Club, Future Farmers of America, and the Southern Baptist Radio and Television Commission. His book *Ain't God Good* is a bestseller—and yes, that's Jerry doing those national radio and TV commercials for Dodge Trucks and Chrysler Motors.

Cochran, Hank

Born: August 2, 1935, Greenville, Mississippi
Married: Jeannie Seely

A writer-singer, better known for the former as composer of the late Patsy Cline's smash "I Fall to Pieces," Burl Ives's "Little Bitty Tear," Ray Price's "Make the World Go Away," and wife Jeannie Seely's "Don't Touch Me" though I personally fancy him as a singer. Listen, for instance, to his "Sally Was a Good Old Girl," which hit top-forty status, and "Has Anybody Seen Me Lately?" a humorous plaint of unrequited love. In 1978, he and old friend Willie Nelson recorded a hit duet, "Ain't Life Hell," written by Hank.

RCA Records and Tapes

Coe, David Allan

No statistics available

He's an ex-convict who spent twenty years in jail, got out in 1967, and decided to be blissfully successful as a backwoods poet and musical prophet. His recording career began, however, in 1968 with "Penitentiary Blues." Later, "How High's the Watergate Martha?" and "Keep Those Big Wheels Humming" brought acclaim, but it was "Would You Lay with Me (in a Field of Stone)" recorded by Tanya Tucker that stirred the emotions of audiences and became number one on all major country charts. His big 1977 release, "Once Upon a Rhyme," reveals yet another aspect of Coe as poet and innovator. In 1978, his biggie was "If This Is Just a Game."

Cornor, Randy

Born: Houston, Texas

A lead guitarist for Freddy Fender and Frenchie Bourque, Randy's first national release of his own, "Sometimes I Talk in My Sleep," for ABC-Dot indicates a promising future. Watch this space.

Randy Cornor

Copas, Cowboy (Lloyd T.)

Born: July 15, 1913, Muskogee, Oklahoma
Died: March 5, 1963, Camden, Tennessee.
Married: Lucy
Children: s. Gary Lee, Michael; d. Katha Loma Hughes

Copas grew up on a ranch where his mother taught him guitar, his father to sing; at eleven, he won an amateur music contest; at fourteen he turned professional on radio shows and country fairs; in 1946, he joined the Opry. His big hits include "Filipino Baby," "Signed, Sealed, and Delivered," "Tennessee Waltz," and "Alabam," his last and biggest single, which seemed to point the way to superstardom for him—when the plane carrying him, Patsy Cline, and Hawkshaw Hawkins crashed.

Cornelius, Helen

Born: Hannibal, Missouri
Birthday: December 6

As a youngster, she sang with her sisters and as she grew older, entered

Helen Cornelius

talent contests in Missouri, graduating in 1970 to the national "Ted Mac Amateur Hour," which she won three times. That same year she began to write songs and sent a tape to a publisher, Columbia Screen Gems. Within a week, she was signed as a writer and soon came to the attention of RCA. The result was her first single release, "We Still Sing Love Songs in Missouri." It was the RCA producer, Bob Ferguson, who matched Helen with Jim Ed Brown as the ideal duet combination. In 1976, they recorded "I Don't Want to Have to Marry You." Within three months, it reached the coveted number-one spot on all three national music trade magazines. This successful combo led to personal appearances, and to Helen's becoming a regular, on Jim Ed's syndicated TV show, "Nashville on the Road." In 1977, their "Saying Hello, Saying I Love You, Saying Good-bye" was another hit. In mid-1978, they moved into the top-ten singles with "If the World Ran Out of Love Tonight" and "I'll Never Be Free," while Helen's solo single "Wha cha Doin' After Midnight?" hit Top Fifty.

Country in the City

Country music fans are finding more and more places to hear their favorite kind of music in the city. From New York to San Francisco, it's possible to see performers— from big-name Opry stars to local bluegrass groups and jug bands. Here is a partial listing of country places. Call for information on acts, show times, and prices.

Arizona

Phoenix

Mr. Lucky's, 3660 Grand Ave., (602) 246–0686. Steve Matherly, general manager.

California

Calabasas

Sagebrush Cantina, 23527 Calabasas Road, (213) 888–6062.

Sundance Saloon, (213) 340–9241.

Helen Cornelius and her family

El Monte
Nashville West, 11910 East Valley Blvd., (Five Points Area), (213) 442–0337. C. J. Sanben, owner-manager.

Los Angeles
The Troubadour, 9081 Santa Monica Blvd., (213) 276–6158.

Mission Viejo
Shade Tree Stringed Instruments, 28722 Marguerite Parkway, (714) 495–5270. Gree Mirken, owner.

Newport Beach
The Cannery, 3010 Lafayette St., (714) 675–5777.

North Hollywood
Palamino Club, 6907 Lankershim Blvd., (213) 765–9256.

Pasadena
The Ice House, 24 N. Mentor Ave., (213) 681–9942.

Reseda
Relic House Diner & Saloon, 7140 Reseda Blvd., (213) 881–9888.

Salinas
Long Branch Steak & Saloon, 425 N. Main, (408) 424–2974.

Santa Barbara
Collywobble's Roadhouse, 16 S. La Cumbre Rd., (805) 967–9305.

Santa Monica
McCabe's Guitar Shop, 3101 Pico Blvd., (213) 828–4497.

Tarzana
Blue Ridge Pickin' Parlor, 5521 Reseda Blvd., (213) 345–1977. Ken Tennesen.

Torrance
Perry's Pizza, 25422 Crenshaw Blvd., at Pacific Coast Highway, Rolling Hills Shopping Plaza, (213) 530–0322.

Florida

Gainesville
Great Southern Music Hall, 233 W. University Ave., (904) 377–3013. Albert Teebagy, producer of shows.

Orlando
Great Southern Music Hall, 44 N. Orange Ave., (305) 423–2308.

Georgia

Atlanta
Country Roads Supper Club, 6400 Hillandale Rd., Lithonia, (404) 482–9131.
Muhlenbrink's Saloon, "Home of the Flaming Hurricane," 48 Old Alabama St., (404) 525–8493. Bobby Beachman, manager.
Rose's Cantina, 688 Spring St. NW, (404) 881–0244. Kerry Stiles, information agent.

Savannah
Night Flight Cafe, 113 E. River St., (912) 234–9565.

Illinois

Chicago area
A & J Lounge, 6336 S. Harlem, Summit, (312) 458–8447
The Alley, Rt. 22 and Green Bay Rd., Highwood, (312) 432–0606.
Amazingrace, 845 Chicago, Evanston, (312) 328–2489
Beef 'n' Barrel, 1932 E. Higgins Rd., Elk Grove Village, (312) 489–4060.
Biddy Mulligan's, 7644 N. Sheridan, (312) 761–6532.
Bar RR, 56 W. Madison, (312) 263–8207. Bill Goldstein, owner.
Charlotte's Web, 728 First Ave., Rockford, (815) 965–8933. Ruby Sky, manager.
Clarite Lounge, 2604 N. Clark, (312) 549–3315.
Clearwater Saloon, 2447 N. Lincoln, (312) 935–6545.
Country Music Inn, Milwaukee & Aptakisic, Prairie View, (312) 541–7670.
D.A.V. Club, 15340 Park Ave., (312) 331–9331.
Durty Nellie's Pub, 55 Bothwell, Palatine, (312) 358–8444.
Gordonsville Depot, 6643 W. Roosevelt, Berwyn, (312) 759–7044.
Harry Hope's, 9000 Cary Rd., Cary, (312) 639–2636.
Iron Rail, 5843 W. Irving Park, (312) 283–4252.
Jimmy's Woodlawn Tap, 1172 E. 55 St., (312) MI3–5516.
Lake 'n' Park Inn, 108th & Roberts, Palos Hills, (312) 974–3066. Jerry Melnitzke, owner.

Minstrel's, 6465 N. Sheridan, (312) 262–6230.
Moose's Lounge, 4553 N. Pulaski, (312) 539–0410, "Moose" Monrotus, owner.
Mr. Kiley's, 1125 W. Belmont, (312) 549–8524.
Nashville North, 101 E. Irving Park, Bensenville, (312) 595–0170. Archie Drury, owner.
North Branch Saloon, 1134 W. Armitage, (312) 281–3428.
Peanuts Tap, 4038 N. Lincoln, (312) 477–1334.
Reilly's Daughter Pub, 4010 W. 11th St., Oak Lawn, (312) 423–1188.
Single File, 934 W. Webster, (312) 525–1558.
Skyline Lounge, 1004 Belmont, (312) 549–9395.
Where Else, 2519 N. Lincoln, (312) 549–9071.

Indiana

Nashville
Little Nashville Opry, (812) 988–2251.

Kentucky

Louisville
Big Moe's, 2217 Goldsmith La., (502) 451–5532. Maurice Wolford, manager.

Missouri

Kansas City
Genova's Chestnut Inn, 2800 E. 12th St., (816) 231–9696. Joe Genova, owner.

New York

New York City
The Bottom Line, 15 W. 4th St., (212) 228–6300.
O'Lunney's Bar and Restaurant, 915 Second Ave., (between 48th and 49th), (212) 751–5470. Hugh O'Lunney, owner-manager.
Sweet Sue's, W. 33rd St., (between 7th and 8th Aves.), 1 Penn Plaza, opposite Madison Square Garden.
Folk City, 130 W. 3rd St., (at 6th Ave.), (212) AL4–8449.
Lone Star Cafe, 13th St. and 5th Ave., (212) 242–1664.
Kenny's Castaways, 157 Bleecker St., (212) 473–9870/1.

Oklahoma

Tulsa

Cain's Ballroom, 423 N. Main St., (918) 582-2078. Robert Bradley, manager.

Tennessee

Nashville

Blue Grass Inn, 1914 Broadway, (615) 327-9974.

Carousel Club, 220 Printers Alley, (615) 256-1802. Buster Merrill, general manager.

Col. Jackson's Picnic in the Woods and Country Music Jamboree, Hermitage Landing, Percy Priest Lake, PO Box 15014, (615) 383-6720 or 297-0572.

Dusty Roads Tavern, 114 Woodland St., (615) 251-9904.

Embers Western Room, 210 Printers Alley, (615) 254-6616.

Exit-In, 2208 Elliston Pl., (615) 327-2784.

Faron Young Jailhouse Lounge, 102 Third Ave. North, (615) 256-9432.

Four Guys Harmony House, 407 Murfreesboro Rd., (615) 256-0188.

Ernest Tubb Record Shop (Saturday Night Jamboree), 1530 Demonbreun, (615) 255-0589.

George Jones Possum Holler, corner of Third and Commerce (615) 254-1431. Bill Swain, general manager.

Old Time Picking Parlor, 105 Second Ave. North, (615) 256-5720.

Station Inn, 104 Twenty-eighth Ave. North, (615) 297-5796.

Tootsie's Orchid Lounge, 422 Broadway, (615) 251-9725.

Texas

Austin

Alliance Wagon Yard, 5555 N. Lamar, suite 123 (Commerce Park), (512) 459-3317. Billy Carmean, general manager.

Armadillo World Headquarters, 525½ Barton Springs Rd., (512) 477-3548. Hank Alrich, manager.

Broken Spoke, 3201 S. Lamar, (512) 442-6189. James White, general manager.

Brushy Creek Saloon, 2015 N. Mays (Old Highway 81) in Round Rock, (512) 255-4846. Chuck Ferguson, general manager.

Bull Creek Inn, 5204 FM2222, (512) 345-7466. Tim O'Connor, general manager.

The Filling Station, 801 Barton Springs Rd., (512) 477-1022.

Rome Inn, 29th and Rio Grande, (512) 476-6111.

Silver Dollar, 9102 Burnet Rd., (512) 837-5950. James Shaw, general manager.

Soap Creek Saloon, 707 E. Bee Caves Rd., (512) 327-9016. Don Dewvall, manager.

Split Rail Inn. 217 S. Lamar, (512) 472-1314. Jim Parish owner.

Dallas

Whiskey River, 5421 Greenville, (214) 369-9221. Jack Roberts, general manager.

General Store and Tipping House, 4820 Greenville Ave., (214) 691-8666. Ralph Sturgeon, owner.

Longhorn Ballroom, 216 Corinth St., (214) 428-3128. Doug Groom, manager.

The Filling Station, 6862 Greenville Ave., (214) 691-4488.

Faces, 4001 Cedar Springs, (214) 526-9004. Bill Tangredi, owner-manager.

Pasadena

Gilley's Club, 4500 Spencer Highway, (713) 941-7990. Sherwood Cryer, general manager.

Wisconsin

Madison

The Church Key, 626 University Avenue, (608) 257-1122. Darrell Hanson, owner-manager.

Milwaukee

Nick's Nicabob, 2538 W. State Street, (414) 342-9931. Nick Beaumont, owner.

Dan Kellams

Hugh O'Lunney in New York City

Country in the City Radio Stations
WAMQ 670—Chicago

Nancy Turner

Charlie O'Neil

Lee Sherwood

Bill Hennes, Program Director

Fred Sanders

Rich Renick

Lon Helton

Burt Sherwood,
General Manager

WHN 1050—New York

Willie Nelson, DJ Lee Arnold, Waylon Jennings

Charlie Cook

Del DeMontreux

Larry Gatlin, Lee Arnold

Jessie Berman

Alan Colmes

Larry Kenney

Ed Baer

Bob "Wizard" Wayne

Country Music Association

In 1958, this organization was formed by people in the country music industry to promote country music in all areas of entertainment around the world. A major force in bringing country stars to network-TV audiences, the Association established the first Country Music Awards in 1967, now an annual TV event as avidly followed as the Oscar and Emmy presentations. The International Country Music Fan Fair, launched in 1972, attracted several hundred thousand fans in 1977 and has become a major annual festival. Cosponsored by the Grand Ole Opry, it offers twenty-five hours of entertainment over five days and the opportunity to meet major artists. *See also* The Country Music Hall of Fame and Museum.

For information: 7 Music Circle North, Nashville, TN. 37203.

Country Music Hall of Fame and Museum

Country Music Association Awards, 1967–1978

Entertainer of the Year

1967	Eddy Arnold
1968	Glen Campbell
1969	Johnny Cash
1970	Merle Haggard
1971	Charley Pride
1972	Loretta Lynn
1973	Roy Clark
1974	Charlie Rich
1975	John Denver
1976	Mel Tillis
1977	Ronnie Milsap
1978	Dolly Parton

Johnny Cash

The White House

Album of the Year

1967 *There Goes My Everything*—Jack Greene—Decca

1968 *Johnny Cash At Folsom Prison*—Johnny Cash—Columbia

1969 *Johnny Cash At San Quentin Prison*—Johnny Cash—Columbia

1970 *Okie From Muskogee*—Merle Haggard—Capitol

1971 *I Won't Mention It Again*—Ray Price—Columbia

1972 *Let Me Tell You about a Song*—Merle Haggard—Capitol

1973 *Behind Closed Doors*—Charlie Rich—Epic

1974 *A Very Special Love Song*—Charlie Rich—Epic

1975 *A Legend in My Time*—Ronnie Milsap—RCA

1976 *Wanted—the Outlaws*—Waylon Jennings/Jessi Colter/Tompall Glaser/Willie Nelson—RCA

1977 *Ronnie Milsap Live*—Ronnie Milsap—RCA

1978 *It Was Almost Like a Song*—Ronnie Milsap-RCA

Female Vocalist of the Year

1967	Loretta Lynn
1968	Tammy Wynette
1969	Tammy Wynette
1970	Tammy Wynette
1971	Lynn Anderson
1972	Loretta Lynn
1973	Loretta Lynn
1974	Olivia Newton–John
1975	Dolly Parton
1976	Dolly Parton
1977	Crystal Gayle
1978	Crystal Gayle

Vocal Group of the Year

1967	The Stoneman Family
1968	Porter Wagoner & Dolly Parton
1969	Johnny Cash & June Carter
1970	The Glaser Brothers
1971	The Osborne Brothers
1972	The Statler Brothers
1973	The Statler Brothers
1974	The Statler Brothers

1975 The Statler Brothers
1976 The Statler Brothers
1977 The Statler Brothers
1978 The Oak Ridge Boys

Single of the Year
1967 "There Goes My Everything"—Jack Greene—Decca
1967 "Harper Valley P.T.A."—Jeannie C. Riley—Plantation
1969 "A Boy Named Sue"—Johnny Cash—Columbia
1970 "Okie From Muskogee"—Merle Haggard—Capitol
1971 "Help Me Make It Through The Night"—Sammi Smith—Mega
1972 "Happiest Girl In The Whole U.S.A."—Donna Fargo—Dot
1973 "Behind Closed Doors"—Charlie Rich—Epic
1974 "Country Bumpkin"—Cal Smith—MCA
1975 "Before The Next Teardrop Falls"—Freddy Fender—ABC-Dot
1976 "Good Hearted Woman"—Waylon Jennings/Willie Nelson—RCA
1977 "Lucille"—Kenny Rogers—United Artists
1978 "Heaven's Just a Sin Away"—The Kendalls—Ovation

Song of the Year
1967 "There Goes My Everything"—Dallas Frazier
1968 "Honey"—Bobby Russell
1969 "Carroll County Accident"—Bob Ferguson
1970 "Sunday Morning Coming Down"—Kris Kristofferson

The Kendalls
Bruno of Hollywood

© 1976 Melinda Wickman

Willie Nelson

1971 "Easy Loving"—Freddie Hart
1972 "Easy Loving"—Freddie Hart
1973 "Behind Closed Doors"—Kenny O'Dell
1974 "Country Bumpkin"—Don Wayne
1975 "Back Home Again"—John Denver
1976 "Rhinestone Cowboy"—Larry Weiss
1977 "Lucille"—Roger Bowling/Hal Bynum
1978 "Don't It Make My Brown Eyes Blue"—Richard Leigh

Male Vocalist of the Year
1967 Jack Greene
1968 Glen Campbell
1969 Johnny Cash
1970 Merle Haggard
1971 Charley Pride
1972 Charley Pride
1973 Charlie Rich
1974 Ronnie Milsap
1975 Waylon Jennings
1976 Ronnie Milsap
1977 Ronnie Milsap
1978 Don Williams

Vocal Duo of the Year (added in 1970)
1970 Porter Wagoner & Dolly Parton
1971 Porter Wagoner & Dolly Parton
1972 Conway Twitty & Loretta Lynn

1973 Conway Twitty & Loretta Lynn
1974 Conway Twitty & Loretta Lynn
1975 Conway Twitty & Loretta Lynn
1976 Waylon Jennings & Willie Nelson
1977 Jim Ed Brown & Helen Cornelius
1978 Kenny Rogers & Dottie West

Instrumental Group or Band of the Year

1967 The Buckaroos
1968 The Buckaroos
1969 Danny Davis & the Nashville Brass
1970 Danny Davis & the Nashville Brass
1971 Danny Davis & the Nashville Brass
1972 Danny Davis & the Nashville Brass
1973 Danny Davis & the Nashville Brass
1974 Danny Davis & the Nashville Brass
1975 Roy Clark & Buck Trent
1976 Roy Clark & Buck Trent
1977 The Original Texas Playboys
1978 The Oak Ridge Boys

Instrumentalist of the Year

1967 Chet Atkins
1968 Chet Atkins
1969 Chet Atkins
1970 Jerry Reed
1971 Jerry Reed
1972 Charlie McCoy

RCA Records/Buddy Lee Attractions, Inc.

Danny Davis and the Nashville Brass

1973 Charlie McCoy
1974 Don Rich
1975 Johnny Gimble
1976 Hargus "Pig" Robbins
1977 Roy Clark
1978 Roy Clark

Comedian of the Year
(eliminated in 1971)

1967 Don Bowman
1968 Ben Colder
1969 Archie Campbell
1970 Roy Clark

Country Music Foundation

The Foundation is the administrative entity encompassing the Country Music Hall of Fame and Museum and also the Country Music Foundation Library and Media Center. It was organized in 1964 by leaders of the country music industry who saw the need for an educational institution that would parallel the promotional activities of the Country Music Association.

The Foundation therefore is the liaison between country music and the university community and works to encourage reissuance of historical recordings and publication of books and articles on country music. The Foundation publishes the quarterly, *Journal of Country Music,* and operates the Country Music Foundation Press, which reprints primary works of historical importance to American music and original manuscripts on country music.

For information: CMF, 700 16th Ave., Nashville, Tennessee, 37203

Country Music Hall of Fame and Museum

Located in the Music City section of Nashville, amidst the studios and offices of the leading country music record companies, publishers, and artists—and across the road from Ernest Tubbs's Record Store! Here is an exciting synthesis of history and scholarship presented with love and integrity. Among the exhibits are:

Performing costumes.
Artists such as Elvis Presley, Minnie Pearl, Hank Snow, Merle Travis, Gene Autrey, Dolly Parton—including Willie Nelson's sneakers and headband!

Three centuries of country music instruments.
Included are such early mountain originals as a fiddle made of a cigar box, banjos made of a roasting pan and groundhog skin, and other items forged from coffee tins and

lard buckets—plus a progression of professional guitars, banjos, fiddles, including historic instruments of such famous instrumentalists as Les Paul, Chet Atkins, Doc Watson, Waylon Jennings, and others.

Grand Ole Opry exhibit.
On display are films, posters, photographs, memorabilia, going back to the show's origin in 1925; a country star's tour bus—a fitted custom Eagle coach—showing how artists 'live on the road; Elvis Presley's gold-plated Cadillac; vintage films of Tex Ritter, Merle Travis, Bob Wills—and a rare copy of the 1929 sound film of Jimmie Rodgers, *The Singing Brakeman,* singing among others, "T For Texas, T For Tennessee."

Opened in April, 1967, as an educational service of the Country Music Foundation, its library and media center have become the foremost research facility on country music in the nation. A half million visitors visit each year.

See How A Record Is Made! You can visit Studio B, still in commercial use as one of Nashville's historic recording studios. Built by RCA at the urging of Chet Atkins, here's where Elvis recorded "Heartbreak Hotel." Jim Reeves's "He'll Have To Go," Roy Orbison's "Pretty Woman," Eddy Arnold's "What's He Doing In My World" etc. Demonstration of multi-track mixing techniques.

Thomas Hart Benton's last mural, "The Sources of Country Music," a poetic tribute to old-time music and musicians.

The Foundation Library and Media Center: early recordings, fan club publications, books, magazines, clippings, films. PLUS a special Roy Acuff archives containing 50 years of memorabilia and a Burl Ives section given by a Michigan man who collected everything Burl did since leaving his Illinois farm in 1936.

Elvis's cadillac

The King owned dozens of Cadillacs but this was reportedly his favorite. A 1960 series 71 limousine, extensively personalized by famed auto customizer, George Barris, it features: two gold-plated telephones, a gold-plated shoe shiner and buffer, gold-plated television set and 45 RPM record player, a gold-plated refreshment tray with gold-plated ice trays and a refrigerator capable of producing ice cubes in two minutes.

The gold theme continues with all the metalwork gold-plated, gold fabric in the interior and six gold records on the interior roof. The exterior is finished in a one-of-a-kind paint—a thick white pearl mixed with gold dust for a rich golden glow. Valued at over $100,000, it was first put on display in the Country Music Hall of Fame on May 5, 1977, and has proved to be the most popular exhibit among museum visitors.

Country Music Magazine

The magazine for country-music fans can be purchased by subscription at great savings. One year for $7.95 (a saving of $4.05 off the newsstand cost of 12 issues) plus free calendar. Two years (24 issues) for $12.95 plus free calendar.

Write, enclosing money to: *Country Music,* PO Box 2560, Boulder, CO 80302.

Country Sales Newsletter

Going into its thirteenth year, this newsletter offers almost anything you can imagine that pertains to country music. Recent editions include "The Bluegrass Directory," old-time sheet music, antique electric trains, instruction guides, magazines, and, of course, records.

The newsletter is free, but the publisher requires at least one order a year in order to remain on the mailing list. Write: PO Box 191, Floyd, VA 24091.

Craddock, Billy "Crash"

Born: June 16, 1939, Greensboro, North Carolina
Married: Mae
Children: s. Billy, Jr., Steve; d. April

As an eleven year old, his "stage" was the barn floor, his "guitar" a broomstick, his "audience," the cows, pigs and chickens—and his older brother Chauncey gave him lessons on a real guitar. That these lessons paid off is evident in eight number-one records since 1972, including "Knock Three Times," "Walk Softly," "Easy As Pie," and "Broken Down in Tiny Pieces." In 1978, "I Cheated On a Good Woman's Love," and "Hubba Hubba" hit the singles charts while LP *Turning Up And Turning On* made the Top Fifty.

Cramer, Floyd

Born: October 27, 1933, Shreveport, Louisiana
Married: Mary
Children: d. Diane, Donna

Floyd Cramer

A distinctive pianist, his work is instantly recognizable on more than two-dozen top RCA albums. In 1951, he joined station KWKH's "Louisiana Hayride" and toured with Hank Williams and Elvis Presley. When Chet Atkins suggested he move to Nashville, he did so and became a studio musician. He wrote his first single for RCA Victor, "Last Date," which sold nearly a million copies. In November 1974, during a performance of the Festival of Music at Opryland, Chet Atkins surprised the startled Floyd with a presentation of an engraved metronome in honor of his fifteen years with RCA Records.

Crawdaddy

Country and western monthly magazine. It sells at $7.95 for 1 year; $14 for 2 years ($10 under newsstand cost); $19 for 3 years ($17 under newsstand cost). Call toll free 800–247–2160, or write to: *Crawdaddy,* PO Box 6330, Marion, OH 43302.

D

Davis, Skeeter

Born: December 30, 1931, Dry Ridge, Kentucky
Married: Ralph Emery
Children: s. Steve

While at high school during the forties, she formed a singing team with classmate Betty Jack Davis (no relation); the Davis Sisters' (as they were called) very first record, "I Forgot More than You'll Ever Know," became the number-one song for 1953. But tragedy struck soon thereafter when Betty Jack was killed in an automobile accident; after a mourning period, Skeeter joined Ernest Tubb and his Texas Troubadours and toured with them. She joined the Opry in 1959. Her own composition "I'm Falling Too" made the top ten for 1960. Other hits are: "My Last Date with You" and "The End of the World."

Dave and Sugar

RCA/Chardon, Inc.

Dave & Sugar

Dave Rowland, Vicki Hackman Baker, and Sue Powell

They started out in 1975 and toured with Charley Pride as his opening act and vocal backup. Dave had previously toured with Elvis Presley, been a member of such well-known groups as the Stamps Quartet and the Four Guys, and regularly appeared on the Opry. Vicki and Sue had each sung with various groups and on radio and TV before joining with Dave as "Sugar." The mix was evidently good because within a year they had recorded their first single, "Queen of the Silver Dollar." It stayed on the charts for twenty weeks and was followed by their first number-one hit single, "The Door Is Always Open." Just to show this wasn't a fluke, their next release, "I'm Gonna Love You," also hit number one, as did their LP, *Dave & Sugar*. The group's travels with Charley Pride have taken them around the world, including Japan and Australia, and have also provided Vicki with a husband, Charley's lead guitar player, Ron Baker. In late 1978, *Tear Time* had hit big as an LP and the singles "It's a Heartache" and "Gotta Quit Lookin' at You Baby," were also hits.

The Devil's Box

Published quarterly by the Tennessee Valley Old-Time Fiddlers Association, it deals with old-time fiddling and related music, history, old-time string bands, rare photographs, and discography, plus reader's forum, record reviews, festival listings, and fiddle tablature.

Subscription: U.S., $5 a year; Foreign, $6 a year. Write: Route 4, Box 634, Madison, AL 35758.

Disc Collector Newsletter

This is a meaty listing of hundreds of rare and wonderful records.

Subscription: 10 issues, $3. Auction lists: 25 cents. Write: Disc Collector Publications, Cheswold, DE 19936.

Dottsy

Born: April 6, 1954, Seguin, Texas

A "country girl" by her own description, with long blonde hair and warm blue eyes, the traditional girl next door, Dottsy has been performing since age twelve. She was discovered by the same man who started Johnny Rodriguez on his career, Happy Shahan who booked her into his Shahan's Alamo Village and became her manager. Her first RCA single, "Storms Never Last" was released in April 1975, and hit the top ten, followed by "I'll Be Your San Antone Rose," another top-charter. Her first album in 1976 was *The Sweetest Thing.* In 1978, her single hit "Play Born to Lose Again" solidified her star status.

Drusky, Roy

Born: June 22, 1930, Atlanta, Georgia
Married: Bobbye Jean Swafford
Children: s. Roy Frank III, Tracy

Roy started in kindergarten as a bandleader and drummer, then studied piano and clarinet, was a talented baseball player, and was about to sign with the Cleveland In-

dians when he joined the Navy instead. That's where he learned to play the guitar and became interested in country music. In the late forties, he formed his own band and played at WEAS, Decatur, Georgia. A DJ and record producer as well as a performer and songwriter, Roy joined the Opry in 1960. His hits include "Anymore" and "Three Hearts in a Tangle." His composition "Alone with You," sung by Faron Young, hit the top ten for 1958.

RCA Records and Tapes

Dottsy

The John Edwards Memorial Foundation, Inc.

Chartered as an educational non-profit corporation in California, the foundation was established to further the serious study of American folk music: to gather phonograph records, photographs, biographical and discographical information, scholarly works, and other material pertaining to folk music; to make available reprints of this information and recordings of the music, and to stimulate academic research in the area of American folk music as part of a cultural heritage. The archives and research facilities are located in the Folklore and Mythology Center at the University of California, Los Angeles. For further details, write to The John Edwards Memorial Foundation, Folklore and Mythology Center, University of California, Los Angeles, CA 90024.

Ely, Joe

Born: Lubbock, Texas

Basically a songwriter-musician, he first traveled with a circus through the Southwest before he formed a small band of musicians in Austin. They played honky-tonk around Texas, including Lubbock's Cotton Club, made famous by Waylon Jennings. Forming the nucleus of the Joe Ely Band are musicians such as Gregg Wright (bass), Steve Keeton (drums), Jesse Taylor (electric guitar), and Lloyd Maines (steel guitar).

MCA Records

Joe Ely

Fairs and Festivals

Typical of these fairs and festivals are livestock competitions, fiddling and banjo contests, horse-racing, quilting bees, canning, square dancing, midway rides, and games of skill—and bright lights and country music, including such superstars as Tammy Wynette, Johnny Cash, and Charlie Pride. Over 160 million visitors flocked to the hundreds of events in 1977. Following is a nationwide listing of annual country fairs and festivals. For specific dates, maps, accommodations, and so forth, write to the individual local agencies, as indicated.

Alabama

June. Jasmine Hill International Folk Festival, near Montgomery; Chalaka Arts and Crafts Show, Noble Park, Sylacauga; Birmingham Square Dance Association's President Ball, Birmingham; Chilton County Peach Festival, Clanton.

July. Spirit of America Festival, Point Mallard Park, Decatur; Glorious Fourth, Fairhope; Annual Lion's Club Barbecue, Prattville; Fourth of July Fair, Talladega; Mentone Crafts Festival, Mentone.

August. Old-Time Fiddlers' and Pickers' Reunion, Chandler Mountain, Steele; Old Home Folks Day, Opp; Marshall County Fair, Boaz; Bluegrass Festival, Sylacauga; Blount County Fair, Oneonta.

September. Etowah County Fair, Attalla; Franklin County Fair, Russelville; World's Largest Contest Day, Castleberry Eclectic School Grounds, Eclectic; Cren-Creek Village, Luverne; Cleburne County Fair, Heflin; Northeast Alabama State Fair, Huntsville; Lawrence County Fair, Moulton; Northwest Alabama Fair, Jasper; Shelby County Fair, Columbiana; Tennessee Valley Exposition (Morgan County Fair), Decatur; Festival in the Park, Oak Park, Montgomery; Kentuck Arts and Crafts Festival, Kentuck Park, Northport; Bibb County Fair, Centreville; Cullman County Fair, Cullman; North Alabama State Fair, Muscle Shoals; Pike County Fair, Double Springs; Autauga County Fair, Prattville; Calhoun County Fair, Anniston; Chilton County Fair, Gragg Field, Clanton; Covington County Fair, River Falls Road, Andalusia; Jackson County Fair, Scottsboro; West Alabama Fair, Tuscaloosa; Annual Tennessee Valley Old-Time Fiddlers' Convention, Athens State College, Athens.

October. Chilton County Singing Convention, Clanton; Butler County Fair, Greenville; Central Alabama Fair, Lion's Fair Park, Selma; Dekalb County Fair, Fort Payne; Lee County Fair, Opelika; Alabama State Fair, Birmingham; Annual Boaz Harvest Festival, Boaz; Annual AAUW Art Show, Confederate Park, Demopolis; Annual White Plains Country Fair, Sharpe's Lake, between Roanoke and LaFayette; Baldwin County Fair, Robertsdale; Annual Old-Time Fiddlers' and Bluegrass Contest, Huntsville; Riverfront Market Day, Selma; Birmingham Square Dance Association Fall Dance, Birmingham; Greater Clarke-Washington County Fair, Jackson; South Alabama State Fair, Montgomery; Greater Gulf State Fair, Mobile; Annual Community Hymn Festival, First United Methodist Church Auditorium, Centre.

November. W.C. Handy's Birthday Celebration, W.C. Handy Museum, Florence; Festival of Harmony, Mobile.

For information, *write:* Bureau of Publicity, State of Alabama, Montgomery, AL 36130.

Debby Boone

Alaska

June. Alaska Festival of Music, Anchorage; Alaska Show and Sourdough Buffet, Captain Cook Hotel, Anchorage; Gold Creek Salmon Bake, Gold Creek Basin, Juneau; King Crab Festival, Kodiak.

July. Golden Days Celebration, Fairbanks; Cry of the Wild Ram, Monashka Bay, Kodiak Island.

August. Tanana Valley State Fair, Fairbanks; Matanuska Valley Fair, Palmer (these two alternate as official state fair: odd-numbered years in Fairbanks, even-numbered in Palmer); Southeast Alaska State Fair, Haines.

October. Alaska Day, Sitka.

For information, write: Division of Tourism, Department of Commerce and Economic Development, Pouch E, Juneau, AK 99811.

Arizona

January. Annual Lost Dutchman Days Celebration, Apache Junction.

February. Annual Square Dance Festival, Yuma; Annual Square and Round Dance Festival, Phoenix.

March. Stagecoach Days, Maricopa; Northern Yuma County Fair, Parker; Frontier Town Celebration BBQ and Dance, Cave Creek/Carefree; South Mountain Festival of Arts, Phoenix; San Xavier Festival, Tucson; Tucson Festival, Tucson.

April. Whoopee Daze Celebration, Tolleson; Sister City Festival, Tempe; Pinal County Fair, Casa Grande; 4H Club Fair, Phoenix; Yuma County Fair, Yuma; Festival Arts and Crafts Fair, Tucson; *La Fiesta de la Placita,* Tucson; *La Fiesta de los Niños,* Tucson; Kearny Pioneer Days, Kearny; Verde Valley Fair, Camp Verde; Annual Pioneer Day, Peoria; Firebird Festival of the Arts, Phoenix.

May. Two Flags Art Festival, Douglas; *Cinco de Mayo Fiestas,* Phoenix, Tucson, and Border Towns; Verde Valley Fair, Cottonwood; Mother's Day Music Festival, *La Noche Mexicana,* Phoenix; Mother's Day Music Festival, Sun City; Annual Yarnell Daze, Yarnell; Gold Camp Days, Oatman.

June. Summer Festival, Flagstaff; Mile High Square Dance Festival, Prescott; Country Music Festival, Payson.

July. Old-Time Fiddling, Pioneer Park, Mesa; White Mountain Square Dance Festival, Pinetop; Pioneer Days, Flagstaff; Sawdust Festival, Payson.

August. Flagstaff Summer Festival, Flagstaff; Buffalo Bill's Wild West Show, Scottsdale; Centennial Celebration, Bisbee; Summer Festival, Pioneer; Coconino County Fair, Flagstaff.

September. Brewery Gulch Days Fair and Pageant, Bisbee; Mohave County Fair, Kingman; Pleasant Valley Fair, Young; 4H Club Fair, Sonoita; Gila County Fair, Globe; Yavapai County Fair, Prescott; Music Fair, Randolph Park, Tucson; Arizona Old-Time Fiddlers' Contest, Payson; Cochise County Fair, Douglas.

October. Old-Time Fiddlers' Contest, Springerville; London Bridge Days, Lake Havasu City; Square Dance Festival, Lake Havasu City; Annual Rex Allen Days, Willcox; Graham County Fair, Safford; Annual *Fiesta de Amigos,* Phoenix; Copper Cities Square Dance Festival, Globe; Autumn Festival and Homecoming, Sedona; Green Valley County Fair, Green Valley; Arizona State Fair, Phoenix; Alpine Festival, Payson.

November. Multi-Cultural Fair, Armory Park, Tucson; Fiesta, Wickenburg; Annual Fountain Festival of Arts and Crafts, Fountain Hills.

December. Gompers Winter Festival, Phoenix.

Charlie McCoy   Monument

For information, write: State of Arizona, Office of Tourism, 1700 West Washington, Room 501, Phoenix, AZ 85007.

California

February. Whiskey Flat Days, Kernville.

March. Van and CB Jamboree, Knotts Berry Farm, Buena Park; Twin Counties Jamboree, Fairgrounds, Santa Maria; Easter County Fair Celebration, Buena Park; Old-Timers Days Carnival, Sunland; Borrego Springs Spring Art Festival, Borrego Springs.

April. Colorado River Country Fair, Blythe; Lakeside Family Fair and Rodeo Days Carnival, Lakeside; Pegleg Liars Contest, Borrego Springs; Lakeside Family Fair and Rodeo Days, Maplewood and Ashwood; Ramona Pageant, Hemet.

May. Valley Center Western Days, Valley Center; May Festival, Hart Park, Orange; Mule Days Celebration, Tri-County Fairgrounds, Bishop; Annual San Ysidro *Cinco de Mayo* Celebration, San Ysidro; Western States Music Tournament, La Mesa; *Fiesta de la Primavera,* San Diego.

June. Wild Wild Wet Summer Grand Opening, Anaheim; Annual Camp Pendleton Rodeo, San Diego.

July. Tri-County Fair, Bishop; Pow Wow Days, Apple Valley.

August. Sounds of Summer, San Diego; Tijuana Home Fair, Rio de Tijuana; Farmers Fair, Hemet; Sports and Arts Festival, Santa Monica.

September. Central Coast Square Dance Association Dances, Santa Maria; Los Angeles City Birthday Celebration, Los Angeles; Los Angeles County Fair, Pomona; Kern County Fair, Bakersfield; Mexican Independence Celebration, San Ysidro; Annual Julian Banjo and Fiddle Contest, Julian.

October. Stagecoach Days, Banning; Fiesta Days Parade, Yorba Linda.

November. Harvest Festival and Country Crafts Market, San Diego; All-Western Band Review, Long Beach.

December. Old Town Posada, San Diego.

For information write: Greater Los Angeles Visitors and Convention Bureau, 505 South Flower Street, Los Angeles, CA 90071

Colorado

All Summer. Mountain-Plains Arts and Crafts Festival, Denver; Flying *W* Chuckwagon Suppers and Show, Colorado Springs; JC Chuckwagon Dinners, Colorado Springs; Bar-*D* Chuckwagon Suppers and Show, Durango; Chuckwagon Suppers at the Lazy *B,* Estes Park; Music in the Mountains Concerts, Estes Park; Square Dancing at Frank Lane's Ranch, Estes Park; Mountain Music Opry, Green Mountain Falls; Square Dancing, Lyons.

May. May Festival, Larimer Square, Denver; *Cinco de Mayo Fiesta,* Henderson; *Cinco de Mayo* Festival, Walsenburg; Music and Cherry Blossom Festival, Canon City; Narrow Gauge Days Celebration, Durango.

June. Wild West Days Carnival, Hugo; Loveland Centennial Pageant, Loveland; Hot Sulphur Days Celebration, Hot Sulphur Springs; Square Dance Festival, Idaho Springs; Kremmling Days Celebration, Kremmling; Chautauqua Arts Festival, Monte Vista.

July. Cottonwood Capers Parade

Wendy Holcombe

and Dance, Alamosa; Range Call Rodeo and Pageant, Meeker; Festival of the West, Jeff. Co. Fairgrounds, Denver; Chuckwagon Supper, Ice-cream Social, Limon; Founders Day Celebration, Rocky Ford; Vail America Day Celebration, Vail; Village Cabaret Melodrama and Musicals, Vail; Tenth Mountain Division Reunion, Vail; Missouri Day Celebration, Fowler; Cattlemen's Days Celebration, Gunnison; Buffalo Bill Days Celebration, Golden; Rocky Mountain Arts and Crafts Fair, Henderson; Gold Rush Days Celebration, Victor; Arts and Crafts Fair, Steamboat Springs; Range Riders Breakfast, Colorado Springs; Craft Show, Barbeque, and Program, Dillon; Mesa County Fair, Grand Junction; St. Anne and St. James Celebrations, San Luis; Crowley Days Barbeque and Dance, Ordway; Western Days Celebration, Grand Lake.

August. Kit Carson County Fair, Burlington; Colorado Day Celebration (Central City/Kremmling/Denver/Loveland/Vail, etc.); Montelores County Fair, Cortez; El Paso County Fair, Calhan; Navajo Trails Fiesta, Durango; Western Welcome Week, Littleton; Gold Rush Days, Idaho Springs; Leadville Boom Days, Leadville; San Miguel Basin Rodeo and Fair, Norwood; Annual Art and Music Festival, Dillon; Evergreen Rodeo and Village Fair, Evergreen; Western Week Celebration, Grand Lake; Bent County Fair and 4H Rodeo, Las Animas; 4H County Fair, Canon City; Night in Old Denver, Larimer Square, Denver; Larimer County Fair and Rodeo, Loveland; Pageant Parade of the Rockies, Colorado Springs; Escalante Days Celebration, Dolores; Archuleta County Fair, Pagosa Springs; 4H Fair and Rodeo, Walsenburg; Arkansas Valley Fair, Rocky Ford; Logan County Fair, Sterling; La Plata County Fair, Durango; Lincoln County Free Fair, Hugo; Colorado State Fair, Pueblo.

September. Garfield County Fair and Rodeo, Rifle; Harvest Festival, Windsor; City Centennial Recognition Day, Loveland; Routt County Fair and Rodeo, Steamboat Springs; Pioneer Day Celebration, Florence; Pioneer Day, Canon City; Middle Park Fair, Kremmling; Harvest Ball, Craig; Grand Junction Art Festival, Grand Junction; Speedboat Races and Octoberfest, Grand Lake; Harvest Festival Entertainment, Limon; Autumn Coloride Fest, Telluride; Pioneer Days Celebration, Norwood.

For information, write: State of Colorado, Division of Commerce and Development, Travel Marketing Section, 500 State Centennial Building, Denver, CO 80203.

Connecticut

June. Hartford Arts Festival, Hartford; Rose Arts Festival, Norwich; Trinity Alive, Hartford.

July. North Stonington Agricultural Fair, North Stonington; Connecticut Agricultural Fair, Durham.

August. Oyster Festival, Milford; Middlesex County 4-H Fair, Durham; Hamburg Fair, Hamburg; Tolland County 4-H Fair, Rockville; Windham County 4-H Fair, South Woodstock; Chester Fair, Chester.

September. Woodstock Fair, Woodstock; Haddam Neck Fair, Haddam Neck; Hebron Harvest Fair, Hebron; North Haven Fair, North Haven; Guilford Fair, Guilford.

October. Berlin Fair, Berlin; Danbury State Fair, Danbury; Glastonbury Grange Fair, South Glastonbury.

For information, write: Connecticut Department of Commerce, 210 Washington Street, Hartford, CT 06106.

Delaware

May. Old Dover Days, Dover.

July. Cape Henlopen Craft Fair and Fold Life Festival, Lewes; Delaware State Fair, Harrington; Annual Brandywine Arts Festival, Wilmington.

For information, write: Delaware State Visitors Service, 630 State College Road, Dover, DE 19901.

Florida

January. Arts and Crafts Festival, Brooksville; Sandy Shoes Festival, Fort Pierce; Country Western Jamboree, North Miami; Annual Square Dance, Panama City; Old Island Days, Key West; Hands of Friendship Across the Border, Daytona Beach Shores; DeSoto County Fair, Arcadia; Collier County Fair, Naples; Manatee County Fair, Palmetto; South Florida Fair, West Palm Beach; Southwest Florida Fair, Ft. Myers; Florida Citrus Festival, Winter Haven.

February. Mount Dora Art Festival, Mount Dora; Everglades Fisherman Seafood Festival, Everglades City; Mardi Gras Carnival, Cape Coral; Annual Florida Citrus Festival, Winter Haven; Illuminated Night Fiesta Parade, Tampa; Ybor City Fiesta Day, Tampa; Haines City Happening, Haines City; Annual George Washington Celebration, Eustin; Grant Seafood Festival, Grant; I Am an American Week,

Lake Buena Vista; Hendry County Fair, Clewiston; Southeastern Youth Fair, Ocala; St. Lucie County Fair, Ft. Pierce; Kissimmee Valley Livestock Show, Kissimmee; Highlands County Fair, Sebring; South Dade County Fair, Homestead; Pasco County Fair, Dade City; Central Florida Fair, Orlando; Hillsborough County Fair and Strawberry Festival, Plant City; Hernando County Fair, Brooksville.

March. Azalea Festival, Palatka; Annual Chalo Nitka Festival and Rodeo, Moore Haven; Davie Orange Festival, Davie; Arts and Crafts Festival, Pompano; Chasco Fiesta, New Port Richey; Largo Patriots Festival, Largo; Lake Worth Spring Festival, Lake Worth; St. Petersburg Folk Fair, St. Petersburg; Frontier Days, Orange City; Fun 'N Sun Festival, Clearwater; Desoto Celebration, Bradenton; Springtime Tallahassee, Tallahassee; Festival of States, St. Petersburg; Highland Games and Festival, Dunedin; Pioneer Days, Sanford; King Neptune's Frolic, Sarasota; County Phillippi Festival and Hobby Show, Safety Harbor; Harvest Festival, Immokalee; Clay Festival, Orange Park; Pinellas County Fair, Largo; Martin County Fair, Stuart; Citrus County Fair, Inverness; Sarasota County Fair, Sarasota; Dade Coun-

ty Youth Fair, Miami; Lake County Fair and Flower Show, Eustis; Bradford County Fair, Starke; Florida State Fair, Tampa.

April. Lake Worth Pioneer Days, Lake Worth; Arts and Crafts Festival, St. Augustine; Arts and Crafts Festival, Dade City; Seven Lively Arts Festival, Hollywood; Scratch Ankle, Milton; Delray Affair, Delray Beach; Annual Suwannee River Area Cracker Folk Arts-Crafts Show, White Springs; Beach Festival and Parade, Jacksonville Beach; Country Day, Vernon; Tarpon Springs Arts and Crafts Show, Tarpon Springs; Putnam County Fair, Palatka; Suwannee River Fair and Livestock Show, Suwannee River; Okaloosa County Fair, Fort Walton Beach; Flagler County Fair, Bunnell.

May. Belleview Founders' Week, Belleview; International Folk Festival, Miami; Zellwood Sweet Corn Festival, Zellwood; Royal Poinciana Fiesta, Miami; Frontier Days, Tampa, Chautauqua, DeFuniak Springs; Old Spanish Trail Festival, Crestview.

June. Orchid Festival, Remuda Beach; Cypress Gardens Festival Month, Cypress Gardens; Billy Bowlegs Festival, Fort Walton Beach; Fiesta of Five Flags, Pensa-

Bill Anderson and Mary Lou Turner

cola; Jefferson County Watermelon Festival, Monticello; Panhandle Watermelon Festival, Chipley; Sea Turtle Watch, Jensen Beach.

July. Gopher Races and Old-Fashioned Fourth, Hudson; Carnival of the Americas and Comparsas, Miami Beach.

August. Fun Day, Wausau; Indian Key Festival, Islamorda.

September. Annual Florida Folk Festival, White Springs; Pioneer Days, Englewood; Panacea Blue Crab Festival, Panacea; Labor Day Festival, Daytona Beach; Labor Day Celebration, Clermont; Bold Cityfest, Jacksonville; Bellview Junction Western Roundup, Pensacola.

October. Rattlesnake Roundup and International Gopher Race, San Antonio; Back to Ybor City, Ybor City; Seafood Festival, Apalachicola; Ocala Week, Ocala; Pensacola Interstate Fair, Pensacola; Florida Forest Festival, Perry; Suwannee County Fair, Live Oak; Jackson County Fair, Marianna; Greater Jacksonville Fair, Jacksonville; Greater Holmes County Fair, Bonifay; North Florida Fair, Tallahassee; Bay County Fair, Panama City.

November. Great Gulf Coast Festival, Pensacola; Central Florida Folk, Arts and Crafts Festival, Apopka; Levy County Fair, Williston; Columbia County Fair, Lake City; Northeast Florida Fair, Callahan; Volusia County Fair and Youth Show, De Land; Alachua County Fair, Gainesville; Hardee County Fair, Wauchula; Broward Country Youth Fair, Hollywood.

December. Parade of Music, Silver Springs.

For information, write: Florida Comments, Florida Department of Commerce, Tallahassee, 32304 or Florida Federation of Fairs and Livestock Shows, 441 Paul Russell Road, Tallahassee, FL 32301.

Georgia

July. Western Square Dance, Andy's Trout Farm, Dillard; July 4th Mountain Style, Unicoi, Helen; Star Spangled Weekend, Stone Mountain Park, Atlanta; Top of Georgia Jamboree, Dillard; Mountain Square Dance, Mountain City; Country Music Show, Country Music Park, Cumming; Arts and Crafts Show, Festival Woods, Jekyll Island; First Saturday Festival, River Street, Savannah; Festival in the

Judd

Park, Cumming; Jerry Clower/Byrd Family Bluegrass Show, Douglas; Sunshine Festival, Neptune Park, St. Simons; Music Festival, Calhoun; Watermelon Festival, Cordele; Square Dance Weekend, Unicoi, Helen; Square Dancing, Elk's Lodge, Brunswick; Chautauqua in Agrirama Dinner Theatre, Tifton; Country Western Show, Grand Opera House, Macon; Country and Western Show, Cobb County Civic Center, Marietta; Bluegrass Festival, Holiday Beach, Douglas.

August. Bluegrass Festival, Fairgrounds, Newman; Appalachian Music Fest, Unicoi, Helen; Georgia Mountain Fair, Hiawassee; First Saturday Festival, River Street, Savannah; Mountain Square Dancing, Playhouse, Mountain City; Top of Georgia Jamboree, Dillard; ·Western Square Dancing, Andy's Trout Farm, Dillard; Square Dancing, Elk's Lodge, Brunswick; Country Music Show, Cumming; Fannin Country Fair, Blue Ridge; Old-Time Fiddlers' Convention, Dalton; Georgia Mountain Eatins' and Squeezins', Unicoi, Helen; Sea Island Festival, St. Simons; Original Sundown to Sunup Gospel Sing, Memorial Stadium, Waycross; Chattahoochee Mountain Fair, Clarkesville.

September. Western Square Dancing, Andy's Trout Farm, Dillard; Coney Grove Bluegrass Festival and Craftsman's Fair, Music Park, Cordele; Flatlanders Fall Frolic Talent Show, Lakeland; Mountain Square Dancing, Playhouse, Mountain City; Top of Georgia Jamboree, Dillard; First Saturday Festival, River Street, Savannah; Flatlanders Arts and Crafts Show, Camp Patten, Lakeland; Flatlanders Fall Frolic Bass Tournament, Ski Show and Gospel Sing, Lakeland; Flatlanders Fall Frolic Horse Show, Fish-Nik and Country Music, Lakeland; Macon Mall Festival of Arts and Crafts, Macon; Western Square Dancing, Andy's Trout Farm, Dillard; Country Music Show, Cumming; Square Dancing Elk's Lodge, Brunswick; Cherokee

Capital Fair, Calhoun; Annual Variety Show, Grand Opera House, Macon; Murray County Fair, Saddle Club Grounds, Chatsworth; Barnesville Buggy Days, Barnesville; All Crafts Show, Griffin; Fall Festival, Crawford; Creative Arts Festival, Dalton; West Central Georgia Fair, Fairgrounds, Thomaston; Annual Georgia Peanut Festival, Sylvester.

October. Western Square Dance, Andy's Trout Farm, Dillard; Country Music Show, Cumming; Country Music Festival, Calhoun; First Saturday "Octoberfest" River Street, Savannah; Houston County Fair, Warner Robins; Annual Okefenokee Agricultural Fair, Waycross; Sumter County Fair, Fairgrounds, Americus; Oglethorpe County Fair, Lexington; Six County Fiesta–Emanuel County Fair, Swainsboro; Yank-Reb Festival, Plaza Parks, Fitzgerald; Square Dancing, Elk's Lodge, Brunswick; Prater's Mill Country Fair, Dalton; Oconee Area Fair, W.B. Williams Park, Milledgeville; North Georgia Fair, Dalton; County Fair, Sylvania; Chattahoochee Valley Fair, Columbus; Fall Country Music Festival, Hiawassee; Sorghum Festival, Haralson Civic Center, Blairsville; Gold Rush Days, Dahlonega; Fall Festival, Watkinsville; Fall Festival, Cleveland; Scottish Festival and Highland Games, Stone Mountain; Colguitt County Fair, Moultrie; Georgia State Fair, Central City Park, Macon; Bluegrass Festival and Old-Time Fiddlers' Convention, Hiawassee; Gospel Music Concert, Cobb County Civic Center, Marietta; Okefenokee Festival, Folkston; Agricultural Fair, Brunswick; Coastal Empire Fair, Savannah.

November. Gospel Concert, Civic Center, Savannah; Fair of 1850, Westville, Lumpkin; Mule Day, Calvary; Million Pines Arts and Crafts Festival, Iva Park, Soperton; Square Dancing, Elk's Lodge, Brunswick; Can Grinding Party, Agrirama, Tifton; Southeastern Arts and Crafts Festival, Macon.

December. Square Dancing, Elk's Lodge, Brunswick; New Year Bluegrass Festival, Jekyll Island.

For information, write: Tourist Division, Georgia Department of Industry and Trade, PO Box 1776, Atlanta, GA 30301

Monument

Don Cherry

Hawaii

January. Narcissus Festival.

March/April. Cherry Blossom Festival.

May. Lei Day.

June. Kamehameha Day.

July/August. Bon Odori; Aloha Week Festivals.

For information, write: Hawaii Visitors Bureau, 2270 Kalakaua Avenue, Honolulu, HI 96815.

Idaho

July. Lions Club July 4th Celebration, Sandpoint; Annual Circle and Swing Square Dance, Sandpoint City Beach, Sandpoint; Bonner County Historical Society Arts and Crafts Show, Sandpoint; Lions Club Annual Beach Barbecue, Sandpoint; 1860 Days, Pierce; Annual Idaho City Arts and Crafts Festival, Idaho City; Snake River Stampede, Nampa; Sagebrush Days, Buhl; Sun Valley Center Music Festival, Sun Valley; Elkhorn Arts and Crafts Festival, Sun Valley; Old-Time Fiddlers'

Jamboree, Shoshone; Livestock Association Anniversary Celebration, Twin Falls; Good Sam Club Jamboree, Twin Falls; Salmon River Days, Salmon; L.D.S. Pioneer Day Celebration and Parade, Pocatello; Fourth of July, Paris; Pioneer Day, Montpelier.

August. Bonner County Fair, Sandpoint; Boundary County Fair, Bonners Ferry; Valley County Fair, Cascade; Countryman's Club Farm/City Nite and Chicken Barbecue, Nampa; Washington County Fair and Rodeo, Cambridge; Camas County Fair, Fairfield; Buckaroo Breakfast, Emmett; Gem County Fair and Rodeo, Emmett; Fayette County Fair and Rodeo, New Plymouth; Lincoln County Fair and Rodeo, Shoshone; Annual Sun Valley Invitational Arts and Crafts Festival, Sun Valley; Gooding County Fair and Rodeo, Gooding; Elmore County Fair-Carnival, Glenns Ferry; Cassia County Fair and Rodeo and Country-Western Jamboree, Burley; Jerome County Fair, Jerome; Custer County Fair, Challis; Bannock County Fair North, Pocatello; Butte County Fair, Arco; Lemhi County Fair, Salmon; Bear Lake County Fair, Montpelier; Franklin County Fair, Preston.

September. Annual Arts and Crafts Festival, Boise; Paul Bunyan Days, St. Maries; Kootenai County Fair, Coeur d'Alene; Lumberjack Days and Clearwater County Fair, Orofino; Nez Perce County Fair, Lewiston; Wagon Days, Ketchum; Twin Falls County Fair and Rodeo, Twin Falls; Eastern Idaho State Fair, Blackfoot; Miss Russet Pageant, Shelley; Idaho Annual Spud Day, Shelley.

For information, write: Division of Tourism and Industrial Development, Room 108, Capitol Building, Boise, ID 83720.

Illinois

April. Old Settler Days, Red Hills State Park, Lawrenceville.

May. Pleasant Plains Spring Craft

Festival, Clayville; River Ramblin' Kidney Benefit Variety Show, Morton; Country Music Show, Timberline Campground, Goodfield; Square Dance, Hennepin; Illinois Old-Timers Fiddlers' Association Jam Session, Shelbyville; Railsplitting Days, Rockome Gardens, Arcola.

June. Illinois Country Opry, Petersburg; Harvard Milk Day Festival and Parade, Harvard; Blue Grass Music Festival, Crazy Horse Campground, Jacksonville; Square Dance, Oregon; Railsplitting Days, Rockome Gardens, Arcola; *Prairie du Rocher-Fort de Chartres Rendevoux,* Fort de Chartres State Park; Homecoming Celebration, Lexington; Gospel Singing Rally, Timberline Campground, Goodfield; Steamboat Days, Henry; Spring Skills from the Hills, Galena; Highland Homecoming Celebration, Highland; Sesquicentennial Celebration and Pageant, Shelbyville; Homecoming Celebration, Sesser; Oswego Days Festival, Oswego; Rock Falls Days, Rock Falls; Old Canal Days Festival, Lockport; Steamboat Days, Peoria; Festival of Crafts, Decatur; Arts and Crafts Festival, Galena; Illinois Old-Time Fiddlers' Association Jam Session, Shelbyville; Sesquicentennial Celebration, Mackinaw; Old Settlers' Festival, Metamora; Carnival, Parade and Chicken Fry, Shelbyville; Heartland Heritage Days, Urbana; Frontier Days, Arlington Heights; Old King Coal Festival, West Frankfort; Pike County Fair, Griggsville; Mississippi River Festival, Southern Illinois University, Edwardsville.

July. Illinois Country Opry, Petersburg; Du Quoin State Fair Agricultural Exposition, Du Quoin; Bluegrass Festival, Timberline Campground, Goodfield; Square Dance, Oregon; Arts and Crafts Fair, Alton; Hanover Days, Hanover; Neoga Days, Neoga; Country Days, Rockford; Fun Days, Mt. Carroll; Illinois Old-Time Fiddlers' Association Jam Session, Shelbyville; Old-Fashioned Days, Hampshire; Blue

Grass and Folk Festival, Sherwood Camping Resort, Ina; Blue Grass Music Festival Jamboree, Arcola; Lake County Fair Trip, Waukegan; Homecoming Celebration, Jewett; Brown County Fair, Mt. Sterling; Champaign County Fair, Fisher; Champaign County Fair, Urbana; Christian County Fair, Taylorville; Clark County Fair, Marshal; Clark County Fair, Martinsville; Clay County Fair, Flora; Clinton County Fair, Carlyle; Coles County Fair, Charleston; Crawford County Fair, Oblong; DeWitt County Fair, Farmer City; Du Page County Fair, Wheaton; Edgar County Fair, Paris; Edwards County Fair, Albion; Fayette County Fair, Brownstown; Ford County Fair, Melvin; Franklin County Fair, Benton; Fulton County Fair, Lewistown; Greene County Fair, Carrollton; Grundy County Fair; Morris; Hamilton County Fair, McLeansboro; Hancock County Fair, Augusta; Henderson County Fair, Stronghurst; Henry County Fair, Cambridge; Iroquois

R. W. and Donna Blackwood

Capitol/Universal Management

County Fair, Crescent City; Jasper County Fair, Newton; Jefferson County Fair, Mt. Vernon; Jersey County Fair, Jerseyville; Jo Caviess County Fair, Elizabeth; Lake County Fair, Grayslake; La Salle County Fair, Ottawa; Lawrence County Fair, Sumner; Lee County Fair, Amboy; Livingston County Fair,

Pontiac; McDonough County Fair, Macomb; Macon County Fair, Decatur; Macoupin County Fair, Carlinville; Madison County Fair, Highland; Marshal-Putnam County Fair, Henry; Mason County Fair, Havana; Menard County Fair, Petersburg; Mercer County Fair, Aledo; Morgan County Fair, Jacksonville; Moultrie-Douglas County Fair, Arthur; Moultrie County Fair, Sullivan; Peoria County Fair, Peoria; Perry County Fair, Du Quoin; Perry County Fair, Pinckneyville; Platt County Fair, Cerro Gordo; Pike County Fair, Pleasant Hill; Randolph County Fair, Sparta; Richland County Fair, Olney; Rock Island County Fair, East Moline; St. Clair County Fair, Belleville; Saline County Fair, Harrisburg; Sangamon County Fair, New Berlin; Schuylerville County Fair, Rushville; Stark County Fair, Wyoming; Vermilion County Fair, Danville; Wabash County Fair, Mt. Carmel; Washington County Fair, Nashville; Wayne County Fair, Fairfield.

August. Illinois Country Opry, Petersburg; Wilmington Catfish Days Festival, Wilmington; Mississippi River Festival, Edwardsville; Homecoming Celebration, Pearl City; Square Dance, Oregon; Northbrook Days, Northbrook; Illinois State Fair, Springfield; Sweet Corn Festival, Mendota; Watermelon Festival, Kankakee River State Park, Bourbonnais; Dairy Days, Galena; Fair, Horseshow and Rodeo, New Windsor; Cobden Peach Festival, Cobden; Corn Boil, Kankakee River State Park, Bourbonnais; Public Chicken Fry, Illinois State Park, Marseilles, Illinois Old-Time Fiddlers' Association Jam Session, Shelbyville; Sweetcorn & Watermelon Festival, Mt. Vernon; Country Music Festival, Silvis; La Salle County Folk Festival, Ottawa; Du Quoin State Fair, Du Quoin; Melon Festival, Spring Bay; Burgoo Day, Chandlerville; Annual Fish Fry and Contests, Chrisman; Adams County Fair, Mendon; Bond County Fair, Greenville; Boone County Fair,

Belvidere; Bureau County Fair, Princeton; Carroll County Fair, Milledgeville; Cass County Fair, Virginia; Cumberland County Fair, Greenup; DeKalb County Fair, Sycamore; Effingham County Fair, Altamont; Jo Daviess County Fair, Warren; Kane County Fair, St. Charles; Kankakee County Fair, Kankakee; Knox County Fair, Knoxville; Livingston County Fair, Cullom; Livingston County Fair, Fairbury; Logan County Fair, Lincoln; McHenry County Fair, Woodstock; McLean County Fair, Bloomington; Marion County Fair, Salem; Monroe County Fair, Waterloo; Perry County Fair, Du Quoin; Pulaski County Fair, Pulaski; Scott County Fair, Winchester; Shelby County Fair, Shelbyville; Stephenson County Fair, Freeport; Tazewell County Fair, Pekin; Union County Fair, Anna; Vermilion County Fair, Georgetown; Warren County Fair, Roseville; White County Fair, Carmi; Whiteside County Fair, Morrison; Will County Fair, Peotone; Winnebago County Fair, Pecatonica.

September. Illinois Country Opry, Petersburg; Fall Festival, Flora; Marigold Festival, Pekin; Du Quoin State Fair, Du Quoin; National Sweetcorn Festival, McFerren Park, Hoopeston; Homecoming Celebration, Grayville; Grape Festival, Nauvoo State Park, Nauvoo; Hog Capitol Festival, Kewanee; Labor Day Roundup and Rodeo, Palestine; Square Dance, Oregon; Yesteryear Fair, Decatur; Marigold Festival, Golden; Melon Days, Thomson; Homecoming Celebration, Shannon; Warren County Prime Beef Festival, Monmouth; Corn Festival, El Paso; Fall Festival, Toledo; Old Settlers' Day, Bishop Hill; Frontier Day, Bunker Hill; Broom Corn Festival, Arcola; Turn of the Century Celebration, Siloam Springs State Park, Clayton; Turn of the Century Day, Long Grove; Apple Festival, Murphysboro; Bluegrass Festival, Lake Wildwood Haven Campground, Bushnell; Homecoming Celebra-

Jim Ed Brown

tion, Chebanse; Autumn Harvest Days, Wheaton; Pumpkin Festival, Warren; Apple and Pork Festival, Clinton; Illinois State Fiddle Contest, Petersburg; Country Show, Rock Island; Barry Apple Festival, Barry; Grundy County Corn Festival, Morris; Calhoun County Fair, Hardin; Christian County Fair, Pana; DeKalb County Fair, Sandwich; La Salle County Fair, Mendota; Ogle County Fair, Oregon; Washington County Fair, Okawville; Williamson County Fair, Marion.

For information, write: Illinois Office of Tourism, 222 South College Street, Springfield, IL 62706.

Indiana

April. Dogwood Festival, Orleans; Sassafras Festival, Vernon.

May. Mayday in Metamora, Metamora; Fair on the Square, Columbus; Freedom Festival, Evansville; May Wine Festival, Indianapolis; Antique and Handcraft Festival, Madison; Banks of the Wabash Festival, Terre Haute.

June. Pioneer Days Festival, Eugene and Cayuga; Adams Mill Folk Festival, Cutler; Indiana Rose Festival, Indianapolis; Limestone Festival, Bedford; Red, White, and Blue Festival, Crothersville; Glass Festival, Greentown; Flag Appreciation Day, Mellott; Talbot Street Art Fair, Indianapolis; Blue Grass Festival, Bean Blossom; June Jamboree, Pendleton; Mermaid Festival, North Webster; Festival of Arts and Crafts, Homer; Summer Festival, Mt. Vernon; Rose Festival, Richmond; Old-Fashioned Days, Kennard; Chicken Barbecue and Flea Market, Versailles; Roann Festival, Roann; Glass Festival, Elwood.

July. Liberty Festival, Liberty; Madison Regatta, Madison; Fourth of July Festival, LaPorte; Salamonie Summer Festival, Warren; Fireman's Festival, Oldenburg; Ethnic Festival, South Bend; Arts and Crafts Festival, Lowell; Art Festival, New Albany; Fourth of July Festival, Pekin; Summer Festival, Wolcott; July Fourth Celebration, Linton; Fiddlers' and Old-Time Musicians' Gathering, Battle Ground; Round Barn Festival, Rochester; Patchwork Fair, Vevay; Summer Festival, Michigan City; Three Rivers Festival, Fort Wayne; Old Timers' Festival, Winchester; Crosierfest, Fort Wayne; Pioneer

Days, Fremont; Historical Days, New Carlisle; Art Festival, Westfield.

August. Old Settlers' Celebration, Delphi; Popcorn Festival, Van Buren; Pietcher Village Art Festival, Nappannee; Garrett Days, Garrett Haynes-Apperson Festival, Kokomo; Fun Fest, North Manchester; V.J. Day Parade and Celebration, Seymour; Free Fair, Moreland; Old Settlers' Meeting, Odon; Harvest Festival, Kewanna; Yeddo Old Settlers' and Lion's Club Fish Fry, Veedersburg; Indiana State Fair, Indianapolis; Blueberry Festival, LaPorte; Holton Jamboree, Holton; Bean Dinner, Fontanet.

September. Fall Festival, Edinburg; Old Settlers' Reunion, Goldsmith; Watermelon Festival, Brownstown; Marshall County Blueberry Festival, Plymouth; White River Catfish Festival, Petersburg; Steamboat Days Festival, Jeffersonville; Beef Barbecue, Hillsboro; Fall Festival, Canaan; Penrod Arts Fair, Indianapolis; Fall Festival, Dale; Pioneer Craft Festival, Ligonier; Pioneer Day, Richmond; Corn Festival, Sullivan; Turkey Trot Festival, Montgomery; Pioneer Days, Whitestown; Persimmon Festival, Mitchell; Pumpkin Show, Versailles; Apple Festival, Cory; Heritage Days, Hope; Farmer's Fair, Aurora; Apple Festival, Bloomfield.

October. Lincoln Hills Arts and Crafts Show, English; Canal Days— Traders Rendezvous, Metamora; Blue River Valley Pioneer Craft Fair, Shelbyville; Two Days to Remember, St. Paul; Morgan County Fall Foliage Festival, Martinsville; Harvest Homecoming, New Albany; West Side Nut Club Fall Festival, Evansville; Orange County Pumpkin Festival, French Lick, West Baden; Old Settlers' Days, Salem; James Whitcomb Riley Festival, Greenfield; Apple Butter Festival, Spencer; Fort Vallonia Days, Vallonia.

For information, write: Governor Robert D. Orr, Tourist Division,

Department of Commerce, Room 336, State House, Indianapolis, IN 46204.

Iowa

May. Country Music Festival, Veterans Auditorium, Des Moines; Annual Tulip Time Festival, Pelia; Kiwanis Pancake Day, Cedar Rapids; Tulip Festival, Orange City; May Fair, Audubon.

June. Bluegrass Festival, Mt. Pleasant; Frontier Days, Fort Dodge; Pioneer Days, Clarksville; Pork Day, Algona; Dairy Day, Fredericksburg; Stockmen's Days, Webster City; Strawberry Days, Strawberry Point; Donkey and Mule Days, Nelson's Timber, Goldfield; Steamboat Days, Burlington; Pioneer Days, Glenwood; Reunion Days, 4H Grounds, Charlton; All Iowa Fair, Hawkeye Downs, Cedar Rapids; Old Settler's Picnic, Rodney; Arts Festival, Dubuque; Folk Music Rendezvous, Des Moines; Mississippi Valley Arts and Crafts Fair, Davenport; Shrine Music Salute to America, Iowa State Fair Grandstand, Des Moines.

July. Polk County Fair, Des Moines; Riverboat Days, Clinton; Allamakee County Fair, Waukon; Coggon Harvest Home, Coggon; Fun and Feed Days, Ankeny; Lu Verne Day, Lu Verne; Centennial Celebration, Grundy Center; Lee County Fair, Donnellson; Old-Fashioned County Fair Days, Marlon; St. Charles Old Settlers, St. Charles; Turkey Days, Grafton; Field Days, Low Moor; Greene County Fair, Jefferson; North Iowa Fair, Mason City; Watermelon Day, Humeston; Corn Carnival, Gladbrook; Humboldt County Fair, Humboldt; Ringgold County Pioneer Museum Center, Ellston; Centennial Celebration, Breda; 4H Fair, Leon; Montgomery County Fair, Red Oak; Black Hawk County 4H Show, Waterloo; Marion County Fair, Knoxville; Shelby County Fair, Harlan; West Liberty Fair, West Liberty; Franklin County Fair, Hempton; Frontier Days Celebration, Forest City; Harrison

County Fair, Missouri Valley; Benton County Fair, Vinton; Worth County Fair, Northwood; Cherokee County Fair, Cherokee; Monroe County 4H and FFA Fair and Fall Festival, Albia; All Iowa Fair, Cedar Rapids.

August. Iowa State Fair, Des Moines; Annual Fiddlers' Workshop and Contest, Tom's Mechanical Music Wonderland, Manly; Washington County Fair, Washington; Tama County Fair, Gladbrook; Mills County Fair, Malvern; Cass County Fair, Atlantic; Hardin County Fair, Eldora; Page County Fair, Clarinda; Van Buren County Fair, Keosauqua; Southern Iowa Fair, Oskaloosa; Woodbury County Fair, Moville; Mitchell County Fair, Osage; Central Iowa Fair, Marshalltown; Mississippi Valley Fair, Davenport; Plymouth County Fair, LeMars; Monona County Fair, Onawa; Wright County District Junior Fair, Eagle Grove; Kossuth County Fair and Free Barbecue, Algona; Winneshiek County Fair, Decorah; Wapello County Fair, Eldon; Hamilton County Fair, Webster City; Bremer County Fair, Waverly; Sweet Corn Days, Elkader; Decatur County Threshing Bee, Leon; Madison County Fair, Winterset; Dubuque County Fair, Dubuque; Great River Days, Muscatine; Monroe Old Settlers, Monroe; Sweet Corn Festival, West Point; Lyon County Fair, Rock Rapids; Watermelon Festival, Montrose.

September. Midwest Old Settlers' and Threshers' Annual Reunion, Mount Pleasant; Council Bluffs Old-Time Country Music Contest and Pioneer Exposition, Council Bluffs.

For information, write: Travel Development Division, Iowa Development Commission, 250 Jewett Building, Des Moines, IA 50309.

Kansas

March. Annual Arts and Crafts Festival, Bonner Springs.

April. Spring Square Dance Festi-

Burl Ives

val, Dodge City; Hutchinson Spring Fair, Hutchinson; Fat City Interdependence Days, Dodge City; Gypsum Hills Arts and Crafts Fair, Medicine Lodge.

May. Ft. Leavenworth Sesquicentennial, Ft. Leavenworth; Johnny Kaw Art Fair, Wamego; Wichitennial River Festival, Wichita; Old Settlers Days, Rock City, Minneapolis; Arts and Crafts Fair, Greensburg; City of Harper Centennial Celebration, Harper; Montezuma Days, Montezuma; Wooden Nickel Day, Waterville; Long Branch Variety Show, Dodge City; Old Fort Days, Fort Scott.

June. Beef Empire Days, Garden City; Farm-City Week, Atchison; Arts and Crafts Fair, Olathe;

Carbondale Days, Carbondale; John Brown Jamboree, Osawatomie; Days of '49, Hanover.

July. Tribal Pow-Wow, Kickapoo Reservation, Horton; Nickel Day, Seneca; July Fourth Fireworks and Free Square Dance, Belle Plaine; Fourth of July, Franklin County Chautauqua Days Celebration, Ottawa; Sumner County Wheat Festival and Rodeo, Wellington; Ottawa County Fair, Minneapolis; Anthony Fair and Race Meet, Anthony; Dodge City Days, Dodge City; Country Threshing Days, Goessel; Tri-City Beef Cook Out Championship, Dodge City; Kiowa County 4H Fair, Greensburg; Cloud County Fair, Glasco; Lane County Free Fair, Dighton; Smith County

Fair, Smith Center; Barton County 4H Fair, Great Bend; Bourbon County Fair, Fort Scott; Sheridan County Free Fair, Hoxie; Labette County Fair, Oswego; Franklin County Fair and Rodeo, Ottawa; Rawlins County Fair, Atwood; Wilson County Fair, Fredonia; Ness County Fair, Ness City; Sedgwick County Fair, Cheney; Pratt County Fair, Pratt; McPherson County Fair, Canton; Russell County 4H Fair, Russell; Parsons Outdoor Arts and Crafts Fair, Parsons; Albany Threshing Bee, Savetha; Butler County 4H Fair, El Dorado.

August. Ford County Fair, Dodge City; Graham County Fair, Hill City; Hodgeman County Fair, Jetmore; Kearny County Free Fair, Lakin; 4H Fair, Larned; Stafford County Fair, Stafford; Mitchell County Fair, Beloit; Crawford County Fair, Girard; Riley County Fair, Manhattan; Sherman County—Norwest Kansas District Free Fair, Goodland; Decatur County Fair, Oberlin; Rice County 4H Fair, Lyons; Jewell County 4H Fair, Mankato; Hamilton County Fair, Syracuse; Neosho County Fair, Erie; Logan County Fair, Oakley; Miami County Fair, Paola; Clark County Fair, Ashland; Rush County Fair, LaCrosse; Cheyenne County Fair, St. Francis; Wallace County Free Fair, Sharon Springs; Washington County Fair, Washington; Cowtown Western Days and Rodeo, Baxter Springs; Annual Threshing Bee, McLouth; Ellsworth County 4H Fun, Fair and Rodeo, Ellsworth; Old Settlers' Picnic, Halstead; Stevens County Art and Crafts Show, Hugoton; Barber County Fair, .Hardtner; Franklin County Fair of Lane, Lane; Kingman County Fair, Kingman; Phillips County 4H and FFA Fair, Phillipsburg; Scott County Free Fair, Scott City; Allen County Fair, Iola; Lyon County Free Fair, Emporia; Cowley County Free Fair, Winfield; Reno County 4H Fair, Hutchinson; Trego County Free Fair, Wakeeney; Johnson County Fair, Gardner; Brown Tri-County Fair, Horton;

Douglas County Free Fair, Lawrence; Wabaunsee County Fair, Alma; Buffalo Bill Days, Leavenworth; Linn County Fair, Mound City; Grant County Free Fair, Ulysses; Scott City Beefiesta, Scott City; Clay County Free Fair, Clay Center; Harper County Fair, Harper; Franklin County—Richmond Free Fair, Richmond; Haskell County Fair, Sublette; Greeley County Fair, Tribune; Wyandotte County Fair, Kansas City; Tri-Rivers Fair and Rodeo, Salina; Ellsworth Cowtown Festival, Ellsworth; Pottawatomie County Fair, Onaga; Leavenworth County Fair, Tonganoxie; Montgomery County Interstate Fair and Rodeo, Coffeyville; Jackson County Fair, Holton; Osage County Fair, Osage City; Thomas County Free Fair, Colby; Anderson County Fair, Garnett; Harvey County Free Fair, Neston; Rooks County Free Fair, Stockton; North Central Kansas Free Fair, Belleville; Chase County Fair, Cottonwood Falls; Morris County 4H Fair, Council Grove; Atchison County Fair, Effingham; Finney County Free Fair, Garden City; Stevens County Fair, Hugoton; Greenwood County Fair, Eureka; Elk County Free Fair, Longton; Morton County Fair, Elkhart; Quad County Old Settlers' Picnic, Mulvane; Five-State Free Fair, Liberal; Coffey County Agricultural Fair, Burlington; Marion County Fair, Hillsboro; Central Kansas Free Fair and Wild Bill Hickock Rodeo, Abilene; Cherokee County-American Legion Fair, Columbus; Osage County-Overbrook Fair, Overbrook.

September. Topeka Kansas Fair, Topeka; Arts and Crafts Fair, Lucas; Old Settlers' Picnic and Kansas State Cow-Chip Throwing Contest, Russell Springs; Sumner County Fair, Caldwell; Old Settlers' Days, Olathe; Community Fair, Elk City; Mission Art Festival, Mission; Tiblow Days, Bonner Springs; Kansas State Fair, Hutchinson; Annual Walnut Valley and National Flat-Picking Guitar Championships,

Zella Lehr

Winfield; Arts and Crafts Fair, Hillsboro; St. Francis Heritage Days, St. Francis; Molasses Days, Alma; Fall Square Dance Roundup, Dodge City; Old Settlers' Day, Marion; Mini Sappa Days, Overlin; Clay County-Wakefield Free Fair, Wakefield.

October. Hesston Fall Festival, Hesston; Cider Sundays Arts and Crafts Festival, Apple Valley Farm, Lake Perry; Whimmydiddle Arts and Crafts Fair, Scott City; Whitewater Fall Festival, Whitewater; Maple Festival Days, Hiawatha; Molasses Days, Alma; Annual Homecoming, Fredonia; Octoberfest and Homecoming, Hays; Neodesha Arts and Crafts Festival, Neodesha; Linn County Jayhawker Festival, Sugar Mound Arts and Crafts Show, Mound City; Linn County Jayhawker Festival, Museum Open House, Pleasanton; Linn County Jayhawker Festival, Quilt Show, Prescott; Linn County Jayhawker Festival, Open House Trading Post Historic Preservation Area, Trading Post; Columbus Day, Columbus; Maple Leaf Festival, Baldwin City; Neewollah Celebration, Independence; Arkalalah Festival, Arkansas City; Fall Halloween Festival, Eskridge; Arts and Crafts

Festival, Emporia; Etude Arts and Crafts Fair, Eureka.

November. Cattlemen's Day, Eureka; Proud to be an American Celebration, McPherson; Annual Arts and Crafts Fair, Anthony.

For information, write: Publications Division; Kansas Department of Economic. Development; 503 Kansas, 6th floor; Topeka, KS 66603.

Louisiana

January. Louisiana Fur and Wildlife Festival, Cameron; Mardi Gras, New Orleans.

March. Amite Oyster Day, Amite.

April. Ponchatoula Strawberry Festival, Ponchatoula; New Orleans Jazz and Heritage Festival, New Orleans; South East Louisiana Dairy Festival and Livestock Show, Hammond; Knights of Columbus Council 5747 Crawfish Festival, Chalmette; South East Louisiana Agri-Dustrial Futurama Expo, Hammond; Louisiana Spring Festival and Fair, Baton Rouge; Holiday in Dixie Festival, Shreveport.

May. Contraband Days, Lake Charles; Breaux Bridge Crawfish Festival, Breaux Bridge.

June. Jambalaya Festival, Gonzalas; South LaFourche Cajun Festival, Galliano.

July. New Orleans Food Festival, New Orleans; France-Louisiana Festival, New Orleans; Louisiana Catfish Festival, Des Allemands; Zigler Museum Bastille Day, Jennings; Louisian Oyster Festival, Galliano; Louisian Soybean Festival, Jonesville; St. Charles Parrish Festival, Norco.

September. Louisiana Shrimp and Petroleum Festival, Morgan City; Bayou Food Classic, Lafayette; La Salle Parish Fair, Jena; Red River Parish Fair, Coushatta; Rayne Frog Festival, Rayne; Bouillabaisse Festival, Larose; Acadiana Fair and Trade Show, Lafayette; Louisiana Sugar Cane Festival and Fair, New Iberia.

October. North Louisiana Cotton Festival and Fair, Bastrop; Natchitoches Historical Tour, Natchitoches; Los Islenos Spanish Heritage Festival, St. Bernard; Terrebonne Livestock and Agricultural Fair, Houma; Claiborne Parish Fair and North West Louisiana Dairy Festival, Haynesville; Calcasieu-Cameron Fair, Sulphur; Ari-La-Miss Industrial and Agriculture Fair, Monroe; Beauregard Parish Fair, DeRidder; Allen Parish Fair, Oberlin; Tangipahoa Parish Fair, Amite; Lagniappe on the Bayou, Chauvin; Gumbo Festival, Bridge City; Livingston Parish Fair, Livingston; North Central Louisiana District Fair, Olla; Rapides Parish Fair, Alexandria; Jeff Davis Parish Fair, Jennings; Quachita Valley Fair, W. Monroe; Louisiana Cotton Festival, Ville Platte; St. Tammany Parish Fair, Covington; West Baton Rouge Parish Fair, Port Allen; Tamale Festival, Zwolle; Washington Parish Fair, Franklinton; International Rice Festival, Crowley; International Acadian Festival, Plaquemine; State Fair of Louisiana, Shreveport; West Carroll Jaycee Fair, Oak Grove; Southwest Trade Exposition and Fair, Lake Charles; Louisiana Dairy Festival, Abbeville;

Louisiana Yambilee Festival, Opelousas; Greater Baton Rouge State Fair, Baton Rouge; Andouille Festival, LaPlace; La Vie La Fourche Festival, Raceland.

November. Louisiana Swine Festival, Basile; Plaquemines Parish Fair and Orange Festival, Fort Jackson; Zigler Museum Festival, Jennings.

For information, write: State of Louisiana, Department of Culture, Recreation and Tourism, Office of the Secretary, Baton Rouge, LA 70804.

Maine

July. Bangor Agricultural Fair, Hermon; Cornish Fair, Cornish; Scarborough Fair, Scarborough Downs; Bangor State Fair, Bangor; Potato Blossom Festival, Fort Fairfield; Maine Broiler Week, Belfast; Maine Dairy Day, Scarborough; Central Maine Egg Festival, Pittsfield; Bean-Hole Bean Festival, Oxford.

August. Taste of Maine Festival, Bangor; Maine Farm Days, Albion; East Pittston Fair, East Pittston;

MCA Records

Vassar Clements

Athens Fair, Athens; Northern Maine Fair, Presque Isle; Cochnewagan Agricultural Fair, Monmouth; Skowhegan State Fair, Skowhegan; North Waterford Fair, North Waterford; Knox Agricultur-

al Fair and State of Maine Blueberry Festival, Union; Piscataquis Valley Fair, Dover-Foxcroft; York Agricultural Fair, Acton; Winslow Lions Club Fair, Winslow; Windsor Fair, Windsor; Seacoast Festival, Kennebunk; Maine Seafoods Festival, Rockland; Lobster Festival, Winter Harbor; New England Blue Grass Festival, Squaw Mountain at Moosehead, Greenville; Last Log Days, Skowhegan.

September. Hancock Country Agricultural Fair, Blue Hill; Lewiston State Fair, Lewiston; Clinton Lion's Club Fair, Clinton; Litchfield Fair, Litchfield; Oxford County Agricultural Fair, Norway; Franklin County Fair, Farmington; North New Portland Lions Club Fair, North New Portland; Cumberland Farmers Club Fair, Cumberland Center; Old-Time Agricultural Fair, Wayne; Labor Day Free Fair, Harmony; Fall Foliage Days, Rangeley; Fall Foliage and Sugarloaf Arts and Crafts Festival, Sugarloaf; Annual Courthouse Dance, Pownalborough Courthouse, Dresden.

October. West Oxford Agricultural Fair, Fryeburg; Sagadahoc Agricultural and Horticultural Fair, Topsham; Skiers' Homecoming, Sugarloaf; Fall Foliage Fair, Boothbay Harbor.

For information, write: Maine Publicity Bureau, Augusta, ME 04333.

Maryland

August. Maryland State Fair, Timonium.

September. Chesapeake Bay Fishing Fair, Stevensville; National Hard Crab Derby and Fair, Crisfield; Museum Birthday Celebration, Ellicott City; Denton September Festival, Denton; Boonesborough Days, Boonsboro (sic); Defenders' Day Ceremony, Baltimore; The Six Days of September, Ocean City; Anne Arundel County Fair, Annapolis; Charles County Fair, LaPlate; Baltimore City Fair, Baltimore; Thurmont-Emmitsburg County Fair, Thurmont; Rockville Heritage

Day, Rockville; Festival of Frostburg, Frostburg; Maryland Folklife Festival, Thurmont; Cumberland Jaycee Seafood Festival, Cumberland; St. Michaels Days, St. Michaels; The Great Frederick Fair, Frederick; St. Mary's County Fair, Leonardtown; National Craft Fair, Gaithersburg; Allegany Bluegrass Festival, Cumberland; Calvert County Fair, Prince Frederick.

October. World Trade Center Weekend, Baltimore; Fell's Point Fun Festival, Baltimore; Springs Folk Festival (Pioneer Days), Springs/Grantsville; St. Mary's County Oyster Festival, Leonardtown; Frederick County Farm Museum Festival, Frederick; New Market Days: Recollection and Recreation, New Market; Autumn Glory Festival, Oakland; Annual Catoctin Colorfest, Thurmont; Community Arts and Crafts Show, Arnold; Smallwood Harvest Festival, Rison; Chesapeake Appreciation Days, near Annapolis.

November. Allegany County Homecoming, Cumberland/Allegany County; Arts and Crafts Fair, Oxon Hill.

For information, write: Maryland Department of Economic and Community Development, Division of Tourist Development, 1748 Forest Drive, Annapolis, MD 21401.

Massachusetts

May. Spring Market Days in Derby, Salem.

June. Middleboro Agricultural Society Fair, Raynham; Brockton Agricultural Society Fair, Raynham; Carver 4H Fair, Carver; St. Peter's Fiesta, Gloucester; St. Peter's Fiesta, Provincetown.

July. New England Crafts Exposition, Topsfield; Barnstable County Fair, Falmouth; Bellingham Country Fair, Bellingham; Barre Fair, Barre; Dedham Lion's 4H County Fair, Dedham; Hampden County 4H Fair, West Springfield; Oakham Youth Fair, Oakham; Pioneer Junior Black and White Fair, Cummington Fairgrounds; Plymouth County 4H Fair, Marshfield Fairgrounds; Westport Fair, Westport.

August. Hillside Agricultural Society Fair, Cummington; Spencer Agricultural Society Fair, Spencer; Union Agricultural Society Fair, Topsfield; Foxborough Fair, Foxborough; Tri-County Fair, Northampton; Rehoboth Fair, Dighton; Franklin County Agricultural Socie-

PBS

Jesse Winchester

ty Fair, Greenfield; Barrington Fair, Great Barrington; Berkshire County Fair, Hancock; Eastern States Exposition, West Springfield; Summerfest, Brockton; Homecoming Week, Beverly; Annual Heritage Days, Salem; Heritage Days, Scituate; Annual Marshfield Fair, Marshfield; Littleville Fair Association, Chester; Martha's Vineyard Agricultural Society Fair, West Tisbury; Highland Agricultural Society Fair, Middlefield; Heath Agricultural Society Fair, Heath; Westfield Fair Association, Westfield; Marshfield Agricultural and Horticultural Society Fair, Marshfield; Adams Agricultural Fair, Adams; Hardwick Fair, Hardwick; Wales County Fair, Wales; Blackstone

Valley 4F, East Douglas; Middlesex County 4F Fair, Westford; West Brookfield 4F Fair, West Brookfield; Worcester Country 4F Fair, Westport; Acushnet Grange Fair, Acushnet; Ashby Community Grange Fair, Ashby; Athol Grange Fair, Athol; Dartmouth Grange Fair, Dartmouth; East Freetown Grange Fair, East Freetown; Fall River Grange Fair, Fall River; Hanson Grange Fair, Hanson; Laurel Grange Fair, West Newbury; Ludlow Grange Fair, Ludlow; Marion Grange Fair, Marion; Mattapoisett Grange Fair, Mattapoisett; Pittsfield Grange Fair, Pittsfield; Shelburne Grange Fair, Shelburne; Shirley Grange Fair, Shirley Center; South Middleboro Grange Fair, South Middleboro; Swansea Grange Fair, Swansea; Upton Grange Fair, Upton; Ware Grange Fair, Ware.

September. Tri-County Fair, Northampton; Annual Fair, Spencer; Franklin County Agricultural Fair, Greenfield; Market Days in Derby Square, Salem; Eastern States Exposition, West Springfield; Festival of the Harvest Moon, Onset; Cranberry Festival, South Carver; Fall Foliage Festival, North Adams; Spencer Agricultural Fair, Spencer; Union Agricultural and Horticultural Society Fair, Blandford; Hampshire, Franklin, and Hampden Agricultural Society Fair, Northampton; Weymouth Agricultural and Industrial Society Fair, Raynham; Barrington Fair Association, Barrington; Foxboro Fair, Foxboro; Bolton Fair, Bolton; Suffolk County Community Fair, Franklin Park Zoo; Norfolk County FFA Fall Exposition, Walpole; Phillipston Fair, Phillipston Center; Boxborough Grange Fair, Boxborough; Boylston Grange Fair, Boylston; Dighton Rock Grange Fair, Segreganset; Easton Grange, North Easton; Fairhaven Grange, Fairhaven; Franklin Grange, Franklin; Holden Grange, Holden; Leicester Grange, Leicester; Leominster Grange, Leominster; Lunenberg Grange, Lunenburg; Massachusetts Grange, West

Springfield; Palmer Grange, Palmer; Richmond Grange, Richmond; Rochester Grange, Rochester; Rutland Grange, Rutland; Stockbridge Grange, Stockbridge; Westboro Grange, Westboro; Williamsburg Grange, Williamsburg; Williamstown Grange, Williamstown.

October. Essex Agricultural Society Fair, Topsfield; Harvest Show, Boston; Harvest Day Festival, Hampden; Buzzards Bay Scallop Festival, Bourne; Harvest Festival, Plymouth; Harvest Festival, Newburyport; Fall Foliage Festival, Easthampton; Annual Music Festival, Worcester.

November. Annual Music Festival, Worcester; Harvest Festival, Worcester.

For information, write: Massachusetts Department of Food and Agriculture, Leverett Saltonstall Building, 100 Cambridge Street, Boston, MA 02202.

Michigan

April. Vermontville Maple Syrup Festival, Vermontville; Maple Syrup Festival, Shepherd; Historical Concert Series (Plantation banjo, ragtime piano, Dixieland jazz), Dearborn.

May. Indian Pow Wow, State Fairgrounds, Detroit; Carson City Frontier Days, Carson City; Michigan Week, Statewide; National Mushroom Festival, Boyne City; Country Fair of Yesteryear, Greenfield Village, Dearborn; American Country Festival, Yack Arena, Wyandotte; Rochester Village Fair, Rochester; Highland Festival, Alma; Toscarora Township Centennial, Indian River; Fort Michilimackinac Pageant, Mackinaw City.

June. Bass Festival, Mancelona; National Asparagus Festival, Hart/Shelby; Bayrama, New Baltimore; Summer Festival, Whittemore; Muzzleloaders Festival, Greenfield Village, Dearborn; Fiesta, Flint; Old-Time Summer Festival, Greenfield Village, Dear-

born; Lake Odessa Fair, Lake Odessa.

July. National Blueberry Festival, South Haven; National Forest Festival, Manistee; West Michigan Seeway Festival, Muskegon; Marion Fair, Marion; National Cherry Festival, Traverse City; Hudson Grange Fair, Hudson; Summerfest, White Cloud; Strawberry Festival, Chassel; Sugar Festival, Sebewaing; Vassar Fair, Vassar; Milan Free Fair, Milan; Mecosta County Fair, Big Rapids; Auburn Corn Festival, Auburn; Bay Country Festival, Bay City; Barry County Fair, Hastings; Berlin Fair, Marne; Montcalm County Fair, Greenville; Fowlerville Agricultural Fair, Fowlerville; Croswell Agricultural Fair, Croswell; Remus Area Centennial, Remus; Pinconning Cheese Festival, Pinconning; Lakeview Muzzleloaders Festival, Lakeview; Farmers Festival, Pigeon; Thornapple Bluegrass Festival, Charleton Park, Hastings; Van Buren County Fair, Hartford; Gladwin County Fair, Gladwin; Lowell Showboat, Lowell; Ottawa County Fair, Holland; Iosco County Fair, Hale; Munger Potato Festival, Munger; Menominee County Fair, Stephenson; Clare County Fair, Harrison; Arts and Crafts Fair, Manistee; Dancing Hippopotamus Arts and Crafts Festival, Ocqueoc; Ferrous

Frolics, Iron County Museum, Caspian; Arts and Crafts Festival, Mich-E-Kewis Park, Alpena.

August. Washtenaw County 4H Fair, Ann Arbor; Tuscola County Fair, Caro; Bay County Fair, Bay City; Gratiot County 4H Fair, Alma; Oakland County 4H Fair, Davisburg; Ingham County Fair, Mason; Ionia Free Fair, Ionia; Huron Community Fair, Bad Axe; Shiawassee County Free Fair, Corunna; Otsego County Fair, Gaylord; Jackson County Fair, Jackson; Cass County Fair, Cassopolis; Branch County 4H Fair, Coldwater; Osceola County 4H-FFA Fair, Evart; Western Michigan Fair, Ludington; Monroe County Fair, Monroe; Sanilac County 4H Fair, Sandusky; Alcona County Fair, Harrisville; Millington Summer Fest, Millington; Gogebic County Fair, Ironwood; Chippewa Lake Days, Chippewa Lake; Oscoda County 4H Youth Fair, Mio; Berrien County Youth Fair, Berrien Springs; VJ Day Celebration, Crystal Falls; Street Fair and Corn Roast, Lake City; Northern Michigan Fair, Cheboygan; Calhoun County Fair, Marshall; Midland County Fair, Midland; Coppertown USA Festival, Calumet; Clinton County 4H Club Fair, St. Johns; Northern District Fair, Cadillac; Kent County 4H Fair, Lowell; Newaygo County

PBS

Mother of Pearl

Fair, Fremont; Manchester Community Fair, Manchester; Armada Agricultural Fair, Armada; Upper Peninsula State Fair, Escanaba; Montmorency County 4H Fair, Atlanta; Paul Bunyan Festival, Oscoda; Kalkaska County Fair, Kalkaska; Lenawee County Fair, Adrian; Alpena County Fair, Alpena; Hudsonville Community Fair, Hudsonville; Kalamazoo County Fair, Kalamazoo; Emmet County Fair, Petoskey; Isabella County Youth Fair, Mt. Pleasant; Chelsea Community Fair, Chelsea; Genessee County Fair, Flint; Michigan State Fair, Detroit; Houghton County 4H Fair, Hancock; Northwestern Michigan Fair, Traverse City; Eastern Michigan Fair, Imlay City; Manistee County Fair, Onekama; Arts and Crafts Fair, Village Green, Saugatuck.

September. Chippewa County 4H-FFA Fair, Kinross; Oceana County Fair, Hart; Dickinson County Fair, Norway; Manton Harvest Festival, Manton; Saline Community Fair, Saline; Michigan Honey Festival, Chesaning; Charlotte Frontier Days, Charlotte; Fall Festival, Leslie; Potato Festival, Edmore; Allegan County Fair; Allegan; Wheatland Bluegrass Festival, Wheatland; Saginaw Fair, Saginaw; Farm City Festival, Mt. Clemens; Coho Festival, Honor; Folk Life Festival, Hastings; St. Joseph County Grange Fair, Centreville; Marquette County Harvest Festival, Marquette; Hillsdale County Fair, Hillsdale; Area Arts and Crafts Show, Hemlock Park, Big Rapids.

For information, write: Michigan Travel Commission, PO Box 30226, Lansing, MI 48909.

Minnesota

January. Old-Tyme Fiddlers' Contest and Dance, Bemidji State University, Bemidji; Paul Bunyan Winter Carnival, Bemidji State University, Bemidji.

February. Annual Mountain Iron Winter Carnival, Mountain Iron.

Barefoot Jerry

March. All Community Review, Winona; Concertina Jamboree and Polka Festival, Gibbon.

April. Annual Spring Carnival, Duluth.

May. Red River Hobby and Talent Show, Breckenridge; Springtime Jubilee, Carver; Springfest, St. Paul.

June. Boyd Good-Time Days, Boyd; Glencoe Festival, Glencoe; Buffalo Days, Buffalo; Ellsworth Dairy Days, Ellsworth; Festival of Lakes, Fairmont; Minnesota State Square Dance Convention, Duluth; Midsummers Day Festival, Erskine; Ramsey House Ice Cream Social, St. Paul; Downtown Summer Mini Festivals, Minneapolis; Sherburn Holiday Festival, Sherburn; Soybean Days, Clara City; Sugar Beet Days, Renville; Hay Daze, Janesville; Town and Country Days, Paynesville; Kaffefest, Willmar; Fortyniner Days, Fridley; Fiesta Days, Montevideo; New Richland's Centennial, New Richland; Cheese Days, Hiawathaland Western Festival, Elgin; Dairy Days, Starbuck; Annual Spudfest, Big Lake; Mora Dala Days and Rodeo, Mora; Svenskarnas Dag, Minneapolis; Mountain Lake Pow Wow, Mountain Lake; Steamboat Days, Winona.

July. Straw Hats and Sunbonnets Day, Verndale; Old-Fashioned Fourth of July, Moorhead; Clay County Fair, Barnesville; Kittson County Fair, Hallock; Annual Swanville Midsummer Carnival, Swanville; Manitou Days, White Bear Lake; Kelliher-Waskish Wild Rice Festival, Kelliher; Rolle Bolle Tournament, Marshall; New Hope Festival, New Hope; Onamia Days, Onamia; Milaca Community Festival, Milaca; Nevis Muskie Days, Nevis; Henning Area Festival, Henning; Otter Taily County Fair, Fergus Falls; Mississippi Melody Festival, Grand Rapids Showboat, Grand Rapids; Polk County Fair, Fertile; Lumberjack Days, Stillwater; Korn Klover Karnival, Hinckley; Hoffman Harvest Festival, Hoffman; Frontier Days, Rushford; Minneapolis Aquatennial, Minneapolis; Faribault County Fair, Blue Earth; Fillmore County Fair, Preston; Waseca County Free Fair, Waseca; Mississippi Melodie Festival, Grand Rapids; Wilkin County Fair, Breckenridge; Wadena County Fair, Wadena; Marshall County Fair, Warren; Logging Days, Park Rapids; Roseau County Fair, Roseau; Festtag, Minnesota Lake; Rice County Fair, Faribault; Annual St. Louis County Fair, Hibbing; Jackson County Fair, Jackson;

Monument

Ramsey County Fair, Maplewood; Scott County Fair, Jordan; Wabasha County Fair, Wabasha; Mahnomen County Fair, Mahnomen; Kolacky Day, Montgomery; Concertina Jamboree and Polka Festival, Givvon; Fireman's Pancake Supper, Pequot Lakes.

August. Todd County Fair, Long Prairie; Rock County Fair, Luverne; Freeborn County Fair, Albert Lea; Olmsted County Free Fair, Rochester; Wright County Fair, Howard Lake; Sibley County Fair, Arlington; South St. Louis County Fair, Proctor; Pine County Annual Fair, Pine City; Redwood County Fair, Redwood Falls; Tamarack Hey Day, Tamarack; Frazee Turkey Days, Frazee; Chatfield Western Days, Chatfield; Kanabec County Fair, Mora; Meeker County Fair, Litchfield; Mower County Fair, Austin; Old-Tyme Threshing Bee, Starbuck; Pipestone County Fair, Pipestone; County Suburban Fair, Anoka; Kandiyohi County Fair, Willmer; Becker County Fair, Detroit Lakes; Carver County Fair, Waconia; Nicollet County Fair, St. Peter; Washington County Fair, Lake Elmo; Old-Fashioned Corn Boil Day, Pequot Lakes; Stacy Daze, Stacy; Chippewa County Fair, Montevideo; Pope County Fair, Glenwood; Aitkin County Fair, Aitkin; Renville County Fair, Bird Island; Blue Earth County Fair, Garden City; Steele County Free Fair, Owatonna; Murray County Fair, Slayton; Nobles County Fair, Worthington; Itasca County Fair, Grand Rapids; Brown County Fair, New Ulm; Salute Blackduck Community Fair, Blackduck; Carlton County Fair, Barnum; Lyon County Fair, Marshall; Summer Festival, Garrison; Cottonwood County Fair, Windom; McLeod County Fair, Hutchinson; Perham Pioneer Festival and Old-Timers' Baseball Game, Perham; Sweet Corn Festival, Ortonville; Douglas County Fair, Alexandria; Houston County Fair, Caledonia; Swift County Fair, Appleton; Minnesota State Fair, St. Paul; Donnelly

Threshing Bee, Donnelly.

September. Boxcar Days, Tracy; Bovey Farmers Day and Old-Timers' Dance, Bovey; Red Rooster Day, Dassel; Sugar Festival, Moorhead; Traverse County Fair, Wheaton; Lac Qui Parle County Fair, Madison; Shindig, Duluth; Wild Rice Day, Mahnomen; Lakehead Harvest Reunion, Proctor; King Turkey Day, Worthington; LaCrescent Apple Festival, LaCrescent; Old-Fashioned Days, Faribault.

October. Potato Day, Williams; Pumpkin Festival, Owatonna.

For information, write: The Tourism Division, Department of Economic Development, 480 Cedar Street, St. Paul, MN 55101.

Mississippi

May. Jimmie Rodgers Memorial Festival, Meridian, Railway Depot Museum (write: Ms. Faye Phillips, Museum Director, PO Box 4153, Meridian, MS 39301).

July. (July through December) Panola Jamboree, Sardis; Grenada Lake Festival, Grenada; Lake Lowndes Folklife Festival, Columbus; Sea Food Festival, Pass Christian; Neshoba County Fair, Philadelphia; Annual Watermelon Festival, Lucedale.

August. Summer Festival, Ruleville; Winston County Fair, Louisville; Family Field Day, Morton.

September. Mississippi Folklife Exhibit, Jackson; Oktibbeha Fall Festival, Starkville; Folklife Festival, Hugh White State Park, Grenada; Lowndes County Fair, Columbus; Central Mississippi State Fair, Kosciusko; Harvest Festival, Florewood River Plantation, Greenwood; Old Trace Crafts Festival, Westwood Park, Tupelo; Old Natchez Territorial Fair, Natchez; Pike County Fair, Magnolia; Gumbo Festival, Necaise Crossing.

October. Yazoo County Fair, Yazoo City; Square and Round Dance Festival, Gulfport; Great River Road

Craft's Fair, Natchez; Oktoberfest, Biloxi; Harvest Festival, French Camp; Mississippi/Alabama State Fair, Meridian; Mississippi State Fair, Jackson; Agri Fair, Jackson; Jackson County Fair, Pascagoula; Oktoberfest, Percy Quinn State Park, McComb.

For information, write: Tourism and Public Affairs Department, Mississippi Agricultural and Industrial Board, PO Box 849, Jackson, MS 39205.

Mercury/Jerry Lee Lewis & Co.

Jerry Lee Lewis

Missouri

June. June Festival of Mountain Folks' Music, Silver Dollar City; Ragtime Festival, St. Louis; West Central Missouri District Fair, Pleasant Hill; Christian County Fair, Ozark; Sullivan Jaycee Youth Fair, Sullivan; National Feeder Pig Show, West Plains; Ozark County Youth Fair, Gainesville; Blackburn Festival, Blackburn; Humphreys 4H Achievement Day and Fair, Humphreys; Logan-Rogersville Junior Livestock Show, Rogersville.

July. National Tom Sawyer Fence-Painting Contest, Hannibal; Andrew County American Legion Youth Fair, Savannah; Vandalia

Area Fair, Vandalia; Barry County Youth Livestock Show, Cassville; Monett Jr. Livestock Show, Monett; Bates County Fair, Butler; Benton County Fair, Ionia; Centralia Youth Livestock Show and Fair, Centralia; Braymer Community Fair, Braymer; Caldwell County Fair, Kingston; Kidder Picnic, Kidder; Auxvasse 4H Fair, Auxvasse; Land of Lakes Youth Fair, El Dorado Springs; Salisbury Fair and Horse Show, Salisbury; Clark County Fair, Kahoka; Clay County 4H Fair, Liberty; Jaycee Cole County Fair, Jefferson City; Cooper County Agricultural and Mechanical Society, Prairie Home; Cooper County Youth Fair, Boonville; Dallas County Fair and Junior Livestock Show, Buffalo; Daviess County Jr. Livestock Show, Gallatin; Jamesport Junior Livestock Show, Jamesport; Clarksdale Picnic and Fair, Clarksdale; Douglas County Fair, Ava; Franklin County 4H Fair, Union; Gerald 4H Youth Fair, Gerald; New Haven Jaycee Youth Fair, New Haven; Gasconade

County Fair, Owensville; Greene County 4H Livestock Show, Springfield; Galt Community Fair, Galt; Laredo Community and 4H Free Fair, Laredo; Cainsville Livestock Show, Cainsville; Harrison County Farmers Fair, Ridgeway; Henry County Fair, Clinton; Annual Urich Reunion, Urich; Hickory County Junior Livestock Show, Hermitage; Squaw Creek Livestock Show, Mound City; Heart of the Ozarks Fair, West Plains; Jackson County Fair, Lee's Summit; Jackson County 4H Fair, Independence; Jasper County Youth Fair, Carthage; Knox County 4H Fair, Edina; Laclede County Community Fair, Lebanon; Lafayette County 4H Fair, Higginsville; Odessa Youth Fair, Odessa; Aurora Tri-County Junior Livestock Show, Aurora; Lawrence County Junior Livestock and Farm Mechanics Show, Mt. Vernon; Lewis County Agricultural Fair, Lewistown; Lincoln County Youth Fair, Troy; Browning Homecoming, Browning; North Central 4H and FFA Fair, Chillicothe; Pork Chop Night, Chillicothe; McDonald County Fair, Anderson; Macon County Town and Country Fair, Macon; Belle Community Fair, Belle; Mercer County Fair, Princeton; Tipton Community Fair, Tipton; Madison Fall Festival, Madison; Paris Monroe County Fall Festival, Paris; Montgomery County Fair, Montgomery City; Newton County Fair, Neosho; Nodaway County 4H and FFA Junior Livestock and Horse Show, Maryville; Oregon County Fair, Alton; Pettis County 4H Livestock Show and Horse Show, Sedalia; Smithton Town and Country Fair, Smithton; Pike County Fair, Bowling Green; Platte County Agricultural Mechanics and Stock Association, Tracy; Polk County Junior Livestock Show and Youth Fair, Bolivar; Ralls County Junior Fair, Center; Purebred Breeders Fair, Huntsville; Randolph County Achievement Days, Moberly; Randolph County Junior Agricultural Show, Moberly; Ray County Fair, Richmond; Youth Fair of St.

Charles County, Wentzville; St. Francois County 4H Roundup, Farmington; St. Genevieve County 4H Fair, St. Genevieve; Saline County Junior Fair, Marshall; Scotland County Agricultural and Mechanics Society, Memphis; Mountain View—Birch Tree FFA and Community Fair, Mountain View; Shelby County Fair, Shelbina; Taney County Fair, Forsyth; Texas County Fair, Houston; Webster County Fair, Marshfield; Wright County Junior Fair, Crovespring.

August. Missouri State Fair, Sedalia; Northeast Missouri District Fair, Kirksville; Northwest Missouri Junior Angus Show, Savannah; Atchison County Livestock Show, Tarkio; Audrain County 4H Fair, Mexico; Hume Fair, Hume; Boone County Fair and Horse Show, Columbia; Buchanan County 4H Baby Beef and Pig Show, St. Joseph; Carroll County Fair, Carrollton; Cass County Junior Livestock Show, Harrisonville; Chariton County Achievement and Exhibit Days, Brunswick; Clinton County Junior Livestock and Home Economics Show, Plattsburg; Crawford County Fair, Cuba; DeKalb County Fair and Horse Show, Maysville; Stewartsville Fall Festival, Stewartsville; Missouri State Peach Fair, Malden; Washington Town and Country Fair, Washington; Ozark Empire Fair, Springfield; Republic Kiwanis Junior Livestock Show, Republic; North Central Missouri Fair, Trenton; Gilman City Fair and Horse Show, Gilman City; Central Missouri District FFA Fair, Windsor; Jasper Harvest Show, Jasper; Johnson County Junior Livestock Show, Holden; Lexington Fall Festival, Lexington; Linn County 4H Fair, Brookfield; Callao Harvest Fiesta, Callao; Palmyra Fall Festival and Marion County Junior Fair, Palmyra; Miller County Fair, Eldon; Moniteau County Fair, California; Monroe City Youth Fair, Monroe City; Morgan County Free Fair, Versailles; Perry County 4H Fair, Perryville; Central Missouri Regional Fair, Rolla; Lucerne Stock

Monument

Boots Randolph

Show, Lucerne; St. Francois County Fair, Farmington; Sweet Springs Festival, Sweet Springs; Schuyler County Junior Livestock Show, Queen City; Jaycee Stoddard County Fair, Dexter; Green City-Comstock 4H Fair, Green City; Sullivan County 4H Jr. Livestock Show, Milan; Tri-County Community Fair, Neston; Winigan 4H Fair, Winigan; Vernon County Youth Fair, Nevada; Marthasville Fall Festival, Marthasville; Warren County Fair, Warrenton; Washington County Fair, Potosi; JFA State Fair, Marshfield; Worth County Fair, Grant City.

September. Cotton Carnival, Sikeston; Atchison County Fair, Rock Port; Lamar's Annual Farm and Indian Expo, Lamar; Cole Camp Fair, Cole Camp; Southeast Missouri District Fair, Cape Girardeau; Stockton Black Walnut and Cheese Festival, Stockton; Dent County Fall Festival, Salem; Delta Fair, Kennett; Northwest Missouri State Fair, Bethany; Calhoun Colt Show, Calhoun; Holt County Autumn Festival, Oregon; Iron County Fair, Ironton; Chilhowee Community Fair, Chilhowee; Holden Free Fall Fiesta, Holden; Concordia Fall Festival, Concordia; Waverly Apple Jubilee, Waverly; Wellington Community Fair, Wellington; Chula Street Fair, Chula; Maries County Fair, Vienna; Hannibal Pork-A-Rama, Hannibal; East Perry Community Fair, Altenburg; St. James Grape and Fall Festival, St. James; Pleasant Hope Jr. Livestock and Home Economics Show, Pleasant Hope; Putnam County Fair, Unionville; Purebred Beef Cattle Show, Moberly; St. Genevieve County Fair, St. Genevieve; Slater Volkfest, Slater.

For information, write: Missouri Division of Tourism, 308 East High Street, PO Box 1055, Jefferson City, MO 65101.

Montana

April. Arts and Crafts Festival, Libby; College Rodeo and Music Festival, Glendive.

May. Annual Cherry Blossom Festival, Polson; Whoop-Up Trail Days Parade and Rodeo, Conrad; Canadian Days and Rocky Mountain Junior Horse Show, Kalispell; Springtime in the Rockies Auction and Party, Red Lodge; Frontier Days and Rodeo, Cylbertson; Square Dance Festival, Missoula.

June. Red Lodge Music Festival, Red Lodge; Belle Creek Stampede Rodeo and Grand Ole Opry, Belle Creek; Pioneer Days, Ronan; Logger Days, Kalispell; Pioneer Fair, Kalispell.

July. Brand New Opry, Harlowton; Flathead Valley Rendezvous, Kalispell; Funsteppers Annual Summer Festival and Campout, Plains; Alberton Street Dance, Alberton; Logger's Days, Libby; Showboat

Willie Nelson   PBS

Around the Bend, Polson; Old-Fashioned Days, Kalispell; Annual Marias Fair, Shelby; Montana State Fiddlers' Championship, Polson; Good Sam Samboree, Libby; Darby Logger Days, Darby; Central Montana Horse Show, Fair and Rodeo, Lewistown; 4H Fair and Stock Sale, Roundup; Last Chance Stampede and Fair, Helena; State Fair, Great Falls; Prairie County Fair and Rodeo, Terry.

August. Gallatin County Junior Fair, Bozeman; Hardin Youth Fair, Hardin; Richland County Fair and Rodeo, Sidney; Phillips County Fair and Rodeo, Dodson; Mineral County Fair, Superior; Copper Empire Show, Anaconda; Daniels County Fair, Scobey; Ronan Junior Fair, Polson; Park County Fair, Livingston; Lake County Junior Fair, Ronan; Northeastern Montana Fair, Glasgow; Flathead Valley Art Festival, Kalispell; Hill County Fair, Havre; Dawson County Fair, Glendive; Yellowstone Exhibition, Billings; Northwest Montana Fair and Rodeo and Horse Races, Kalispell; Madison County Fair, Twin Bridges; Fallon County Fair, Baker; Tri-County Fair, Deer Lodge; Prairie County Fair, Terry; Rosebud County Fair, Forsyth; Western Montana Fair, Missoula; Eastern Montana Fair and Rodeo, Miles City; Roosevelt County Fair, Culbertson; Beaverhead County Fair, Dillon; 4H Fair, Red Lodge; Silver Bow County Fair, Butte; Roosevelt County Youth Fair, Wolf Point; Crow Fair and Rodeo, Hardin.

September. Ravalli County Fair, Hamilton; Sanders County Fair,

Plains; Chouteau County Fair, Fort Benton; Blain County Fair, Cinook; Knothead Squaredance Jamboree, West Yellowstone; Community BBQ, Lima; Gallatin Lions Fiddle Contest, Bozeman; Missoula Logger Days, Missoula.

For information, write: Montana Travel Hosts, Montana Chamber of Commerce, PO Box 1730, Helena, MT 59601.

Nebraska

May. Camp Clarke Days, Bridgeport; Brownsville Spring Festival, Brownsville.

June. Official Nebraska State Country Music Championship, Waterloo; Fun Day Festival, Norfolk; Annual Society for Preservation of Bluegrass Music of America—Family Bluegrass Festival, Waterloo; Nebraskaland Days, North Platte; Days of '56 Rodeo and Celebration, Ponca; Big Sky Jubilee, Anselmo; Brownsville Historical Society Square Dance, Brownsville.

July. Fur Trade Days, Chadron; Old Settlers' Picnic, Hickman; Sugar Valley Singers' Concert, Wildcat Hills Amphitheatre, Scottsbluff/Gering; Seneca Days, Seneca; Summer Music Festival, Brownsville; Oregon Trail Days, Gering; Summer Festival, Gothenburg; The Diller Picnic, Diller; Old Settlers' Picnic, Western; Harvest Festival, Trenton; Winside Old Settlers' Picnic, Winside; Nancy County Fair, Fullerton; Hitchcock County Fair, Culbertson; Columban Festival, Bellevue; Burt County Fair, Oakland; Red Willow County Fair, McCook; Polk County Fair, Osceola; Minden's Centennial, Minden; Nuckolls County Fair, Nelson; Platte County Fair, Columbus; Wayne County Fair, Wayne; Winnebago Pow Wow, Winnebago; Madison County Fair, Madison; Clay County Fair, Clay Center; Crystal Springs Camp-in, Fairbury.

August. Dodge County 4H Fair, Fremont; Summer Music Festival, Brownsville; Harlan County Junior

Fair, Orleans; Pawnee County Fair, Pawnee City; Gage County Fair, Beatrice; Fillmore County Fair, Geneva; Sioux County Fair, Harrison; Cedar County Fair, Hartington; Rock County Fair and Rodeo, Bassett; Annual Pawnee Days, Genoa; Custer County Fair, Broken Bow; Box Butte County Fair, Hemingford; Deuel County Fair, Chappell; Cass County Fair, Weeping Water; Saunders County Fair, Wahoo; Dawson County Fair, Lexington; Thayer County Fair, Deshler; Sarpy County Fair, Springfield; Webster County Fair, Bladen; Thomas County Fair, Thedford; Garfield County Fair, Burwell; Butler County Fair, David City; Haynes County Fair, Haynes Center; Colfax County Fair, Leigh; Dodge County Fair, Scribner; Lincoln County Fair, North Platte; Country Music Festival, Ainsworth; Hay Springs Friendly Festival, Hay Springs; Grant

County Fair, Hyannis; Johnson County Fair, Tecumseh; Knox County Fair, Bloomfield; Keith County Fair, Ogallala; Washington County Fair, Arlington; Adams County Fair, Hastings; Dundy County Fair and Rodeo, Benkelman; Kearney County Fair, Minden; Scottsbluff County Fair, Mitchell; Nemaha County Fair, Auburn; Dixon County Fair, Concord; Frontier County Fair, Eustis; Jefferson County Fair, Fairbury; Greeley County Fair, Spalding; Holt County Fair, Chambers; York County Fair, York; Lancaster County Fair, Lincoln; Dawes County Fair, Chadron; Furnas County Fair, Beaver City; Sheridan County Fair and Rodeo, Gordon; Dakota/Thurston County Fair, South Sioux City; Cherry County Fair, Valentine; Gosper County Fair, Elmwood; Perkins County Fair, Grant; Boyd County Fair,

Dave & Sugar

RCA/Chardon,

Spencer; Loup County Fair, Taylor; Saline County Fair, Crete; Hooker County Fair, Mullen; Stanton County Fair, Stanton; Douglas County Fair, Waterloo; Cuming County Fair, West Point; Hall County Fair, Grand Island; Buffalo County Fair, Kearney; Arthur County Fair, Arthur; Wheeler County Fair, Bartlett; Sheridan County Fair and Rodeo, Gordon; Pierce County Fair, Pierce; Santee Sioux Pow Wow, Santee; Seward County Fair, Seward; Cass County Country Music Contest, Weeping Water; Merrick County Fair, Central City; Otoe County Fair, Syracuse; Omah Pow Wow, Macy; Chase County Fair, Imperial; Howard County Fair, St. Paul; Logan County Fair, Stapleton; Garden County Fair, Lewellen; Antelope County Fair, Neligh; Morrill County Fair, Bridgeport; Hamilton County Fair, Aurora; Popcorn Days, North Loup.

September. Nebraska State Fair, Lincoln; Brown County Fair, Johnstown; Hay Days Celebration, Cozad; Keya Paha County Fair, Norden; Richardson County Fair, Humboldt; Nebraska Polka Days, Omaha; Kass Kounty King Korn Karnival, Plattsmouth; Western Regional 4H Events, Omaha; Annual Prairie Schooners Square Dance Festival, Sidney; Nebraska State Square Dancing Convention, Grand Island.

October. Nebraska State Square Dancing Convention, Grand Island.

For information, write: Travel and Tourism Division, Department of Economic Development, Box 94666, 301 Centennial Mall South, Lincoln, NB 68509.

New Hampshire

July. Stratham Fair, Stratham; Cheshire Fair, Keene.

August. North Haverhill Fair, N. Haverhill; Canaan Fair, Canaan; Cornish Fair, Canaan; Belknap County 4H Fair, Laconia; State Fair, Plymouth.

September. Hopkinton Fair, Contoocook; Coos and Essex Agricultural Fair, Lancester; Hilsborough County Fair, New Boston; Rochester Fair, Rochester; Deerfield Fair, Deerfield.

October. Sandwich Town and Grange Fair, Sandwich.

For information, write: New Hampshire Division of Economic Development, Concord, NH

New Mexico

February. The Wagon Wheels, Square and Folk Dance, Grants.

March. Home Town Grand Ole Opry, Alamogordo.

April. Annual Pioneer Days Arts and Crafts Fair, Roswell.

May. Old Time Fiddlers' Contest, Truth or Consequences; Annual Moreno Valley Fish Fry and Square Dance Festival, Eagle Nest; Annual Butterfield Trail Days, Deming; Annual Memorial Day Square Dance Festival, Red River.

June. Annual *Fiesta de la Primavera, Los Cerrillos;* Annual Santa Rosa Day and Community Picnic, Santa Rosa.

July. Annual Sierra County Farm Bureau Cotton Extravaganza, Truth or Consequences; Annual Fourth of July Fiestas, Las Vegas; Independence Day Celebration, Santa Fe; Outdoor Social and Fiddlers' Contest, Holloman; Outdoor Social and Fiddlers' Contest, Tularosa; Annual Old-Timers' Day, Estancia.

August. Annual Northeastern New Mexico Tri-County Fair and Rodeo, Las Vegas; Annual Los Alamos County Fair and Junior Rodeo, Los Alamos; Taos Mountain Rodeo Arena; County Fair and Horse Show, Taos; Outdoor Social and Fiddlers' Contest, Weed; Old-Time Fiddlers' Contest, Truth or Consequences; Annual Old Lincoln Days, Lincoln; Annual Summer Festival, Corona; Outdoor Social and Fiddlers' Contest, Cloudcroft; Annual Lea County Fair and

Rodeo, Lovington; Annual Chama Days, Chama; Village Fair and Horse Show, Bosque Farms; Rio Arriba County 4H/FFA Fair, Española; Annual de Baca County Fair, Fort Sumner; Roosevelt County Fair, Portales; Annual Zuni-McKinley County Fair and Rodeo, Zuni Pueblo; Annual Lincoln County Fair, Capitan; Catron County Fair and Junior Rodeo, Reserve.

September. Union County Fair, Clayton; Annual McKinley-Valencia Uranium Bi-County Fair, Prewitt; Socorro County Fair and Rodeo, Socorro; Annual Labor Day Square Dance Festival, Red River; Annual Fiesta de Santa Fe, Santa Fe; Annual Hatch Valley Chili Festival, Hatch; Annual Apple Festival, Hillsboro; Annual Pioneers' Picnic, Bloomfield; Annual Curry County Fair, Clovis; Annual Piñata Festival, Tucumcari; Quay County Fair, Tucumcari; Annual Valencia County Fair, Belen; Annual San Juan County Fair, Farmington; Annual Colfax County Fair, Springer; Annual Otero County Fair and Rodeo, Alamogordo; Annual Hidalgo County Fair and Junior Rodeo, Lordsburg; Annual Sierra County Fair, Truth or Consequences; Annual New Mexico State Fair, Albuquerque; The Aspencade, Red River; Annual Aspen Festival and Paul Bunyan Days, Eagle Nest; Annual Eastern New Mexico State Fair and Rodeo, Roswell; Annual Southern New Mexico State Fair, Las Cruces.

October. Annual Mule-O-Rama, Ruidoso; Harvest Festival, Old Cienega Village Museum, La Cienega; Annual Cliff-Gil-Grant County Fair, Cliff; Annual Taos Festival of the Arts, Taos; Annual Southwestern New Mexico State Fair and Quarter Horse Show, Deming; Oktoberfest, Angel Fire; Annual Wild West Night, Farmington; Annual 49ers Celebration, Socorro; Annual Peanut Festival and Arts and Crafts Fair, Portales.

November. Annual Southwest Arts and Crafts Festival, Albuquerque;

Annual Northern New Mexico Arts and Crafts Fair, Los Alamos.

For information, write: Tourist Division, New Mexico Department of Development, 113 Washington Avenue, Santa Fe, NM 87503.

New York

January. Annual Winter Festival, Lake George.

February. Annual Winter Carnival, Malone; Annual Winter Carnival, Saranac Lake; Annual Winter Carnival, Cooperstown.

April. Annual Central New York Maple Festival, Marathon; Annual Western New York Maple Festival, Franklinville; Annual Schoharie County Maple Festival, Jefferson.

May. Annual Dogwood Festival, Dansville.

June. Annual Steuben County Dairy Festival, Bath.

July. Annual Fourth of July Celebration and Field Day, Narrowsburg; Annual Stone House Day Tours, Hurley; Glenora Music and Arts Festival, Glenora.

August. Festival of American Heritage (Newport Jazz Festival), Performing Arts Center, Saratoga Springs; New York State Woodsmen's Field Days, Boonville; Dutchess County Fair, Rhinebeck; New York State Fair, State Fairgrounds, Syracuse.

October. Cohocton Fall Festival, Cohocton.

For information, write: New York Tourist Bureau, East 42nd Street, New York, NY 10017.

North Dakota.

June. Irrigation Days, Oakes; Annual Sugarbeet Festival, Grafton; Old-Time Fiddlers' Contest, Dunseith; Bottineau County Fair, Bottineau; Jubilee, Crosby Wells County Fair, Fessenden; Grand Forks County Fair, Grand Forks; Upper Missouri Valley Fair,

Williston; McLean County Fair, Underwood.

July. Stutsman County Fair, Jamestown; Chautauqua, Devils Lake; Roughrider Days, Dickinson; Towner County Fair, Cando; Pembina County Fair, Hamilton; Burke County Fair, Flaxton; Summer Festival, Hazen; Red River Valley Fair, West Fargo; Griggs County Fair, Cooperstown; McKenzie County Fair, Watford; North Dakota State Fair, Minot; Fort Totten Days Pow Wow, Fort Totten; Tri-County Fair, Wishek.

August. Dickey County Fair, Ellendale; Morton County Fair, New Salem; Grant County Fair, Carson; Ransom County Fair, Lisbon; Mercer County Fair, Beulah; Pioneer Days, Bonanzaville USA, West Fargo.

September. Golden Valley County Fair, Beach; Sargent County Fair, Forman; Kidder County Fair, Steele; Bowman County Fair, Bowman; Chancellor Square Fair, Bismark; Fall Festival, Richardton; Annual Fall Festival, Hebron.

October. Octoberfest, Rugby.

For information, write: State Travel Division, Capitol Grounds, Bismark, ND 58505.

Ohio

May. Cherry Blossom Festival, Barberton; Moonshine Festival, New Straitsville.

June. National Clay Week, Uhrichsville/Dennison; Festival of the Fish, Vermilion; Swiss Cheese Festival, Middlefield; Bellevue Cherry Festival, Bellevue.

July. Canal Days, Canal Fulton; Ohio Hills Folk Festival, Quaker City; Pottery Festival, Roseville/Crooksville.

August. Salt Fork Arts and Crafts Festival, Cambridge; Ohio State Fair, Columbus; Coshocton Canal Festival, Coshocton; Parade of the Hills Festival, Nelsonville; Sweet Corn Festival, Millersport.

September. Melon Festival, Milan; Tomato Festival, Reynoldsburg; Honey Festival, Lebanon; Johnny Appleseed Festival, Lisbon; Apple Festival, Jackson; Grape Jamboree, Geneva.

October. Holmes County Antique Festival, Millersburg; Ohio Sauerkraut Festival, Waynesville; Bob Evans Farm Festival, Rio Grande; Fall Festival of Leaves, Bainbridge; Pumpkin Show, Circleville.

For information, write: Ohio Festivals and Events Association, State Capitol, Columbus, OH.

Oklahoma

April. Square Dance Festival, Tulsa; Oklahoma City Festival of the Arts, Oklahoma City; Spring Fever Bluegrass Festival, Bluegrass Kingdom Park, Cement.

May. Tri-State Music Festival, Enid; Veterans' Day Pow Wow, Carnegie; No Man's Land Pioneer Celebration, Guymon; Central District Square Dance Jamboree, Oklahoma City; Western Oklahoma Bluegrass Festival, Weatherford; Rooster Day Celebration, Broken Arrow; Western Days, Durant; Bigheart Day, Bamsdall.

The Oak Ridge Boys

June. Bluegrass Festival, Eufaula; Old Settlers' Day and Rodeo, Checotah; Love County Frontier Days, Marietta; Bluegrass Festival, Bluegrass Kingdom Park, Cement; Little River Bluegrass Festival, Gallaher Pecan Grove, Norman; Western Heritage Days, Cushing; Wagoner Lake Festival, Wagoner; Bluegrass Festival, Eagle Park, Cache; Texomaland National Sand Bass Festival and Carnival and Entertainment, Lake Texoma; Reunion Days, Stigler; Pushmataha County Annual Homecoming, Antlers; Grant's Gospel Jubilee, Hugo; Green Corn Festival, Bixby; Annual Homecoming Celebration, Boswell; Blue Mountain Western Festival, Hartshome.

July. Old Santa Fe Trail Days, Shawnee; Powderhorn Park Bluegrass Festival, Langley; Kiamichi County Music Festival, Robbers Cave State Park, Wilburton; Davis Bluegrass Festival, Davis; Kiowa County Fair, Hobart; Frontier Days and Rodeo, Poteau; Greer County Pioneer Reunion, Mangum; Round Spring Park Bluegrass Festival, Disney; Jolly Roger Festival, Cleveland; International Roundup Cavalcade, Pawhuska; All Night Gospel Sing, Holdenville.

August. Old Settlers Reunion and

ABC Dot Records
The Jim Halsey Co., Inc.

Rodeo, Velma; Bluegrass Festival, Hugo; Western Week, Holdenville; Grant's Bluegrass Festival, Hugo; Peach Festival, Porter; Watermelon Festival, Rush Springs; Western Heritage Days, Bristow; Canadian Valley Day, Seminole; Pioneer Day Celebration and Rodeo, Skiatook; Eufaula Fair, Eufaula; All Night Gospel Sing, Seminole; Osage County Fair, Pawhuska; Latimer County Fair, Wilburton.

September. Choctaw County Fair, Hugo; Jefferson County Fair, Waurika; Garvin County Free Fair, Pauls Valley; Kiowa County Fair, Hobert; Hinton Free Fair, Hinton; Tri-County Fair, Carnegie; Pioneer Days Celebration, Cache; Annual Homecoming, Clayton; Bluegrass Festival, Bluegrass Kingdom Park, Cement; Labor Day Homecoming, Ralston; Rodeo and Parade, Elk City; Garfield County Fair, Enid; Lincoln County Fair, Chandler; Comanche County Fair, Lawton; Okfuskee County Fair, Okeman; Woodward County Fair, Woodward; Chelsea Fair and Jamboree, Chelsea; Greer County Fair, Mangum; Marshall County Fair, Madill; Heritage Day, Spencer; Old Settlers' Day, Chandler; Custer County Fair, Clinton; Murray County Fair, Sulphur; Washington County Fair, Dewey; Cherokee County Fair, Tahlequah; Pontotoc County Fair, Ada; Noble County Fair, Perry; Cimarron County Fair, Boise City; Canadian County Fair, El Reno; Marshall County Fair, Madill; Cherokee Strip Celebration, Perry; Open Air Art Show and Festival, Elk City; Pioneer Week, Cushing; Carter County Free Fair, Ardmore; Cimarron County Fair, Boise City; Creek County Fair, Bristow; Fall Festival and Rodeo, Coweta; Oklahoma State Fair, Oklahoma City; Tulsa State Fair, Tulsa.

For information, write: Oklahoma Tourism and Recreation Department, Division of Tourism Promotion, 500 Will Rogers Building, Oklahoma City, OK 73105.

PBS

Tracy Nelson

Oregon

June. Strawberry Festival, Lebanon; '62 Days Celebration, Canyon City; Vacation Daze, Dallas; Buckaroo Square Dance Roundup, Roseburg; Pioneer Day, Burns; Phil Sheridan Days, Sheridan; Linn County Pioneer Picnic, Brownsville; Beachcombers' Days, Waldport; Pioneer Day, Jacksonville; Arts Festival, Lake Oswego; Arts and Crafts Festival, Princeville; Rockhound Pow Wow, Fairgrounds, Princeville; Happy Days, Fairgrounds, Hillsboro; Arts Festival, Monmouth; Territorial Days, Oregon City.

July. Annual Country Western Show, Baker; Dexter Daze, Dexter; Jetty Jubilee, Port Orford; Square and Round Dance Festival, Fairgrounds, Roseburg; 4H Fair, Fairgrounds, Eugene; Sandy Mt. Festival, Sandy; Opera County Classic, Wilsonville; Bohemia Mining Days, Cottage Groves; Crazy Days, Albany; Western Days, Hillsboro; Yamhill County Fair, McMinnville; Lincoln County Fair, Newport; Horseracing and Crazy Days, Lakeview; County Fair, Hood River; Crazzee Days, Woodburn; Garibaldi Days Celebration, Garibaldi; Friendship Jamboree, Vernonia;

Applegate Trail Days, Veneta; Fair, West Linn; Krazee Daze, Dallas; Multnomah County Fair, Portland; Old-Timers' Picnic, Dayton.

August. Washington County Fair, Hillsboro; Umatilla County Fair, Hermiston; Thunderegg Days, Nyssa; Union County Fair, La Grande; Crazy Days, Newport; Applegate Trail Days Festival, Veneta; Deschutes County Fair and Rodeo, Redmond; Arts and Crafts Festival, Seaside; Boones Ferry Days, Wilsonville; Wallowa County Fair, Enterprise; Antique Powerland Farm Fair, Brooks; Town and Country Days, Tigard; Jackson County 4H and FFA Fair, Central Point; Douglas County Fair, Roseburg; Tillamook County Fair, Tillamook; Columbus County Fair, St. Helens; Jefferson County Fair, Madras; Benton County Fair, Corvallis; Curry County Fair, Gold Beach; Huckleberry Festival, Warm Springs; Sunset Bar-B-Que, Sunset Park, Banks; Crawfish Festival, Tualatin; Josephine County Fair, Grants Pass; Clackamas County Fair, Canby; Lane County Fair, Eugene; Malheur County Fair, Ontario; Crook County Fair, Prineville; Coos County Fair and Rodeo, Myrtle Point; Morrow County Fair and Rodeo, Heppner; Grant County Fair, John Day; Western Exposition Fair, Cottage Grove; Pioneer Days, Canyonville; Oregon State Fair, Salem.

September. Lake County Fair and Roundup, Lakeview; Fun Festival, Coos Bay; Harney County Fair and Rodeo, Burns; Gilliam County Fair, Condon; Oktoberfest, Mt. Angel; Oktoberfest, Holladay Park, Portland; Melon Festival, Winston; Portage Days, Hood River; Cranberry Festival, Bandon; Linn County Fair, Albany; Fall Festival, Corvallis.

October. Octoberfest, La Grande; Turkey and Dollar Days, Newport.

For information, write: Oregon Department of Transportation, Travel Information Section, Salem, OR 97310.

Red Sovine

Pennsylvania

March. Pennsylvania Maple Festival, Meyersdale.

May. Northern Appalachian Crafts Festival, Bedford.

June. Du Bois Gateway Fair, Du Bois.

July. Lycoming County Fair, Hughesville; Jefferson Town and Country Fair, Sykesville; Plainfield Farmers Fair, Pen Argyl; Kimberton Community Fair, Kimberton; Troy Fair, Troy; Butler County Fair, Butler; Jefferson Township Fair, Mercer; Clarion County Fair, New Bethlehem; Agricultural Americana Folk Festival, Dauphin; Kutztown Folk Festival, Kutztown.

August. Morrison Cove Dairy Show, Martinsburg; Goshen Country Fair, West Chester; Clearfield County Fair, Clearfield; Fayette County Fair, Uniontown; Great Dallastown Fair, Dallastown; Jacktown Fair, Wind Ridge; Mercer County Grange Fair, Mercer; Potter County Fair, Millport; Union County West End Fair, Laurelton; New Stanton Farm and Home Fair, New Stanton; Great Allentown Fair, Allentown; Great Bedford Fair, Bedford; McKean County Fair, Smethport; Wayne County Fair, Honesdale; Lebanon Area Fair, Lebanon; Butler County Farm Show, Butler; Mountain Area Community Fair, Farmington; Greene County Fair, Waynesburg; Tioga County Fair, Whitneyville; Warren County Fair, Pittsfield; Wolf's Corners Fair, Tionesta; Clinton County Fair, Mill Hall; Cochranton Community Fair, Cochranton; Harrold Free Fair, Greensburg; Delaware Valley Fair, Milford; Rostraver Community Fair, Belle Vernon; Cameron County Fair, Emporium; Montour-DeLong Community Fair, Washingtonville; Sewickley Community Fair, West Newton; Dayton Fair, Dayton; Kutztown Fair, Kutztown; Carlisle Fair, Carlisle; Middletown Community Fair, Middletown; Washington County Fair, Washington; Huntingdon County Fair, Huntingdon; Lawrence County Fair, New Castle; Venango County Fair, Franklin; Elk County Fair, Kersey; Middletown Grange Fair, Wrightstown; Franklin County Fair, Chambersburg; Somerset County Fair, Meyersdale; Westmoreland County Fair, Greensburg; Harford Fair, Harford; Crawford County Fair, Meadville; Bullskin Township Fair, Wooddale; Fulton County Fair, McConnelsburg; Hookstown Fair, Hookstown; Transfer Harvest Home Fair, Transfer; Blue Valley Farm Show, Bangor; Perry County Fair, Newport; Mount Nebo Grange Fair, Sewickley; Centre County Fair, Centre Hall; Wattsburg Fair, Wattsburg; West End Fair, Gilbert; Sullivan County Fair, Forksville; Greene-Dreher-Sterling Fair, Newfoundland; Big Knob Grange Fair, Rochester; Great Stoneboro Fair, Stoneboro; Philadelphia Fold Festival, Philadelphia.

September. Bear Lake Community Fair, Bear Lake; Juniata County Fair, Port Royal; South Mountain Fair, Arendtsville; Cambria County Fair, Ebensburg; Waterford Community Fair, Waterford; Ox Hill

Community Fair, Home; Spartansburg Community Fair, Spartansburg; Pymatuning Community Fair, Jamestown; Dallas Area Fair, Dallas; York Inter-State Fair, York; Bellwood Antis Farm Show, Bellwood; Green Township Community Fair, Commodore; Greenfield Township Community Fair, Claysburg; Southern Lancaster County Fair, Quarryville; Albion Area Fair, Albion; West Alexander Fair, West Alexander; Berlin Brothers Valley Fair, Berlin; Oley Valley Fair, Oley; North East Community Fair, North East; Beaver Community Fair, Beaver Springs; Gratz Fair, Gratz; Ephrata Fair, Ephrata; Keystone County Festival, Blair County, Altoona; Mountain Craft Days, Somerset; Sinking Valley Community Farm Show, Sinking Valley; Harmony Grange Fair, Westover; Williamsburg Community Fair, Williamsburg; Bloomsburg Fair, Bloomsburg; Elizabethtown Marketplace Fair, Elizabethtown; Morrison Cove Community Fair, Martinsburg; West Lampeter Community Fair, Lampeter; Tri-Valley Community Fair, Hegins; Holidaysburg Community Fair, Holidaysburg; Manheim Community Fair, Manheim; Unionville Community Fair, Unionville; Dillsburg Community Fair, Dillsburg; Unionton's Poultry and Farm Products Show, Uniontown.

For information, write: Department of Agriculture, Bureau of Markets/Fair Funds, 2301 N. Cameron Street, Harrisburg, PA 17120, and Pennsylvania Festivals Association, Box 90, Kempton, PA 19529.

Rhode Island

May. Providence City Celebration, Providence; Village Fair, Kingston; Annual Earth Fair, Touro Park, Newport.

June. Flag Day Jonnycake Festival, North Kingston; Fourth of July Celebration, Bristol; Festival of Music, Foster; Greenville Arts and Crafts Festival, Greenville.

July. Annual South Country Heritage Festival, Wakefield; Annual Lions Beer Festival, Westerly; Summer Festival, Tiverton; Charlestown Historical Society County Fair, Charlestown; Newport County 4H Fair, Portsmouth; Tercentenary Carnival, East Greenwich; Annual Warren Summer Festival, Warren; Annual Foster Country Fair, Foster

Reba McEntire

Mercury

Center; Blessing of the Fleet Festival, Galilee; Southern Rhode Island 4H Fair, East Greenwich; Annual Columban Fathers Outing, Bristol.

August. Washington County Fair, Richmond; Annual Summer Fair, Little Compton; Gloucester Heritage Day Fair, Chepachet; Rocky Hill State Fair, East Greenwich.

September. Warwick Historical Society Annual Colonial Affair, Warwick; Butterfly Festival, Providence; Annual Harvest Fair, Bristol.

October. Annual North Smithfield Heritage Fair, Slatersville; Oktoberfest, Fort Getty, Jamestown; Annual Usquepaug Jonnycake Festival, Usquepaug.

For information, write: Rhode Island Department of Economic Development, Tourist Promotion Division, One Weybosset Hill, Providence, RI 02903.

South Carolina

April. The Governor's Annual Frog Jumping Contest, Springfield; Fiesta, Columbia; Wagons to Wagener, Wagener; Annual Murrells Inlet Outdoor Arts and Crafts Festival, Murrells Inlet.

May. Hell Hole Swamp Festival, Jamestown; South Carolina Landmark Conference, Greenwood; Upstate Heritage—Past and Present, Abbeville; Square Dance, Greenwood.

June. Square Dance, Oconee State Park, Walhalla (through August 26); Annual Sun Fun Festival, Myrtle Beach; Colonial Crops and Crafts at Charles Towne Landing, Charleston; Ridge Peach Festival, Trenton; Hampton County Watermelon Festival, Hempton-Varnville.

July. Mountain Rest Hillbilly Day, Mountain Rest; Stand Up for America Day, Greater North Augusta Area.

August. Springdale Fun-D Day, Springdale; Grape Festival, York; Annual Foothills Festival, Easley.

September. Indian Summer Days,

Myrtle Beach; Myrtle Beach Square and Round Dance, Myrtle Beach; Kingstree Old-Fashioned Days Festival, Kingstree; Annual Labor Day Observance at Charles Towne Landing, Charleston; Raylrode Daze Festival, Branchville; Anderson Fair, Anderson.

For information, write: South Carolina Division of Tourism, Room 15, PO Box 71, Columbia, SC 29202.

South Dakota

June. South Dakota Biennial, Brookings; Harvest Festival, Elkton; Rhubarb Festival, Leola; Pioneer Days, Dupree; Old Settlers' Days, De Smet; June Festival, Parkston; Red Rock Arts and Crafts Festival, Dell Rapids; Old Settlers' Days, Highmore; Aberdeen Arts Festival, Aberdeen; Gala Days Celebration, Bison.

July. Heart of the Hills Days and

Universal Management

Blackwood Rhythm Band

Timber Show, Hill City; Square Dance Festival, Rapid City; Gold Discovery Days, Custer; Whitewood Days, Whitewood.

August. Union County 4H Achievement Days and Fair, Alcester; Clay County Fair and Achievement Days, Vermillion; Fall River County Fair and Achievement Days, Degemont; Annual Days of '76, Deadwood; Tri-County Festival, Philip; Ft. Randall Pow Wow, Lake Andes; 4H Achievement Days, Huron; Harvest Festival and 4H Achievement Days, Salem; 4H Achievement Days, Tyndall; Summer Arts Festival Rapid City; Central States Fair, Rapid City; Sioux Empire Fair, Sioux Falls; Day County Fair, Webster; Oahe Days, Pierre; Potter County Fair, Gettysburg; Hutchinson County Fair, Tripp; Bennett County Fair and Achievement Days, Martin; 4H Achievement Days, Yankton; 4H Achievement Days, Watertown; Tripp County Fair, Winner; Moody County Fair, Flandreau; Custer County Fair, Hermosa; Butte County Fair, Nisland; Sully County Fair, Onida; Brown County Fair, Aberdeen; Pow Wow and Fair, Ft. Thompson; White River Frontier Days, White River; Montrose Community Frolic Day, Montrose; Meade County Fair and Achievement Days, Sturgis; Turner County Fair, Parker; Canton Corn Carnival, Canton; Harding County Fair and Rodeo, Camp Crook; South Dakota State Fair, Huron.

September. Cheyenne River Sioux Fair, Eagle Butte; Labor Day Weekend Celebration, Wagner; Labor Celebration, Buffalo; Corn Palace Festival, Mitchell; Sunflower Daze, Groton.

October. BHSC Swarm Day Homecoming, Spearfish; Yankton College Pioneer Day Homecoming, Yankton; Huron College Pow Wow Days Homecoming, Huron; South Dakota and Open Fiddlers' Contest, Yankton; NSC Gypsy Days Homecoming, Aberdeen; DWU Blue and White Day Homecoming, Mitchell;

Dakota Day Homecoming, USD/Vermillion; Founders' Day Homecoming, USD/Springfield; Augustana Viking Days Homecoming, Sioux Falls; Hobo Day Homecoming, SDSU/Brookings.

For information, write: South Dakota Division of Tourism, Pierre, SD 57501.

Tennessee

January. Red Boot Square Dance, Gatlinburg.

February. Curt Payne Square Dance, Gatlinburg; Allen Tipton Square Dance, Gatlinburg.

April. Paris Fish Fry, Paris; Ramp Festival, Cosby.

May. Annual Strawberry Festival, Dayton; Memphis Cotton Carnival, Memphis; Memphis Cotton Pickin' Music and Craft Fair, Memphis.

June. International Country Music Fun Fair, Nashville; State Square and Round Dance Festival, Chattanooga; Grinders Switch Arts and Crafts Show, Centerville; Grandmaster's Fiddling Contest, Opryland, Nashville; Rhododendron Festival, Roan Mountain; Townsend Arts and Crafts Fair, Townsend.

July. Old-Time Fiddlers' Jamboree and Crafts Festival, Smithville; Frontier Days, Lynchburg; Rutherford County Heritage Week, Murfreesboro.

August. Annual Country Music and Crafts Festival, Nashville; Korne Pone Day, Sparta; International Banana Festival, South Fulton; Davy Crockett Days and Davy Crockett Arts and Crafts Festival, Lawrenceburg; Giles County Fair, Pulaski; Rutherford County Fair, Murfreesboro; Okra Festival, Belles; Roane County Fair, Roane County Park, Kingston; Rhea Rural Fair, Spring City; Opryland Crafts Festival, Nashville; Memphis Waterfront Fair, Memphis.

September. State Fair, Nashville; Mid-South Fair, Memphis; Coffee County Fair, Manchester; Folk Festival of the Smokies, Cosby; Country Fair, Nashville; Opryland Square Dance Festival, Nashville; Annual Outdoor Tuckaleechee Cove Arts, Crafts and Music Festival, Townsend; Reelfoot Arts and Crafts Festival, Tiptonville.

October. Hillbilly Day, Madison; National Quartet Convention (Gospel Music Festival), Nashville; Annual Chattanooga Choo Choo Square-Dance Festival, Chattanooga; Old Timers' Day, Manchester; Anniversary of the Grand Ole Opry, Nashville; Meriwether Lewis Arts and Crafts Fair, Meriwether State Park, Columbia; Gatlinburg Craftsman's Fair, Gatlinburg; Craftsman's Fair of the Southern Highlands, Knoxville; Memphis Ocktoberfest, Memphis; Older Americans' Days, Silver Dollar City; National Crafts Festival, Silver Dollar City; Annual Fall Color Cruise and Folk Festival, Chattanooga.

November. Foot Hills Craft Guild Show and Sale, Oak Ridge.

For information, write: Department of Tourist Development, State of Tennessee, 505 Fesslers Lane, Nashville, TN 37210.

Texas

April. Western Day Festivities, Mathis; Square and Round Dance Festival, Lubbock; Country Fair, Carrizo Springs; Miss Freer Pageant (Parade, Barbecue, Rattlesnake Fry), Freer; Bluegrass Picnic and Jam Sessions, Glen Rose; Dogwood Fiesta (Square Dance), Quitman; Old Fiddlers' Contest, Llano; Tyler County Dogwood Festival, Woodville; Wildflower Trails of Texas (Music Festival, Gospel Sing, and Street Dance) in Avinger, Hughes Springs and Linden; Rangerette Revels, Kilgore; Jamboree, Smithville; Fiesta San Antonio, San Antonio; Country Gospel Concert, Stephenville; Arts and Crafts Festival, Killeen; San Jacinto Week and Strawberry Festival, Old-Time Fiddlin', Pasadena; Buccaneer Days, Corpus Christi; State Championship

Fiddlers' Contest, Hallettsville; Shrimp Festival, Galveston; Gospel Sing Convention, Stephenville; Spring Fling (Fiddlers' Contest), Wichita Falls; Great Southwest Music Festival, Amarillo; Cornyval (Old Fiddlers' Contest), Helotes; Square Dance, Stephenville; Historical Pilgrimage, Jefferson.

May. *Cinco de Mayo* Celebration, Hondo; Mayfest, Fort Worth; Fiesta Bandana, Alice; Roundup Days, Ingleside; Village Fair, League City; Frontier Fair, Brackettville; Square Dance Festival, Fort Stockton; Fiddle Festival, Groesbeck; Cajun Fais Do-Do Festival, Houston; Texas Tall Tales Contest and Square Dance, Kingland; Sheriff's Posse Rodeo and Dance, Giddings; Stagecoach Days,

Eddie Rabbitt

Marshall; Folk Festival, Kerrville; Old Fiddlers' Reunion, Athens; Bluegrass Jamboree, Glen Rose; Salt Festival and Rodeo and Dances and Gospel Nite, Grand Saline.

June. Fun-Tier Nights, San Antonio; Rodeo and Dances, Llano; Leather Tom-Tom Festival and Rodeo and Dance, Yoakum; Square

and Round Dancing, Houston; Folk Fest, Austin; Annual International Cowboy Campfire Cookoff and Western Heritage Festival, Abilene; Folk Fete, Cameron; County Rodeo and Old Settlers' Reunion, Archer City; Watermelon Jubilee and Old Fiddlers' Contest, Stockdale; Peach Jamboree and Rodeo, Stonewall; Gospel Quartet Festival, Woodville; Corn Festival, Holland; Annual Watermelon Thomp (Fiddlers' Contest), Luling; Fiesta de San Juan, Fort Stockton; Western Days, Grand Prairie; Family Fun Carnival (Old Fiddlers' Contest), Belton.

July. Willie Nelson Picnic, Gonzales (July 4); Rodeo, Parade and Fiddlers' Contest, Clarendon; Texas Cowboy Reunion (Dances), Stamford; Homecoming and Fiddlers' Contest, Hale Center; Western Week, Dennison; Old Settlers' Rodeo and Old Fiddlers' Contest, Childress; Western Days Rodeo and Dance, Elgin; Black-Eyed Pea Jamboree, Athens; Fair and Rodeo, Burnet; Gospel Jubilee, Kerrville; Great Country Roundhouse Jamboree, San Antonio.

August. Last Frontier Days, Morton; Annual Texas Folklife Festival, San Antonio; Annual Old Settlers' Reunion, Rodeo, Dance, and Fiddlers' Contest, Camp Ward; Texas Old Fiddlers' State Championship, Burnet; Fiddlers' Festival, Gatesville; Homecoming Celebration, D'Hanis; County Fair and Rodeo, Canton; Howdeo and Dance, Waskom; Old Fiddlers' Convention and Contest, Burnet; County Fair, Gainesville; Sutton County Day, Sonora; County Fair, Greenville; Old Settlers' Reunion, Matador; County Fair, Fredericksburg; Annual Old Settlers' Reunion, Brownfield; Country Fair, Brownwood; Chili Cookoff, Thorndale; Fish Fry, Earth; County Fair, Comanche.

September. Dove Festival and Fair, Hamilton; Country Fair, La Grange; Bluegrass Festival, Kerrville; County Fair and World Championship Barbecued Goat Cookoff, Brady; County Fair, Boerne; Central East Texas Fair, Marshall; Pecan Festival, Groves; County Fair, Dumas; Agricultural and Livestock Fair, Seguin; Country Fair on the Square, Kyle; West Texas Fair, Abilene; County Fair, Caldwell; County Fair and Rodeo, Hempstead; Town and Country Days, Karnes City; Southern Gospel Music Meet, Stephenville; County Fair, Woodville; Folk Festival and Barbecue Cookoff, Pasadena; Busch Gardens Arts and Crafts Fair, Houston; County Picnic, Memphis; Tri-State Fair, Amarillo; County Fair and Livestock Exposition, Longview; County Fair, New Braunfels; Pioneer Days, Pittsburg; Square Dance Convention, Stephenville; Boll Weevil Festival, Taft; County Fair, Coleman; Arts and Crafts Fair, Beaumont; Arts and Crafts Festival, Gladewater; East Texas Fair, Tyler; Come and Take It Celebration Carnival, Street Dance and Rodeo, Gonzales; County Fair, Mt. Pleasant; County Fair and Rodeo, (Fiddlers' Contest) Rosenberg/ Richmond; Texas Rice Festival (Fiddlers' Contest), Winnie;

Bluegrass Reunion, Glen Rose; Border Folk Music Festival, El Paso; Country Fair, Snyder; County Fair, Tulia.

For information, write: State Department of Highways and Public Transportation, Travel and Information Division, Austin, TX 78701.

Utah

March. Utah Round Dance Association Annual Festival, Salt Lake.

May. Big U Jamboree, Square Dancers, Vernal.

June. Square Dancing, Liberty Park, Salt Lake; Strawberry Days, Pleasant Grove.

July. Pioneer Dance, Salt Lake; Tri-Valley Days of '47 Street Dance, Salt Lake; Pioneer Days, Ogden; Annual Festival of the American West, Great West Fair, Old West Cookout, Logan.

August. Wasatch County Fair, Heber City; County Fair and Rodeo, Morgan; County Fair, Duchesne; Salt Lake County Fair, Murray; Cache County Fair and Rodeo, Logan; Rich County Fair and Roundup Rodeo, Randolph; West Desert Fair, Bagley Ranch, Callao; Utah County Fair, Spanish Fork; Garfield County Fair, Panguitch; South Utah County Fair, Richfield; Sweetwater Daggett County Fair, Rock Springs, Wyo., Millard County Fair, Deseret; Davis County Fair, Farmington; Kane County Fair, Orderville; Washington County Fair, Hurricane; Summit County Fair, Coalville; Wayne County Fair, Loa; Juab County Fair, Nephi; Box Elder County Fair, Tremonton; Sanpete County Fair, Manti; Piute County Fair, Junction; Golden Spike National Historic Site, Promontory; Servier County Fair, Richfield; Beaver County Fair, Minersville.

For information, write: Utah Travel Council, Council Hall, Capitol Hill, Salt Lake City, UT 84114.

Vermont

January. Annual Green Mountain Opry, Barre.

March. Annual Weaving Exhibit of Green Mountain Weavers Guild, North Bennington; Annual Green Mountain Country Music Contest, Barre; Annual Maple Sugar Square Dance Festival, Burlington.

April. Annual Vermont Maple Festival, St. Albans.

June. 4H State Day, Barre; Vermont Dairy Festival, Enosburg Falls; Annual Summer Solstice Festival, Springfield; Annual Strawberry Festivals, Plymouth and Londonderry.

July. Annual A-Fair, Bristol; Annual County Fair, Windsor; Annual Tri-Church Bazaar and Chicken Barbecue, Bradford; Bluegrass Contest, Randolph; Annual Mad River Valley Craft Show, Waitsfield; Swanton Summer Festival, Swanton; Cracker Barrell Bazaar, Newbury; Country Field Days, Hyde Park; Arts and Crafts Show, Wilmington; Field Day, Reading; Bennington County 4H Field Day, Sunderland; Annual Fiddlers' Contest, Craftsbury Common; Missisquoi Arts and Crafts Show, Swanton; Passumpsic Valley Guild Arts and Crafts Fair, St. Johnsbury; Connecticut Valley Fair, Bradford.

August. Annual Craft Festival at Frog Hollow, Middlebury; Craft Producers' Crafts Fair, Mount Snow; Annual Arts and Crafts Fair, Newport; Washington County Field Days, Waterbury Centre; Peru Workshop Craft Fair, Manchester; Old-Time Fiddling Contest, Chelsea; Old Home Day, Craftsbury Common; Banjo Contest, Hardwick; Addison County Fair and Field Days, New Haven; Orleans County Fair, Barton; 4H State Dairy Day, Burlington; Community Fair, Danville; Caledonia County Fair, Lyndonville; Annual Deerfield Valley Farmers' Day, Wilmington; Champlain Valley Exposition, Essex Junction.

September. Vermont State Fair,

Rutland; Guilford Fair, Guilford; World's Fair, Tunbridge; Bondville Fair, Bondville; Banjo Contest, Craftsbury Common; Holiday in the Hills, Victory and Granby.

October. Square Dance Festival, Montpelier; Fall Festival of Vermont Crafts, Montpelier; Colonial Day, Castleton; Fall Foliage Festival, Johnson; Annual Harvest Bazaar, Mendon; Annual Octoberfest Dinner and Bazaar, Hancock and Granville; Oktoberfest, Stowe; Leaflookers' Supper, Manchester Village; Oktoberfest at Sugarbush Ski Area, Warren; Apples and Crafts Fair, Woodstock; Apple Pie Festival, Dummerston Centre; Annual Fall Handcraft Fair, Montpelier.

November. Vermont Handcrafters' Annual Bazaar, Burlington.

For information, write: Agency of Development and Community Affairs, Office of the Secretary, Montpelier, VT 05602.

Washington

April. Puyallup Valley Daffodil Festival, Tacoma; Washington State Old-Time Fiddlers' Show, Yakima; Washington State Apple-Blossom Festival, Wenatchee; North Washington Fair, Colville; Annual Arts and Historical Festival, Port Orchard; Asotin County Fair, Asotin.

May. Dam Hot-Foot Daze, Metaline Falls; Lewis County Spring Dairy Show, Chehalis; Manson Apple Blossom Festival, Manson; Orcas Island Family Festival, Eastsound; Spokane Lilac Festival, Spokane; Clam Diggers' Breakfast, Ocean Park; Manson County Forest Festival, Shelton; Rhododendron Festival, Port Townsend; Aberdeen Rain Fair, Aberdeen;Fort Vancouver—Ham Fair, Vancouver; University District Street Fair, Seattle; Northwest Regional Folklife Festival, Seattle Center; Dayton Days, Dayton; Wild Goose Bill Days, Wilbur.

June. Chelan's Diamond Jubilee,

Crystal Gayle

Chelan; Salty Sea Days, Everett; Kahlotus Days Celebration, Kahlotus; Fire Festival, Seattle; Lummi Stommish Water Festival, Bellingham; Treaty Day Celebration and Rodeo, White Swan; Tiinowit International Dancing Competition, White Swan; Square Dance Federation, Spokane; Quincy Canal Days, Quincy; Planters Day Celebration, Woodland; Berry Dairy Days, Burlington; Hilander Summer Festival, Kelso; Lakewood Summer Festival, Lakewood Center; Stevens County Pioneer Picnic, Colville; Stillaguamish Valley Frontier Days, Arlington; La Center Community Fair, La Center.

July. Pioneer Days, Cle Elum; Marymoor Park Heritage Festival, Redmond; Fathoms O'Fun, Port Orchard; Country Fair, Woodinville; Festival of American Fiddle Tunes, Port Townsend; Ezra Meeker Days, Puyallup; Moss Bay Festival, Kirkland; Pioneer Picnic, Colfax; Lynn-O-Rama South City Community Festival, Lynnwood; Krazy Daze, Chehalis; Skagit Squares Annual Conference, Mt. Vernon; Harvest Days, Battleground; Bear Festival, McCleary; Summer Festival, Belfair; Whaling

Days, Silverdale; Pacific NW Arts and Crafts Festival, Bellevue; Community Fair, Kalama; Apple Pie Jamboree, Pateros; Old Settlers' Annual Picnic, Ferndale; Old-Timer Days, Buckley; King County Fair, Enumclaw; Sandy Bend Community Fair, Castle Rock; Kalama Community Fair, Kalama; Castle Rock Fair, Castle Rock; Evergreen Community Fair, Orchards.

August. Waterland Festival, Des Moines; Skagit County Pioneer Picnic, LaConner; Summer Festival, Sumner; Pioneer Days Parade, Lake City; Cheney Festival, Cheney; Snake River Days, Clarkston; Logger's Jubilee, Morton; Hamfair 1977, Graham; Chelan County Old-Timers' Picnic, Leavenworth; Makah Days, Neah Bay; Washing-

APA/Monument

Larry Gatlin

ton Old-Time Fiddlers' Campout, Richland; Cowlitz County Fair and Rodeo, Longview; Thurston County Fair, Lacey; Stanwood Camano Fair, Stanwood; Southwest Washington Fair, Chehalis; Clark County Fair, Ridgefield; Pierce County Fair, Graham; Skagit County Fair, Mount Vernon; Jefferson County Fair, Port Townsend; Northwest Washington Fair, Lynden; Yakima Valley Junior Fair, Grandview; Grant County Fair and Rodeo; Moses Lake; Grays Harbor County Fair, Elma; Wahkiakum County

Fair, Skamokawa; San Juan County Fair, Friday Harbor; Deer Park Community Fair, Deer Park; Mason County Fair, Shelton; Kitsap County Fair and Rodeo, Bremerton; Benton-Franklin Counties Fair and Rodeo, Kennewick; Skamania County Fair, Stevenson; Pend Oreille County Fair, Cusick; Island County Fair, Langley; Pacific County Fair, Menlo; Clallam County Fair, Port Angeles; Evergreen State Fair, Monroe; Southeastern Washington Fair, Walla Walla.

September. Annual States Day Celebration, Prosser; Apple Valley Street Fair, Wenatchee; Sugar Beet Festival, Harrah; Pioneer Fall Festival, Waitsburg; Autumn Leaf Festival, Leavenworth; Oktoberfest, Richland; Adams County Fair, Ritzville; Ferry County Fair, Republic; Kittitas County Fair, Ellensburg; Lincoln County Fair, Davenport; Chelan County Fair, Cashmere; Okanogan County Fair, Okanogan; Northeastern Washington Fair, Colville; Palouse Empire Fair, Colfax; Columbia County Fair, Dayton; Darrington Community Fair, Darrington; Klickitat County Fair, Goldendale; Spokane County Fair, Spokane; Adams County Fair, Othello; North Central Washington Fair, Waterville; Garfield County Fair, Pomeroy; Western Washington Fair, Puyallup.

October. Central Washington State Fair, Yakima.

For information, write: Department of Commerce and Economic Development, General Administration Building, Olympia, WA 98504.

West Virginia

May. WV Country Fling Quilt Show, Harpers Ferry; WV Heritage Festival, Huntington; Strawberry Festival, Berkeley Springs; Webster Springs Woodchopping Festival, Webster Springs; Kanawha County Fair, Charleston; Memorial Day Celebration; North Bend State Park, Cairo; Homecoming Weekend, Glen Dayle.

June. West Virginia Strawberry Festival, Buckhannon; Calhoun County Wood Festival, Grantsville; Daniel Boone Weekend, Cairo; Rhododendron State Outdoor Arts and Crafts Festival, Charleston; Mountain Heritage Arts and Crafts Festival, Harpers Ferry; West Virginia State Folk Festival, Glenville; Fireman's Carnival, Wardensville; Wild'n Wonderful West Virginia Weekend, Cairo; St. George Days, St. George; Harpers Ferry Annual Art Festival, Harpers Ferry; Belmont VFD Fireman's Festival, Belmont; Downtown Action Council Arts and Crafts, Morgantown; Arts and Crafts Festival, Wheeling; Mountain State Arts and Crafts Fair, Ripley.

July. Virginia Point Days, Kenova; July Jamboree, Fayetteville; July Fourth Celebration, Cairo; Mountaineer Days, Thomas; Frontier Fourth Celebration, Pricketts Fort State Park, Fairmont; Old Guyandotte Days, Guyandotte; Braxton County July Fourth Celebration, Sutton; Sistersville Lions Club Fourth of July Celebration, Sistersville; Pioneer Days, Marlinton; Jackson County Junior Fair, Cottageville; West Virginia Poultry Convention and Festival, Moorfield; 4H Wood County Fair, Parkersburg; Beverly Community Week, Beverly; Huntington Square and Round Dance Festival, Huntington.

August. Primitive Crafts Invitational, Fairmont; Magnolia Fair, Matewan; Hughes River Holidays, Harrisville; Watermelon Day and Homecoming, Independence; Tyler County Fair, Middleboune; Paw Paw District Fair, Rivesville; Mason County Fair, Pt. Pleasant; WV Square and Round Dance State Convention, Salem; Cherry River Festival, Richwood; Logan County Arts and Crafts Fair, Logan; Mountain Jubilee, Cairo; Monongalia County Fair, Westover; Town and County Days, New Martinsville; Square Dance Festival, North Bend State Park, Cairo; French Creek Pioneers' Homecoming, French

Creek; State Fair of West Virginia, Fairlea; John Henry Folk Festival, Camp Virgil Tate, Charleston; Cross Roads Community Smorgasbord, Fairmont; Jeffery County Fair, Charles Town; Nicholas County Fair, Summersville; Annual Barbour County Fair, Philippi; Berkeley County Youth Fair, Martinsburg; Frontier Days, South Charleston.

September. Lions Fall Festival, Eureka; Labor Day Celebration, Cairo; Appalachian Arts and Crafts Festival, Beckley; Webster County Fair, Camp Caesar, Webster Springs; Pendleton County Fair, Circleville; Hick Festival, Hendricks; Lincoln County Tobacco Fair, Hamlin; Stonewall Jackson Jubilee, Weston; Braxton County Homecoming, Sutton; Roane County Homecoming, Gandeeville; Annual Ox Roast, Rowlesburg; Horton Whitmer Homecoming, Whitmer; Tucker County Fair and Fireman's Homecoming, Parsons; U.S. Coal Festival, Beckley; Helvetia Community Fair, Helvetia; Nicholas County Potato Festival, Summersville; Shinnston Frontier Days, Shinnston; Downtown Action Council Arts and Crafts Festival, Morgantown; King Coal Festival, Williamson; Treasure Mountain Festival, Franklin; Annual Harvest Moon Festival, Parkersburg; Molasses Festival, Arnoldsburg; Heritage Weekend, Hardy County, Moorefield; Quilt Fair, Bluefield; West Virginia County Fling (Fall), Harpers Ferry; Annual Apple Festival, Fairmont; Preston County Buckwheat Festival, Kingwood; Mountain Heritage Arts and Crafts Festival, Harpers Ferry.

October. Mountain State Forest Festival, Elkins; Kermit Fall Festival, Kermit; Arts and Crafts Festival, Bluefield; Ritchie County Heritage Weekend, Cairo; West Virginia Black Walnut Festival, Spencer; Homecoming, Buckhannon; Arts and Crafts Festival, Welch; Annual A–B College Arts and Crafts Fair, Philippi; Apple Butter Festival, Berkeley Springs;

Little Jimmy Dickens

West Virginia Turkey Festival and Shooting Match, Mathias; Cross Roads Community Bazaar, Fairmont; Blackwater Rendezvous, Davis; Bethany College Mountain Music Festival, Bethany.

November. Annual Mountaineer Week Crafts Fair, Morgantown; Arts and Crafts Festival, Weirton; Snowflake Festival, St. Albans; Capital City Arts and Crafts Show, Charleston.

For information, write: Travel Division, Department of Commerce, State Capitol, Charleston, WV 25305.

Wisconsin

June. June Dairy Days Celebration, Markesan; Summer Frolic Festival, Mount Horeb; Newburg-Trenton Fireman's Picnic, Newburg; Sunfish Days Festival, Onalaska; Dairy Days Festival at Fairgrounds, Viroqua; Arts and Crafts Fair at Paquette Park, Portage; Wisconsin Folk Festival at Fairgrounds, Fond du Lac; Brady Street Festival, Milwaukee; Fun Fest, Durand; Old Kilbourne Weekend Festival, Wisconsin Dells; Arts and Handicrafts Fair, Elkhart Lake; Heritage Days Festival, Watertown; Barbecued Pork Festival, Fairgrounds, Janesville; Annual Outdoor Arts Festival, Sheboygan; Fur Trade Rendezvous, Villa Louis Historical Site, Prairie du Chien; Fireman's Festival, Cottage Grove; Heritage Days Festival, Prairie du Chien; Village Crafts Fair, Janesville; Heart Concert, Arts

and Crafts Fair, Polka Concert, Milwaukee; Charity Arts and Crafts Fair, Sheboygan; Farmers Fair, Jefferson; Summer Festival, Lake Mills; Summer Festival, Oregon; Hodag Holidays Community Festival, Rhinelander; Olde Ellison Bay Days, Ellison Bay; Gree County Dairy Day, Juda; Mid-Summer Festival, Wakefield; Central Wisconsin Polka Festival, Fairgrounds, Merrill; Okauchee's Okassion, Okauchee; Arts and Crafts Fair, Spring Green; Arts and Crafts Fair, Clintonville; Fair Fun Days, Gays Mills; Chicken Barbeque, Milton; Strawberry Festival, Alma; Square Dance Rally, Minocqua; Summerfest, Milwaukee.

July. Pow Wow Days, Tomahawk; Annual Pig Roast, Pelican Lake; Chicken Barbecue, Walworth; Celebration Days, Bruce; Fourth of July Celebration—Beach Party, Square Dance, Janesville; Old-Fashioned Fourth of July Celebration, Eau Claire Lakes, Barnes; Mining Heritage Day Festival, Shullsburg; Fourth of July, Land O'Lakes; Cattle Fair, Princeton; Summerfest, Berlin; Old-Fashioned Days Festival, Taylor; Wisconsin Dairyland National Tractor Pull, Carnival, and Arts and Crafts Show, Tomah; Outdoor Craft Fair, Oak Creek; Hodag Holidays Parade, Rhinelander; Arts and Crafts Fair, Whitefish Bay; Summer Festival, Big Bend; Old Peninsula Days Festival, Fish Creek; Fireman's Picnic, St. Lawrence; Old Crafts Day at Historic Galloway House and Village, Fond du Lac; Fireman's Picnic, Kewaskum; Chicken Barbecue and County Queen Coronation, Kingston; Annual Creative Crafts and Fine Arts Exhibit, Three Lakes; Cutagamie County Fair, Seymour; LaCrosse Interstate Fair, West Salem; Elroy Fair, Elroy; Waukesha County Fair, Waukesha; Bluegill Festival, Birchwood; Sunfair Arts and Crafts Fair, Milwaukee; Country Fair, Millard; Blueberry Festival, Iron River; Arts and Crafts Fair, Echo Park, Burlington; Fireman's Festival, Princeton; National Square Dance Campers Meeting, Elkhorn; Sauk County Fair, Baraboo; Crazy Day Celebration, Merrill; Crazy Day Sales and Entertainment, Princeton; Ridiculous Days Sales and Entertainment, Superior; Eau Claire County Junior Fair, Eau Claire; Lafayette County Fair, Darlington; Jefferson County Fair, Jefferson; Dance County Junior Fair, Madison; Dunn County Junior Fair, Menomonie; Milwaukee County 4H Junior Fair, Wauwatosa; Kewaunee County Fair, Luxemburg; Juneau County Fair, Mauston; Summerfest Days, Hazelhurst; Wild Rice Festival, Mole Lake; River Falls Days Gay '90s Celebration, River Falls; Annual Fish Day, Port Washington; Arts and Crafts Fair, Williams Bay; Farmers Fair, Cambridge; Krazy Daze Street Sale, Kewaskum; Carnival and Street Dance, Sayner; Pepin County Junior Fair, Arkansaw; Columbia County Fair, Portage; Tri-State Fair, Superior; Fond du Lac County Fair, Fond du Lac; Green County Fair, Monroe; Barron County Fair, Rice Lake Washington County Junior Fair, Slinger; Door County Antique Show and Fair, Fish Creek; Trempealeau County Fair, Galesville; Taylor County Youth Fair, Medford; Monroe County Fair, Tomah; Central Burnett County Fair, Webster; Holland Days Festival, Cedar Grove; Pioneer Days Festival, Butternut; Tobacco Days Festival, Edgerton; Annual Marsh Days Festival, Horicon; Arts and Crafts Fair, Edgerton; Fish Day Festival, Port Washington; Street Dance and Festivities, Elcho; Art Fair USA, Milwaukee.

August. Rock County 4H Fair, Janesville; Lincoln County 4H Fair, Merrill; Northern Wisconsin State Fair, Chippewa Falls; Old-Fashioned Day Festival, Baraboo; Cattle Fair, Princeton; St. Croix County Fair, Glenwood City; Green Lake County Junior Fair, Green Lake; Clark County Fair, Neillsville; Racine County Fair, Union Grove; Jackson County Fair, Black River

Falls; Ozaukee County Fair, Cedarburg; Buffalo County Fair, Mondovi; Flambeau Rama Festival, Park Falls; Polk County Fair, St. Croix Falls; Marquette County Fair, Westfield; Fair-Fest Festival, Cudahy; International Polka Festival, Milwaukee; Iron County Fair, Saxon; Summer Fun Days, Woodruff; Fair Fest and Art Fair, Cudahy; Annual Corn Roast and Picnic, Pearson; Tri-State Arts and Crafts Fair, Waterfront Park, Bayfield; Golden Fun Days, De Forest; Arts and Crafts Fair, Rice Lake; Langlade County Youth Fair, Antigo; Village Days Art Fair, Greendale; St. Ann's Festival Arts and Crafts Fair, Stoughton; Washburn County Junior Fair, Spooner; Wisconsin Valley Fair, Wausau; Muskie Jamboree; Boulder Junction; Door County Fair, Sturgeon Bay; Kenosha County Fair, Wilmot; Burnett County Fair, Grantsburg; Ashland County Fair, Marento; Wisconsin State Fair, Milwaukee; Price County Fair, Phillips; Golden Fun Days, De Forest; Vilas County Fair, Eagle River; Fort Fest Celebration, Port Atkinson; Wisconsin Square Dance and Round Dance Convention, Mecca, Milwaukee; Aquarama Festival, Minocqua; Blue Grass Festival, Mole Lake; Community Fair, Sheldon; Farmers Fair, Lake Mills; Arts and Crafts Fair, Wisconsin Rapids; Corn Ball, Melrose; Stumpfvenshun (Stumpf Fiddle), at Sheboygan; Arts and Crafts Fair and Ice-Cream Social, Janesville; Outdoor Art Festival, Watertown; Farmers Fair, Jefferson; Brown County Fair, De Pere; Winnebago County Fair and Exposition, Oshkosh; Western Days Festival, Superior; Pierce County Fair, Ellsworth; Crawford County Fair, Gays Mills; Oconto County Youth Fair, Gillett; Sawyer County Fair, Hayward; Bayfield County Fair, Iron River; Waushara County Fair, Wautoma; Waupaca County Fair, Weyauwega; Annual Picnic, Adams; Fireman's Picnic, Fillmore; Fireman's Ball, Washington Island; Sweet Corn Festival, Sun Prairie; Picnic and Parade, Allenton; Fire-

man's Festival, Fish Creek; Milwaukee Sentinel Active Americans, Milwaukee; Manitowoc County Exposition, Manitowoc; Dodge County Fair, Beaver Dam; Fair, Athens; Forest County Fair, Crandon; Adams County Fair, Friendship; Rusk County Fair, Ladysmith; Grant County Fair, Lancester; Near North Fair, Wausaukee; Frontier Festival, Butler; Good Neighbor Festival, Middleton; VFW Country Fair Days, Muskego; Summer Art Fair, Green Bay; Arts and Crafts Show, Middleton; Annual Fisherman's Party, Milltown; Picnic and Barbecue, Markesan; Walworth County Fair, Elkhorn; Central Wisconsin State Fair, Marshfield.

September. Iowa County Fair, Mineral Point; Sheboygan County Fair, Plymouth; Shawano County Fair, Shawano; Calumet County Fair, Chilton; Rosholt Community Fair, Rosholt; Trout Boil, Green Lake; Stonewood Village Art Fair, Brookfield; Great River Festival of Traditional Crafts and Music, La Crosse; Flórence County Fair, Florence; Old Wade House Arts and Crafts Fair, Greenbush; Harvest Festival, Hawkins; Fireman's Corn and Bratwurst Picnic, Marquette; Labor Day Celebration, Merrillan.

For information, write: Department of Business Development, Wisconsin Division of Tourism, PO Box 7606, Madison, WI 54707.

Wyoming

April. Big Horn Festival of the Arts, Greybull; Wyoming Polkathon, Casper.

May. High School Rodeo, Lovell, Gillette, Cody; Western Concert, Lander Valley H.S.; High School Rodeo, Thermopolis; Wyoming State Old-Time Fiddle Contest, Shoshoni.

June. Pinedale Rodeos, Pinedale; Big Horn 50, Big Horn Mountains; Labor Day, Bighorn Canyon National Recreation Area, Lovell Visitor Center; Rawlins Saddle Club Fun Night, Rawlins; Northern

Rocky Mountain Barbed Wire Collection, Sheridan; Days of '49 Rodeo, Greybull; National High School Rodeo, Riverton; Junior Livestock Show, Thermopolis; Hoback River Regatta, Jackson Hole; Wood Chopper's Jamboree, Encampment.

July. Cache Creek Posse Shoot-out, Jackson; Jim Bridger Wagon Trek, Evanston to Ft. Laramie, Evanston;

Rawlins Renegade Days, Rawlins; Rodeo and Chuck Wagon Days, Big Piney; Chuckwagon Breakfast, Lander; Jubilee Days, Laramie; Grand Teton Music Festival, Teton Village; Cheyenne Frontier Days, Cheyenne; Central Wyoming Fair and Rodeo, Casper.

August. Laramie County Fair, Cheyenne; Crook County Fair, Moorcroft; Big Horn County Fair,

Basin; Wyoming State Fair, Douglas.

September. Ft. Bridger Muzzle-loading Rendezvous, Ft. Bridger; Little Britches National Finals Rodeo, Cheyenne.

October. Oktoberfest, Torrington.

For information, write: Wyoming Travel Commission, 1-25 Etchepare Circle, Cheyenne, Wyoming 82002.

Fairchild, Barbara

Born: November 12, 1950, Knobel, Arkansas
Married: Randy Reinhard
Children: s. Randall Reinhard II; d. Tara Nevada, Randina Sierra

As a singer-composer, she cut her first record at fifteen, "A Brand New Bed of Roses." A year later she and a friend headed for Nashville, where they met producer Jerry Crutchfield. He listened to their songs, advised them to write at least six more, and then come back. Barbara wrote fifteen—and Crutchfield signed her with Kapp Records as a writer.

Crutchfield subsequently took Barbara to a well-known producer and CBS/Nashville vice president of A & R, Billy Sherrill, who promptly signed her to Columbia Records. Her first album with Columbia was *Someone Special,* which was followed soon after by another album, *Love's Old Song.* A single entitled "Color My World," released from the latter album, hit number nineteen on the national charts. But it was Barbara's third album, *A Sweeter Love,* that finally established her as one of the top women vocalists and songwriters in country music. The album included Barbara's first number-one hit single, "The Teddy Bear Song."

Kid Stuff, Barbara's fourth album and single by the same title, soon came next. Barbara often refers to these singles as her "nursery songs," and it was with a certain fear of being typecast that Barbara went into the studio and launched her

Columbia

Barbara Fairchild

next album. The result was *Love Is a Gentle Thing,* followed by an equally mature sixth album, *Standing in Your Line.*

The same year *Standing in Your Line* was released, Barbara was nominated Top Female Vocalist of 1975 by The Academy of Country Music in California.

Her seventh album, *Mississippi,* was released to critical acclaim and afforded Barbara another hit in "Cheatin' Is."

Barbara's eighth album for Co-

lumbia, *Free and Easy,* once again fulfills her ongoing goal: to make each album better than the one before. The album offers a diverse selection of songs and styles, shifting from "Painted Faces," a song featuring strong native American drum rhythms, to the gently melodic ballad "When the Morning Comes," to the tongue-in-cheek "She Can't Give It Away." In late 1978, her "It's Sad to go to the Funeral (of a Good Love That Has Died)" was in the top hundred.

Fan Clubs

Most country music stars welcome the formation of fan clubs and do their best to relate to their fans through the club.

Most clubs collect dues—usually no more than a couple of dollars a year—to cover the cost of producing a newsletter and maintaining a mailing list. Almost all performers are very happy to promote their clubs, and some are extremely active in this field.

Possibly the best source of fan-club information is the Johnson sisters—Loretta, Loudilla, and Kay—who run the International Fan Club Organization from their ranch in Colorado. The organization's address is PO Box 177, Wild Horse, CO 80862.

Fan Club Listings

A

Allen, Rex
Wilma Orr, Pres.
160 El Bonita
Benicia, CA 94510

Anderson, Bill
Lorraine Plante, Canada Rep.
Ste. Anges de Dundee
Huntington, Quebec, CANADA

Anderson, Lynn
Linda Palmer, Pres.
17 N. Wabash Ave.
Battle Creek, MI 49017

Ashworth, Ernest
Connie Ludwick, Pres.
1033 Westwood Dr. NW
Cedar Rapids, IA 52405

B

Bluegrass Fan Club
Chaw Mank, Pres.
Box 30
Staunton, IL 62088

Burgess, Wilma
Cheryl Duffey, Pres.
PO Box 5532
Orlando, Fla.

Butler, Carl & Pearl
Opal Hardman, Pres.
1008 S. Oak St.
Champaign, IL 61820

Byrd, Jerry
Millie Annis, Pres.
3122 Clyde Park SW
Wyoming, MI 49509

C

Campbell, Glen
Suzi Olds, Pres.
PO Box 8372
Universal City, CA 91331

Carter Family
Mr. Freeman Kitchen, Pres.
Drake, Ky.

Carter, Wilf
Eleanor Burdo, Pres.
Box 151
Florence, MA 01060

Johnny Carver Fan Club
Betty Allen, Pres.
PO Box 40006
Detroit, MI 48240

Johnny Cash Society
Mable Samland, Rep.
1625 N. Wildwood Ave.
Westland, MI 48185

Johnny Cash Society
Reba Hancock, Pres.
2200 Gallatin Rd.
Madison, IN 37115

Johnny Cash Society
David & Pat Deadman
"Saskatoon"
106 Queen Elizabeth's Dr.
New Addington
Croydon, Surrey
England

Johnny Cash Fan Club
Charles & Virginia Stohler
1110 W. Hartman Rd.
Anderson, IN 46011

Roy Clark Fan Club
Jim Halsey Agency
3225 S. Norwood
Tulsa, OK 74135

Brian Collins Fan Club
Roger Jaudon
1024 Sixteenth Ave., S.
Nashville, TN 37212

Collins, Tommy
Bonnie Daily, Pres.
812 Fillmore St.
Taft, CA 92368

Compton Brothers
Ronnie Rhoads, Pres.
RT 1
Mertztown, PA 19539

Cooper, Stoney & Wilma Lee
Billie Martz, Pres.
2709 Martha Pl.
Hammond, IN

Country Folk—Western Club
Glen Temple, Pres.
1605 West Victoria Blvd.
Burbank, CA 91506

Country Gentlemen Fan Club
Box 387
Hagerstown, MD 21740

Country Scene, The
(All Star Fan Club)
Libby Roberts & Dorothy Mann, co-Pres.
4747 Twelfth Ave., S.
St. Petersburg, FL 33711

Billy Craddock Fan Club
Earlene Morris, Pres.
PO Box 1585
Nashville, TN 37202

D

Davis, Skeeter
Barbara McCroy, Pres.
9890 Moorish Rd., RT. 3
Birch Run, Mich.

Dean, Jimmy
Loretta Geisler, Pres.
4403 Scotta Rd.
Baltimore, MD 21227

Dickens, Jimmy
Mary Ann Sauber, Pres.
6749 King Rd.
Jackson, MI 49201

The Dillards Society
Frances Bylund, Pres.
4731 Scenario Dr.
Huntington Beach, CA 92647

Dollar, Johnny
Mrs. Evelyn Bernat
180 Springfield Ave.
Philadelphia, PA 19127

Capitol

Merle Haggard

E

Emmons, Blake
Charlotte Maehl, Pres.
4850 Kathryn Ct.
Fremont, CA 94536

Emmons, Buddy
Mrs. Barbara Allen, Pres.
1068 Louis Dr.
Benton Harbor, Mich.

F

Barbara Fairchild Fan Club
504 West Spruce
Jerseyville, IL 62052

Fairchild, Barbara
Kay Brooks, Pres.
5997 Bond Ave.
East St. Louis, IL 62207

Donna Fargo Fan Club
Linda Culp, Pres.

PO Box 15881
Nashville, TN 37215

Narvel Felts Fan Club
Suite 303
Music Park Bldg.
107 Music Circle
Nashville, TN 37214

Freddy Fender Fan Club
Jim Halsey Agency
3225 S. Norwood
Tulsa, OK 74135

G

Gately, Jimmy
Sharon Young, Pres.
1244 South 20th Ave.
Maywood, IL 60153

Gibson, Don
c/o Virginia Pontesso, Pres.
2625 S. 8th Street
Terre Haute, IN

Glaser Brothers
Peggy Motley, Pres.
916 19th Ave., S.
Nashville, TN 37212

Grammer, Billy
Marie Kirby, Pres.
RT 1, Box 105
Mulberry, KS

Greene, Jack
Sandra Orwig, Pres.
PO Box 786
Harrisburg, PA 17108

Gunn, Stan
Donna South, Pres.
Box 374
Wood River, IL 62095

H

**Merle Haggard
International
    Fan Club**
Ken Gilmore, advisor
PO Box 1027
Sun Valley, CA 91352

Haggard, Merle
Flossie Haggard
1303 Yosemite Dr.
Oildale, CA 93308

Hamilton, IV, George
Dodey Varney, Pres.
6646 Old Plum Rd.
Ft. Idward, NY 12828

Hank the Drifter
c/o New England Records
12606 Carlsbad
Houston, TX 77045

Hart, Freddie
Naomi Collins, Pres.
2120 Sherwood La.
Pueblo, CO 81004

Roy Head Fan Club
Kip Bates
2011 W. 34th
Houston, TX 77018

Husky, Ferlin
Mary Dunn
207 Dunlap
Lansing, Mich.

J

Jackson, Stonewall
Ethel Hammock, Pres.
RT 3
Bethpage, Tenn.

**Sonny James & Friends
Assn.**
Wanda Jones, Pres.
RT 1, Box 207-A
Kilgore, TX 75662

Jennings, Waylon
Ian George, Pres.
PO Box 4733 - Station B
Columbus, OH 43202

Jim and Jesse
Jean S. Osborno
404 Shoreline Dr.
Tallahassee, FL 32301

Jones, George
Shirley Phillips
PO Box 8100
Nashville, TN 38107

George Jones-National
Fran Maloney, Pres.
4243 Hein Road, N.
San Antonio, TX 78220

**Jones, George
Tammy Wynette National**
Mildred Lee
RT 1, Box 100
Red Bay, AL 35582

K

K-T Country Roundup
Blance Trinajstick
2730 Baltimore Ave.
Pueblo, CO 81003

L

Lee, Brenda
Windy Tindell
RT 1, Box 183
Poplar Grove, AR 72374

Lewis, Bobby
Rachel Jones, Pres.
345 Central Ave.
Decatur, IL 62521

Linton, Sherwin
Mary Ann Linton, Pres.
10414 Terrace RD., NE
Minneapolis, MN 55433

Locklin, Hank
Margaret Mack
714 Phospher Ave.
Motairie, IA

MCA Records

Loretta Lynn

Long, Shorty
Cleta Wade, Pres.
RD 2
Birdsboro, PA 19508

Lord, Bobby
Luane Kelley, Pres.
8492 Eastruver Blvd.
Minneapolis, MN 55421

Luman, Bob
Bernice Kauffman, Pres.
423 E. Mistletoe
San Antonio, TX 78212

Lynn, Judy
June Hucker, Pres.
PO Box 14927
Las Vegas, NV 89114

Lynn, Loretta
Loretta, Loudilla & Kay
Johnson, Pres.
Box 177
Wild Horse, Colo.

M

McCall, Darrell
Sarah Freeman, Pres.
RT 3, Box 146
Hattiesburg, MS

Barbara Mandrell International Fan Club
PO Box 665
Madison, TN 37115

Martel, Marty
Jean Ireland, Pres.
RD 4, Box 121
Burgettstown, PA 15021

Martin, Jimmy
Mary Ann Garrison, Pres.
PO Box 46
Hermitage, TN 37076

Mason, Sandy
Bud Reinsel, Pres.
3388 Sardis Rd.
Marysville, PA 15668

Mathis, Dean
Goldie Smith, Pres.
112 West 104 Terrace
Kansas City, MO 64114

Mize, Billy
Beverly Sorenson, Pres.
Box 672
Martendale, IA

Monroe, Bill
Glen Mowery, Pres.
RT 3, Box 219
Claremore, OK 74017

Montgomery, Melba
Mary Ann Cooper, Pres.
RT 7, Box 406
Decatur, IL 62521

N

Olivia Newton-John does not have a fan club as yet (one is being set up). Write her care of United Fan Mail Service, 8966 Sunset Blvd., Hollywood, CA 90069.

O

Osborne Bros.
Elizabeth Pinach, Pres.
PO Box 1043
Cuyahoga Falls, OH

Tommy Overstreet Fan Club
Dorothy, Pres.
PO Box 1254
Nashville, TN 37212

Ozark Mountain Trio
Velma Grovers
RT 3, Box 273
Hillsboro, Mo.

P

Parker, Billy
Joanne & Janice Vogt, Pres.
121 S. Ninth
Broken Arrow, Okla.

Johnny Paycheck Fan Club
333 Gallatin Rd. E-24
Madison, TN 37115

Phillips, Bill
Alma Devine, Pres.
103 Broadmoor Dr.
Willow Street, PA 17584

Pillow, Ray
Bobbie Gainey, Pres.
RT 2, Box 284-A
Defuniak Springs, FL 32433

Pierce, Webb
Evelyn Otteson, Pres.
1026 Santa Marie Rd.
Lakes Wales, FL 33853

Pierce, Webb
Norma Preston, Pres.
103 S. Valley Rd.
Hendersonville, TN 37075

Price, Ray
Sandra Orwig, Pres.
PO Box 786
Harrisburg, PA 17108

Ray Price Fan Club
PO Box 34886
Dallas, TX 75234

Pride, Charley
Laura Lagge, Pres.
811 Tenth Ave., W.
Dickenson, ND 58601

R

Rainwater, Marvin
Jeanie Lloyd, Pres.
108-54 42nd Ave.
Corona, NY 11168

Reeves, Del
Mary Ann Cooper
RT 7, Box 406
Decatur, IL 62521

Reeves, Del
Donna Hay, Pres.
3803 Hilltop La.
Nashville, Tenn.

Reeves, Jim
Janet Cameron, Pres.
Green Head Hotel
Dailly, Ayrshire
Scotland

Reno, Don
Carmia Sue Dabe, Pres.
2433 Indiana Ave.
Columbus, OH 43202

Reno, Jack
Sandy Davis, Pres.
2215 N. Bigelow
Peoria, IL 61604

Riley, Jeannie C.
3106 Belmont Blvd.
Nashville, TN 37212

Ritter, Tex
Texas Jim Cooper, Pres.
2001 Williams La.
Carrollton, TX 75006

Robbins, Marty
Peggy Ann Munson, Pres.
3811 Wylly Ave.
Brunswick, Ga.

Roberts, Jack
Dorothy Sawyer, Pres.
PO Box 1743
Seattle, WA 98111

Rogers, David
Perky Cowan, Pres.
RD 4, Box 128
Burgettstown, PA 15021

S

Scott, Sandi
Ron Lamontagne, Pres.
PO Box 372
Ft. Collins, CO 80521

Hank Snow Fan Club
2218 Colfax Ave.
Columbus, OH 43224

Stearns, June
Judy Long, Pres.
PO Box 382
Dodge City, KS 67801

Glen Campbell

Stewart, Wynn
Frances Fuller, Pres.
PO Box 6448
Minneapolis, MN 55423

Nat Stuckey Fan Club
PO Box 102
Brentwood, TN 37027

Stuckey, Nat
Linda Barthel, Pres.
PO Box 40
Roland, OK 74954

T

Hank Thompson Fan Club
Jim Halsey Agency
3225 S. Norwood
Tulsa, OK 74135

Tillis, Mel
Larry Little, Pres.
909 W. Iona St.
Lansing, Mich.

Tillman, Floyd
Helen Lewis
8022 ½ Signet St.
Houston, TX 77029

Trail Blazers Fan Club
Al Grennawalt, Pres.
PO Box 25
Barto, PA 19504

Trail Blazers Fan Club
Ann Wright, Pres.
PO Box 194
Plymouth, PA 18651

Tubb, Ernest
Mrs. Norma Barthel, Pres.
Box 219
Roland, OH

Twitty, Conway
Elizabeth Rich, Pres.
2521 W. Hayes St.
Peoria, IL 61605

W

**Wells, Kitty/
Johnny Wright**
Magi Rosenkotter, Pres.
Box 214
Pierce, NB 68767

**Wells, Kitty/
Johnny Wright**
Ruby Hiles
906 Riverview Dr.
St. Joseph, MO 64503

Wilburn Brothers
Reva & Imogene Choate, Pres.
929 Neuhoff La.
Nashville, TN 37205

Don Williams Fan Club
Pauline Cochran
95 Pinehurst Dr.
Hopeville, GA 30354

Williams, Hank, Jr.
Jean Sopha, Pres.
806 Sixteenth Ave. S.
Nashville, TN 37203

Williams, Leona
Donna Dunlap, Pres.
Old Monroe, MO 63369

Wright, Sonny
Darlene Halvorsen, Mildred Wright & Billy Claycolm, co-Pres.
2089 Hanover St.
Aurora, CO 80010

Wynette, Tammy
Mildred Lee, Pres.
RT 1, Box 100
Red Bay, LA 35582

Y

Young, Faron
Dempsey Jenkins, Pres.
1314 Pine St.
Nashville, Tenn.

Fargo, Donna

Born: November 10, 1949, Mount Airey, North Carolina
Married: Stan Silver

Teaching high school in Covina, California, she had no ambition to be a country performer until she met record producer Stan Silver who taught her the guitar and married her. Her first hit, "The Happiest Girl in the Whole U.S.A." in 1972 was a gold record that crossed over to become a pop smash hit. Other number-one country hits followed: "Funny Face" (another gold and pop hit), "Superman," "You Were Always There"—and "Little Girl Gone," which merely hit the number-two spot. Since then she has written such singles as "What Will the New Year Bring?" "Hello Little Bluebird," and "It Do Feel Good," and recorded the songs of Shel Silverstein, "A Couple of More Years"; Neil Sedaka's "Sing Me"; Harry Chapin's "I Wanna Learn a Love Song," all in her LP *Fargo Country.* In 1978, her hit singles included "Another Goodbye" and her big LP was *Dark-Eyed Lady.*

Donna Fargo

Freddy Fender
by
Freddy Fender

My real name is Baldemar G. Huerta. I was born (June 4, 1937) in the south Texas valley border town of San Benito. I'm a Mexican-American, better yet, a Tex-Mex. I just picked up my stage name, Freddy Fender, in the late fifties as a name that would help my music sell better with *gringos.* Now I like the name.

Music was part of me, even in my early childhood. I can still remember sitting on the street corner facing Pancho Galvin's grocery store, plunking at my three-string guitar. It didn't have a back on it, but it sure sounded pretty good to me and the crowd of little kids listening. Music kept a lot of us happy, even when it was hard for our mamas to put beans on the table.

We began migrating north as farm workers when I was about ten. We worked beets in Michigan, pickles in Ohio, baled hay and picked tomatoes in Indiana. When that was over, it was cotton-picking time in Arkansas. All we really had to look forward to was making enough money to have a good Christmas in the Valley, where somehow I'd always manage to get my mother to buy me a guitar if the old one was worn out.

When I was sixteen, I dropped out of high school and joined the Marines for three years. I got to see California, Japan, and Okinawa; but mainly I got my point of view from the time I spent in the brig. It seemed that I just couldn't adjust myself to such a disciplined way of life. I always liked to play the guitar in the barracks and to drink, so much so that sometimes I forgot where or who I was.

The late fifties found me back in San Benito, playing beer joints, Chicano dances, and starting a singing career. I even began recording some all-Spanish Chicano records, and by 1958 these were doing great in Texas and Mexico. Next I turned to some Tex-Mex rockabilly music for recordings and cut "Holy One" and my big hit in 1959, "Wasted Days and Wasted Nights." In 1960, I cut "Crazy, Crazy Baby." Everything went beautifully until May—Friday the thirteenth—in 1960. I was busted for grass in Baton Rouge, Louisiana. I'm not bitter about that; but if friends ask, I still say that the three years I had to spend in Angola State Prison was a long time for such a little mistake.

My time in prison was hard, but music made it better. I can remember when my bass player and I (we were busted together) walked into Angola, carrying our

guitar and bass instead of our clothes. Then every Saturday and Sunday we would play on the "walk" for our fellow convicts. I even recorded an album of Chicano songs on a portable tape recorder at the prison.

In July 1963, I headed home from prison on a Trailways bus, but soon came back to Louisiana, singing at Papa Joe's on Bourbon Street in New Orleans until 1968. It was there that I played music with such cats as Joe Berry, Joey Long, Skip Easterling, and Aaron Neville.

By 1969, I was back in the Valley, playing again with a Chicano orchestra and learning new trades. I was beginning to feel that maybe I was getting too old and should go ahead and hang up my gloves. So I went to work as a mechanic and played music on weekends, getting $1.60 an hour and $28 a night picking so that I didn't starve to death. I took the GED test, received my high school diploma, and even went to college for two years.

By 1974, I was living in Corpus Christi, Texas, where a friend told me about Huey Meaux, a recording producer from Houston who had produced some big hits on B.J. Thomas, Joe Berry, and my good friend, Doug Sahm. He accepted my material and started recording.

It was in one of these sessions that I first cut my country and pop hit "Before the Next Teardrop Falls" on Huey's Crazy Cajun label. ABC-DOT Records purchased the record and signed me when it started happening on country stations in Houston. I couldn't be prouder. After twenty years of trying, I finally got my first national hit record!

Fiddler's News

Its objectives are to preserve and promote the art and skills of old-time fiddling, and give news of contests, picnics, and related events in Vermont. Certainly worth getting if you live in the area or are planning a New England trip.

Membership dues are $4 a year. Write to Pauline Dubois, 77 Ferguson Avenue, Burlington, VT 05401.

Fifty Years of Country Music

The three-hour NBC–TV Big Event on January 22, 1978, was one of the greatest arrays of country music stars ever assembled for a prime-time TV special. The hosts were Glen Campbell, Roy Clark, and

Dolly Parton

Dolly Parton, each presiding over one hour. Johnny Cash, Ray Charles, and Loretta Lynn were special guest stars. Also starring were Roy Acuff, Chet Atkins, The Carter Family, Danny Davis and the Nashville Brass, Larry Gatlin, Crystal Gayle, Merle Haggard, Doug Kershaw, Bill Monroe and the Bluegrass Boys, the Oak Ridge Boys, Minnie Pearl, Charlie Rich, Johnny Rodriguez, the Earl Scruggs Revue, the Statler Brothers, the Stony Mountain Cloggers, Mel Tillis, Ernest Tubb, Kitty Wells, The Bob Wills Texas Playboys, Tammy Wynette. Introduced to network TV audiences was Carlene Carter. Also included were seven members of the Country Music Hall of Fame (Acuff, Atkins, the Carter Family, Monroe, Minnie Pearl, Tubb, and Wells) and seven winners of the Entertainer of the Year Award

(Campbell, Clark, Cash, Lynn, Haggard, Rich, and Tillis).

Flatt, Lester Raymond

Born: June 28, 1914, Sparta, Tennessee
Died: May, 1979
Married: Gladys Stacy
Children: d. Brenda

Best known for his twenty-one-year partnership with Earl Scruggs, Lester Flatt joined Bill Monroe's Bluegrass Boys in 1944, singing tenor and playing the mandolin and guitar. There he met Earl Scruggs, with whom he became good friends; they left Monroe in 1948 to form their own Foggy Mountain Boys, taken from an old Carter Family tune. After splitting with Earl, Lester formed a new group—Lester Flatt and the Nashville Grass—considered one of the best bluegrass bands in the country, playing bluegrass festivals from coast to coast, sometimes attracting as many as ten thousand visitors.

Forman, Peggy

Born: Centerville, Louisiana
Married: Wayne
Children: d. Cindy Jo

A songwriter-artist, she landed a recording contract with MCA through the help of Conway Twitty, who has recorded many of her songs, as have Loretta Lynn, Mary Lou Turner, and Connie Cato.

Lefty Frizzell

ABC Records

Frizzell, Lefty (William Orville)

Born: March 31, 1928, Corsicana, Texas
Married: Alice
Children: s. Marlon, Rick; d. Lois

MCA Records

Inspired by the early recordings of Jimmie Rodgers, Lefty earned his first five dollars at age fifteen in a songwriting contest in Dallas. He played and sang in local bars there until he cut a record for a man named Jim Beck who took it to Columbia Records. In 1950, he signed a recording contract that began an incredible hit-making string. One record made history with both sides hitting the number-one spot: "If You've Got the Money, Honey, (I've Got the Time)" and "I Love You a Thousand Ways." In 1952, he joined the Opry but soon moved to California and appeared on Town Hall Party in Compton for five years and the "Country America" TV show in Hollywood for a year. By 1962, he was back in Nashville. Other hits through his near quarter-century of performing and writing are: "Always Late," "Saginaw, Michigan," "Mom and Dad Waltz," "The Long Black Veil," "Cigarette and Coffee Blues," and "Confused."

Gatlin, Larry

Born: May 2, 1948, Seminole, Texas
Married: Janis
Children: s. Joshua; d. Kristin

When Larry was six years of age, he sang with his younger brothers Steve and Rudy in a gospel group that appeared at family and church gatherings.

Their father was an oil driller who moved from job to job, taking his family to eight different towns in one year alone. Through all their travels, music and religion were their mainstays. They settled in Odessa, Texas, when Mr. Gatlin became an engineer there. Whenever such gospel groups as the Blackwood Brothers or the Statesmen came to town, the Gatlin family all went to see them.

Larry began writing his own religious lyrics to familiar pop songs. After winning several local talent contests, the Gatlin brothers spent two years on a weekly television show in Abilene, Texas. Later their younger sister Donna joined the group. As they grew older, the Gatlins sang together less often.

While attending the University of Houston on a scholarship, Larry heard that the Imperials, a gospel group, would be backing Elvis Presley at Las Vegas and they needed a

Dann Moss Associates/APA/Monument

Dann Moss Associates/APA/Monument

baritone. Although he didn't get that job, Larry had an opportunity to work with the Imperials for a month during a later engagement in Vegas. Also on the bill was singer Dottie West who recorded two of those eight songs, "Once You Were Mine" and "You're the Other Half of Me," and helped get others recorded. She also played one of Larry's tapes for Kris Kristofferson, who alerted Fred Foster, president of Monument Records. Fred signed Larry, as well as the Gatlins, and he produced Larry's first album, *The Pilgrim,* which was released in January of 1974.

Highlights of *The Pilgrim* album include "Pennie Annie," "Bitter They Are, Harder They Fall," "It Must Have Rained in Heaven," and, of course, "Sweet Becky Walker." Larry wrote over one hundred songs before he had ten he felt were strong enough to include in his debut album. Gatlin followed *The Pilgrim* with his second Monument album, *Rain Rainbow,* which features the single, "Delta Dirt." *Larry Gatlin With Family and Friends* also features a hit single, "Broken

Lady," which made the number-one spot in 1976. Other number-one singles followed: "Statues Without Hearts" and "I Don't Wanna Cry," "I Just Wish You Were Someone I Love," in 1977, "Night Time Magic" and "Do It Again Tonight" in 1978. His album *Love Is Just a Game* hit the top ten in early 1978, followed by *Oh! Brother,* out in mid-1978. In honor of the two friends he most admires, he and Janis named their daughter Kris, for Kris Kristofferson, and son Joshua Cash for Johnny Cash.

Gayle, Crystal (Brenda Gail Webb)

Born: January 9, 1951, Paintsville, Kentucky
Married: Bill

One of seven children, her older sister is Loretta Lynn, and her other sister Peggy Sue and brother Jay Lee are also professional singers. Brothers Don, Herman, and Junior also play and sing for charities and civic organizations. In 1955, the Webb family moved to Wabash, In-

United Artists Records

Crystal Gayle

diana. By 1967, Gayle was touring country fairs and jubilees with big sister Loretta, developing her voice and performing skills, then she began appearing regularly on the Jim Ed Brown TV show, "Country Place." Loretta wrote Crystal's first recording hit, "I Cried the Blue Right Out of My Eyes," in 1970, which made the country singles charts. In January 1973, she signed with United Artists Records where producer Allen Reynolds masterminded her career, beginning with "Restless" as a hit single, which was then included in her first album, *Crystal Gayle,* along with "Wrong Road Again" and "This Is My Year for Mexico." Next came "Somebody Loves You" and her first number-one record—"I'll Get Over You," which was followed by "Crystal." Her 1977 hit "Don't It Make My Brown Eyes Blue" proved the Academy of Country Music was right when it named her Most Promising Female Vocalist of 1977 and 1978. In 1978, her singles and LP hits included "We Must Believe in Magic" and *When I Dream.*

Gentry, Bobbie (Roberta Streeter)

Born: July 27, 1944, Chickasaw County, Mississippi
Married: William Harrah (div.)

Her "Ode to Billy Joe" made her an instant major star as both songwriter and performer in 1967. The song zoomed to the number-one spot on the charts, winning the raven-haired, leggy Mississippi beauty a Grammy. She never would say exactly what was thrown off the famous Tallahatchee Bridge (the movie version came out in 1976), nor can anyone explain why her subsequent efforts have not measured up to her first success. Subsequent discs include "Papa, Won't You Let Me Go to Town with You," "Lazy Willie," "Okolona River Bottom Band," "Louisiana Man"—and two duos with Glen Campbell, "Let It Be Me" and "All I Have to Do Is Dream."

Don Gibson ABC Hickory/Top Billing, Inc.

Gibson, Don

Born: April 3, 1928, Shelby, North Carolina
Married: Bobbi
Children: d. Autumn

Don Gibson made his debut with Knoxville's WNOX "Tennessee Barn Dance." Discovered by Roy Acuff's partner, Wesley Rose, Don was signed to a writer's contract with Acuff-Rose and an artist's contract with RCA Victor. First known for "Oh Lonesome Me" and "I Can't Stop Loving You," subsequent number-one-chart records include "Sensuous Woman," "Country Green," "Touch the Morning," and "One Day at a Time." Ray Charles's recording of "I Can't Help Loving You" is one of the all-time top money earners listed with BMI. For ABC Hickory, Don rerecorded his 1977 hit single "I'm All Wrapped Up in You" as the title song of his album. His 1978 singles hit was "Oh, Such a Stranger" with "I Love You Because" on the flip side.

Glossary of Music-Industry Terms

A & R Man Abbreviation for Artist & Repertóire, referring to an employee of a phonograph record company whose duties include: 1. Selecting and/or approving songs to be recorded by artists. 2. Supervising and directing the recording of these songs. Staff producer.

A-440 Standard piano tuning (Standard tuning note) an A note which has 440 vibrations per second.

AM Abbreviation—amplitude modulation, i.e., AM radio.

A Side 1. The side of a 45-RPM single recording which the record company suggests that radio stations play on the air. 2. The side of a single record that has the most commercial appeal.

Acoustic Guitar Unamplified stringed musical instrument, as opposed to an electronically amplified guitar.

Acoustics The qualities of a room, studio, auditorium, theater, etc., that have to do with how clearly sounds can be heard or transmitted within said area.

Ad Lib Abbreviation for *ad libitum* meaning at pleasure, at will, usually referring to an unplanned or unprepared speech or other public performance. Syn—*Impromptu.*

A. F. of M. Abbreviation for American Federation of Musicians. A musician's union.

AFTRA Abbreviation of American Federation of Television and Radio Artists. A union of and for singers, actors, and announcers.

AGAC Abbreviation for American Guild of Authors and Composers.

Air Check A recording made for reference purposes from radio or TV broadcast.

Amp Abbreviation for amplifier. as a guitar *amp,* meaning guitar amplifier. Electronic mechanism or device that reproduces picked up audio sounds through speakers at a higher volume level.

Arranger One who makes music arrangements for recording of songs, live concerts, etc. One who designs a musical work to fit a style for a specific person or group.

ASCAP American Society of Composers, Authors, and Publishers. A performance rights organization.

Assign To legally transfer all or part of the earnings or ownership of a copyrightable composition to another person.

Audition A trial or test performance designed to evaluate a song, a singer, a musician, etc.

Axe Musician's term referring to a musical instrument.

BMI Broadcast Music Incorporated—Performance rights organization.

Booking Agent A person who arranges live performances for entertainers, for singers and musicians in theaters, clubs, etc.

Capitol

Lee Clayton

Bottleneck The act of fretting a guitar with a piece of glass or metal to create a slide or steel effect.

Bridge 1. That part of a stringed instrument over which the strings pass. It carries the vibrations of the strings to the sound box. 2. The melodic part or passage of a song that deviates from the theme often called the release or middle part.

b/w Backed with. Other side of a single record. Syn—*c/w.*

C & W Country and western music.

Capo A clamp-type device that fits on the neck of a stringed instrument, e.g., guitar, ukulele, etc., to stop all strings at the same fret. Changes in keys are made by affixing capo up or down on the neck.

Cartridge Tape Endless recording tape packaged on a single reel within a plastic container.

Charts 1. Written musical arrangements. 2. Popularity polls used to gauge public acceptance of recorded music.

CMA Country Music Association.

CMF Country Music Foundation. Owners and operators of Country Music Hall of Fame and Library.

Commercial 1. An advertisement placed into the programming of radio or TV shows. 2. Having sales potential or sales record. 3. Entertainment either live or recorded having mass appeal with revenue earning potential.

Copyright (statutory) Written registration with the US Library of Congress to establish ownership of creative product, e.g., poetry, music, books.

c/w Abbreviation meaning coupled with. A recording released with any other recording or recordings on record or tape. Syn. —*b/w.*

Demo 1. Abbreviation or slang—demonstration recording. 2. Slang referring to a dub. 3. Slang abbreviation referring to demonstration recording session where an artist or writer records on tape his compositions for reference or presentation.

Distributor A phonograph record and tape wholesaler.

Dobro A six-string guitar with a metal sound box. Tones created have a metallic or tinny sound.

Drum Cage A small room or enclosure within a recording studio that is designed to restrict the drum sound to one specific area of the studio.

Dub 1. An acetate disc used for limited play only of a recording needed for presentation or reference purposes. 2. Slang for demonstration recording. 3. An acetate disc recording used for temporary reference.

Dub Cutter Machine used to transfer taped songs to acetate discs for temporary use in presenting material to producers and artists.

Echo Chamber A man-made room lined with a hard surface that reflects sounds emitted from a speaker and received by a microphone giving a delayed or echo effect to recorded music.

Equal Billing Referring to artists or acts performing a given event that are to receive the same attention in all promotion and advertising of said event, e.g., same type size on posters and same size letters on auditorium marquee.

Exposure Used in entertainment world in referring to public attention focused or given to a performer, record, etc.

Fade The process of diminishing the volume at the end of a song to keep it from ending abruptly.

Fan Club An organized group of followers who are devoted to the same entertainment personality.

Feedback When the source of input picks up sound from the source of output in the same electrical circuit, this is called feedback. Feedback results in a loud roar or high-frequency squeal.

Finger Pick A plectrum that fits on the end of the guitarist's or banjoist's finger of his strumming hand, used by five-string banjoists and thumb- and finger-guitar stylists.

Flat Top A round hole Spanish guitar with a bridge that is glued to the body and secures the non-tunable end of the strings to the sound board, as opposed to an F hole or arch-top guitar.

FM Frequency Modulation—a radio band.

Front Man A performing master of ceremonies who introduces acts and generally readies the audience for the stars of the show. Generally a salaried member of a traveling pre-packaged show who usually works as musician or singer with the show.

Funky Slang—earthy; without superfluous adornment.

Gas Descriptive term to indicate something great or impressive.

Gear Slang for key or scale in which a song is being played.

Gig Slang word, meaning a job,

i.e., singing, playing instrument, etc.

Gut String Slender cord made of animal tissue (or synthetics) stretched on a musical instrument to be plucked, bowed, or strummed to create musical sounds. Gut strings are used on certain guitars, ukeleles, and on most bowed instruments like violins and bass fiddles.

Half tone Printer's term for a glossy black- and-white photograph.

Harp/Harpoon Harmonica or mouth harp that is blown by the player to vibrate small wooden or brass reeds that create musical sounds.

Headphones Small speakers or sound- reproducing mechanisms that fit over the head and ears so that only the user may hear what is being reproduced through the phones.

Head Session A recording session in which there is no written arrangement and the ideas are developed in the musicians' heads as a song is presented by the artist.

Heavy slang—important, meaningful, outstanding.

High String A flattop or open-hole guitar that is strung with a high G or G-string tuned an octave higher than standard guitar tuning. Some high-string guitarists use higher-octave tunings on 3rd, 4th, 5th, and 6th strings.

Elektra

Kenny Rogers

Hillbilly 1. An inhabitant of the hills, usually referring to low-income, uneducated farm people. 2. Once this was a descriptive term used for a music form that has evolved to what is now Country Music.

Hype 1. To overrate or oversell. 2. To exaggerate the qualities of an artist or record for the purpose of selling.

In the Can A master recording that has been set aside for future release.

Independent Producer A record producer who is not on salary from a record company. He derives his income from a percentage of sales and/or fees for his services. A record producer who contracts on individual basis to record specific artists under contract to a label.

IPS Abbreviation—inches per second. Referring to the speed that a tape transport carries recording tape over the recording or playback heads of a tape recorder. Standard speed for home recorders is 7½ IPS; professional master tapes are recorded at 15 or 30 IPS.

Jam Session An impromptu musical performance between two or more musicians strictly for the entertainment of the participants.

Jock Nickname for disc jockey.

Lead A group singer or group musician who sings or plays the melody line.

Lead Sheet Sheet music for copyright purposes by publisher and for reference by artists, arrangers, producer, etc., when recording songs. Sheet music not printed for sale to public.

Liner Notes The part of an album that contains written information on the artist or the album.

Lip Sync Slang for *lip synchronization*—the process of moving the lips to mimic the sounds produced by previous recording usually used in TV and motion-picture production. Used for special-effect purposes. Also used by singers to duplicate the same unattainable sound of their studio recording.

Lyrics The words to a song.

Master The original tape recording from which copy tapes or discs are reproduced, the master tape is the first step in the process of making records.

Mechanical Payments 1. Monies collected from record companies for the sale of records that are paid to artist, publisher, and writers. 2. Monies collected and paid for the sale of copyrighted works, e.g., sheet music.

Mike Abbreviation for microphone.

Mixer Audio engineer. One who operates a console which electronically combines sounds channeled from several different microphones. Process is used in TV, radio, motion pictures, and recording studios.

Performance Rights Organization The organization that collects money from radio, TV clubs, etc., for performance of song—to be paid to writers and publishers. *See* ASCAP, BMI, SESAC.

Performance Royalties Monies collected by performance-rights organizations from radio, TV, club performances of songs, to be paid to publishers and writers.

Pick 1. The act of playing a musical instrument; originally referring to the plastic, felt, or tortoise-shell pointed object used to strike the strings of a guitar, uke, mandolin, etc. 2. A phonograph record chosen by a radio station or trade magazine as having hit potential.

Play Back The act of listening, in the studio, to material just recorded for the purpose of analysis by the persons in charge of the recording session.

Producer The person who is in charge of a recording session; sometimes he represents the record company to which the artist is signed; in other cases, the producer functions independently of a record company and awards his product to the highest bidder.

Professional Manager The person in charge of everyday operation of a music-publishing company.

Progression 1. (harmonic) the advancement from one chord to another. The chord patterns of a song. 2. (melodic) the advancement from one tone to another. The melody of a song.

Promo Man Abbreviation for Promotion Man—a person whose job it is to secure airplay and other forms of public and/or industry exposure for his recorded product or artist.

Publisher A songwriter's agent. The publisher usually assumes all business and management functions in relation to commercial use of musical compositions, including the copyrighting, collection, and distribution of royalties, providing financial assistance to writers and the promotion of recordings.

R & B Abbreviation—Rhythm and blues music.

Rack Jobber A phonograph-record merchandiser who vends his product via display counters or racks, placed in department stores or other retail outlets. The racks are serviced by the jobbers who periodically replenish and update the stock.

Reel-to-Reel Tape Vinyl recording tape that is rolled off a reel or spindle and onto another reel while passing over the recording heads of a tape machine. Process is opposed to single reel cartridge or packaged casette tape.

Re-Mix The process of editing multitrack tape recordings to rearrange the combinations of recorded sounds.

Re-Verb A mechanical/electronic method of creating an echo based on a system of vibrating springs.

Rhythm A regularly recurring system of strong and weak beats or heavily and lightly stressed tones.

RIAA Record Industry Association of America. Membership is derived from record companies. Chief function of the RIAA is to unbiasedly certify claims of one million sales on single records or the million dollars worth of album sales.

RPM Revolutions per minute.

SESAC A performance organization.

Session The occurrence of a group of musicians gathering with an artist, producer, and other recording personnel at a recording studio for the purpose of creating recorded product.

Session Leader The musician responsible for all other musicians on that session.

Sideman Musician who accompanies or backs up an artist on either personal appearances or recording session.

Vern Gosdin

Skull Orchard A nightclub having a reputation for rough-housing.

Slap Back Echo effect created by the use of recording tape and a series of recording and playback heads. Also used to create multiple recurrences of the same sound.

Sleeper A phonograph record that is slow to receive commercial acceptance but maintains a steady gaining pace and often turns out to be a hit.

Slinky Uncommonly narrow gauged metal guitar and banjo strings chosen for their ability to be easily stretched.

Snuff Queen A female follower of performers who characteristically hangs around places frequented by country music artists.

Song Plugger Person who presents tapes or acetates of published songs to record label A&R men and artists for the purpose of getting the material recorded on a commercial record.

Stampers Nickel-plated discs that are used to form or stamp vinyl into disc recordings used for sale to the public. Process is called pressing.

Statement Accounting of royalties, a written accounting of monies due a publisher/writer or artist for sales or performance of a song during a specified period.

Stone Country A form of country music that is most earthy or basic.

Straight Pick A plastic or turtleshell plectrum used to pluck the strings of a guitar, uke, banjo, mandolin, or other stringed instruments.

Sweetening A term used to indicate the addition of soft sounds, such as violins or other strings to recorded product.

Tape Deck The transport or mechanical portion of a tape recorder. The part of a recorder that mechanically transports the tape across the head which in turn relays electronic impulses to an amplifier.

Thumb & Finger Style of guitar playing that utilizes the thumb and fingers of the hand that plucks the strings, as opposed to straight-pick strumming.

Thumb Pick A plectrum that fits around the thumb and is made of plastic or shell.

Tight Well rehearsed; generally referring to a group of musicians who work well together musically. Smooth, flawless interaction of group in a performance or session.

Trades Nickname for trade publication usually referring to any magazine or publication which specializes in news or subject matter dealing with a specific industry, e.g., for record business *Record World, Cash Box,* and *Billboard* magazines.

Turn Around Instrumental break in the middle of a song.

Vamp The instrumental introduction to a song.

Video Tape Magnetic vinyl tape used to record audio and visual signals. VTR, as it is called, has largely replaced film in television delayed broadcasts.

VTR Video Tape Recording.

Goldsboro, Bobby

Born: January 18, 1941, Marianna, Florida
Married: Mary Alice Watson
Children: s. Danny; d. Terri

A former guitar player for Roy Orbison, Bobby has hit it big on his own with "See the Funny Little Clown," "Voodoo Woman," "Little Things," and—in 1968—"Honey," the biggest worldwide selling single for that year. He has received some sixteen BMI awards. In addition to

Elektra/Universal Management

Vern Gosdin

being a songwriter and a performer, he is also a music publisher.

Gosdin, Vern

Birthdate: August 5
Born: Woodland, Alabama
Married: Cathy (div.)
Children: s. Steve; d. Chris

He and brother Rex as the Gosdin Brothers recorded with Gene Clark and did "Sounds of Goodbye" for Capitol in 1968 and did a concert tour of Japan. The next year, the brothers split up and Vern retired to Georgia. In 1976, at the urging of friends like producer Gary Paxton, Vern resumed recording as a solo performer. His first Elektra/Asylum song, "Yesterday's Gone," climbed swiftly up the country charts. In 1977, the flip side, "Hangin' On," also became a hit. In June 1977, he released the album *Till The End,* with both the album and the title single making the country top-ten charts. At the end of 1977, his "Mother Country Music" became his next hit followed by "Break My Mind" in 1978.

Grammer, Billy

Born: August 28, 1925, Franklin County, Illinois
Married: Ruth
Children: s. Billy; d. Donna, Dianne

One of thirteen children, Billy learned to play the violin at five from his father, and soon moved on to guitar, banjo, and mandolin, performing as a youngster at local events. After the army, he started his professional career at radio station WARL, Arlington, Virginia. By 1958, he had his own band, and his first record, "Gotta Travel On," went over the million mark. An Opry regular by 1959, his next biggies were "Bonaparte's Retreat" and "The Kissing Tree." Albums include *Billy Grammer* and *Country Guitar,* both Decca releases. He has his own music publishing company and has an interest in a guitar company.

Grand Ole Opry

Grand Ole Opry
by Terry Strobel

The Grand Ole Opry moved into its grand new home at Opryland on March 16, 1974, and the magnificent new auditorium is filled every Friday and Saturday night with country music fans who come from around the world, fifty-two weekends a year, to see the live country music radio stage show that is now in its fifty-second year. Although the new house has a seating capacity of 4,400, there are always capacity crowds during the peak vacation season, and the Opry has added weekend matinees during the summer to take care of the visitors who are unable to get tickets for the evening shows.

The Grand Ole Opry is as simple as sunshine. It has a universal appeal because it is built upon good will, and with folk music expresses the heartbeat of a large percentage of Americans who labor for a living.
— George D. Hay, founder of the Grand Ole Opry.

The Roaring Twenties were turbulent and exciting years for America and the world. It was a decade that saw Man O'War win the Belmont and Preakness Stakes, the beginning of airmail service between New York and San Francisco; and a young cornetist named Louis Armstrong came from New Orleans to Chicago, joined Joseph "King" Oliver's Creole Jazz Band and made musical history.

The early twenties also saw great developments in the radio field. Before the end of the decade, this infant medium would have a profound influence on the social, economic, and entertaining life of the United States. And nowhere was this influence more felt than in Nashville, Tennessee.

It began in the early fall of 1925. The headlines in the local papers read: "Construction of Radio Station Here is Begun . . . Call Letters WSM Assigned to National Life." In those days of crystal sets—and very few at that—it was hard to imagine this event having such a profound effect on the character and international image of the city it serves.

That Nashville should be known as "Music City USA" is a result of WSM and the Grand Ole Opry, which have always been the nerve center of the country music industry. For over half a century, the Opry and the radio station have directly influenced the city's economic and physical growth. Without its dedication to country music and its nurturing of talent, it is doubtful the industry would have centered in Nashville.

The Opry had its beginning on November 28, 1925, in the fifth floor WSM Studio of the National Life and Accident Insurance Company. Legend has it that the featured performer on that show was Uncle Jimmy Thompson, an eighty-year-old fiddler who boasted that he could fiddle the "taters off the vine." His early appearance, however, was restricted to one hour. Not quite enough time to prove his reputation of knowing a thousand fiddle rounds.

The announcer was one of America's pioneer showmen. George D. Hay, a reporter for the Memphis Commercial Appeal, started his radio career when he was appointed radio editor for the newspaper. He first went on the air over the Commercial Appeal's station, WMC, in June of 1923. A year later he went to Chicago and was appointed chief announcer of Radio Station WLS. Here he was voted America's most popular radio announcer in a nationwide contest conducted by *The Radio Digest*. Here, also, he originated the WLS Barn Dance, later to become known as the National Barn Dance.

On October 5, 1925, Hay came to Nashville for the dedicatory ceremony inaugurating WSM. One month later he joined the station as its first director.

Then at eight P.M. on November 28, 1925, he announced himself as The Solemn Old Judge (although he was only thirty years old) and launched the WSM Barn Dance. Two years later he gave it the title The Grand Ole Opry.

WSM, a member of the National Broadcasting Company network, was also carrying on Saturday nights "The Music Appreciation Hour" conducted by a celebrated personality, Dr. Walter Damrosch. The station followed that hour with three hours of "barn dance" music.

Hay later recalled the moment in a 1945 pamphlet. "Dr. Damrosch always signed off his concert a minute or so before we hit the air with our mountain minstrels and vocal trapeze performers. We must confess that the change in pace and quality was immense. But that is part of America—fine lace and homespun cloth.

"The monitor in our Studio B was turned on so that we would have a rough idea of the time which was fast approaching. At about five minutes before eight, your reporter called for silence in the studio. Out of the loudspeaker came the correct, but accented voice, of Dr. Damrosch and his words were something like this: While most artists realize there is no place in the classics for realism, nevertheless I am going to break one of my rules and present a composition by a young composer from Iowa, who sent us his latest number, which depicts the onrush of a locomotive. . .

"After which announcement the good doctor directed the symphony orchestra through the number which carried many 'shooshes' depicting an engine trying to come to a full stop. Then he closed his program with his usual sign-off.

"Our control operator gave us the signal which indicated that we were on the air. We paid our respects to Dr. Damrosch and said something like this: Friends, the program which just came to a close was devoted to the

George D. Hay, founder of the Grand Ole Opry, with Uncle Jimmy Thompson, 1925.

classics. Dr. Damrosch told us that it was generally agreed that there is no place in the classics for realism. However, from here on out for the next three hours we will present nothing but realism. . . It will be down to earth for the earthy.

"In respectful contrast to Dr. Damrosch's presentation of the number which depicts the onrush of locomotives, we will call on one of our performers— DeFord Bailey, with harmonica to give us the country version of his 'Pan American Blues.'

"Whereupon, DeFord Bailey, a wizard with the harmonica, played the number. At the close of it, your reporter said: 'For the past hour we have been listening to music taken largely from Grand Opera, but from now on we will present "The Grand Ole Opry." ' "

It wasn't long before the crowds clogged the corridors of the WSM studio to observe the performers. This led to a decision. Edwin W. Craig, a National Life official, was the man of early and continuous vision. A strong supporter of the station and the Opry, he suggested that all the observers be allowed to watch in a studio so their reactions could add to the program. His suggestion led to the construction of Studio C, an acoustically designed auditorium capable of holding five hundred enthusiastic fans.

Soon the auditorium-studio could no longer accommodate the throngs, so the search for an appropriate home began. The first move was to the rented Hillsboro Theatre, a former movie house in what was then the southwest part of the city. When the audience continued to grow, Opry officials sought another hall.

A huge tabernacle across the Cumberland River in East Nashville was available. Although the floor was covered with sawdust and the splintery benches were crude, the audience outgrew this location in two years.

In July, 1939, the show moved to the newly constructed War Memorial Auditorium; an entrance fee of twenty-five cents was imposed in an effort to curb the crowd. It didn't work, the weekly crowds averaged better than three thousand. The move to the Ryman Auditorium in 1943 was a necessity.

The Ryman had been built in 1891 by riverboat captain Tom Ryman who came to a religious tent meeting to heckle the preacher, only to stay and be converted. He built the structure for the Reverend Sam Jones.

The first real country band to appear on WSM was headed by a genial physician, Dr. Humphrey Bate. At the time of Dr. Bate's death in 1936, Judge Hay wrote, "As a matter of fact, Dr. Bate played on the station even before the barn dance started." Dr. Bate was a graduate of Vanderbilt University Medical School, and played harmonica. He joined the Opry with six of his neighbors and named them the "Possum Hunters." At the piano was Dr. Bate's thirteen-year-old daughter, Alcyone, who has performed for fifty years each Saturday night. Other outstanding string bands were: The Gully Jumpers, The Fruit Jar Drinkers, The Crook Brothers, Arthur Smith and his Dixie Liner, The Binkley Brothers and their Clod Hoppers, Uncle Ed Poplin and his Ole Timers, The Delmore Brothers, and Jack Jackson and the Bronco Busters.

Uncle Dave Macon, "The Dixie Dewdrop," joined the Opry in 1926 after several years in vaudeville. He remained its top star for many years.

Until 1938, the Grand Ole Opry placed virtually all emphasis on instruments. There were some singers, but they were subordinate to the band. Then came young Roy Acuff and the Smoky Mountain Boys. A short time later, one of the instrumentalists in the band of Pee Wee King and his Golden West Cowboys stepped forward to sing. That was the start of the career of Eddy Arnold, "The Tennessee Plowboy." Arnold later formed his own group, and the rush was on. Red Foley became a hit, then Ernest Tubb, Cowboy Copas and Hank Williams.

On came the Duke of Paducah, Whitey Ford. He had been the star of a network radio show "Plantation Party." Then Minnie Pearl and Rod Brasfield, Curly Fox, Texas Ruby and the Fox Hunters. Those were the days of minstrels, and the Opry produced Jamup and Honey. Bill Monroe arrived to introduce Bluegrass Music.

Others included Uncle Joe Mangrum and Fred Schriver, Asher Sizemore and Jimmy, the Vagabonds, Lew Childre, Zeke Clements, Paul Howard, Curly Williams and Clyde Moody.

In 1939, the Opry was carried on the NBC network for the first time. Sponsored by Prince Albert, the first show featured Uncle Dave Macon, Roy Acuff, Little Rachel, the Weaver Brothers and Elviry, and the Sol-

The Possum Hunters, first band to play on WSM.

emn Old Judge. This same group made the first Grand Ole Opry movie a year later. Vito Pellettieri, Opry stage manager since 1934, handled all the complicated stage traffic.

The 1940s and 1950s brought new stars to the Opry: Lester Flatt and Earl Scruggs, Lonzo and Oscar, Ray Price, Johnny and Jack, the Carlisles, Mother Maybelle Carter, Ferlin Husky, the Jordanaires, Stringbean, Cousin Jody, Marty Robbins, Hank Snow, Don Gibson, The Stoney Mountain Cloggers, The Ralph Sloan Dancers, Billy Grammer, Charlie Louvin, Jean Shepard, Little Jimmy Dickens, Justin Tubb, Kitty Wells, The Willis Brothers, Margie Bowes, George Morgan, Bobby Lord, Hank Locklin, Hawkshaw Hawkins, Del Wood, Faron Young, Jim Reeves, Jimmy Newman, Roy Drusky, Johnny Cash, Grandpa Jones, Archie Campbell, The Everly Brothers, Stonewall Jackson, Patsy Cline, Bill Anderson, The Wilburn Brothers, Wilma Lee and Stoney Cooper, Porter Wagoner, George Hamilton IV, Skeeter Davis, and the list continues.

The 1960s brought no let-up in new and great talent. They include Marion Worth, LeRoy Van Dyke, Dottie West, Tex Ritter, Bobby Bare, Connie Smith, Bob Luman, Billy Walker, Sonny James, Ernie Ashworth, Loretta Lynn, The Osborne Brothers, Jim and Jesse, The Glaser Brothers, Jim Ed Brown, Jack Greene, Dolly Parton, Del Reeves, Mel Tillis, Jeannie Seely, Stu Phillips, Charlie Walker, The Four Guys, Ray Pillow and others. The Opry has since added: David Houston, Barbara Mandrell, Jerry Clower, Jeanne Pruett, George Jones, and Tammy Wynette.

The Grand Ole Opry family is unique. But like every other family it shares many human emotions. It has not always had the happiest of times. Tragedy has been a sad chapter in its history.

In 1953, at the age of twenty-nine, Hank Williams died in the back seat of a car somewhere between Knoxville, Tennessee, and Oak Hill, West Virginia. Ten years later, Patsy Cline, Hawkshaw Hawkins, Cowboy Copas and his son-in-law, Randy Hughes were killed in an airplane crash. Then Jack Anglin, Betty Jack Davis, Texas

Ruby Owens, Jim Reeves, Ira Louvin and Sam McGee were lost in tragic accidents. Probably the most publicized disaster occurred in 1973 when Stringbean and his wife, Estelle, were murdered at their farm after a Grand Ole Opry performance. The 1970s also claimed the lives of: Tex Ritter, George Morgan, Staley Walton, Ed Hyde, Claude Lampley, Jimmy Widener, and Cousin Jody.

From every state in the Union and many foreign countries 750,000 Opry fans annually travel an average of 470 miles one way to see the Friday and Saturday performances. It has been estimated that an additional seven to eight million see Opry stars themselves journey three million miles a year in making these appearances. Today Nashville's music industry, an offshoot of the Opry, is a billion dollar a year business. The statistics are impressive indeed. Nashvillians are employed by recording studios, record pressing plants, talent agencies, trade papers, recording companies and performing rights organizations. Through the Opry, WSM has created a musical family that has in turn made Nashville "Music City, U.S.A." In fact David Cobb, retired WSM personality, is responsible for dubbing the town "Music City" many years ago. The first recording studio, Castle, was put together by three former WSM engineers: Aaron Shelton, George Reynolds and Carl Jenkins. And the man generally considered the father of Music Row's recording industry was Owen Bradley, former musical director of WSM. Bradley succeeded Beasley Smith who penned such famous songs as: "The Old Master Painter from the Faraway Hills" and "Lucky Old Sun."

Bradley was succeeded by Marvin Hughes, who later became a producer for Capital. Hughes' successor was Bill McElhiney, whose most recent successes have included arranging for Danny Davis and the Nashville Brass. Roy Acuff and Fred Rose both worked at WSM. They teamed to form Acuff-Rose, the publishing and talent management empire. Chet Atkins, one of Nashville's musical giants and a key RCA executive, came to WSM as a sideman with the Carter Family. Jack Stapp, who had been program director and produced the old Opry network shows for NBC, formed Tree Publishing Company. Frances Preston, head of BMI in Nashville, had worked for the station in the promotion department. There was also Dinah Shore, Snooky Lanson, Tennessee Ernie Ford, Phil Harris, Kitty Kallen, James Melton, Francis Craig, and Anita Kerr among others.

The body and soul of music is the musician. In Nashville he has prospered. WSM and the Grand Ole Opry have been patrons of music for more than five decades. Now there is a boom in Country Music. But during the long, lean, early years, music was always present in the studios and halls of WSM.

There are performers who have been members of the Grand Ole Opry or members of the WSM staff band for twenty, thirty, and even fifty years. The disbursement of weekly and monthly monies has not been confined to a few. Witness the hundreds of stars and thousands of

"sidemen" who have performed on the Opry, and the dozens of staff musicians employed by WSM in the pop field. The fact that WSM has possibly the last remaining studio staff orchestra in America speaks for itself. The station has recently formed its own record label, Opryland Records, to further the advancement of music and musicians.

Continuing in the traditional role of vanguard for new concepts in broadcasting, WSM gave America its first commercial frequency modulation radio station in 1941. Retired WSM President, John H. DeWitt, who manned the audio controls at the first Opry broadcast, was the principal force behind this new venture. WNV47 is now a part of broadcast lore, partly because people were uninterested in buying a converter or receiver to pick up the station's signal. In the early sixties, interest in FM revived. WSM-FM (95.5) made its debut in 1968 with 100,000 watts. The station broadcasts in stereo with vertical and horizontal polarization. It covers a one hundred-mile radius surrounding Nashville.

In 1950, WSM brought Nashville its first television station. The video facility set up a series of five microwave relay stations between this city and Louisville, thereby becoming the first TV network affiliate in town. The station also brought this area its first color programs and installed the first color film processor in Nashville.

WSM's latest influence on the growth and economy of Nashville is the construction of a $28 million family

Hickory Records, Inc./Acuff-Rose Artists Corp.

Roy Acuff

The Grande Ole Opry House at Opryland USA. It is the world's largest broadcasting facility, seating 4,400. Opryland USA is a 369-acre entertainment/amusement complex.

WSM/Les Leverett

entertainment park and music center. Of course, the $15 million Opry House is the focal point of this project.

In the summer of 1968, Irving Waugh, president of WSM, Inc., and National Life executives, Edwin Craig and Bill Weaver, talked of plans to build a new Opry House. When they began thinking in terms of space of parking and other considerations, the plan for a park was conceived.

At the 1968 Grand Ole Opry Birthday Celebration, Waugh announced to the thousands of disc jockeys and music industry notables that a feasibility study would be undertaken to determine if such a complex were economically sound. At the 1969 birthday celebration, Waugh stated that all systems were go.

Opryland USA, a 369-acre complex, is designed to be "The Home of American Music." The park is divided into entertainment areas that combine live musical shows, natural animal habitat areas, restaurants, gift shops, and sensational thrill rides. Opryland opened its gates to the public in the spring of 1972, and two years later the Grand Ole Opry show moved to the new 4,400 seat Opry House. In 1975, National Life and Accident Insurance Company officials announced plans for Oprytown . . . Tennessee's largest hotel-convention-exhibition center. . . .

The Grand Ole Opry is, and has always been, entertainment, pageantry, vaudeville and music of all the people packaged into one presentation. The rapport between the Opry artists and the audience is unlike anything else in the world.

The music is genuine, down-to-earth, and honest. It is realism. And as Judge Hay explained once, "The principal appeal of the Opry is a homey one. It sends forth the aroma of bacon and eggs frying on the kitchen stove on a bright spring morning. That aroma is welcomed all the way from Maine to California."

Guitar Player

This is the guitar magazine devoted totally to music. Each monthly issue is filled with interviews, feature articles, columns on instrument design, manufacture, care ... electronics and musical equipment, playing techniques, music business. It's written by top guitar artists for both the amateur and professional player.

Write, enclosing $12 for 1 year or $24 for 2 years, to *Guitar Player,* Box 615 FN, Saratoga, CA 95070.

Guthrie, Woody (Woodrow Wilson)

Born: July 14, 1912, Okemah, Oklahoma
Died: October 4, 1967
Married: Marjorie
Children: s. Arlo

The first country singer with a social conscience, he hard-traveled across America in the twenties and thirties looking for work—and hope. He rode freight trains,

Woody Guthrie and Mary Lou

slept in ditches, joined the Dust Bowl refugees on the trek to California, and helped the workers to organize into unions. A warm, witty, wiry man of wry perception and deep humanity, he wrote hundreds of songs including "So Long, It's Been Good to Know You", "Hard Travelin'," and the exuberant hymn to America, "This Land Is Your Land." An inspiration to Bob Dylan, Burl Ives, Pete Seeger, and Ramblin' Jack Elliott among oth-

ers—including his son, Arlo, who wrote the brilliant, "Alice's Restaurant," Woody died tragically of a hereditary nerve disease, Huntington's Chorea. His autobiography, *Bound for Glory*, which depicts his years of wandering, has been made into a film starring David Carradine as Woody. Several LPs are available including an outstanding Library of Congress retrospective, *Woody Guthrie*, comprising three hours of conversation about things like home brew, Texas oil fields, bankers and hoboes, government camps, and outlaws Pretty Boy Floyd and Jesse James, plus such songs as "Worried Man Blues," "Greenback Dollar," "Dirty Overalls," "Dustbowl Refugees," and "Goin' Down That Road Feelin' Bad."

H

Hagers, Jim and John

Born: Chicago, Illinois

Identical twins, who are regulars on "Hee Haw" and tour with Buck Owens, they made their first professional appearance at East Street, a nightclub in their native Chicago. Now they both live in Los Angeles with their respective families.

Haggard, Merle

Born: April 6, 1937, Bakersfield, Calif.
Married: Bonnie Campbell Owens (div.); Leona Williams
Children: s. Marty, Noel; d. Dana, Kellie.

Son of a dust-bowl Okie migrant, Merle's life and artistry reflect the pain and hopes of the thousands who lost everything in the Depression and expected to find paradise in California—but wound up starving in Hoover Camps. Born in a converted boxcar, Merle started getting in trouble when he was only fourteen. He landed in San Quentin at twenty, with a one-to-fifteen-year sentence for burglary. Paroled in 1960, he returned to his family in Bakersfield, dug ditches by day and played and sang country music at night in local saloons and dance halls that catered to the ranch hands and oil workers. His first record, "All My Friends Are Gonna Be Strangers," led to a contract with Capitol Records. He soon formed his own band, married Bonnie, and together they recorded "Just Between the Two of Us." On his own, Merle wrote and sang "Mama Tried" and "Hungry Eyes" about his childhood; "Branded Man" and "Sing Me Back Home" about his prison years; and "Workin' Man Blues" and "White Line Fever" about his days of backbreaking

Capitol

Merle Haggard

manual labor. With his singles hitting number one on the charts and his albums zooming, Merle's rising stardom took a dramatic turn with "Okie from Muskogee" in 1969 and his subsequent "Fightin' Side of Me." Merle's working man's songs had made him something of a Woody Guthrie to his fans, who reacted with dismay at the "patriotic" ideals his two new hits expressed. But these were days of campus unrest and fierce anti-Vietnam War activism. And patriotism was something of a dirty word at that time. "Fightin' Side" expressed the resentment and self-pride of the working man as he watched the college kids doing their wild thing. Though stunned by the reaction, Hag kept

his own council and continued to write about the world he knew and the people in it. "They're Tearing the Labor Camps Down" depicts the plight of today's migrants; "Irma Jackson" sensitively portrays an inter-racial love affair.

In response to Bob Dylan's "Like a Rolling Stone," Merle wrote "I've Done It All." One of his most touching songs, "If We Make It through December," topped the charts in 1975. Among his LPs are: *Same Train, A Different Time* (the great songs of Jimmie Rodgers) and *A Tribute to the Best Damn Fiddle Player in the World* (Bob Wills). With his band, The Strangers, he has won over thirty major country music awards since 1965.

Merle Haggard by Lawrence Linderman

With very little fanfare indeed, Merle Haggard has quietly risen to the pinnacle of country-music success—and in the process has helped down-home country music achieve sudden prominence. An endangered musical species only a decade ago, the country sound has since become the hottest-selling item disced out by U.S. record companies. Haggard, an intensely proud man, has been a leader in its resurgence, along with such other country luminaries as Johnny Cash, Waylon Jennings, Charley Pride, Charlie Rich, Willie Nelson, and Kris Kristofferson.

Of them all, however, the man they call The Hag perhaps best expresses the country singer's traditional preoccupation with such eternal verities as respect, loyalty, and friendship—and with such time-honored potential nemeses as whiskey, women, and the law. Like the best country balladeers, Haggard has "lived" what he calls his "hurtin' songs" to such a thorough extent that when he sings "I've Done It All," he is merely reporting on a life that, until 1960, appeared to be totally misspent.

Born in Bakersfield, California, on April 5, 1937, Haggard is the son of a hard-working farm couple that headed west from Oklahoma during the depression. When the family settled in Bakersfield, Haggard's father went to work for the Santa Fe railroad. Merle was nine when his father died, and with his mother, Flossie, working during the day, he soon became an adventurous wanderer. By the time he was fourteen, he was regularly cutting school. At a juvenile correctional institution, he got in with youthful criminals and became an outlaw in the truest sense of the word. By the time he was twenty-three, he had already served six years behind bars. Freed from prison in 1960, Haggard straightened out his life and began singing at a series of small clubs. After several hit records had established him on the corn-pone circuit, "Okie from Muskogee" made him both a superstar and a millionaire. Since then, Haggard has solidified his position as one of the most gifted and respected performers in country-music history.

After *Penthouse* sent freelancer Lawrence Linderman to track down the thirty-nine-year-old singer, Linderman reported: "The word on Merle Haggard is that he goes his own way and is so unconcerned with the press that he's virtually impossible to interview, unless you happen to bump into him on the road and he feels like talking that day. With that in mind, I took my chances and headed for Las Vegas, where Haggard was appearing at the Sahara Hotel. When I drove into town, I got in touch with Fuzzy Owen, Haggard's manager. He arranged for the *Penthouse* interview sessions to be conducted in Haggard's dressing room, between Merle's two nightly performances.

"The first evening I came by, however, Haggard

wasn't up to talking. Earlier in the day he'd arm-wrestled every member of the band, and he was in such acute pain as to be unable to play his fiddle. The Sahara management dispatched a doctor to Haggard's dressing room, and the young MD—a country boy himself—told Haggard he'd torn chest muscles away from the bone. Haggard was asked to lie on the floor and was given a concerted, somewhat painful massage—during which he nonetheless giggled like a kid every time the doctor's fingers pinpointed down into the affected muscle. Five members of Haggard's crew, slugging away at their beers, laughed even louder. The group acts much like a close-knit family.

"The next night I watched Haggard perform (he's got a beautifully clear and strong voice), and he received a warm, enthusiastic reception from an SRO audience. When we later sat down to talk, Haggard mentioned that Las Vegas crowds are tamer than the audiences he used to play for, and that remark led to the opening question of our interview."

Penthouse: Until just a few years ago, you and your band had a reputation for somehow igniting assorted brawls, mayhem, and general violence wherever you played. Was that a bum rap?

Haggard: No, cause it really *did* happen. For a long time, we were like the late Bob Wills's band. Roy Nichols, my lead guitar player, says that Wills's music would make you want to either fuck or fight, and a helluva lot of both went on at any dance Bob played at. We were like that, too. I still don't know what it was, but our music would just get everybody goin'. I remember one night in Amarillo. The owner of the dance hall we were playing picked us up when we got to town and told me, "Merle, we've had this club for five years. We have a real fine reputation, and we never had a fight yet." I said, "Well, I hate to tell you this, but we'll fix that reputation right quick." And sure enough, we hadn't been playin' twenty minutes when the damnedest fight broke out that you ever seen. They tore that whole sonofabitch up!

Penthouse: Are we correct in assuming you've played more than your share of the kind of grubby country bars that Glen Campbell calls "fightin' and dancin' clubs"?

Haggard: When I was coming up, I worked in every kind of club you can think of; and yeah, some of 'em were rougher than others. I can recall one really unfriendly place down in Hugo, Oklahoma. I was onstage, playin' and watchin' guys beat each other to a pulp, when somebody came runnin' up to me and said, "Hey, a couple of ole boys are tryin' to break into your camper to get at your wife." I stopped what I was doing, ran and got my pistol, and bluffed those jokers out. All *kinds* of crazy things used to happen in them dance halls.

Penthouse: Do you ever miss those days?

Haggard: Yeah. And about two years ago I made the mistake of thinking I'd enjoy gettin' back into that scene; so I agreed to play the Reo Palm Isle dance hall

in Longview, Texas. The place was built to hold about nine hundred people; and when we got there, a crowd of about three thousand was waitin' for us. People were all over the stage and all over Roy Nichols and my bass player, and I couldn't get a decent note out of *none* of the guys. That was the last time we played one of them places; it's just a lot easier playing coliseums and show-rooms.

Penthouse: And a lot more lucrative, especially since the nation's appetite for country music has increased to the point where even singers like Andy Williams are starting to come on like Ferlin Husky. Does this sudden profusion of supperclub, rhinestone cowboys disturb you?

Haggard: Not a whole hell of a lot. I know of big entertainers who haven't done very well in their own fields for

a long time and who've seen the success of country music; so they've cut a couple of country records. They do well for a short period of time, but I don't think they're going to shit the country-music public for long. I've never seen anyone who *can* shit 'em. The A-number-one rule about country music is sincerity. I've found that my audiences look for that, and I just try to be honest with them.

Penthouse: Is the business side of country music similarly sincere?

Haggard: No, and I found that out right quick. And it *irritates* me. I think you should be able to depend on a man's handshake, but you can't do that in this business. It's like a man's word is worth nothing and a piece of paper is worth *everything,* and that's just no good. People in my organization have never needed more than a handshake; and I've never even signed a contract with my manager, Fuzzy Owen, and we've been together for fifteen years. I'd better correct that a little: I believe we may have drawn up some kind of thing to protect his family, but we never signed anything to protect us against each other. Anyway, I just don't like how people act when they get to talkin' business. So I always say that it's not my bag and that I'm not business minded. Maybe I'm not, 'cause the truth is, I'd rather go fishing than negotiate a contract—and I've actually done just that on a couple of occasions. The thing is, I just won't do what I don't *want* to do.

Penthouse: Has that attitude ever hurt your career?

Haggard: I don't think so, but it has got me into a couple of jams. One time I was hired by CBS-TV to play Curly in Rodgers and Hammerstein's *Oklahoma,* which is a show where people sing "Everything's Up-to-Date in Kansas City" and stuff like that. Minnie Pearl and Jeannie C. Riley were in the cast; so I guess it was all right. The one thing I told the producers at the beginning was that I wouldn't do a bunch of dancin' and crap like that. And they said fine: we'd have six days of rehearsal, and they'd film it for worldwide television.

But then they went back on their word. As the week progressed . . . they had some funny boys around there —in fact, I think the whole goddamn crew was funny— who kept insisting that I dance, until the thing really got on my nerves. During rehearsal one night, I saw Fuzzy Owen standin' behind the curtain, and as me and Jeannie C. Riley danced by, I said to him, "Fuzzy, on my next round past you I'm goin' straight to the bus."

Well, the people from the show all followed me out there and wanted to know what the hell was wrong. I told 'em, "Look, it's a big mistake for me to do this show, because you got me doin' what you said I wouldn't have to do—all this dancin' and choreography crap. I just don't see what my fans are gonna identify with. Those truck drivers ain't gonna *understand* all this, and I don't blame 'em. It's bad for me, and I don't enjoy it; so I'm gettin' out."

They argued and said there was only one day left before filming started. But I told 'em I wasn't gonna do it, and if they wanted to file a lawsuit to just go on and get the thing over with. It actually ended up okay: they got somebody to take my place, and I never heard a word about it afterward.

Penthouse: Country music is currently bigger than it's ever been and still growing. What's responsible for that?

Haggard: I think you can put it all down to the exposure country music's gotten in the last ten years—which is more exposure than it's ever had before. There's also been a change of attitude about it. Not so many years ago, country music was looked down on, and you wouldn't see well-dressed people admitting they liked it. But that's changed now. I happen to think the desire for it has always been there, and I personally can't see why anybody wouldn't like country music. Myself, I like all music, and I think there's only two kinds: good and bad, and nobody's opinion on what's good really counts except your own. If nothing else, that's one thing the hippie uprising did for us all: it suggested that we do our own thing and be proud of it.

Penthouse: Praise for hippies is about the last thing we'd expect from the man who wrote and recorded the ultimate hippie put-down, "Okie from Muskogee." Could it be that you're a closet longhair?

Haggard: Hell, no. And I didn't write "Okie from Muskogee" with the idea of gettin' back at hippies. Me and the band were on a bus in Oklahoma when we passed a sign sayin', "Muskogee, 100 miles" or something like that, and somebody said, "I bet they don't smoke marijuana in Muskogee." I thought that was a funny comment, so we started making up some more lines, and in about twenty minutes we had us a song.

Penthouse: Did you expect "Okie from Muskogee" to be the monster hit it turned out to be?

Haggard: Yeah, and I'll tell you why. The night after we wrote it, we played a non-commissioned officers' club at an air force base down in North Carolina, and I sang it there. At the end of the song, some sergeant came walking up to the stage and just completely stopped the show and asked if I'd sing it again. I said okay; so we did it again. And *again.* We left scratchin' our heads, and I told everybody, "I think we might have somethin' here, but this hasn't been a fair trial, cause it's a military base."

The next night, though, we played a regular coliseum —and at the end of "Okie from Muskogee," people climbed past the orchestra pit and up to the stage. We knew then that we had a product to record live, and I thought that it was a natural. Funny thing is, "Okie from Muskogee" turned out to be a very, very bad record. The musicianship on it, the singing—we just weren't up to par.

Penthouse: Why not?

Haggard: It was our own danged fault. We were doing dates in Texas and the Southwest and trying to put together an album that was gonna be called *Six Nights in a Row.* We decided to do the recording ourselves. But instead of hiring a company that specializes in that sort of thing, we just took along the eight-track machine— out of a little ole dingbat studio we have in Bakersfield, California,—stuck it in a van, and headed off. As it turned out, we didn't have a correct power supply. We were short three or four little things to make the equipment work right. We ran into all *kinds* of problems.

Anyway, we got down to the last night of the trip, which was also the most important night, 'cause we were playing in Muskogee, Oklahoma. I remember walkin' around sayin', "We're not going to make no record *this* trip," for I was sure something new would go wrong with the recording gear that night. I wasn't really mistaken, 'cause the record's full of technical sounds—poppin', wires hissing, just about everything went slightly haywire. But in spite of all that, the damned record was the biggest thing we ever had.

Penthouse: Why do you think it became such a huge success?

Haggard: "Okie from Muskogee" said something to those particular people who were called "the silent majority." Finally *they* were having something said in their behalf, and they really came unwound when they heard it said the way they wanted to hear it said. We got reactions like that for three or four years, and in some places we still get wild reactions.

Penthouse: Did you get much criticism about the song from the liberal press?

Haggard: I really figured that would happen, but it didn't—at least, not very much. Oh, there were some jokes and some kidding, but nothing really hot. The song kicked up some controversy in both directions, but I don't think it got any more attention than it had coming to it. The song was about something that was happening in this country, and the controversy was between the people and not really directed toward me or toward "Okie from Muskogee."

Capitol

Penthouse: Were you very down on the hippies?

Haggard: I sure was. During the uprising that started in 1968 and 1969, which is what the song was directed toward, those people had all the gripes and bitches and were going around sayin', "Down with everything!" But they had no answers.

Penthouse: Soon after "Okie from Muskogee," you recorded "The Fightin' Side of Me," a song that criticized war protesters and "warned" them: "If you don't love it, leave it." Do you really think that people who disagree with a nation's war policy should either shut up about it or be subject to a love-it-or-leave-it ultimatum?

Haggard: No. I wasn't saying that. I've never thought things are perfect in this country and that we should take it the way it is or leave it. The song said *love* it or leave it, which is something very different.

Penthouse: In what way?

Haggard: I think that if you don't love this country, you damned sure can't or won't have the initiative to really change it and help it; if you don't love America, the only reason you're gonna be here is to tear it down. For instance, if you're raising a child and you hate that kid, how you gonna raise it right? So I think if you don't love the country, you *should* leave it. And if you love it, then stay here and try to *fix* the sonofabitch.

Penthouse: Political dissidents would claim that's precisely what they try to do. Do you automatically assume that people who've supported unpopular causes—such as the antiwar movement of the sixties—hate the nation?

Haggard: No, but I still think you've got to love the country enough to take the good with the bad, to put up with its problems, and to defend it when it *needs* defending. Look, we really have to take orders from the people in charge and to have confidence in their decisions. And if they make the wrong decisions, *we're* the ones at fault, because we put 'em in office. People seem to be saying, "Okay, let's argue and talk about what we should do, but let's not fight each other. Let's not tear up any more schools or burn down any more buildings." Stuff like that went on not too many years ago, and it just didn't make any sense to me. It's *still* going on, and now it's really gettin' dangerous. . . .

Penthouse: Does that lead you to conclude that America will suffer from stepped-up guerrilla-style activity in the future?

Haggard: I hate to think so, but I believe that it's probably inevitable and that it *will* happen here. As our country grows in population and as our standard of living keeps going down—which it has—we're gonna be in for more and more trouble. Our economy seems to have peaked out in the late fifties, at a time when we were probably living better than any other society in modern history. But as we get an increase in people and as our food supply declines, there's bound to be serious agitation. People get *uncomfortable* when they get hungry; if there's a whole mess of folks starving to death and one ole boy has a bunch of food in his house, they're gonna come around and tear down his door. And if they're cold at night and another ole boy has all the heatin' oil in town, they're gonna take that, too.

Penthouse: When do you see all this happening?

Haggard: Unless we find some new energy sources to replace the ones we're using now—the cost of which is screwing up our entire economy—we're gonna be in bad shape in fifteen years. We just can't depend on oil for energy anymore—that's what we've got to get away from. Coal is one of the main resources being talked about to replace oil with, but coal is one of the worst air polluters there is.

I know a lot of people who are studying all this, and

they claim there's a lot more oil around than we know about or have found yet. But that still may not mean too much. You see, there's things like production and transportation costs to consider. How much will it *really* cost to get oil down here from Alaska, and by the time it gets here, how many more people will need how much more oil?

Penthouse: You sound very pessimistic about the future. Are you?

Haggard: No, 'cause I think that we're *going* to find other sources of energy. If I'm wrong and we don't, then we're in for bad times. But I think we'll learn how to use the sun and the oceans for producing energy. We're on the verge of breaking through in both areas right now, or at least that's what I'm told. Solar research is really coming along fast, and if we can harness the sun's energy, it means we'll have energy for as long as the sun comes up. And the day it *don't* come up, well, we probably won't need energy

Penthouse: Do you think your interest in the energy issue will eventually cause you to write songs about it?

Haggard: Could be. But if I don't, other people will—you almost always find a song in the country charts that gives you a picture or an explanation of a subject that's on everybody's mind. That's why it's fair to say that country music is journalism set to music. But that's only part of what country music is.

Penthouse: What's the rest?

Haggard: To me, it's a way of life—and country music was my way of life before it became my profession. It's hard to explain, but it begins with the difference between a country-music fan and a fan of some other kind of music. For a lot of people, music is something to create an atmosphere with or something to enjoy by yourself. Country-music fans are different, because they literally worship their idols, and they're not satisfied just to play their records, they've got to get everybody else in the neighborhood listening, too. I was like that myself when I was a kid.

Penthouse: And who were the country musicians *you* used to tell people about?

Haggard: I liked the three guys who were big in 1950, which is when I was first jumping out of the nest: Hank Williams, Bob Wills—who was beginning to go down in popularity about that time—and Lefty Frizzell. They were the top country artists in America, and when any of them came to my hometown of Bakersfield, I'd get so damned excited that I'd act a little crazy. I was in high school the first time Frizzell ever came to Bakersfield, and it was such an event for me that I got drunk the night *before* his appearance and stayed drunk all that night and the next day, and wound up barely able to make it to the dance. He played at a place called the Rainbow Garden, and it was such a madhouse you could hardly hear him. Frizzell was a young, good-looking guy with a lot of class, and a fifteen year old, like I was, could really admire him. He also turned out to be the first musician of any stature ever to get me up on the

bandstand.

Penthouse: How did that come about?

Haggard: The second time Frizzell came through town was in 1953, and by then I'd gotten to playin' guitar and singing; and my friends liked what I did so much that when we'd go to parties, I'd wind up havin' to sing all night. Anyway, when Lefty came to play the Rainbow Garden again, my friends went backstage before the show and asked Frizzell if he'd like to meet a guy who sang like he did. He said sure; so I was allowed to go backstage and sing a couple of songs for him, and he seemed pretty pleased. Just as I finished up, one of the club owners came by and told Lefty it was time to start the show, and Frizzell said, "I want this kid to sing a song out there before I go on." The owner looked at Lefty like he was crazy and told him, "Hey, that crowd didn't pay to hear their own local yokel sing. They came to hear Frizzell."

But Lefty refused to go on if I wasn't allowed to sing, so he got his way, and I got to use his guitar and have his band play behind me. It was quite a thrill. I did two or three songs, and they were well accepted. Other than Frizzell's songs, I only knew songs by Jimmie Rodgers, and I remember singing one of 'em, called "My Rough and Rowdy Ways."

Penthouse: That may have been a particularly appropriate choice. How rough and rowdy were *you* as a kid?

Haggard: Well, if it means anything, nice girls' parents wouldn't let their daughters go out with me. I wasn't a *bad* kid, just mischievous. My one big disagreement with life in those days was that I didn't want to go to school. So I was always takin' off with a good friend of mine, Dean Corlson, who's always been in my band. We'd wind up workin' some harvest and usually makin' it rough on ourselves when we didn't have to. Both of us were well taken care of at home, but we somehow would always end up on a trip somewhere, broke and hungry. It's kind of fun to think about now, 'cause we had us some good times.

Penthouse: Such as?

Haggard: Well, one time we decided to go to Missouri; so Dean and I and another fella and a girl just up and left town in a '41 Plymouth. The girl was fourteen, I was sixteen, and Dean and this other boy were both seventeen, and we didn't think anything about it. But the law did. After we were gone one night, the girl's folks got the police out lookin' for us, and when we drove through a place called Ash Fork, Arizona, two police had us pull over and said, "Yup, these are the ones we got that all-points bulletin on."

The Ash Fork, Arizona, law officers stopped us on Highway 66 and had us follow them to another highway, where they told us, "Listen, we're the only officers on duty out here, and we can't leave our posts. This is a two-way highway that goes to a town called Prescott, and there's no roads off it in either direction. You kids drive into Prescott—police will be waiting for you at the city limits. Meanwhile we're gonna wait right here until we get radioed that you're in custody."

That was our orders, so we left for Prescott, but we weren't feelin' too hot. The police had told us we were guilty of white slavery and that we'd be going to jail; so instead of driving to Prescott, we just turned off the highway and cut a path right through the damned desert —we drove a good twenty miles out into the sand. When we stopped, we covered that old Plymouth up with tumbleweeds and then just sat there for three days. By then we'd gone through all the beer, sandwiches, and candy we'd brought with us, and we were dyin' of thirst and hunger. We'd held out for as long as we could; so we decided to try to make it past the police roadblock in Prescott. We started toward that town at three in the morning; and as we got there, we saw the police road-block, just past an alleyway. As luck would have it, the police officer on duty was talking to somebody and had his back to us. And before he could turn around to see our car, we ducked into the alley, went around the back of the building, and were able to get back on the high-way. We drove straight home.

We didn't know, of course, that the Arizona police had already radioed California authorities that they had us in custody. The Arizona police were probably a little annoyed about us slipping by 'em, because the day after we all got home the juvenile authorities picked us up on charges of white slavery and escape. I told 'em we didn't escape from no one, 'cause Arizona never really had us. They just *thought* they had us. Me and Dean did a cou-ple of weeks in the clink for that one. Something like that was always goin' on.

Penthouse: Why do you think you got into so many scrapes with the law?

Haggard: I honestly think it began with my dislike for school. California has a strict truancy law, and the first time they came down on me for not going to school, I wound up being sent to a little ole road camp. I stayed in that place five days.

Penthouse: Did that short stretch teach you anything?

Haggard: Actually, my sentence was longer than five days. The reason I was able to leave is that I stole a car, which was the *real* beginning of my troubles with the law. After that, it was just one thing after another, a lot of it involved in trying to get away from someplace. I was still a kid when I got into trouble for writing hot checks in Phoenix, and then I took to running with some ex-cons and experienced thieves, and I pulled a few jobs with 'em. I ended up tryin' to pull some jobs on my own, and I got caught. One night me and a few guys were drinkin', and we decided to rob a café in Bakersfield. The law got us, and all of a sudden I was headed for San Quentin.

Penthouse: Were you frightened by the prospect of being sent to San Quentin?

Haggard: I sure was. My sentence was from six months to a fifteen-year top, and I remember bein' *real* worried about going to the joint. San Quentin was a dreaded name. I'd already been sent to a couple of places for boys sixteen to eighteen years old, and they'd been pret-ty mean institutions. I recall thinking, "Goddamn, if San Quentin's any rougher than *those* sonofabitches, Lord, what am I in for?" But San Quentin turned out different than I thought. If you had to be sent to prison in 1957, it was actually a good place to be, because you were allowed to do your time in peace, and you were treated like a man.

MCA Records

Penthouse: You once said, "I'm not sure it works like that often, but I'm one guy the prison system straight-ened out. I know damned well I'm a better man for it." Why?

Haggard: For me, San Quentin was like the army would probably be for any other young man: I learned a lot of values there. I went to San Quentin when I was nineteen, and I just kind of grew up there. The joint's changed in a lot of ways since then; but at the time there was a lot of respect and honesty to be found inside San Quentin. You'd tell a man you were going to do something, and it had best be done on that day, 'cause there'd be no place to hide. After you saw a few guys killed, you learned how important honesty is. It seems like life was cheap and honesty meant everything. Besides that, I re-alized that I had to grow up. So I made a choice to get out.

Penthouse: Was San Quentin as violent then as it is now?

Haggard: No, and that's because the age spread of cons when I was there was something like eighteen to sixty. There were enough guys my own age to talk to, and there were enough older fellas to keep things settled down. The problem now is that San Quentin has a younger class of inmate. Most of 'em today are eighteen to thirty years old. The result of having all these young kids bunched up in one place is that San Quentin's been sectioned off into black gangs, white gangs, and Mexi-

can gangs. Whoever's in charge of California's correctional deal is making a big mistake, because if San Quentin had more thirty-five- and forty-year-old guys who could handle themselves and whose heads are on straight, that gang crap wouldn't be *allowed* to go on.

Penthouse: Why not?

Haggard: Because old cons will run a joint, and they just want to do their time and be left alone. Young cons live in a dream world, and I'd say that about eighty percent of 'em are halfway proud of bein' in San Quentin, which is why they walk around with a gung-ho, I'm-a-crook attitude. You don't see that in a more mature penitentiary. Most older cons are damned sorry to be in pris-

on.

Penthouse: How involved were you with music while you were in prison?

Haggard: For the first year I was there, not at all. They used to have five different classifications of custody: maximum custody, close custody, medium custody, medium *B,* and minimum. I was on close custody during my first year, because I'd run away from all those juvenile joints. In other words, I had an escape record. That meant I couldn't get to play no music. But after a year, a friend of mine got my classification changed to medium custody, because they wanted me to play in the warden's show. Every week we'd play for different organizations, like Moose Hall or police or firemen and their wives, or whoever else would come visit the joint. It was actually a pretty good show, with everything from magicians and dancers to country singers.

Penthouse: Had you decided by then to earn your living as a musician?

Haggard: No. I had hopes of it, but when I got out of San Quentin in 1960—I served two years and nine months—I was like a lot of people: I had no idea how to get into music as a professional. So I went to work for my brother, who was an electrical contractor. And after a little while I got a job, playing four nights a week at a place called High Pockets, in Bakersfield. I finally went into music full time when I got a job for six nights a week in another club.

Right about then I met Fuzzy Owen, who had a little record and music-publishing company, and he became my manager. I was awfully naive about business, and Fuzzy could've taken me for whatever he wanted to, because I'd have believed anything he said. Luckily, Fuzzy turned out to be an honest guy, and we wound up workin' together. Everything was goin' along fine until 1961, when I went to Las Vegas and worked for a year at the Nashville-Nevada Club.

Penthouse: What was the problem?

Haggard: I got to gambling. When I got to Las Vegas, I had me a new car and a few thousand dollars in the bank —and before I left, I'd lost everything. My game was "twenty-one"; that's all I ever played, and I guess I shouldn't have. But even though I had to go back to Bakersfield and start all over, my year in Las Vegas didn't turn out all bad, because while I was there I cut my first record, "Sing Me a Sad Song," which made the national and *Billboard* charts. When I got back to Bakersfield, I did a record for Fuzzy's label, called "All My Friends Are Gonna Be Strangers," and it got to be the number-two song on country charts throughout the nation. It also made Capitol Records sit up and take notice, and when they wanted to buy me from the small label Fuzzy owned, we both agreed that we'd better do it.

Penthouse: Most country music stars seem to live in or around Nashville. Is there any particular reason why you don't?

Haggard: Yeah, there is. Since we were looking to get ahead in country music, it didn't make sense to us to go where everybody *else* was. Instead of going to Nashville and gettin' lost in the shuffle, we thought we'd get more notice by workin' steady and stayin' away. You gotta understand that country music isn't like the movie business: to get into films, you pretty much have to go to Hollywood or do well on Broadway. But you can make a record anywhere. Another thing that decided me against going was that I've never known of anyone becoming a star out of Nashville since it became the center of country music. A lot of country stars live there, but they don't *start* there.

Penthouse: Is being a star different from what you im-

agined it might be like when you were a kid?

Haggard: Hell, yes. You fantasize that there's the top of a mountain, but there ain't none. *I* sure don't know of people who've gotten to the top of the mountain, and if there *is* such a place, I bet they were so damned busy they didn't know they were there. Some folks think *I'm* there.

Penthouse: Are you?

Haggard: Only in this sense, there's eight or ten entertainers—not too many more—who can consistently draw audiences across the country, and I think I'm in that bracket. But I can't afford to get sick, and at times that's a terrible weight. It's a scary feeling to carry around, because there's times I *have* been sick. But you've gotta go onstage, 'cause if you don't, it won't just end in a reprimand. You're gonna get sued, and you're gonna pay for it in months to come, 'cause when you come through that town again, people are gonna be bad-mouthin' you.

Penthouse: What goes through your mind when you perform when you're ill?

Haggard: I just get mad, mostly at myself for not puttin' my foot down and sayin' the hell with it and goin' back to my room. It's a strange life, believe me. We probably do 150 days on the road every year, even though we always start out with the intention of only doing eighty.

Penthouse: What effect does being on the road so much have on you?

Haggard: It makes me feel like a stranger when I go home. In fact, I don't really feel like I *have* a home. I've been movin' on down the road for twelve years now. My wife traveled with me for about ten years, and that finally became too much of a problem for her and the kids.

But when I go home, I sit around for two or three days. And then I get to feelin' that you ought to be somewhere; so I *go* somewhere. I wouldn't recommend this kind of life to anybody, and if there was any other way I could make the kind of money I do, I'd change my life in a minute. The money part of it is good, *very* good. But there's a whole lot of things that go with it that sometimes makes me wonder if it's worth it.

Penthouse: What *would* make it worth it?

Haggard: My big dream is to take a year off, and I want to do that before I get too old to enjoy some of the things I've accumulated, like a houseboat and a couple of other things I like to relax with. The trap is a financial one: I have to figure out a way to maintain the band and our organization while I lay around doin' nothing. My real problem, I guess, is that I'm the type of guy who worries about tomorrow the day before yesterday, to the point where if I have to work on Tuesday, I won't be able to enjoy going fishing on Monday. I guess the thing that upsets me most about all this is that I don't know if I can change my ways. And if I don't, that year will never come.

Halsey, Jim

Birthday: October 7
Born: Independence, Kansas
Married: Jo Ann Sherman
Children: s. Sherman Brooks; d. Gina

Jim is personal manager to many major performers and songwriters and head of a vast empire of related businesses, including Thunderbird Enterprises, Jim Halsey Radio Properties, and the Jim Halsey Agency. He served on the Board of Directors of the Academy of Country and Western Music (1969–1970) and on the CMA Board of Directors (1963–1964; 1970–1971).

Hamilton, George, IV

Born: July 19, 1937, Winston-Salem, North Carolina
Married: Adelaide "Tinky"
Children: s. Edwin, George V; d. Mary

While in high school, he formed a three-piece combo; as a freshman at the University of North Carolina in 1956, his recording of "A Rose and a Baby Ruth" was released and sold over a million copies. Ironically, this happened at precisely the time he appeared on the Arthur Godfrey "Talent Scouts" TV Show—and lost! Godfrey later invited the dapper young star back many times afterwards. Torn between pop and country, he made the commitment to the latter in 1959 when he began to appear regularly on the Grand Ole Opry. His country hits for RCA include: "West Texas Highway," "Break My Mind," and the long-time number one, "Abilene" as well as "Before This Day Ends," and "Three Steps to the Phone." In 1977, he completed the longest international concert tour in country music history by performing a total of seventy-three consecutive concerts over a three-month period. The tour included the British Isles and the Scandinavian countries, with George as master of ceremonies at the First International Festival of Country Music in Helsinki. Host of

his own TV show in Canada, Hamilton's more than twenty albums include *West Texas Highway, Canadian Pacific, Fine Lace and Homespun Cloth,* and *Bluegrass Gospel.*

Harris, Emmylou

Born: April 2, 1949, Birmingham, Alabama
Married: Brian Ahern
Children: d. Hallie

She floated around as a folk singer until the Flying Burrito Brothers heard her sing at the Cellar Door in Washington, D.C., in 1971 and asked her to join them. That's when Gram Parsons—known by some as the doomed genius—invited her to work on his Warner's album, *GP.* She traveled with Gram on his spring 1973 tour and that summer assisted on his last LP, *Grievous Angel.* Parsons's strange death shook Emmylou, and instead of pursuing her singing career, she returned to Washington and formed her Angelband. But Parsons had left her a legacy—*her* voice on his last LP so impressed Warner's that they signed her, and by early 1975, her own *Pieces of the Sky* established her as a major artist. The breadth of the material on this top-rated album is wide: Dolly Parton's "Coat of Many Colors"; Merle Haggard's "The Bottle Let Me Down"; plus songs by the Everly Brothers, Waylon Jennings, the Beatles, and the Louvin Brothers' "If I Could Only Win Your Love," which was also released as a single and became a number-one country single. In 1976 her second LP, *Elite Hotel,* featured Buck Owens's classic, "Together Again," the Beatles' "Here, There and Everywhere," Hank Williams's "Jambalaya" and her mentor, Gram Parsons's "Sin City" and "Wheels," plus three country hits, including the number one, "One of These Days." In 1977, *Luxury Liner* offered a slew of famous friends (Emory Gordy, Hank deVito, James Burton, Albert Lee, Glen D. Hardin and—Dolly Parton!). Early 1978 started the new year in fine style with "Quarter

Moon in a Ten Cent Town," produced by Brian Ahern and with the backing of the Hot Band. From this has come "Burn that Candle," "Beneath Still Waters," "Defying Gravity" and Dolly Parton's top-charter, "To Daddy"—and a mid-1978 top-hit single, "Two More Bottles of Wine."

Hart, Freddie

Born: December 21, 1933, Lochapoka, Alabama
Married: Virginia Trendall
Children: s. Freddie, Victor, Joe, Andrew

Helped into the music business by his friend Lefty Frizzell, Freddie Hart signed a recording contract with Capitol in 1953—and subsequently recorded for other companies such as Columbia, Monument, and Kapp before returning to Capitol in 1969. His hits include "The Key's in the Mailbox," "Togetherness," and his 1971 number-one, "Easy Lovin'," which won the CMA Song of the Year Award in 1971 and 1972, followed by "Super Kind of Woman," "The First Time," "Why Lovers Turn to

Warner/Reprise
Dan Reeder

Emmylou Harris

Strangers," among others. In 1972, he made a clean sweep of the CMA Awards, winning Best Entertainer, Top Male Vocalist, Best Song, Best Record, and Best Album. 1978 saw his "Top to Toe" in the top fifty. With his business partner Buck Jones, Hart also owns a trucking firm called Hartline, the trucks being instantly recognizable by the big red hearts on their sides.

Minnie Pearl
South Curtiswood Lane, Nashville
(Next door to the governor's mansion.)

Custom Productions, Inc.

Capitol

Freddie Hart

Homes of Country Music Stars

Exclusive photographs from the *Nashville Tour Map.* For your copy, send $1 to Custom Production Marketing, 102 Linden Drive, Hendersonville, TN 37075.

Custom Productions, Inc.

Custom Productions, Inc.

Tammy Wynette
Franklin Road, Nashville

Eddy Arnold
Granny White Pike, Nashville, Tennessee

Custom Productions, Inc.

Custom Productions, Inc.

Custom Productions, Inc.

Ronnie Milsap
Franklin Road, Nashville

Johnny Cash
Caudill Drive, Hendersonville, Tennessee

Homes of Country Music Stars

Custom Productions, Inc.

Johnny Rodriguez
Hillview Drive, near Brentwood, Tennessee
(Reached from Old Hickory Boulevard.)

Roy Acuff
Moss Rose Drive, Nashville
(Note tour group on the lawn.)

Porter Wagoner
Franklin Road, Nashville
(He has sold this house and will probably move soon.)

Custom Productions, Inc.

Custom Productions, Inc.

Marty Robbins
Long Valley Road, near Brentwood, Tennessee

Custom Productions, Inc.

Roy Orbison
Caudill Drive, Hendersonville, Tennessee

Custom Productions, Inc.

Waylon Jennings
Old Hickory Boulevard, Brentwood, Tennessee
(Newly purchased home.)

Webb Pierce
North Curtiswood Lane, Nashville

137

Howard, Harlan

Born: September 8, 1929, Lexington, Kentucky
Married: Jan Howard (div.)
Children: s. Kenneth, Harlan, Jr.; d. Donna Gail Taylor

Winner of ten BMI songwriting awards in 1961, he is one of country music's most prolific songwriters. "Pick Me Up on Your Way Down" was his first hit in 1958, followed by "Heartache by the Number," "I Fall to Pieces," "Sunday Morning Christian," "Down to Earth," and "Three Steps to the Phone."

Hunley, Con

Born: 1945, Luttrell, Tennessee

In 1963, he was working as a bundle boy at a Knoxville mill, playing the piano at night at the Corner Lounge, a local club. After a stint in the air force and a series of gigs with various groups, he formed his own band and signed with Warner Records. In 1978, his singles releases included, "Cry, Cry Darlin', " "Hangin' On," and "You've Still Got a Place in My Heart."

Husky, Ferlin

Born: December 3, 1925, Flat River, Missouri
Married: Marvis Thompson (div.); Betty (div.), with four subsequent wives and divorces
Children: s. David, Kelly, Terry, Preston; d. Donna, Dana, Denise

One of the most colorful and diverse personalities in country music, Ferlin (his real name) first performed in Bakersfield, California, under the name of Terry Preston while also doing comedy routines as Simon Crum. As Terry Preston, his first hit was "A Dear John Letter" in 1953, then he switched back to Ferlin for "Gone" (1957), which sold over a million. In 1958, his Simon Crum made the charts with a comedy song "Country Music Is Here to Stay," while Ferlin himself became a movie star in *Country Music Holiday* with Zsa Zsa Gabor.

Warner Bros.

Con Hunley

Subsequent hits include "Wings of a Dove," "Champagne Ladies and Blue Ribbon Babies," and a retrospective, *The Country Sounds of Ferlin Husky.*

Jackson, Stonewall

Born: November 6, 1932, Tabor City, North Carolina
Married: Juanita Carmene Wair
Children: s. Stonewall, Jr.

While serving in the navy in the early fifties, he wrote songs and put on shows for his fellow crewmen. On release from duty in 1954, he went to Nashville and played some of his material for Wesley Rose, of Acuff-Rose, who arranged for his audition with the Grand Ole Opry. Stonewall (his real name) became an Opry regular and soon signed a recording contract with Columbia. His first number-one song was in 1958, "Life to Go"; his first million seller was "Waterloo" in 1959. Other records include "Sadness in a Song," "Stamp Out Loneliness," and *Greatest Hits,* Vols. 1 and 2.

"Jamboree USA"

Every Saturday night in Wheeling, West Virginia, you can attend this live broadcast on radio station WWVA. Big-name guest artists include Charlie Rich, Loretta Lynn, Johnny and June Cash, Mel Tillis, Buck Owens, and others. One of the oldest country music radio shows in the country (second probably to the Grand Ole Opry), "Jamboree USA" first went on the air in January 1933. In 1969, it found a permanent home in the new Capitol Music Hall, which seats 2,466 people. There are other things to see and do around Wheeling, including exhibitions of mountain crafts, historic sites, and be lavished by southern cooking. For complete details on dates, package tours, and facilities, write: WWVA Jamboree USA, Capitol Music Hall, Wheeling, WV 26003, (304) 232-1170.

James, Sonny

Born: May 1, 1929, Hackleburg, Alabama
Married: Doris

After several years of being voted among the top five of male country music performers by *Billboard, Record World* and *Cash Box,* he was accorded the singular honor of being named Country Music's Male Artist of the Decade by *Record World* in 1977. Starting with his multimillion seller "Young Love" in 1956, he has had a string of phenomenal hits. For seven years, every single he released became a national hit. That's twenty-seven number-one records in a row, the longest string of top records in country music history. His *200 Years of Country Music* album traces the history and basic styles of country music, with many of the original bands and musicians. James's phrasing, authentic sound, and historic integrity make this a classic. As producer-arranger, he is responsible for three award-winning LPs by Marie Osmond, starting with the multimillion selling *Paper Roses.* A multitime Grammy and CMA nominee, he and his group, The Southern Gentlemen, appear regularly on major TV shows and at country fairs, rodeos, and concert halls across the country. (In 1976, he made over 130 personal appearances.) The Country Music Hall of Fame has on display a homemade guitar that Sonny James's father made for him when he was three years old. Among his LPs are *Guitars of Country Music, A Mi Esposa Con Amor, Country Artist of the Decade,* and *When Something Is Wrong.*

Jennings, Waylon

Born: June 15, 1937, Littlefield, Texas
Married: Jessi Colter

An RCA Records ad for his "Are You Ready for the Country" advises: "Take him or leave him. He's been called abrasive because he's

Waylon Jennings

twice with two LPs making their debuts on the *Cash Box* charts in the number one position. They were his *Waylon and Willie* (with Willie Nelson, of course) on February 11, and *I've Always Been Crazy* on October 21, which made further history by being the first country LP to "ship gold"—more than one million copies!

Jones, George Glen

Born: September 12, 1931, Saratoga, Texas
Married: Tammy Wynette (div.)
Children: d. Tamala Georgette

Since 1955, he has recorded hit after hit, his number-one songs including "White Lightning," "She Thinks I Still Care," "A Good Year for the Roses," and "Walk Through This World with Me." In 1962 and 1963, *Cash Box* and *Billboard* voted him Number One Male Vocalist. Amazingly, all of his one-hundred-plus albums and countless singles have made the country top ten since 1956. When his six-year marriage to Tammy Wynette ended, she responded with solo recordings of "D-I-V-O-R-C-E" and "Stand by Your Man," and then the two got together for "Golden Ring" and "Near You" among others on their joint album, *We Go Together.* His big 1978 LP was *George Jones: Bartender's Blues.* His Possum Holler Club in Nashville has been so successful that now he's opened branches in Topeka, Kansas, and Mobile, Alabama.

Jones, "Grandpa" (Louis M.)

Born: October 20, 1913, Niagra, Kentucky
Married: Ramona Riggins
Children: s. Mark; d. Eloise, Alisa

A member of the Grand Ole Opry since 1946, he took the name "Grandpa" in 1935 when he was only twenty-two! As a performer-comedian, he sings and plays the banjo on "Hee Haw" and records for Monument and Decca.

Waylon Jennings and Willie Nelson's wife Connie.

©1974 Melinda Wickman

honest to a fault. He's been called a beauty because he's Waylon to the core. He's been called a hard ass, a pussycat, an outlaw, a sweetheart, and a whole lot more!" *Seventeen* magazine has called him "the Humphrey Bogart of country music." The CMA named him Male Vocalist of the Year for 1975. He and Willie Nelson have given a new meaning to the word "outlaw." All of this means he's come a long way since the early fifties when he was one of the youngest disc jockeys in radio history (in Littlefield, Texas), moving on eventually to Lubbock, where rock star Buddy Holly invited him to join his group as electric bass player. Fate kept him from the plane flight that took Buddy Holly's life. A shaken Waylon then formed his own group, The Waylors, appearing in clubs where Chet Atkins happened to hear him and signed him for RCA. His major hits include

"Heartaches by the Number," "Honky-Tonk Heroes," "Good-Hearted Woman," "Ruby, Don't Take Your Love to Town," "I'm a Ramblin' Man," "Ol' Waylon," and "The Outlaws" with Willie, Jessi, and Tompall Glaser. In 1978, he made country music chart history

RCA Records and Tapes

The Kendalls, Royce and Jeannie
Royce

Born: Sept. 25, 1934, St. Louis, Missouri
Married: Melba
Children: Jeannie

Jeannie

Born: Nov. 13, 1954, St. Louis, Missouri

This father-and-daughter duo won the 1977 Best Country Group Grammy award for "Heaven's Just a Sin Away," one of country music's top sellers that year and the CMA award for Best Single of 1978. The next record, "It Don't Feel Like Sinnin' to Me," followed the first up the charts in early 1978. As a boy, Royce and his brother Floyce had played and sung on small Arkansas radio stations. After a stint in the army, Royce moved around, married Melba, and settled down in St. Louis where they ran a combination barbershop and beauty salon. Their only child, Jeannie, loved singing duets with her daddy. When she was fifteen, they went to Nashville to cut a custom record. A local producer heard it and signed them with STOP, a small Nashville label. Their first commercial session included John Denver's "Leaving on a Jet Plane," "Two Divided by Love," and "You've Lost that Loving Feeling." The next few years, they moved to ABC Dot and United Artists, trying to find their own identity until finally, in 1976, they found producer Brien Fisher at Ovation and recorded *Making Believe* and a single, "Live and Let Live," a good song and doing fine—except that the radio stations were swamped with demands for the *B* side of the record, a little number called "Heaven's Just a Sin Away." Next came "It Don't Feel Like Sinnin' to

The Kendalls   Bruno of Hollywood

Me," and, from the LP *Old-Fashioned Live*, "Sweet Desire," "The Pittsburgh Stealers" and the title single.

Kershaw, Doug (Douglas James)

Born: January 24, 1936, Tiel Ridge, Cameron Parrish, Louisiana
Married: Elsie Carol (div.), Pam
Children: s. Doug, Jr., Victor, Zachary

The "Ragin'" Cajun made his first public appearance at age eight, singing and playing the fiddle at a place called The Bucket of Blood where performers worked behind a protective screen of chicken wire. With his brother Rust, he recorded "Louisiana Man" for Hickory Records in 1961. In the late sixties, he and Bob Dylan were the only two guests on Johnny Cash's first TV show, which led to his being signed by Warner Brothers Records. Hits include *The Ragin' Cajun, Spanish Moss, Mama Kershaw's Boy, Alive and Pickin,* and *Flip, Flop & Fly.* On the road, his wild and wonderful fiddling is augmented by his band, Slidin' Jake, comprised of Max Schwennsen, lead singer and guitar; Al Kaatz, vocals and guitar; Rose deArmas, vocals, guitar, and percussion; Marty

Doug Kershaw   Warner/Reprise

Vadalabene, drums; and Brian Smith, bass.

Kosser, Michael

Born: December 19, 1941, Mt. Vernon, New York

Songwriter for such artists as Barbara Mandrell, George Jones, Ray Price, Skeeter Davis, Tammy Wynette, Tommy Overstreet, Bill Anderson, Billy "Crash" Craddock —and his 1978 hit, "It Don't Feel like Sinnin' to Me" for the Kendalls —Michael is author of a songwriter's do-it-yourself book, *Bringing It to Nashville*. (For details, write: Cumberland Valley Books, Box 643, Brentwood, TN 37027.)

Here is some advice from the book to all aspiring songwriters headed for Nashville.

Once you decide to go, plan what you'll need to take. Basics include the following:

Money. It's not a bad idea to put together enough cash to carry you three to six months in Nashville. It's impossible at this point to estimate how much that will be a year from now, so I won't try. Don't—DON'T come to Nashville with several thousand dollars in cash. Put a few bucks in your pocket and get a cashier's check at the bank for the rest. When you arrive in Nashville, one of the first things you'll want to do is deposit that check in a bank convenient to Music Row.

Car. At this time the Nashville metropolitan area does not have the best public transportation in the world, and a person operating in the opportunistic business of music does not want to be at the mercy of bus schedules anyway, so get yourself a car and put it in good working order before you leave for Nashville.

Clothes. Nashville's Music-Row dress requirements are flexible, but a newcomer can hurt himself if his taste in personal appearance is too exotic. Few people on Music Row wear suits, but that doesn't mean you shouldn't. At this writing, denims and tasteful westernwear are in, but not rhinestones and glitter. It's sufficient to say that you're in Nashville to show people your songs, so don't try and wow 'em with weird sartorial flourishes or some of musicdom's less charitable citizens will mark you down as strange and unfit for them to associate with. You the new songwriter have enough problems without stirring up people's biases.

No matter how you dress, you'd better have at least one good suit, with tie and clean matching shirt because (1) sooner or later you'll have to look for a job, and (2), if you happen to run afoul of the law, you'll probably get better treatment from the judge if you come to court dressed in respectable attire.

Tools of the trade. Bring the instrument you compose with, of course, guitar, electric piano, whatever. I'm assuming you are not only a lyricist, but do your own tunes. It's fair to say that if you're strictly a lyricist,

Warner/Reprise

Doug Kershaw

your chances of making it as a new writer in Nashville are almost nil. While most Nashville writers think of themselves as stronger either in words or music, almost all are capable of writing a complete song themselves. Take a look at some old sheet music published in New York's Tin Pan Alley. Chances are the credits read something like this: Music by Joe Doakes, lyrics by Sam Schwartz. You almost never see that kind of billing in Nashville. Cowritten songs in Nashville almost always read something like: words and music by Joe Doakes and Sam Schwartz. Nashville writers generally regard a song as being an inseparable marriage of melody and lyrics, and cowriters generally participate in creating both. I do not know one reputable Nashville publisher who as a matter of policy will consider taking a poem or lyric (other than a recitation) without a melody, so if you can't do the music, learn how before you come to Nashville.

This doesn't mean you have to *read* music. Most Nashville songwriters, many of whom play guitar quite well, can't read a note.

In addition to your instrument, you must bring tape copies and lyric sheets of all your songs. The following information is important.

Do not take huge tapes with twelve songs to a reel. Take a bunch of five-inch reels with no more than three songs to a reel. You don't need elaborate studio demos, just a well-done home tape with someone singing the lyric clearly and one instrument (probably piano or guitar) supplying chords and rhythm in the background. Although you'll hear stories of producers who heard hit songs through terrible demos, it helps you professionally if the singing and picking on the tape are good. Make sure the voice is far enough out front of the instrument for every word to be easily understood.

The tapes should be recorded at 7½ inches per second. Tapes should be brand new, or at least wiped clean with a magnetic bulk eraser before recording, because home ma-

chines are generally quarter track stereo, and publishers' machines are usually half track, so if you use a previously recorded tape, the publisher's machine might pick up some old signals you'd forgotten existed, making your tape worthless.

Most publishers in Nashville work entirely with reel-to-reel tape, so if you walk in with casettes or cartridge tapes, you'll meet with a lot of unnecessary disappointment.

Copyrights. Your songs are protected by law whether or not you've copyrighted them, but without a copyright it could be difficult to prove that you wrote the song, in the event of someone's stealing it. Copyrighting is an expensive process, and song theft is not considered a pressing problem in Nashville. In fact, publishing companies generally do not copyright a song until it is either recorded or scheduled to be performed on the air. This does not mean that there aren't people in the Nashville music scene who would steal you blind. Generally, these so-called song sharks are after your money, not your songs (they probably wouldn't be able to get them recorded anyway), so I can't see any necessity of filling out copyright forms and sending them along with your hard-earned dollars to Washington.

The new writer in town does run the risk of bringing his song into an unethical publisher who might like the idea of your song enough to steal the idea and write his own song around it. It would be almost impossible to prove such a theft in a court of law, so there's no sense worrying about it. Besides, most publishers bend over backwards to avoid such situations.

Along with your tapes, it's important that you bring along a tape recorder (again, reel-to-reel), so you can remember the tunes you've just written, and so you can make your own demos to pitch to the publishers as you write them. Everybody has heard stories of the great new writer who walks into the publisher's office with his battered guitar and proceeds to knock him out with a series of songs played right at him live, but today if a publisher likes your song, he's going to want a tape he can play at his leisure so he can decide whether he really believes in the song before he takes you into the studio to make a more sophisticated demo.

Some amateur writers pay good money to get professional lead sheets made of their songs. Lead sheets show the music and chords as well as the lyric, but few professional Nashville writers make their own lead sheets unless they have their own publishing companies. All the Nashville publisher needs is that tape and a neatly typed or hand-printed copy of the lyric. If you happen to own a typewriter, bring it. It'll come in handy.

Those two- and three-song demo tapes you take to the publishers should be neatly boxed. The boxes should have labels listing the songs on the tape, plus your name, address, and phone number.

Additional materials. Keep on hand a supply of blank tape and reels, typing paper, large note pads (legal pads or spiral notebooks), and a supply of pens and pencils. It's a good idea to carry around a pocket-sized note pad at all times. The basis of that hit song is a great idea, and ideas can pop up at any time. When that idea comes, write it down, or it'll slip your mind. Keep a pad at the side of your bed when you go to sleep. There's nothing more frustrating for a writer than to wake up in the middle of night with a great idea, only to lose it because you were too groggy to get up and hunt for a piece of paper to put that idea on. Keep that pad by your bed, so you only have to grope for a pen to scribble enough to remind you when you wake up in the morning.

A radio is a necessity! Whatever music you're writing, if you want to be commercial, it makes sense to keep in touch with what's happening. Ronny Light, who produced hit records with Waylon Jennings, Kenny Price, and Skeeter Davis, bought

copies of every record that broke into the *Billboard* Top Twenty charts, country *and* pop, while he produced for RCA.

Another useful item is an attache case. Publishers and producers get scared to death when they see someone walk into their office with a half-dozen tapes under his arm. If you walk in with an attache case you look neat, streamlined, less threatening. Even if the publisher sees a dozen tapes in the case when you open it to give him one, he might figure you just happen to be carrying them around. But if he thinks you intend to play him everything you ever wrote, he's liable to hate you instantly.

It might not be a bad idea to bring all these materials with you to Nashville, so that when you arrive you can devote your entire attention to the problems at hand—finding a place to stay and making those first difficult inroads into the strange world of Music City, USA.

Kristofferson, Kris

Born: June 22, 1936, Brownsville, Texas
Married: Fran Beir (divorced); Rita Coolidge
Children: d. Casey (1974)

The son of a retired Air Force major general, Kris moved to San Mateo, California, as a teenager and seemed headed for an academic career. At Pomona College, he majored in creative writing and won first prize in an *Atlantic Monthly* short story contest. A superb athlete (football and boxing) and campus leader, he won a Rhodes Scholarship to Oxford University in England and wrote two novels. Unhappily, they were rejected by publishers so he joined the Army, went to jump school, Ranger school, flight school, married Fran, became a pilot, and was stationed in Germany as a helicopter pilot. By 1961, he was writing songs and performing at NCO

Kris Kristofferson and his wife, singer Rita Coolidge.

Kris with Burt Reynolds and Brian Dennehy in the movie Semi-Tough

in concert led to his being cast in his first movie, a cameo role in Dennis Hopper's *The Last Movie.* Fans who never turned on to country music suddenly discovered Kris. Other movies followed: *Cisco Pike* with Gene Hackman, *Blume in Love* with George Segal, *Pat Garrett & Billy The Kid* with James Coburn and Bob Dylan, *Alice Doesn't Live Here Any More,* and *The Sailor That Fell from Grace with the Sea* with Sara Miles—and then superstardom opposite superstar-plus Barbra Streisand in *A Star Is Born. Semi-Tough* with Burt Reynolds and Jill Clayburgh and *Convoy* with Ali McGraw have clinched his unique position as the only country star who is also a rock star and also a movie star who could have, if he had chosen, merely stayed home and concentrated on song-writing and still made history. In 1978, he shaved off his beard to play a World War II pilot in *Hanover Street.*

clubs. In 1965, transferred stateside to become an English instructor at West Point, he took a two-week leave in Nashville that changed his life. Playing his guitar, singing, hanging out with people like Johnny Cash, he knew that this was where he belonged. He quit the Army and took a job as janitor at Columbia Records Nashville studios for $58 a week. It took four years of poverty, odd jobs, and constant striving before Monument Records launched him as the major singer-poet of the seventies with "Me and Bobby McGee," "Sunday Morning Coming Down," "Help Me Make It through the Night," and others. In November, 1973, both his single, "Why Me" and his LP, *The Silver Tongued Devil and I* made gold, followed two weeks later by the LP *Jesus Was a Capricorn.* In 1974, he and his new wife, Rita Coolidge, cut their first two dual LPs, *Full Moon* and *Breakaway.*

Personal appearances on TV and

Lee, Brenda (Brenda Mae Tarpley)

Born: December 11, 1944, Augusta, Georgia
Married: Charles R. Shacklett
Children: d. Julie Leanne, Jolie Lenee

She made her debut at six and was discovered by Red Foley at twelve. Her first big record was Hank Williams's "Jambalaya," followed by "One Step at a Time," "I'm Sorry," "Baby Face," "Coming on Strong," and "All Alone Am I."

Her "Rocking Around The Christmas Tree" was one of three million-selling singles. *Billboard* and *Cash Box* named her Most Programmed Female Vocalist for 1961–1965. Among her 1978 appearances was Glen Campbell's TV Christmas special.

Lee, Dickey (Dickey Lipscomb)

Born: September 21, 1941, Memphis, Tennessee
Married: Linda
Children: Danna, Amanda

His "Patches" was a million seller in 1962. "I Saw Linda Yesterday," "Laurie (Strange Things Happen)," and "The Girl from Peyton Place" became top-ten hits in the seventies. His RCA single, "Never-Ending Song of Love," was number one on the country charts in 1971. "Ashes of Love" and "Baby Bye-Bye" reached top ten prominence. As a writer, his material has been performed and recorded by Jerry Lee Lewis, George Jones, Glen Campbell, Brenda Lee, and others. In 1978, his hit single as a performer was "It's Not Easy."

Joni Lee

Lee, Joni

Born: 1958
Married: Chris Prater

Joni Lee, Conway Twitty's daughter, began her career in a duet with her father, "Don't Cry Joni," followed by "I'm Sorry Charlie." In 1976, *Angel on My Shoulder* came out as both an album and a single.

Dickey Lee

147

Zella Lehr

Lehr, Zella

No statistics available.

Her father was a descendant of a long line of performers whose show-business roots can be traced back to seventeenth-century England—and he wasn't about to go against that much tradition!

Mr. Lehr packed up his wife, two sons, and Zella, and left Burbank, California, for Europe, where he put together a vaudeville act. The act consisted of rope spinning, unicycle riding, juggling, singing, and dancing. Zella learned to ride the unicycle and juggle on the family's tour of Europe and Asia and made her singing debut in England—all at the ripe old age of six! The act was a big hit in Europe and only returned to

the United States following the death of Zella's father.

The return to the United States signaled the end of the act, and Zella started out on her own, singing in local clubs in New York and doing TV commercials. Zella's first love, like her father's, was country music, and when she received an offer to appear at the Flamingo Hotel in Las Vegas, she organized her own group, built a routine around country music, and began working the Las Vegas-Tahoe circuit.

As her fame grew, Zella began appearing on national television, doing guest spots on such shows as "The Steve Allen Show," "The Rosie Grier Show," and "The Real Tom Kennedy Show." She also landed herself an appearance on "Hee

Haw" by riding a unicycle into the producer's office, a stunt that so thoroughly intrigued them, they signed her on the spot.

An appearance at a local nightclub in Nashville proved to be the break Zella had been waiting for. RCA executive Jerry Bradley and producer Pat Carter caught her show and subsequently signed her to an RCA recording contract. In 1978, her rendition of Dolly Parton's "Two Doors Down" reached top-twenty status followed by "Danger, Heartbreak Ahead.

Lewis, Jerry Lee

Born: September 29, 1935, Ferriday, Louisiana

His first record on the Sun label that spawned Elvis Presley was "Crazy Arms," which became a respectable hit but was only the preliminary to "Whole Lotta Shakin' Going On," which surfaced in June 1957 and has sold over six million copies. Following that was "Great Balls of Fire," a mere five-million seller. Both of these incredible hits were number one on the pop, country, and R & R charts. (Only Elvis has matched this distinction.) Like many fifties' rockers, he suffered a slump in the sixties, complicated by public reaction to his marrying his thirteen-year-old cousin. His concerts continued to draw huge crowds, and in 1968, he cut his first full-blown country music session. "What Made Milwaukee Famous Has Made a Loser Out of Me," "Your Cheatin' Heart," and "You Win Again" are among his early country hits. With over twenty-five albums, he has released some of his best singles in a series of *The Best of Jerry Lee Lewis* collections. In 1978, Vol. 2 includes "Chantilly Lace," "Would You Take Another Chance on Me," "Middle Age Crazy," "There Must Be More to Love Than This," and "Let's Put It Back Together Again." His many TV appearances include the "Rolling Stone 10th Anniversary TV Special" and he is also in a film based on the life of Alan Freed.

Lingo

Locomotive Whistles

Trains figure prominently in folk and country music—*Wabash Cannonball, Fireball Mail, Orange Blossom Special,* to name but a few. While lonesome whistles beckon men in trouble and women in pain, locomotive whistles are in fact used as signals of communication between the engineer and the other trainmen.

Here are some of the most frequently used signals:

One Short Apply brakes, stop. This signal has two meanings and is used ordinarily in emergencies. When an engineer sees some other movement that is in danger, he will whistle one short sound to them, meaning "stop." Or, an engineer may whistle one short to a brakeman or switchman, meaning that he should set hand brakes on cars.

Two Short Answer to a signal. This the engineer uses to acknowledge that he has heard or seen a signal that affects his movement.

Three Short Back up. When an engineer wants to make a reverse movement or receives a signal to make a reverse movement, he gives three short whistles.

Four Short Call for signals. This the engineer uses when he wants someone to give him a signal so he will know what move to make.

One Long Approaching stations. This is used when approaching a station, to notify employees there that the train is coming.

Two Long Release brakes. Proceed. Used to notify members of his crew that the engineer is ready to move ahead, and to release any brakes that they may have applied.

Two Long, One Short and **One Long** Approaching highway and street crossings.

One Long and **Three Short** Flagman protect rear of train. When the train stops, this signal reminds the flagman at the rear of the train that it is necessary for him to go back with a red signal and torpedoes and fusees to stop any following train.

Four (or Five) Long Recall flagman. When engineer is again ready to proceed, he whistles either four long or five long sounds, depending on the direction the flagman has gone, to recall him to the train.

Talking "Southern"

From the Atlantic seaboard moving west through the states of Kentucky, Alabama, Tennessee, Mississippi, Missouri, and into Texas, the southern vocabulary and pronunciation is a mixture of two things: regional dialect and self-mocking exaggeration. As a Northerner often accused of having chicken fat in my ears, I've listened long and hard to certain lyrics, feverishly trying to fathom them until in a sudden revelation they make sense. One of my earliest challenges was Johnny Cash singing about an "exican dog" that drove me crazy until I realized it was an "egg-sucking dog." More recently, Jimmy Buffett's "lost shaker of salt" in his song "Margaritaville" had me apoplectic with frustration—until a kind friend eased my pain with a

Jerry Lee Lewis

Jerry Lee Lewis & Co./Mercury

translation. Southern lingo includes talk from Virginia, Charlestonese, Mountain, Nashville and Texlish (Texas-English), many of these overlapping. The examples here are given phonetically and are fun to read aloud.

A

Abode   A piece of wood, as "han' me *a bode* to hit this mule."

Aboot   Approximately.

Ah   The thing you see with and the personal pronoun denoting individuality. "*Ah* think *Ah*'ve got somethin' in mah *ah*."

Ahmoan   An expression of intent. "*Ahmoan* have a little drink. You want one?"

Aint   Sister of your parents.

Air   What you could hear with: "Friends, Romans, countrymen, lend me your *airs*."

Argon   A Pacific Coast state just north of California.

Arm   I am.

Armageddon   I'm gonna get.

Arn   Iron.

Aster   "Ah *aster* last night."

At'tair   Contraction used to indicate the specific item desired: "Pass me *at'tair* gravy please."

Auto   An expression of intent. "I *auto* go to work, but Ah'm tared."

Awl   A dark fluid used to lubricate engines. "Ah like that car, but it sure does use a lot of *awl*."

Aw Riot   All right.

Ax   "Ah *ax* you this."

B

Bah   Bye, as in "So long!"

Balks   A container, such as a match*balks*.

Bare   A beverage made from malt and hops.

Barn   "I was *barn* in Kentucky."

Barter   Something to spread on bread.

Bawl   What water does at 212 degrees Fahrenheit. "That gal can't even *bawl* water without burnin' it."

Beckon   Meat from a pig, often eaten with a-igs for brake-fuss.

Bob Wahr   Barbed wire.

Bone   Blessed event as, "I was *bone* in the South."

Bottle   A military engagement.

Bow-At   Something you sail in.

Boy   To purchase.

Braid   What you make toe-est from, to go along with beckon and a-igs for brake-fuss.

Bread   (Raised) "Ah was *bread* in Caintucky."

Bucks   Something the library is full of.

Bud   What wobbles sweet in the springtime.

Bull   Nickname for William. (Another nickname: Wolly)

Bum   An instrument of destruction, as the H-*bum*.

Bun   Consume by heat, as "When you make toe-est, don't *bun* the braid."

Bus'   Upper part of the female body.

C

Cad   To tote, as "I *cad* ma bride over the threshold."

Caller   Part of a shirt that goes around the neck.

Canada   Politician running for public office.

Cane Chew   Aren't you able to, as "*Cane chew* talk like a good Southerner?"

Caught   A little bed.

Caw   Whut you ride in (a Fode *caw*)

Cheer   (Whut you sit on) "Pull up a *cheer* and set down."

Chess   A strong balks (box).

Chile   A youngun'.

Coal   Ailment that causes sniffles.

Coarse   Certainly.

Coat   Where they got that jedge an' all, as "Stannup for hizzoner, *coat's* in session."

Coined   Humane. "He was always coined to animals."

Conduit   Impossible to accomplish.

Cup   A place called home by hens, as "Where's Wolly?" "Wolly's paintin' the hen *cup*."

Cyst   "Can Ah *cyst* you with those packages, ma'am?"

D

D'Earth   The world in which we live.

Des Moines   They belong to me.

Did   Not alive, as "He's *did*."

Dollar   Less sharp, as "My knife was *dollar* than his-own."

Drug   Hauled.

E

Etlan-na   The city General Sherman burned during the War for Southern Independence. "*Etlan-na* is kind of like a New York with pecan trees."

F

Faints   A barricade of wood or brick.

Famine   Tilling the soil, as "I've been *famine* all ma life."

Fan Ella   The flavor of white ice cream.

Far   A burnin' pile of sticks.

Far'm   To take off the payroll, as "If he don't wake up, *far'm!*"

Feel   An open space.

Flow   What you stand on in a house.

Fode   1. A caw. 2. Tennessee Ernie's last name.

Foe   Whut comes after three.

Forks   Bushy-tailed animal hunted by riders in red coats.

Frustrate   Tops; initial ranking.

Fur   Over yonder.

Fussed   Whut comes before second.

G

Garner   A man who tends to flowerbeds.

Gate   To obtain.

Gay-yet   Opening in a fence.

Go-it   A smelly animal which eats tin cans.

Granite   Conceded or given, as "He was *granite* a pardon by the guv-ner."

Griyuts   What no southern breakfast would be complete without—grits. "Ah like *griyuts* with butter and sawt on 'em, but Ah purely love 'em with red-eye gravy."

Groan   Increasing in size.

Gull   A young female human.

H

Hail   The abode of integrationists, some Damn Yankees, and other evil spirits.

Hair   At this place.

Hale   Where General Sherman is going fow what he did to Etlanna. General Sherman said, "War is *hale*," and he made sure it was.

Halo   A greeting similar to "How do you do" (see *Higher*), as "*Halo,*

Gid Tanner

Woolly, what are you doing hanging around here?" or "Higher, Bubber, I'm just hanging around for the hail of it."

Harmony   Cooked grits.

Hate   Heat.

Hawsers   Hay-eating quadrupeds.

Heide   Greeting as in "*Heide,* folks."

Hep   1. assist, "*Hep* stamp out iggnorants." 2. Whut you holler when you're drowning.

Herring   The auditory function, as "Pappa's hard of *herring.*"

Higher   See Halo.

Hominy   What number?

Hone   Something on an auto that you blow.

I

Ice Cool   A school for younguns before college.

J

Jell   Place of confinement for criminals.

K

Key-Yard   A heavy piece of paper, like a post-*key-yard.*

Kin   Something usually made of tin that food comes packed in.

L

Lack   Enjoy, as "I *lack* fried chicken."

Lane   Lying down.

Lawn   Not short.

Layman   A fruit from which *layman*-ade is made, as "Is that your *layman*-ade?"
"No, that's pappa's zone."
"Well, poet back in the pitcher, 'cause pappa's now drinking bare."

Lean   A little road, as "Lovers' *lean.*"

Lease   The smallest.

Likker   Whisky, either the amber kind bought in stores or the homemade white kind the federal authorities frown upon.

Loin   Storying. Not telling the trut'.

Lore   To let down.

Loss   To mislay, as "He *loss* his match balks."

Lot   "Jeannie with the *lot*-brown hair."

Lucid   Leggo it.

M

Mah   My, as in "*Mah* fella Markins."

Mare   Hizzoner, a city's chief executive.

Marge   Marriage.

Mihyonaire   Millionaire.

Mine-eyes   Salad dressing.

Minuet   You and I have dined.

Mow   "Pass me some *mow* 'lasses," fussed time say "Pass the 'lasses."

Muttered   A yellow condiment that goes well with hot dogs.

N

Nawth   Yankeeland.

Noise   Pleasant, as "*Noise* weather we're having."

O

Oil-and   A body of land surrounded by water.

P

Packing   Maneuvering an auto to the curb.

Pain   A writing instrument mightier than the sword.

Pastor   Field where cows graze.

Pat   Portion, but not all.

Paunch   Blow struck with the fist.

Pea-Pickers   Folks from the South.

Pie-sun   What you put out to kill roaches, which they usually thrive on.

Pin   Whut you keep hogs in—"a hog *pin.*"

Play-it   Something you eat grits off of.

Poach   A verandah.

Poet   To transfer a liquid, as "*Poet* from the pitcher to the glass."

Police   Term of polite request.

Prayed   A large public procession, as "That was some *prayed* they had downtown."

Pre-shade   Grateful for, as "I *preshade* the compliment."

R

Rah Chair   Where you are at.

Rat Cheer   Not there, here, like "lay it *rat cheer.*"

Rilly   Really.

Rot   Perfectly agreeable, such as "It's all *rot* with me."

Rum   An enclosed space within a building.

S

Sandy Claws   The fat jolly man who comes down the chimney every Christmas: "Did *Sandy Claws* bring you a lot of presents?"

Sane   Speaking, as "I can hardly hair what he's *sane.*"

Send-wishes   Items of food made with bread, handy for a picnic.

Sex   One less than seven.

Shore   Same as *show*; sure.

Shot   Not long.

Show   Yes.

Snow   To breathe loudly and heavily while sleeping.

Sprang   When the buds wobble sweet.

T

Tarred   Weary, as "Ah'm too *tarred* to go bowlin' tonight."

Teax-issss   Texas.

Thud   Whut comes after second, as "This only my *thud* mint julep."

Tin-Sin-Stow   Where everything used to cost a foive and doyme: "Les go in the *tin-sin-stow.*"

Toad   Past tense of tell; "Ah *toad* you never to do that."

Toil   Thin slabs of baked clay.

Toll   Past tense of tell.

Ton   To swerve; to *ton* around.

Tone   Ripped.

Toy   Cravat.

Toyed   Something that ebbs and flows off the shore.

Traffic   Something stupendous.

Loretta Lynn

MCA Records

True Hurled, as "He *true* the ball."
Tuck Removed.

V

Varmit A pesky two- or four-legged pest.
Version The kind of queen that Elizabeth I of England was.
Vertigo "What happened to him?"
Violet Violent.
Voice A squeezing tool, attached to a workbench.

W

Wheel The sort of a mammal that Moby Dick was.
Wretched The first name for which "Dick" is the nickname.

Y

Yawl Mode of address used by N'Yawkers when visiting in the South, as "*Yawl* come to see me."
Year To listen.

Lynn, Loretta

Born: April 14, 1935, Butcher's Hollow, Kentucky
Married: Oliver V. (Mooney) Lynn
Children: s. Jack Benny, Ernest Ray; d. Betty Sue, Clara Marie, Patsy Ellen, Peggy Jean

The following is a touching excerpt from the autobiography Coal Miner's Daughter *by Loretta Lynn.*

At first, I had to work clubs to sell for the jukeboxes, to get known. You'd have to work three or four shows a night to make any money, and that was hard work. Also, you'd get guys who'd been drinking and think that gave 'em the right to grab you and hug you. I don't mind some old boy if he's with his family or something. But the way some guys in those drinking clubs grab you—now that's not family!

I don't have anything against people drinking, as long as they don't mess up other people's lives. But I've got to be honest and say I don't like playing clubs because of the hard work and the way a few guys carry on.

I was still kind of backwards when I got to Nashville for the first time. Doo had to stay back with the babies, so Mr. Burley hired me a girl to travel with. She was a big redhead, I think her name was Mack—and she was something else. She was supposed to promote me and my record, but she had other ideas to attract attention.

The first thing she did was to hire convertibles and get us bikini bathing suits. I never had one in my life and I wouldn't wear it. She said you had to show off what you got. I said I wouldn't have it. That's not the way my mommy and my daddy raised me, and my husband would die if he found out, after killing me first.

"That's the way everybody does it," the redhead said.

"If it is, I better get out right now," I replied. But I didn't get out, and things were getting worse.

We were in some towns where she would go out on a date with some disc jockey. I didn't know what was going on. Then she said, "You better go out on dates with disc jockeys, too. That's the way it's done." I said I was married and didn't go out on dates with nobody. It was a shaky situation.

We got to Nashville and this redhead had me on a radio station. I'm not gonna mention the station, but it wasn't WSM. I figured we were done with the town, but Mack said if we stayed around until Tuesday, they'd play my record.

I told her I didn't have to do that. Then I asked her, "What do they expect from us if we stay?" She shrugged her shoulders, and I knew what she meant—if you want to make it in this business, you've got to sleep with those men.

I got real scared. I was over my head with this girl. I picked up the phone and started calling my husband. Mack got mad and started throwing ashtrays around the room, yelling, "Do that and I'll tear up your contract."

Finally I got Doo on the phone, and I was crying. He told me if I didn't quit crying, he was gonna make me quit the business. I started telling him what was going on. Doo said I shouldn't do nothing, just move on to the next town, which was Cincinnati, and he'd join me. So I told Mack I wasn't gonna sleep with no disc jockeys

this time or any time, and we should go to Cincinnati. When Doo arrived, he told me Mr. Burley said, "You tell that redheaded bitch Loretta doesn't have to sleep with anybody." And they fired the redhead. I've tried to forget about her. I don't like to remember bad situations.

That kind of thing never happened to me again, I'm glad to say. My husband stayed closer to me after that, and other people like the Johnsons watched out for me, too. But I was getting some kind of education in the ways of the world.

I guess growing up in Butcher Holler just didn't prepare me for the facts of life, just like I didn't know anything about sex when I got married. In fact, I was still pretty ignorant even with four kids. I didn't even know there was such a thing as a lesbian until my daughter came home from *grade* school and told me. I couldn't believe it then—but now I can.

I think there's a few of my fans who are lesbians—maybe more than a few. But they're my fans, and they visit me, just like anybody else, and it don't bother me. I've even got one friend who tells me about her personal life, and she'll even fix my hair or something. But she would never do anything that would upset me. It's not your friends who are the problems anyway. I've had a couple of women I didn't know proposition me, or even try something. That's why I've gotten more careful about seeing a lot of strangers.

Working in those clubs I got to see it all. I'd see a husband coming in with someone else's wife. A wife coming in with someone else's husband. It was all the same, the public and the musicians. It started to seem like the whole world was like that. Then I got to worrying if Doo was doing the same thing, see, because everyone else was. It was a bad time for me in that respect, because of what I saw.

The only good thing was I started writing more songs. Everyone says all my songs are about myself. That's not completely true, because if I did all the things I write about, I wouldn't be here, I'd be all worn out in some old people's home. But I've seen things, and that's *almost* the same as doing 'em.

Like one of my songs was, "You Ain't Woman Enough to Take My Man." This one I didn't really write about myself. There was a little girl, she was a bit on the plump side, not much. She came backstage one night, crying, and she said, "Loretta, my husband is going with another woman, so he brought her here tonight. See that guy sitting out there? See that girl sitting beside him?"

I looked at that other girl and I thought, "My God, don't tell me you're going to let something like that take your husband away from you!" Cause, to me, she was twice the woman that other gal was. So I looked back at her and said, "Why she ain't woman enough to take your man!" Just like that, as soon as I said it, I knew I had a hit song. She was all prepared to take a backseat because her husband fell for another woman. But that's not something I'd let myself do. By the way, that girl fought for her man, and a few months later she wrote to me and said they were back together again. I still see her, and she's still married to that same guy.

That's the same way I wrote "Fist City." There was a gal in Tennessee who was after my man, like I said before. I was up singing every night and she'd come around to the clubs and she'd hang around him. So finally I wrote this song that said, "You better lay off my man . . . or I'll grab you by the hair of your head and lift you off of the ground."

And I would. I've been in a couple of fights in my life. I fight like a woman. I scratch and kick and bite and punch. Women are much meaner than men. So I warned any girl making eyes at Doo then, and I'm still jealous enough to warn 'em today—if you see this cute little old boy near me wearing his cowboy hat, you'd better walk a circle around us if you don't want to go to Fist City. (Although I guess I'd better be careful what I say. For all I know, there might be a dozen gals out there ready to take me on.)

Doolittle knows he don't have to worry about me, even if we're not together on the road all the time. Once in a while he'll pick up some rumor, but Nashville is famous for rumors. After twenty-five years of being married, I ain't cheated on him.

People ask me sometimes, doesn't it get lonely on the road? Don't you ever meet a man you'd like to spend some time with? Usually I just answer a flat-out no. But that's really too simple an answer. The truth is, everybody finds themselves attracted to different people at different times. Anybody who says that ain't true is just a liar. I'm normal in that respect. I've met men I *could* like—but I haven't ever seen one yet who could take the place of my family. So I stay out of trouble.

I wrote a song about that once called, "I'm Dynamite," and in it was a line, "Please don't light the fuse." See, the way I look at it, it's up to the woman to keep out of trouble. Maybe if I was the type who liked to go to parties and drink, I'd get in trouble. That's why I don't condemn Doo for what he's done. As long as you keep up with this traveling life, with all the people and parties, there're bound to be temptations. As for what Doo has done, it's not anything I haven't thought about doing myself.

But I've seen what happened to women when they started messing around. They lost their families and they went downhill in a hurry. I've had friends like that. I'd rather write a song about it—that's my way of staying out of trouble. My marriage means too much to take a chance.

Besides, if I wasn't married I couldn't do the same things I do now. I couldn't be friendly with a lot of men, hug 'em and tell 'em I love 'em. They might take it the wrong way, and that would spoil things for me.

But sometimes men take your personality wrong. They see me up on the stage and they think I'm just waiting for their telephone call. Like this doctor from Texas who followed me around whenever I played that part of the country. He wouldn't take no for an answer. He'd be calling up and wanting to meet me. One night I was taking a bath and he called me from the lobby and said, "Well, I've found you." I didn't know how he got my room number, but he did. He said he wanted to watch TV in my room. I said it was too late, the TV was off.

He said he wanted to talk, so I said he could talk on the phone. Then he started telling me about his troubles with his wife, which is about the worst approach a man can use. I said, "Why don't you write to Dear Abby?" He hung up, and I haven't heard from him since. But he knows who he is.

But just because you don't go for that kind of stuff, doesn't mean it's not there. You just look around you. That's why I think country music is so popular with ordinary people. Because not everybody can appreciate poetry or classical music, and they don't like words that say one thing and mean another thing. Country music is real. Country music tells the story the way things are. People fall in love and then one of 'em starts cheating around, or both of 'em sometimes. And usually there's somebody who gets hurt. Our country songs are nothing but the truth. That's why they're so popular.

It's like that song Conway Twitty and I did in 1974, "As Soon As I Hang Up the Phone." It starts with the phone ringing and Conway, in a choking kind of voice, tries to tell me good-bye. Now, for a while, I don't pay any attention to what he's saying, but he keeps bringing the subject back to him leaving. Finally he says it's true, and I sing, "Ohhhh, noooo. . . ."

Now how many people have gotten bad news on the phone about their man or woman? Lots. And I bet most of 'em react the way I do in that song. Well, that song started being played on the jukeboxes over and over again because it was real.

You just look around at the problems that people keep having. Divorces and split-ups and extra boyfriends and girlfriends all over the place. I don't know how they find the time for it. And another reason country songs are so popular: some of the songs are about ourselves, really. We ain't no better than anybody else.

As for me, I ain't slept with nobody except my husband. I'm always getting letters from Conway's fans who say I was responsible for breaking up his marriage. Those fans hear Conway and me singing on our records, or they know that we're partners in a talent agency. But that's the *only* way we're partners. I've heard rumors about me and every singer in country music. There were even rumors about me and Ernest Tubb, and he's like a father to me. As far as I'm concerned, Ernest Tubb hung the moon. But my friends know me better than that. I also know you don't have to sleep with anybody to make it in this business. If I do sleep with anybody, it will be for my own accord. Like I told that redhead back in 1961, that ain't the way my mommy and my daddy raised me.

Maggard, Cledus (Jay Huguely)

No statistics available.

Actor, director, and producer of TV commercials for an ad agency in Greenville, South Carolina, he wrote "The White Knight" as a means of exploring CB lingo. Everyone loved it so he pressed two thousand copies for local distribution. "I figured the agency would be giving these away as Christmas presents for the next twenty years!" he recalls. As the record caught on, Mercury Records stepped in and offered to buy the master. The result was the huge country and pop single that led to the LP of the same name, which rose to top-ten listing on the charts. Why the name Cledus Maggard? Jay Huguely explains: "About twenty years ago, I was doing skits at a radio station. One of the continuing characters was Cledus Maggard who gave reports on local traffic conditions. When 'The White Knight' was going into release, Cledus Maggard just popped into my mind."

Mail Order

Write for   Here is a country roundup of goods, publications, and catalogs available by mail. Details given are correct at press time.*

The Alvarez Guitars
Over fifty handmade models that have been customized in the Alvarez shop. Built for sound and playability, these guitars are played by some of America's best folk rock and western stars. The instruments are priced from $125 to $1,600.

For a free catalog, write to St. Louis Music Supply Company, 1400

The author and publisher take no responsibility for the quality and value of goods listed.

Cledus Maggard

Ferguson Avenue, St. Louis, MO 63133 *or* Pacific Music Supply Company, 1143 Santee Street, Los Angeles, CA 90015.

Bean's Chino Pants
L.L. Bean are manufacturers of outdoor sporting trousers made in soft chino twill, polyester, and combed cotton. Also available are their chino trousers lined with chamois cloth for extra warmth.

For free catalog, write to L.L. Bean, 6954 Casco Street, Freeport, ME 04033.

Carvin Products
Available direct only, thus eliminating costly retail markups, Carvin are manufacturers of the following high-quality stereo equipment: stereo mixers, horn loaded lo-end systems, radial horns, bass amps, tube stacks, and stereo guitars.

For free color catalog, write to Carvin Systems Engineering, Department Cm-10, 1155 Industrial Avenue, Escondido, CA 92025.

The CB Times

This is the monthly journal featuring current news about CB clubs, personalities, FCC rulings, new equipment, campers and hikers, police information, truckers' and boaters' activities. An exclusive *CB Times* news bureau in Washington, D.C., will report directly on FCC actions plus special CB features and regular columns aimed at keeping you up-to-date on activities coast to coast. One year's subscription costs $9.95 (save $5.05 over newsstand price); 2 years costs $18.95 (saving $11.05); and 3 years costs $26.95 (saving $18.05).

Write, enclosing money, to *The CB Times,* 1005 Murfreesboro Road, Nashville, TN 37217.

CMH Records

Here is a large selection of contemporary recordings by America's greatest bluegrass artists such as Mac Wiseman, Don Reno and Bill Harell, and Lester Flatt available in two-record sets, twin-pack cartridges and cassettes. Plus twenty-four brand new recordings of The Singing Cowboy, Songs of the Silver Screen, and newly recorded deluxe five-record box set of the country music history covering one hundred songs plus a sixteen-page booklet.

For free catalog, write to CMH Records, PO Box 39439, Los Angeles, CA 90039. Telephone: (213) 663-8073.

Conn Guitars

Stocked by fine music dealers in over three hundred cities coast to coast, Conn are the manufacturers of many types of guitars including classical, grand concerts, and dreadnoughts with six- and twelve-string models.

Write for Conn's Super-Monster Chord Chart, enclosing $1 for handling, to Conn Guitars, 616 Enterprise Drive, Oak Brook, IL 60521. Telephone: (312) 325-7080.

Country Music Films for Rent

There are over fifty vintage films of various lengths going back to the thirties, with such artists as Roy Acuff, Roy Rogers, Judy Canova, Lulubelle & Scotty; films include *The Nashville Sound,* a ninety-minute documentary starring Johnny Cash, Doug Kershaw, Dolly Parton, Hank Snow, Bobby Goldsboro and a dozen more. For catalog (which includes a free Beatles poster!), send $1 to Ivy Films, 165 West 46 Street, New York, NY 10036.

Jimmie Rodgers

Country Style

For back issues of this magazine to augment your collection, write, enclosing one dollar per issue, to *Country Style* Back Issues, 11058 West Addison Street, Franklin Park, IL 60131.

Crafts from Tennessee

Here are old-fashioned mountain crafts including corn-shuck dolls with corn-silk hair, games and puzzles like acorn-in-a-knothole, and one of the oldest toys in America—the dancing hillbilly who does a jig and swings his arms *without* batteries.

For free brochure, write to Tennessee Crafts, 274 Capitol Hill Building, Nashville, TN 37219.

Fender Pedal Steel Guitars

Fender has got three new pedal steel guitars: the Artist Dual 10, the Artist Single 10, and the Student Single 10. All have interchangeable tuning; new, more responsive pickups; smooth, quiet pedal action; and a simple string-changer system.

Write for free color catalog to Fender, Box 3410, Department S75, Fullerton, CA 92634.

Fifty-five Years of Recorded Country-Western Music

A price guide to over twenty thousand country-western recordings and listing of thirteen hundred record collectors, buyers, sellers, and general nostalgia nuts. This book also contains over one hundred rare photographs and an exclusive interview with Gene Autrey.

For further details write to Bruce Hamilton, Scottsdale, Arizona.

The Gibson Guitar

This is the traditional Gibson guitar streamlined by the latest scientific technology: a change in the shape of the bridge and repositioning of the structural braces enhances the sound of this guitar, and, in addition, a slight arc at the head of the instrument will combat weather deterioration.

For catalog, send $1.75 for postage and handling to Norlin Music, Advertising, 7373 North Cicero Avenue, Lincolnwood, IL 60646.

Glen-Bel's Country Store

This is a three-hundred-page catalog of old-fashioned-style articles from wood-heating stoves to grandfather clocks; horse drawn wagons to coffee grinders; spinning wheels to corn shellers. Over three thousand items are available, all of which are, in fact, brand new.

For catalog, write, enclosing $3, to GlenBel's Country Store, Route

5, Department CG, Crossville, TN 38555.

Grand Ole Opry

Grand Ole Opry History Picture Book, 156 pages of color photos and stories of the Opry and its stars. $3.50. Write: Director of Merchandise, 2800 Opryland Drive, Department D, Nashville, TN 37214.

Gretsch Guitars

Gretsch Guitar models include the Super Chet, Country Gentleman, Nashville, and the Tennessean. The guitars have ebony fingerboards and double Filter Tron pickups to eliminate any hum and distortion.

For free catalog, write to Gretsch, 1801 Gilbert Avenue, Cincinnati, OH 45202.

Guild Guitar

The new Guild D-40 C Florentine Cutaway enables you to play all the high frets with greater ease and no cramping or stretching of fingers and without loss of sound quality.

For free catalog, sheet number 8241-E, write to Guild Guitars, 225 West Grand Street, Elizabeth, NJ 07202.

The Mel Tillis Guild Guitar—handmade in the USA.

For free color catalog 8082-B, write to Guild Guitars, 225 West Grand Street, Elizabeth, NJ 07202.

Lone Star Dude Hat

Created for the Lone Star Bunch with a pull-tab crease, this hat, which comes in tan, has a brim width of 3 1/2 or 4 inches. The crown height is 6 1/2 inches with or without hand-painted, hand-tooled Lone Star or Long Neck emblem. Bands can have tooling or shotgun shells or stars between the emblems.

Lone Star Dude Hat costs $35; add a further $25 for hand-tooled, hand-painted band, plus 5% sales tax and $4 for postage.

Send money and order to Texas Hatters, 2058 South Lamar, Austin TX 78704. Telephone: (512) 444-9485.

Morninglory Songbooks

These songbooks, featuring music by such varied artists as the Eagles to Conway Twitty, Linda Ronstadt to Charlie Rich, contain lyrics, piano music, guitar chords, and photos. For two dollars you will receive the world's finest catalog of songbooks four times a year.

For catalog, write, enclosing $2, to Morninglory Music, PO Box 6407, Santa Barbara, CA 93111.

The New Dodge Street Van

The first van that comes factory customized. Complete for the street with fat tires, flashy chrome wheels, extra-bright trim, high-back bucket seats with fold-down armrests, and thick carpeting up front. Plus, every street van comes complete with a Dodge Customizing Idea Kit: loaded up with trick paint designs for the outside; full-size templates for the inside custom work, and much more. In addition, you get a one-year membership in the new Van Clan—a van association that gives you travel services, van theft protection, and more.

For free catalog, write to The Van Clan, PO Box 125, Birmingham, MI 48012.

Ohio Country and Western Music Association

A nonprofit organization chartered by the state of Ohio, the purpose to create, stimulate, and promote interest in country and western music, to promote social activities among its members, to study music and encourage new talent. Dues: $8 annually, which includes subscription to *The Buckeye Music News*; annual events include Summer Jubilee, Ohio State Fair, and Awards Banquet. For information, write Box 11542, Columbus, OH 43215, (614) 455-8784.

1001 Jumbo Songbook

This spiral-bound book has 510 pages of popular songs, from the hits of today right back to the Gay Nineties' songs of yesteryear. Music for all ages . . . songs for every musical taste, from country to rock, pop, and jazz. In addition, there are special instructional sections for playing pop music on piano, guitar, or organ.

For book, enclose check for $12.95 plus 70¢, postage paid, to Mail-A-Music, 620 Kinderkamack Road, River Edge, NJ 07661.

Peer-Southern Publications

They publish sheet music, folios, solos, and musical arrangements plus instructional manuals and books on the history of American music. For free catalog, write to Peer-Southern Publications, 1740 Broadway, New York, NY 10019.

Schwann Record and Tape Guides

They publish monthly and semi-annual catalogs and booklets on all recorded music from classical to popular, jazz to juvenile. For details of catalogs, write to Schwann Record and Tape Guides, ABC Leisure Magazines, 130 East 59th Street, New York, NY 10022. Telephone: (212) 826-8355.

Sheplers Incorporated

The world's largest Western store, so they say! Free ninety-six-page color catalog fully illustrated and featuring a comprehensive collection of Western wear, boots and outdoor casual apparel for men, women, and children. Everything for the horse and rider, too, in the complete Saddle and Tack Department.

Write to Sheplers, 6501 West Kellogg, Department 103, PO Box 202, Wichita, KS 67201.

Stud Hat

In lustrous finish high-quality wood felt, the modern styling of this hat is accentuated by a rugged leather hatband and its brass studs and decorative feather. This gambler-style hat, which has a rolled brim, is available in buffalo-brown or black. For free catalog, write to Fun Wear Brands, CM-116, Estes Park, CO 80517. Telephone: (303) 586-3361.

Uncle Jim O'Neal

A very large selection of records by top artists from Roy Acuff to Elvis Presley, Marty Robbins to Stonewall Jackson, at discount prices. Record albums listed at $4.98 sold at $2.98 each (outside USA, $3.50), plus 50¢ for handling.

For free catalog, write to Uncle Jim O'Neal, Box A, Arcadia, CA 91006.

The Underground Berkshire Guide

A guide that reports on all kinds of esoterica that are hard to discover: where to get the last living grilled-cheese sandwich for thirty-five cents, the times you can come by and watch cows milked at a working dairy farm, how to contact local people who will let you live in their homes, how to hire a Sufi to clean your attic. And much more about auctions, museums, spiritual dancing, and so forth. Send $1.50 for Guide to PO Box 7228, Stockbridge, MA 01262.

United Farm Agency

United Farm Agency's latest catalog describes and pictures over twenty-five hundred selected real estate values from coast to coast. When writing for free catalog, please specify type, property, and location desired, to United Farm Agency, 612-CG West 47th Street, Kansas City, MO 64112. Telephone: (816) 753–4212.

Mandrell, Barbara

Born: December 25, 1948, Houston, Texas
Married: Kenneth Dudney
Children: s. Matthew; d. Jaime

In addition to singing, she plays pedal steel guitar, five-string banjo, saxophone, and bass guitar. Part of a family band, she toured with Johnny Cash in 1961 and entertained troops in Korea and Vietnam in 1967. With her own band, the Do-Rites, she has traveled thousands of miles in a custom bus. At one point she was the youngest member of the Opry.

Barbara Mandrell

Her major recordings include: "Treat Him Right," "Do Right Woman," "Playing around with Love," "After Closing Time," "Standing Room Only," and her top-ten hit, "Married but Not to Each Other." In 1978, her career took on superstardom proportions, with frequent network TV appearances and the top-ten song "Sleeping Single in a Double Bed" and the LP *Moods*.

Miller, Roger

Born: January 2, 1936, Fort Worth, Texas
Married: Leah Kendrick (div.), Mary Arnold

The "King of the Road" quit school at puberty, worked on a farm, rode in rodeos, and served in Korea with the army, where he first performed before an audience. Going to Nashville, he worked in a hotel while peddling his songs. In 1958, Ray Price recorded his "Invitation to the Blues." In 1960, Roger signed with RCA and made two hits, "You Don't Want My Love" and "When Two Walls Collide." By 1963, he switched over to Smash Records and the top of the charts with "Dang Me," "King of the Road," and "Chug-a-Lug." Many of his hits have become classics that continue to sell and to be played on country stations, including "Do Wacka Do," "Engine, Engine, Number Nine," "England Swings," and "Little Green Apples."

Milsap, Ronnie

Born: Jan. 16, 1946, Robbinsville, North Carolina
Married: Joyce
Children: s. Todd

Born blind because of congenital glaucoma, he attended Raleigh State School for the Blind and was soon playing the violin, the piano, and by age twelve, the guitar. Winner of the CMA Male Vocalist Award in 1974 and 1976, his early hits, "Let's Fall Apart," "I Hate You," and "Pure Love," were just the preparation for

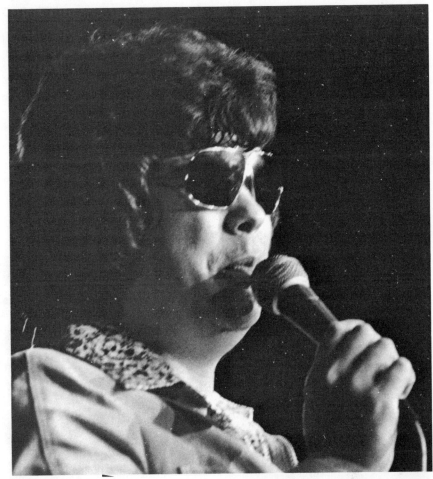

Ronnie Milsap

Country

his Album of the Year for 1975 and Grammy-award winning *A Legend in My Time,* "Too Late to Worry, Too Late to Cry," "(I'm a) Stand by Your Woman Man." "Let My Love Be Your Pillow" was number one in early 1977, followed by "What a Difference You Made in My Life," "Let's Take the Long Way Around the World," and the LP *Only One Love in My Life.* His *Ronnie Milsap Live* and *It Was Almost Like a Song* won Album of the Year awards in 1977 and 1978.

Montgomery, Melba

Born: October 14, 1938, Iron City, Tennessee
Married: Jack Soloman

Melba learned to sing with her father at the Methodist Church in Florence, Alabama. In the mid-1950s, her family moved to

Melba Montgomery

Nashville, where she and her brothers were finalists in a talent contest. Roy Acuff heard her and invited her to join his Smokie Mountain Boys tour. In 1962, her solo career began with two singles, "Happy You, Lonely Me" and "Just Another Fool along the Way"—both major hits. Early in 1963 she teamed up with George Jones, resulting in a long line of joint successes, including "We Must Have Been out of Our Minds," which she wrote. A gifted duet singer, she recorded many hit albums with Jones and also had her own first number-one single in "No Charge," written by Harlan Howard. Melba has recorded with Gene Pitney "Baby Ain't that Fine," and Charlie Louvin; on TV she appears often on "Hee Haw," "Mike Douglas Show," "Pop Goes the Country," and "The Jim Ed Brown Show."

Mountain Music Shindig Tape Club

A unique lending-library-by-mail for hearing mountain music on tape. Old 78s, interviews, new records, special features. The club works on a lend-send basis. Listen to the tapes within five days, dub off any material you like, and then send the tape to the next member on the circuit listed on the box.

The cost is four dollars for six tapes. The club has been going for seven years, so it must work! For details, write Mountain Music Shindig Tape Club, 124 East Main Street, High Bridge, NJ 08829.

Music Row, Nashville

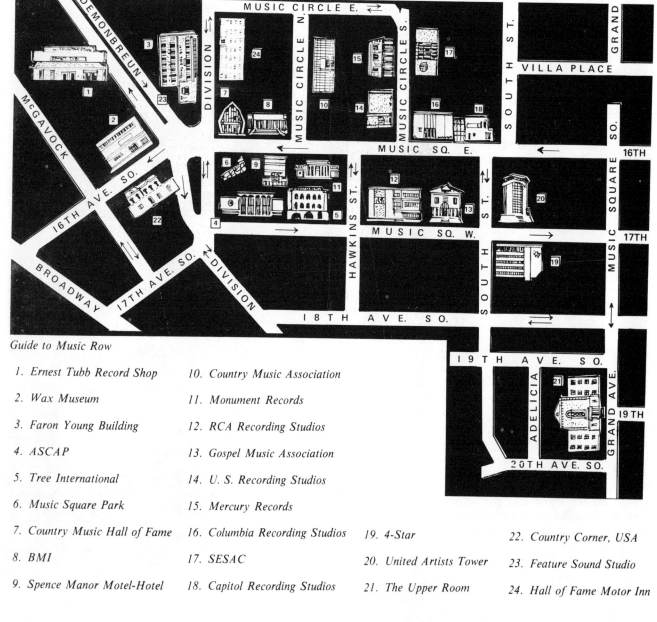

Courtesy of the Tennessee Guide

Guide to Music Row

1. *Ernest Tubb Record Shop*
2. *Wax Museum*
3. *Faron Young Building*
4. *ASCAP*
5. *Tree International*
6. *Music Square Park*
7. *Country Music Hall of Fame*
8. *BMI*
9. *Spence Manor Motel-Hotel*
10. *Country Music Association*
11. *Monument Records*
12. *RCA Recording Studios*
13. *Gospel Music Association*
14. *U. S. Recording Studios*
15. *Mercury Records*
16. *Columbia Recording Studios*
17. *SESAC*
18. *Capitol Recording Studios*
19. *4-Star*
20. *United Artists Tower*
21. *The Upper Room*
22. *Country Corner, USA*
23. *Feature Sound Studio*
24. *Hall of Fame Motor Inn*

Nelson, Willie

Born: April 30, 1933, Abbott, Texas
Married: Connie
Children: d. Lana, Paula Carlene

"The Red-Headed Stranger," as he is sometimes called, traveled a long, hard winding road to superstardom. He learned to play the guitar at six, played in a dancehall band at ten, sold Bibles and vacuum cleaners door to door, joined the air force, and by 1959 was a part-time disc jockey in Fort Worth, Texas. The first songs he wrote included "Family Bible" and "Night Life," which have been recorded by over seventy performers and sold more than thirty million copies. Going to seek his fortune in Nashville in the early sixties, he wrote such hits as "Crazy" for Patsy Cline, "Hello, Walls," for Faron Young, and "Ain't It Funny How Time Slips Away" for Ray Price, performer and part owner of Pamper Publishing. In other words, Nashville liked him as a writer but not as a performer.

During a dozen years in Nashville, he recorded over twenty albums, none of them successful. Part of the reason was the Nashville method of backing a performer with studio musicians who are excellent at instantly picking up on a tune or style—but who are strangers to the performers and lack the intimacy that comes with traveling and playing together. As an "outsider" in Music City, Willie was in such good company as Waylon Jennings, Tompall Glaser, and Kris Kristofferson. In 1972, when his house burned down, Willie returned to Texas and found his personal and musical home in Austin. The first Fourth of July picnic concert at Dripping Springs was held in 1972 and starred his old friends Kris, Waylon, and Tom T. and is said to have been the start of the Austin Sound, later becoming known as Outlaw Music because of the maverick approach of Willie and friends—and the "Ladies Love Outlaws" song. Since 1972, Willie Nelson has become a cult figure of mythic proportions. His 1976 RCA LP *Outlaws* with Waylon, Jessi, and Tompall was the first country LP ever to go platinum. In 1978, *Waylon and Willie* went gold in two weeks and includes such hit singles as "Mamas, Don't Let Your Babies Grow Up to Be Cowboys" and "If You Could Touch Her At All." Other 1978 chart-breakers include duets with Waylon: "I Could Get Off on You" and "Whiskey River." As a change of pace, his April 1978 LP *Stardust* made new hits out of such old classics as "Georgia on My Mind," "Someone to Watch Over Me," and "Unchained Melody." In Austin, he is the backbone of the "Austin City Limits" TV series, often making unannounced appearances. Further, Charley Pride proudly gives Willie

© 1974 Melinda Wickman

Willie and daughter Paula Carlene

credit for making him the first black country music star. Tom T. Hall once called him the Shakespeare of Country Music. *Newsweek* columnist Pete Axthelm wrote the following brilliant tribute to Willie and the Outlaws in 1976.

Songs of Outlaw Country

by Peter Axthelm

The strapping rodeo bull rider grabbed Jerry Jeff Walker's arm in a vicelike grip and stared angrily at the singer, who bore a beatific, faraway expression on his face. "Didn't you hear me, boy?" he growled. "I told you to play that song about red-necks. Now play it. Fast."

Willie with rock star Leon Russell

Backstage at the Texas Opry House, Austin, Texas, 1974. Left to right: Billy Cooper; Alex Harney, "Delta Dawn" songwriter; Waylon Jennings; Willie Nelson; Lee Clayton; Ray Wylie Hubbard, composer of "Up Against the Wall, Redneck Mother."

Stoned and drunk and uncertain if he was in a honky-tonk in Austin or in Oklahoma City, Walker struggled to concentrate on his dilemma. If he played the song, which he knew the cowboy hated, he would probably be beaten up. If he refused the request, he would also be beaten up. Finally, he began to play. The cowboy hit him three times, smashed his guitar and left him bloody. "Situations like that," Jerry Jeff explains cheerfully, "are what being an outlaw is all about."

The outlaws of country music need all their dark memories these days; tales of brawls, drug busts and rejection slips seem to be their best means of coping with the fact that they are suddenly rich and fashionable. Perennial outsiders like Waylon Jennings and Willie Nelson have found themselves at the center of the music business, accepting its awards and watching their records climb on pop as well as country charts. Outlaw writers are reaching red-necks and hippies alike with their raw, honest lyrics. And Nelson, the leader of the Austin-based movement known rather imprecisely as "progressive country," is now running his own record label and building an impressive economic base.

Honky-Tonk Heroes

"Even outlaws are entitled to free enterprise," Nelson was saying, . . . "I like spending a lot of money just as much as I once liked spending what little I had. And now I can give chances to the bright pickers who've been unnoticed just because the Texas honky-tonks aren't on the road between Nashville and Los Angeles. I can see it as a spiritual movement. . . ." The bearded face with the wild, penetrating eyes twisted into a self-mocking grin. "I better have a beer," he said. "I'm starting to sound so serious, I must be getting close to sober."

Austin was a refreshing place to be. . . . While millions of viewers saw an Academy Award bestowed on an insipid, fake-country song from the condescending movie *Nashville,* it was bracing to wander through honky-tonks like the Soap Creek Saloon and Armadillo World Headquarters, where down-to-earth musicians swilled beer in longneck bottles and shared their songs and dreams. "I don't worry about anybody copying what's going on here," said Jerry Jeff Walker's wife, Susan. "If you need a lot of publicity men to make you look real and crude, then you ain't crude."

From his cowboy hats and red bandanas to his tennis shoes, Willie Nelson is crude. He is small, but he carries himself with the cocky assurance of one who never has backed down. He has been writing hits for twenty years; but for most of that time he was told by the "experts" in Nashville and L.A. that his straightforward arrangements, intense personal statements, and strange, slightly nasal voice would never make him a star. Too long-haired for the red-necks, too "country" for the kids, Willie seemed either behind or ahead of his time. . . .

Then, after all the disappointments of Nashville and the road, Nelson went home and rediscovered Texas. Three years ago, in an inspired stroke, he gave the first of his huge annual Fourth of July picnics, where hardened cowhands and sandaled kids found happiness together. Later he translated the anguish of his divorce into the critically acclaimed album *Phases and Stages*. And last year he evoked the oral tradition of the Old West in his haunting tale of the *Red-Headed Stranger*.

The Long Battle

That album, about a hero who kills two women in his wild sorrow over lost love, seemed to incorporate all the simplicity, sentimentality and implacable individualism that had always kept Nelson from stardom. It sold half a million copies and helped him win his long battle against the Nashville Establishment and its formula songs and syrupy string arrangements.

The success of the Austin scene has not been without its price. "Five years ago we had a sense of mission and outrage," says entrepreneur Eddie Wilson of Armadillo World Headquarters. "Now Vietnam's over, long hair is routine and possession of marijuana is only a misdemeanor. About the only thing left to be mad about is people capturing too many armadillos."

On the grimmer side, musicians and kids have helped to make Austin such a drug capital that it has witnessed some gory shoot-outs among dealers. But on the whole, the mood in the honky-tonks is as carefree as Nelson himself. Jerry Jeff may crawl onstage in his jockey shorts at Castle Creek; his friend Bud Shrake, the novelist, may show up at a bowling-alley bar dressed as a polar bear. "But the beauty of it," says Nelson, "is that hardly anybody will be surprised. Around here everybody hits the streets at sundown and expects something wild to happen." It's what being an outlaw is all about.

(*See also:* Austin City Limits)

Willie, Emmylou Harris, and President Carter

The White House

MCA Records/Solterst Roskin, Inc.

Newton-John, Olivia

Born: September 26, 1948,
Cambridge, England

She was raised in Melbourne, Australia, where her father was appointed headmaster of Ormond College. While still at school, she formed a group with three girl friends, calling themselves the Sol Four. It didn't last very long. At sixteen, she won a talent contest, which sent her to England where she teamed up with Pat Carroll, another Australian. They were appearing in top cabarets and on the BBC when Pat's visa expired. She then returned to Australia and Olivia cut her first single, Bob Dylan's "If Not For You," which brought her instant international attention. In 1973, "Let Me Be There" earned her first Grammy as Best Country Vocalist, and since then her awards could fill the walls of a five-room house. Among her hits are such singles as "If You Love Me, Let Me Know," "Have You Ever Been Mellow?", "Please, Mr., Please," "Let It Shine," "Come On Over," "Don't Stop Believing," and such albums as *First Impressions, Long Live Love,* and *Clearly Love.* Making her first movie with John Travolta, the spectacular *Grease,* she has since settled in Malibu, California, with two cars, four dogs, and five horses.

Her many awards include:

Country Music Association: Top Female Vocalist of the Year, 1974.

Grammys: Best Country Vocal, Female, 1973 ("Let Me Be There"); Record of the Year, 1974 ("I Honestly Love You"); Best Pop Vocal Performance, Female, 1974 ("I Honestly Love You").

Billboard: No. 1 Awards for LPs and singles, 1974; Favorite Female Country Singles Artist, 1975; Favorite Female Country Album Artist, 1975: Favorite Female Pop Singles Artist, 1975; Favorite Female Pop Album Artist, 1975.

Cash Box: No. 1 New Female Vocalist, Singles, 1974; No. 1 New Female Vocalist, Albums, 1974; No. 1 Female Vocalist, Singles, 1975; No. 1 Female Vocalist, Albums, 1975.

American Music Awards: Favorite Female Vocalist–Pop/Rock, 1974; Favorite Single–Country, 1974 ("I Honestly Love You"); Favorite Female Vocalist–Country, 1974; Favorite Album–Country, 1974 (*Let Me Be There*); Favorite Female Vocalist—Country, 1975; Favorite Female Vocalist–Pop/Rock, 1975;

Favorite Album–Pop/Rock, 1975 (*Have You Ever Been Mellow*); Favorite Female Vocalist–Pop/Rock, 1976.

The Oak Ridge Boys with Roy Clark (center) on "Hee Haw."

ABC Dot/The Jim Halsey Co., Inc.

Joe Bonsall

Oak Ridge Boys

Vocals: Bill Golden, Richard Sterban, Duane Allen, and Joe Bonsall.
Band: Mark Ellerbee, Harold Mitchell, Garland Craft, and Don Breland.

William Lee Golden
Born: January 12, 1939, Brewton, Alabama

Joe Bonsall
Born: May 18, 1948, Philadelphia, Pennsylvania

Duane Allen
Born: April 29, 1943, Taylortown, Texas

Richard Sterban
Born: April 24, 1943, Camden, New Jersey

Duane Allen

Richard Sterban

Formed in 1957 as a gospel group, The Oak Ridge Boys have converted to country. They are international favorites, and travel as much as three hundred days a year. To rave reviews, they have appeared in such farflung places as Las Vegas, Wembley in England, The Gold Buffet in Kansas City, country fairs, and college campuses—and on such top TV shows as "Tonight," "Merv Griffin," "Mike Douglas," and "Dinah Shore." They have been winners of the Gospel Music Association's Dove Awards many times over for Best Album, Best Male Group, Best Instrumental, and Gospel Song of the Year. Their 1976 Grammy for Best Gospel Song was for "Where the Soul Never Dies." In 1977, they really hit their stride with "Y'All Come Back Saloon" for ABC-Dot and appeared at New

Bill Golden

The Oak Ridge Boys

ABC Dot/The Jim Halsey Co., Inc.

ABC Dot/The Jim Halsey Co., Inc.

York's Carnegie Hall in concert with Mel Tillis, Donna Fargo, and Alvin Crow and the Pleasant Valley Boys. In early 1978, "You're the One" moved to the top of the charts followed by "Cryin' Again" and the LP *Room Service*. They won two of the CMA awards for 1978—Vocal Group of the Year and Instrumental Group of the Year.

Oak Ridge Boys International Fan Club

Members receive a one-year subscription to the official club newsletter (beautifully illustrated and informative), plus special offers on T-shirts, records, and tapes.

Annual dues: $5. For membership application, write: 329 Rockland Road, Hendersonville, TN 37075.

Old-Time Country Music Club of Canada

They are dedicated to preserving and promoting authentic country, old-time, and bluegrass music. Projects and benefits include record library, social events, concerts, barn dances, and so on. They publish a newsletter twice annually.

Club membership: $2 a year. Write: Bob Fuller, Secretary, 1421 Gohier Street, St. Laurent, Quebec, Canada H4L 3K2.

Old-Time Music

A quarterly devoted to old-time music, including stringband, cowboy, Cajun, bluegrass, Tex-Mex, American-Irish; also western swing and commercial country music of the thirties and forties, plus present-day old-time activity.

Subscription: $6 a year (surface rate); $9 air mail. For details, write: Old-Time Music, 33 Brunswick Gardens, London W 8 4AW, England.

They also publish two books that are generally unavailable in the United States: *The Grand Ole Opry: The Early Years, 1925--35,* by Charles K. Wolfe ($5.95 postpaid); *Jimmie The Kid,* by Mike Paris and Chris Comber, a biography of Jimmie Rodgers with discography, photographs, and illustrations ($8.95 postpaid).

Gid Tanner and His Skillet Lickers

Old Time Roots

by Paul Wells

Country music before World War II was vastly different from that of today. An amazing variety of sounds and styles existed, from solo fiddlers, string bands and banjo pickers, to singing cowboys, yodelers, family groups, and even a few crooners. Beginning with the recording of Texas fiddler Eck Robertson in 1922, much of what was waxed in the early days of country music reflected regional differences in folk music traditions. Fiddlers from Georgia sounded a lot different from those from Virginia, and North Carolinian Charlie Poole's finger-style banjo playing was far removed from the flailing of Lillie Mae Ledford of Kentucky's Coon Creek Girls.

Carson Robison and His Pioneers

Fiddlin' John Carson

The Coon Creek Girls

Traditional music comprised only a portion of the whole, however, as new material was composed and new styles soon emerged with an eye towards satisfying the demands of the new-found country music market. The Great Depression caused a sharp decline in record sales, which hastened the professional demise of many of the older-style acts. The 1930s saw the growth of pro-

Milton Brown and His Brownies

Carl T. Sprague

Gene Autry

The Carlisle Brothers

Carson J. Robison

Moss Photo, N.Y.

fessionalism and sophistication among country performers. There was a general trend toward mellowness as vocal harmonies became smoother and bands became tighter.

While country performers had appeared on radio since the early 1920s, this medium became increasingly important during the thirties. Powerful stations such as WSM in Nashville, WLS in Chicago, KVOO in Tulsa, KWKH in Shreveport, and several stations south of the Mexican border (which, being free from FCC control, blasted their signals into the states with tremendous power) carried the sounds of The Carter Family, Uncle Dave Macon, Gene Autry, Bill Monroe, and many others far from their home regions. This increased media exposure, plus the breakdown of regional cultures brought about by World War II, was both good and bad for country music—good, because it helped bring the music to national attention, but bad because much of the old regional variety and vitality was lost.

173

The Blue Sky Boys

The Hillbillies

Byrd Moore's Hot Shots

The Delmore Brothers

Who were some of the personalities of country music in the days before the War? Let's meet a few of them.

Paul Wells is manager of the record series issued by the John Edwards Memorial Foundation. Holder of an M.A. in Folklore and Mythology from UCLA, his writings on folk and country music have appeared in *JEMF Quarterly, Pickin', The Journal of American Folklore,* and elsewhere.

Maybelle, Sara, A.P. Carter

Outlaw Blues

There are six country songs in this hilarious 1977 film of ex-convict Peter Fonda who writes a song, "Outlaw Blues," which is then stolen by "beloved" country star James Callahan. Fonda plays and sings for the first time on film. Apart from the title song, others include "Whisper in the Velvet Night" by Lee Clayton and "Jailbirds Can't Fly" by Harlan Sanders. Susan St. James plays a singer who makes a star of the fugitive Fonda by creating perilous promotion stunts that result in spectacular car crashes and a speedboat chase that careens over the top of a 150-foot dam.

The Cast

Bobby Ogden...Peter Fonda
Tina Waters..Susan St. James
Buzz Cavanaugh....................................John Crawford
Garland Dupree....................................James Callahan
Hatch..Michael Lerner
Elroy...Steve Fromholz
Associate Warden..........................Richard Lockmiller
Billy Bob...Matt Clark
Cathy Moss......................................Jan Rita Cobler
Leon Warback...Gene Rader

The Credits

Executive Producers......................Fred Weintraub and
Paul Heller
Produced by..Steve Tisch
Directed by....................................Richard T. Heffron
Written by...B. W. L. Norton
Edited by.................................Danford B. Greene and
Scott Conrad
Director of Photography..........................Jules Brenner
Music by...Charles Bernstein
Presented by...Warner Bros.
Running time: 101 minutes
Rated PG.

Peter Fonda

Susan St. James

Overstreet, Tommy

Born: September 10, 1937, Oklahoma City, Oklahoma
Married: Nancy
Children: s. Tommy III; d. Lisa

His first hit in 1969 was "Rocking a Melody," the next in 1970, "If You're Looking for a Fool," followed by a spate of hits: "I Don't Know You Anymore," "Heaven Is My Woman's Love," "Send Me No Roses," "From Woman to Woman," and "If Love Was a Bottle of Wine." He tours with the five-piece band, The Nashville Express. In 1977, he hit the charts with Mike Kosser's "Don't Go City Girl on Me." In 1978, his big single was "Fadin' In, Fadin' Out," his LP, *Better Me.*

Owens, Buck (Alvis Edgar)

Born: August. 12, 1929, Sherman, Texas
Married: Bonnie (div.), Phyllis (div.), Jana Grief
Children: s. Buddy Alan, Mike, Johnny

It seems as if every established country entertainer has had a hard-luck life prior to stardom, and Buck Owens is no exception. In the arid corner of Texas called Sherman, Buck's family life in the Dust Bowl was comparable to that of his neighbors; sharecropper parents, the bare necessities of life and few frills or extras, but the music was always there. "As long as I can remember, we always had a piano around the house," he recalls. "And mama would sit and play all the old hymns and we'd sing with her. She taught me most of 'em."

Buck grew to a strapping size and began to work trucks to help pay grocery bills. In the evenings he would listen to the radio with his family. Bob Wills, Red Foley, and Roy Acuff were the artists who impressed him; so much so that his father rigged up an electric guitar for him, using that trusty radio as an amplifier. Crude as it was, young Buck practiced and worked with his guitar every spare moment.

When he was sixteen, the entire Owens family packed up and trekked to California. "It was like *The Grapes of Wrath,*" Buck recalls, "except that we didn't make it to California. We were all packed into a little car—five adults and five kids —with the mattress on top. We ended up in Arizona because the trailer broke down."

Warner Bros. Records

Buck Owens

In Mesa, Buck again worked at whatever he could find for himself. "But I was also trying to learn to be a performer, from anybody who would take the time to teach me." Buck married at seventeen and became a father at eighteen. Mesa, Arizona, did not fulfill its promise of a solid future, and a move to California was next. The lush San Joaquin Valley, with its abundant crops and its booming oil industry was home for many of the Oklahoma-Texas emigrants, so Buck and his young family headed there, settling in the largest town in the Valley—Bakersfield.

This city had quite naturally become the entertainment center for the hundreds of music-loving agricultural migrants. Small clubs flourished, providing country and western music to cater to the southern and southwestern tastes of their clientele. It was here that Buck began performing, trying, in his words, "to become a *good* guitar player." He was called on to do many sessions in Los Angeles, picking for such stars as Tommy Sands, Tennessee Ernie Ford, and Sonny James. Eventually, and curiously enough not willingly, he became a singer.

"I just wanted to be a picker, and the boss told me to fill in for the singer who was gone that night. It was either sing or lose my job, so I sang." He was signed to Capitol Records in 1958. "Under Your Spell Again" followed, and, in 1962, he formed his backup group, the Buckaroos. Everything came up roses from then on.

His recordings "Act Naturally," "Love's Gonna Live Here" and "I've Got a Tiger by the Tail" topped the country record charts in 1963, 1964, and 1965, and he had more than twenty-six consecutive number-one hits, with twelve albums hitting number one also. An innovator and trendsetter at the right time, Buck was one of the first to recognize the importance of a strong percussion sound in country music, perhaps as a remnant from the early days when he played dance music. He put a solid drum beat on "Act Naturally" and many subsequent hits. Never one afraid to try something new, he approached the Paul Simon tune "Bridge over Troubled Water," and over the protests of doubtful record executives, turned it country—and into a hit.

His songwriting talents are a major part of Buck Owens's successful career. Not only are his tunes chart busters, but they have also been recorded by such artists as the Beatles, Dean Martin, Ray Charles, and Barbra Streisand. Perhaps it's the disarming combination of simple, honest lyrics and catchy melodies that account for the popularity of Buck's music; whatever magical ingredient they contain, his songs take on an even greater meaning when he performs them. He can hold an audience spellbound during a ballad, captivate them completely with joyous novelty numbers, and literally raise the roof with foot-stompin' bluegrass.

Warner Bros. Records

He's played to capacity houses all across the country, and his trips overseas have broken every attendance record on the books. He has played three SRO shows at the London Palladium and has sold out halls in Holland, Germany, Sweden, Ireland, and Japan. His performance at the Sydney Opera House is one that stylish institution will long remember, for, during the middle of the show, a group of excited females boldly rushed the stage. They came away waving Buck's shirt as a trophy while a bewildered and amused Buck Owens began the next song. That, in part, is the kind of adulation he inspires: a kind of total open communication with his audiences. It's this honesty that made him country music's number one artist five years in a row. It's the reason the "Buck Owens Ranch Show" and "Hee Haw," both shows which he has hosted, have endured.

All through his remarkable career, he's continued to give precious time and monies to charitable causes. In the past few years, he's pushed himself, despite his hectic schedule, to devote even more time —his primary cause being the Kern Community Cancer Center in Bakersfield. This community-based cancer research and treatment center promises to be the most modern of all. Buck has personally underwritten the first $250,000 of the estimated $1 million-plus budget.

Nor has Buck's interest ever diverted from his music. The summer of 1976 saw the release of his first Warner Brothers' Album, *Buck 'Em.* Recorded in Nashville with Norro Wilson producing, *Buck 'Em* accurately portrayed Buck as one country artist whose evolution and maturation is a vital, ongoing process; tunes from such diverse hands as the Eagles ("Hollywood Waltz"), Bob Jones ("California Oakie"), and Lennon and McCartney ("Lady Madonna") shared space with some of the strongest Owens originals to date ("Rain on Your Parade," "Child Support"). Among his 1977–1978 releases is the hit-single, "Nights Are Forever without You."

Parton, Dolly

Born: January 19, 1946, Sevierville, Tennessee
Married: Carl Dean

In the fall of 1977, Barbara Walters visited with Dolly Parton in Kansas City, Missouri. The resulting interview appeared on the prestigious Barbara Walters Special on the ABC-TV Network, December 6, 1977. Here, for the first time in print, is the edited transcript of this historic meeting between two outstanding women.

"The Barbara Walters Special"

Dolly Parton with Barbara Walters*

* Barbara Walters Special No. 5, with Lucille Ball and Gary Morton; Dolly Parton; Henry Winkler and Stacey Weitzman. Air date: Tuesday, December 6, 1977, 10:00 –11:00 PM , NYT, ABC TV. Produced by JoAnn Goldberg, Don Mischer; directed by Don Mischer.

Barbara on camera, speaking to the TV audience.
BARBARA: Success . . . how do you get it? What do you do with it? And what if you lose it?

The larger-than-life phenomenon known as Dolly Parton, described as a cross between Mae West and Norman Vincent Peale, performing for us and telling of her fierce determination not to be just a country music superstar, but a superstar period . . . and you'd better believe it.

"Here You Come Again" is Dolly's biggest hit record. Born in the Tennessee mountains, Dolly was singing with the Grand Ole Opry at ten. Now thirty-one, she's a giant country music star, but with her crazy wigs, stunning figure, and unique style, she's trying to win all kinds of fame—to branch out, knock 'em dead. And she sure does go. Like most country music stars, home to Dolly is her custom-designed bus. Cost . . . 130,000 dollars. Traveled last year 150,000 miles for 300 days.

Barbara and Dolly, interior of bus.

BARBARA
When you wake up, do you know where you are?

DOLLY
Sometimes I do, sometimes I don't. I'm just happy with myself, and I'm happy within my group, so I always feel content. And I'm kinda like a gypsy. I think we all are. It's something inside you. It's like truck drivers . . . you need it. It's a way to survive. That excitement of the motion underneath your feet or, the wheels rolling. But

Elektra

I like it. But I do enjoy home, too.

BARBARA
You really like this? To me it seems like horror. Every night in the bus. Every day a different place, and you like it?

DOLLY
Yeah, I do like it. It's excitement to me. Because I guess bein' brought up in the mountains where you have little time to do anything but work and things are so quiet. And things are so calm. That you grow restless if you have restless blood. And you grow more restless as the years go on and you want to get out. And when you do, you enjoy it. I love to go home, but if I'm home more than two weeks straight, I get restless and bored, and I wanna get back on the bus and I wanna go.

BARBARA
Some of the country music stars have two buses. One for themselves and one for the band. You just have one. Why?

DOLLY
Well, it is cramped, but up till now it's been fine, because I do have my own small room with my own bathroom, my own hot and cold water, and that sort of thing. And I really love the people in my group. We're like a family.

BARBARA
Is there any "hanky panky" in the bus? To pass the time?

DOLLY
Hanky-panky! Well, that depends on what you mean by *hanky panky*. We do lot of celebratin' on the bus. Let's put it that way. If there's really something to celebrate, if we want to stop and buy some wine or some champagne, if there's somethin' really nice. So it's all fun, but it's very rare that anybody in the bus . . . I don't have anybody in my group involved with each other as lovers. I have worked in groups where there were people, the musicians or singers, whatever, were involved. It makes it very hard for everybody because if they have a lovers' quarrel or that sort of thing, then it affects everything.

BARBARA
Describe the bus to us. What's in it?

DOLLY
I'd love to.

Tour of bus interior. Well, we've arrived. [inside the bus].

BARBARA
Looks like a dormitory room.

DOLLY
Well, it kinda does. These are the boys' bunks. And, of course, there's eleven people that travel with me.

BARBARA
I'd hate to be the guy in the bottom bunk.

DOLLY
You have to be good friends to live this close. Right.

BARBARA
Can we see your little room?

DOLLY
Yeah, let's do that. Okay. Now this is my couch. Also, this is my bed. And this lets down from this point. There's a piece in the back and it makes a full bed. It comes all the way out to the wall, so I have lots of room to sleep. And then up here in these cabinets are my wigs. So here's another Dolly . . . and another one . . . and another one. So that makes it really nice for me. It keeps it pretty nice. Actually, I have three closets in this room. But this one is the most special because this holds all of my stage clothes. . . .

Barbara and Dolly walk from bus to arena.

BARBARA
When Dolly isn't traveling on the bus, home is a twenty-three-room mansion outside Nashville. She's been married for eleven years to a contractor named Carl Dean. They have no children, see each other a total of about six weeks a year, but she says the marriage is perfect. Dolly writes her own songs. Many about her childhood when she was, she says, dirt poor, but much loved.

(Dolly Sings "Coat of Many Colors.")

Dolly and Barbara on camera.

BARBARA
Tell me about your childhood.

DOLLY
Well, there's really quite a bit to tell. I don't know how far back you want to start.

BARBARA
Let's start at the beginning.

DOLLY
Okay. I was born in a little log cabin on the banks of the Little Pigeon River. And, of course, at that time we only had three other children. There's twelve children. There's eight younger than me.

BARBARA
Dolly, where I come from, would I have called you a hillbilly?

DOLLY
If you'd had of, it would've been somethin' very natural, but I would've probably kicked your shins or somethin'. (LAUGHS) No. . .

BARBARA
Dolly, you said—and maybe you were talking about when you were a kid—you said, "I felt that I never belonged. I felt I was always different."

DOLLY
I wanted more than to just be a farmer's daughter, even though I'm proud to be. I just wanted pretty things. I wanted money to buy the things that I had always been impressed with as a child. I wanted to, I guess, to be a star.

BARBARA
Dolly, did you look like this when you were a kid?

DOLLY
Not quite.

BARBARA
I mean you didn't have the . . . the blonde wig. . .

DOLLY
No. . .

BARBARA
But when you went to school. When you were eleven, twelve, thirteen. Was it . . . this about you?

DOLLY
Well, you mean . . . the . . . full figure?
(LAUGHS)

BARBARA
Yeah, that's what I'm after.

DOLLY
Yeah, I thought that's what you meant. Well, actually, I've always been pretty well blessed. As a child I grew up fast. . . .

BARBARA
My assistant asked me something—and I'm going to blame it on her 'cause I wouldn't have had the nerve otherwise—is it all you?

DOLLY
(CHUCKLES) Well, I can't show you here right on television (BARBARA LAUGHS).

BARBARA
I'll take your word for it. . . .

DOLLY
I'm not all that curvy in this outfit.

Barbara Walters

BARBARA
No, it's not bad. Do you give your measurements?

DOLLY
No. I always just say that I weigh a hundred and plenty.

BARBARA
You don't have to look like this. You're very beautiful. You don't have to wear the blonde wigs. You don't have to wear the extreme clothes, right?

DOLLY
No. It's certainly a choice. I don't like to be like everybody else. I've often made this statement . . . that I would never stoop so low as to be fashionable. That's the easiest thing in the world to do. So I just decided that I would do somethin' that would at least get their attention. Once they got past the shock of the ridiculous way I looked and all that, then they would see there was parts of me to be appreciated. I'm very real, where it counts, and that's inside. And as far as my outlook on life and the way I care about people and the way I care about myself and the things that I care about. But I just chose to do this. Show business is a money-makin' joke and I just always liked tellin' jokes (CHUCKLES). . . Like I say, I am sure of myself as a person. I am sure of my talent. And I'm sure of my love for life and that sort of

Parton

thing. I'm very content. I like the kind of person that I am, so I can afford to piddle around and do-diddle around with makeups and clothes and stuff, because I am secure with myself. . . .

BARBARA
Listen, tell me about this marriage of yours. You don't see him very much. You're on the road most of the time. You've said, "I know that this marriage will always last. This man gives me everything I need." How do you know?

DOLLY
Well, I need freedom. The man gives me freedom.

BARBARA
So why get married?

DOLLY
Well, why not?

BARBARA
Why? I mean if what you want most is freedom, why have a husband . . . tucked away someplace that you see six weeks a year?

DOLLY
He has the same freedom. See the thing of it is, you don't find a person that you can be happy with and that can accept you the way you are and can share the things and the plans for the future and to enjoy your home. We have our foundation, we have our roots, we have all the things that everybody's lookin' for, and that's happiness in the marriage.

BARBARA
Well, what about when you're on the road. Weeks at a time. No temptations?

DOLLY
Well I didn't say that we've never had temptations.

BARBARA
When you have these temptations (DOLLY LAUGHS), does anything happen that he could be jealous of?

DOLLY
No, not really, because he's the kind of person that if bein' apart, if we should meet somebody I would never tell him. He would never know and it wouldn't hurt him. And it's the same way with him. I wouldn't want to know it. As long as he loves me and as long as he's good to me and as long as we're good to each other . . . I don't think that it happens, but I'm just sayin' I wouldn't want to pry in it. I've got better things to do than to sit around in my room thinkin', *Oh, what's Carl doin' tonight? I wonder if he's with somebody and this and that?*

BARBARA
I don't know too much about country music. But what I did know about you before we met was that you started and still are with the Grand Ole Opry. That you'd been with a very prominent country music singer named Porter Wagoner for six years. You worked with your family. Had the whole band together. And then, in the last year, good-bye Porter Wagoner, a new Hollywood agent. Good-bye to the family band. And I hear the folks back home saying, "She's gone Hollywood. Dolly's changed." (DOLLY CHUCKLES) Or "Dolly might change." Not that she's changed yet. Tell us about all that.

DOLLY
Well actually I think a lot of what I'm doin' musically has been distorted quite a bit with so much press and dwellin' on the same thing. I'm not makin' a crossover from country to pop. I'm trying to be accepted in the pop field as well as the country field. I feel my music is its own music, just like I'm my own person. I write 'em, I sing 'em. I have my own way of singin' 'em, my own way of doin' it, and as a business person I like to think that there's more money to be made than the money I've been makin'. I've been workin' too hard, too long, for too little.

BARBARA
What do you make? What did you make as a country star?

DOLLY
Well, I made a great deal. I usually don't . . . I would probably [say] the most money that I've made as a country artist would probably be maybe five, six hundred thousand dollars a year. But, you've got to pay expenses and all this sort of thing. Of course, that's not countin' records and this sort of thing, but when you say that you can make millions compared to thousands and if you are going to be in this business, if you are talented, if you do love it, then why not touch as many people. My dream was always to make as many people happy as I could in this life. . . .

Well, I want to be a star. A universal star. I would like to be a superstar. I guess all people dream of that. So in order to be a superstar you can't be just a superstar in one area. That means you have to appeal to a majority of people, and that's what I'm trying to do.

BARBARA
When is all this gonna happen?

DOLLY
It's happenin' now.

BARBARA
Are you there yet? Are you a superstar yet?

183

DOLLY

No. No. No. No. I'm not near where I dream of being.

BARBARA

Do you think that this superstardom will be here, let's say, in five years?

DOLLY

Yes.

BARBARA

Dolly, you've said of yourself that you live in your own imagination. That sometimes you remind yourself of a fairy tale. I want to try a fairy tale on you . . . once upon a time there was a little girl from the Smoky Mountains. Her name was Dolly Parton and—

DOLLY

She lived in a small town in the mountains, which she loved, because it was a comfort, because she knew there was love and security there, in her family. But she was a child, very curious. And she wanted all the things that she had always been impressed with. Like the fairy tales of Mother Goose stories and the Cinderellas and the lost slipper. Well, I guess she kinda wanted to find the other slipper in sort of a way so she worked hard and she dreamed a lot. And one day, it came true. She was a fairy princess and she lived happily ever after.

Dolly going off stage in arena.
Dolly in car with roses.

Parton, Stella

Born: May 4, 1949, Locust Ridge, Sevier County, Tennessee
Married: Jim Molloy
Children: s. Timmy

The sixth of twelve Parton children, Stella at age nine sang *You are My Sunshine* with sister Dolly, age twelve, on a local Tennessee radio station. Singer, songwriter, instrumentalist (she plays guitar and autoharp), Stella wrote her first song in 1975, "I Want to Hold You in My Dreams Tonight." It made it to number seven on the *Billboard* country chart without benefit of a major label. In 1976, she joined Elektra/Asylum in Nashville and released her first album *Country Sweet* in 1977, including three of her own compositions, "If You're a Dream,"

"I've Got to Have You for Mine," and "The More I Change." Her first big 1977 single as a performer was "I'm Not that Good at Good-bye," cowritten by Don Williams and Bob McDill. Her top-chart hit, "Danger of a Stranger," is by Shel Silverstein and Even Stevens. In mid-1978, her "Four Little Letters" hit the charts followed by "Standard Lie Number One" and "Stormy Weather."

Harry Langdon

Stella Parton

Harry Langdon

Paycheck, Johnny

Born: May 31, 1941, Greenfield, Ohio

"Take This Job and Shove It," made him into a working man's cult hero early in 1978, a position further solidified by flip side "Colorado Cool Aid" and follow-up "Me and the IRS"—all of this just a few months after his 1977 smash, "I'm the Only Hell My Mama Ever Raised." Johnny's career has been a series of fits and starts, highs and lows. He began in the late fifties as a bass guitarist sideman for artists like Porter Wagoner, Faron Young, George Jones, and Ray Price, later switching to steel guitar and changing his name briefly to Donny Young. Back to being Johnny Paycheck, he did such honky-tonky hits as "Lovin' Machine," "Jukebox Charlie," "I've Got Someone to Kill," and "You'll Recover in Time." In 1966, he wrote Tammy Wynette's first hit, "Apartment Number Nine," followed by "Touch My Heart," a top-ten triumph for Ray Price. Troubles began with the business failure of his company, Little Darlin' Records, and a self-confessed alcoholism. Taking the cure, he bounced back in the early seventies with famed Epic producer Billy Sherrill, starting with "She's All I Got," "Someone to Give My Love To," and leading through trial and error to "Mr. Lovemaker," "Song and Dance Man," and "For a Minute There." His albums include *11 Months and 29 Days* (which refers to his suspended jail sentence for passing a bad check) and *Take This Job and Shove It*. His late 1978 hit single was "Friend, Lover, Wife."

Pearl, "Cousin" Minnie (Sarah Ophelia Colley Cannon)

Born: October 25, 1912, Centerville, Tennessee
Married: Henry Cannon

An admirer once called Minnie Pearl the "Jack Benny of country—all she has to do is step onstage and people start laughing!" Even on radio where you can't see the famous hat with the dangling pricetag and the "yeller" dress, the one joyous word, "how-deeeeee!" instantly identifies "Cousin" Minnie Pearl as she's about to impart some country wisdom such as, "The chicken is the only animal that can gain weight and not show it in the face!" As Sarah Ophelia Colley, she studied drama at Nashville's stylish Ward-Belmont College and taught dancing while slowly developing her Minnie Pearl character. The hat with the pricetag evolved from her actually forgetting to remove it once before a performance; the yellow mountain woman's dress came from a second-hand store in North Carolina; the "good-luck" shoes have been carefully worn for nearly forty years. Grinder's Switch actually exists—not as a town but as a railroad switching station where her father Thomas, a sawmill owner, took his logs. "Cousin" Minnie joined the Opry in 1940 and has become one of the most beloved characters in American humor. Elected to the Country Music Hall of Fame in 1975, she appears regularly on "Hee Haw," the "Tonight Show," and top country fairs, where she still cracks up audiences with her wistful desire to "ketch a feller."

Epic

Presley, Elvis

Born: January 8, 1935, East Tupelo, Mississippi
Married: Priscilla Beaulieu (div.)
Children: d. Lisa Marie
Died: August 16, 1977, Memphis, Tennessee

The following is an extract from
The Illustrated Elvis by W.A. Harbinson.

He is born in a two-room plank house in Tupelo, Mississippi. The house is raised off the ground on legs of concrete and brick, has a porch, three windows and a pointed roof. Small, narrow, redolent of poverty, it resists the heavy rains and the summer's dry heat, but otherwise doesn't amount to much. The floors are bare. There is no running water. Outside is a shit-house, a pump, some trees and untended grass. A few miles north-east, in the Princeville Cemetery, his twin brother is buried not forty-eight hours after he is born. Life is raw in Tupelo, Mississippi.

It is January, 1935. Highway 78 runs from Memphis to Alabama, passing close to the Presley home in Tupelo. The land rises and falls, drinks the rain, fights the sun, and is webbed with dried creeks and stooped fences. This is Black country. There are cottonfields and sugar cane plantations; there is white trash and black scum. You can hear the two groups singing with evangelical fervor in those nights when God keeps them from madness; they both sing the same songs.

About a year after the birth of Elvis Aron Presley and the almost simultaneous death of his brother Jesse Garon, one of history's more catastrophic tornados tears through Tupelo. It spirals blackly to the sky, splitting the dark clouds, ripping through the land with the cold blind malevolence of nature. It's a nightmare, a dreamer's deep trap, the howling eye of oblivion. It kills a few hundred people, injures more than a thousand, and destroys a great number of homes. It takes thirty-two seconds. But the Presley shack, in the east side of Tupelo, remains untouched.

Now we see them. They are a family of three. The mother has a face of extraordinary beauty, her hair pulled back tight over delicate ears, her eyes dark and luminous. The features are fragile, hinting at deprivation and the sort of religious faith that can move mountains. She is wearing a cheap, patterned dress, a belt buckled at the waist; her left hand is looped over the shoulder of her equally sombre husband. He wears a faded shirt, a hat tipped back on his head; is lean, hungry and radiating the innocence of a man who does not hope for too much.

They are workers and they know it.

The boy, Elvis Aron, stands between them. He is two or three years old, a real sharecropper's kid. He is wearing dungarees, a grubby two-toned shirt, and has a hat on his head just like Dad. The hat is tipped cutely to the right, slanting down over huge, fine eyes whose pupils seem enormous and give him a penetrating look which is at odds with his round baby face. The nose appears to be flattened, the cheeks are too chubby, and already the now famous curl is distorting his fat lips. He is, in short, an unlovely but irresistible kid—the kind normally doomed to oblivion in a land that eats cheap labor.

Some time later when the boy is six, there is another photograph. It is a head shot. He has developed some of his mother's more delicate features, is golden-haired, wide-eyed, and beautiful. But the famous lip is there, twisted down to the left, giving the angel a mischievous look, again irresistible. When at the age of eight he is photographed again, he is taller, slimmer and quite docile; every mother's dream child.

In this six years the parents have aged considerably. The mother is heavier, her hair is loose but cropped short, and the curve to her legs speaks of hard work. The father wears baggy trousers, a worker's leather jacket and a cheap shirt. The boy, now called Elvis, is dressed in local style, with a long-sleeved white shirt, open at the neck, and ragged trousers tugged chest-high by braces; he is Huckleberry Finn.

The great myths of America lie behind him. Born of a family that is scourged by its own poverty, maybe he already dreams some heady dreams. In this land that he roams, through the cottonfields and swamplands, the air is heavy with the romance of its own history. The Union and Confederate armies have clashed on these slopes, the town has been razed in the fury of civil strife, and the Indians have left names that will roll on the tongue with all the magic of ancient hieroglyphics: this land is a dreamer's masque.

The boy will sense this if he doesn't quite realize it. He will learn to love God, to respect even his worst elders, and to stand by his country right or wrong. He wanders through the bellied fields and the sloping swamplands, puts his ear to the wind and listens closely. The air is filled with singing that came out of slave ships, now pours from black lips, fills white churches. It is the singing of the Blacks who have given to the white man a culture he will never acknowledge: it is American Gospel. His parents and his country and the First Assembly of God church are the meaning and marked horizons of his life: there is no other way.

His mother has lived in Lee County all of her life, has five sisters, three brothers, a hard time. Her folks had farmed some, but were otherwise anonymous; just another large underfed family, struggling along. When she met Vernon Presley, a man as poor as she, they had a quick courtship and got married; a romantic endeavor. Her husband was a quiet man, grabbing work where he could, doing his best to get on in this county where work wasn't plentiful at the best of times. From sun-up to sunset he hoed cotton and corn, humped bales, delivered milk, sorted lumber—tried just about everything. So he did the rounds, working here, working there, while his wife climbed from bed in the cold dawn to make breakfast, then work in the garment factory—twelve long hours a day. Now the child sees them, is enfolded in

their love, but knows nothing of how they survive. His mother embraces him, comforts him, making up for her lost child, soothing this one's clinging fears. He will always be loved.

They have breakfast, the dawn breaks, the day begins; it is Sunday, it is time for church. His mother takes him by the hand, and with a wave to his father walks him down to the small church on Adams Street, where they stand and worship.

It is the Day of our Lord in America in 1943.

Here, and in the fields, and in Beale Street in Memphis, he learns everything he will ever need to know.

Black and white are apart, but their cultures have merged, and it is nowhere more obvious than in music. No one will acknowledge it—it is a tacit understanding —but black religion fills white churches in ways that aren't questioned, and this white boy feels black in his bones. The preacher chants fervently, the congregation shrieks "Praise God!" and gazing out at the cotton-fields, he hears the noise from the other churches, the raving gospel of the blacks, and takes their rhythm into his bloodstream: when he sings, it's with tainted breath.

The singing comes as naturally as breathing: it is part of his heritage. He lives in the very seat of American folk music where white man and black man swop minor traits. White music is hillbilly, black music is the blues, and some day the two will have to meet. His singing, therefore, is not unusual; it is something he grows with. It is the enthusiasm with which he steps forward to do it and the angelic repose of his face as he utters the words which are remarkable. But he learns early and well. He sings gospel in the churches, folk songs on the porches, and he sometimes sways his body in childish emulation of the Blacks he has watched in the fields.

Out of his untutored eyes he observes his parents' withering poverty. They both rise with the dawn and they work hard all day and they don't have too much time for pleasure. His father keeps changing jobs, they have to keep changing houses, endlessly, it seems. He sees his mother's face, feels the tension in her flesh, and he swears one day he'll mend things.

He is at that time of life when the golden haze of childhood must give way to the first buffetings of reality. It is possible that he now sees behind their shielding smiles to the hopelessness lying beyond, to the land's clinging poverty. He sings to his mother when the storms drive them from home; he stands up to sing at school and in church, clear, tremulous, uncertain, with an arresting sincerity that brings tears to the eyes. The songs are bathetic in the country and western vein, tied to blue moons and broken hearts and trains howling lonesome on those tracks that lead back into history—the songs of deprived folk. Or they are hymns, the spirituals of his church, and they are spun with a high Southern drawl. They are songs at the crossroads.

He's a spoilt child, but he carries it well. Later it will show in contradiction—in his narcissism and in his private humility—but for now it protects him. No one who remembers him will complain of his manners. Sweet and unfailingly polite, quiet and respectful, the hint of rebellion has never touched him. Poor but decent, average at school, he gathers flowers with the other kids, fools around, rarely gets into mischief: an anonymous boy.

Some things, however, are prophetic. At the tender age of ten Elvis Presley is entered for the annual singing contest of the Mississippi-Alabama Fair. He stands up on a chair, sings Red Foley's "Old Shep" and walks off with the five-dollar second prize. He's sung it at school, and to his parents and friends, and he will sing it many times in the future—a favourite song, a real tear-jerker. Some day he will sing it to the masses.

Now he has a guitar in his hands, bought by his parents. He learns to play it by listening to the radio, to the hillbilly stations—to Jimmie Rodgers and Roy Acuff and Ernest Tubb and many others—all of them steeped in country music. He listens to the blues, to the proliferating black men, to Big Bill Broonzy, Otis Span, B. B. King, John Lee Hooker, to Jimmy Reed and Chester Burnett and Booker White—all steeped in "gutter" music. And finally, most always, he sings in church with his folks, and adds spirituals to his broadening repertoire;

he picks them up, he plays tricks with them.

His family moves close to Shakerag, Tupelo's black ghetto, and Elvis finds himself at a new school. He is thirteen years old and is photographed looking threatening in a cowboy suit in front of a painted western landscape. He is, in this photograph, remarkably similar to what he will later become: his eyes are dark-shadowed, his face is lean and narcissistic and a fancy cravat dangles from his neck; he wears a broad belt that is studded and glittering over a pair of real fancy two-toned pants. He is still thirteen years old when the family moves yet again, migrating like the blacks and the other poor whites from the harsh fields to the bright lights of Memphis—the home of the blues.

In Memphis things are bigger, more frightening, more exciting: the alien streets run for miles. There's a new kind of life here, and a new breed of people; there are cinemas and cars and televisions and juke joints, and the kids are slick and strangely restless. The whole world is changing, and while he doesn't comprehend it, he responds to its secret siren call: he yearns for material things.

It is Tennessee's largest city, and though they live near the commercial centre, they are as poor as they ever were before. They have a one-room apartment and share a bath with three families; the walls are ragged with holes and filthy. He goes to a huge school where the strangeness terrifies him, but eventually he adjusts, makes some friends, dates some girls, and starts to change fast without knowing it.

Memphis envelops him.

While both his parents work, his father moving from job to job, Elvis finds his way about the streets and local customs. He is growing, getting acne, putting grease on his hair, and, though he is still quiet and polite, he is finding the confidence he needs. All the kids now have crew cuts but he wears his hair long, and his sideburns cause more than one fight—he is not slow to swing. Yes, for all his charm, for all his shyness and gentility, he has a violent temper and a certain arrogance that seem totally at odds with his character: he'll cut loose if he's pushed.

They move again. This time they are imprisoned in a three-story brick building that looms over the leaning shacks of the poorest blacks. Here there are drug stores, beer parlours and factories—and just half a mile away, burning bright in the night, is Beale Street, the home of the blues. There he wanders, past the pimps and the whores, around the winos and the junkies, walking under the bright lights, treading with care, thrilled by the danger, by the strangeness of it all. Blue eyes wide and innocent, drinking it in he listens to the music of the honky-tonks, the beer parlours, the crumbling rooms. The songs are different from his own, they are crude and exciting; they are shocking words growled by these raw, battered blacks to the rhythm of guitars and harmonicas: they are fresh, more vital. And now the music of his childhood, the country songs and the spirituals, are being fused in his mind with what he hears in this street and will make him the future white negro.

Now sixteen years old he buys his clothes in Beale Street—Black clothes, bright and flashy—he shows a peculiar preference for garish pink and black in the age of the grey flannel suit. Take this, and his long hair and his ever-growing sideburns, place it down in its context, in the Eisenhower years, and you have something outrageous on the loose.

Naturally, he continues to sing, to carry his guitar around. He plays occasionally for his friends, in the school's variety show, at picnics and at the local boys' club—never professional. He isn't showy with it, is more often reluctant—it's just something he does—but once he starts he really gets into it.

The length of his hair now appears to be tied to his desire to become a truck driver like his father. But he's like most other kids: trailing the sweater girls, doubling up to go to movies, taking rides at the fair, throwing balls at milk bottles, longing for a car to go cruising in —a pretty average All American Boy.

The adolescents hang out around the drug stores and juke joints, bored by the past, embalmed by the present, and casting their hazy eyes towards the romantic future. This God-given country is going through its dullest phase, and they can't stand their parents for suffering it. It's excitement they want, and it's excitement they will get, but at the moment they just don't know where to turn. The atmosphere is heavy, desolation clouds the brain; they are affluent and don't know how to spend it —*it's all such a drag*. The girls in their sweaters have bobbed hair and lipstick; the guys—slacks and jumpers, domes neatly crew-cut—play sport. On the radio they listen to Rosemary Clooney and Doris Day, to Vic

Damone and Eddie Fisher, and that crap's enough to make you want to weep. There is, it is true, a slight rebellion in the air, most noticeably against parents in grey suits, against all that's static. Yet some things are beginning to happen: Marlon Brando is a brute who sends shivers down the spine, there are people called Beatniks in the most alluring cities and, most important, four-beats-to-the-bar are now drawing crowds back to the dance halls. Yes, changes are coming, but no one quite knows what they are—they only know that they are waiting for the Phoenix to rise from the ashes of postwar mediocrity, for some cool and dangerous and sexy redeemer, some Lazarus.

He is here amongst them and he goes quite unnoticed. He is normal. A growing lad. But that's not to say he's ignored.

In 1953 Bill Haley and his Comets have a hit with an item called "Crazy Man Crazy," which words henceforth enter the Language. The changes have started.

Towards the end of his school years Elvis starts working part-time to help out his struggling parents. He works as an usher at Loew's State Theatre, but has to quit when he punches a fellow usher. He works the evening shift at the Marl Metal Products Company which is rough, and makes him fall asleep at school. For this reason he quits again.

His parents are still badly off. They are harassed by the Housing Authority, and they never know when they'll have to move again. The debts are piling up, the kid mows lawns for pocket money, yet no matter how poor they might be, they always look after him. They even go so far as to buy him a Lincoln coupe, which ostensibly is for all of the family, but he uses it. Life sways on a tightrope, but considering the circumstances, he has a very good time—goes to parties, does the bop, hangs on juke boxes, gets his oats—but he never runs short on the gratitude: he returns all the love he gets.

He leaves school in the June of 1953, gets a factory job, then moves to the Crown Electricity Company. Finally he is a truck driver and he loves it: he is earning his keep. People notice that he likes to comb his hair and that he doesn't give a damn who sees him do it. In fact, so little does he think of the opinions of others that he has his hair trimmed in the beautician's instead of the barber shop.

All life is an accident; so might fame be. Certainly, in his case, he comes by it casually enough.

One of the places the kid drives past in his battered Ford pick-up is the Memphis Recording Service on Union Street. It's a modest offshoot of the Sun Recording Company who specialize in private recordings. The kid has never been in there, but he knows all about it, and he wants to cut a platter for his mother—four dollars, two sides.

It is the summer of 1953. A hot, busy Saturday. Every hustler in Memphis carries a guitar, and thinks he's gonna make it real big when he trembles his tonsils. The office is crowded. There must be some tension in the air.

The kid sits in a chair, slicks back his greased hair, and waits his turn. The office manager at this time is one Marion Keisker who has recently been Miss Radio of Memphis. She asks him what he can sing, to which he replies: "Anything." Unperturbed, she then asks him who he sounds like: "I don't sound like nobody," he says. He is shy and polite but he really doesn't know what else to say: it is the innocence of genius.

The kid, now dwelling in the safety of this innocence, goes in to cut the disc for his Ma. He sings one of his favorites—the Ink Spots' "My Happiness"—then he tries "That's When Your Heartaches Begin," a real country tear-jerker.

He doesn't like the sound of his own voice.

This studio is sitting at the crossroads where black music meets white. The owner, Sam Phillips, who loves black music and sells it, is on the lookout for a white man who can sing it: this development must come. If the kid is a genius who will never comprehend it, then Sam Phillips is his reasoning second half. Already Sam has cut records that will go down as classics—though neither he nor his staff are yet to know it. It is even likely that the kid in his studio has been influenced by some of the material: Joe Hill Louis' "We All Gotta Go Sometime," Rufus Thomas' "Bear Cat," perhaps even "Walkin' in the Rain" by the Prisonaires, who sound just like his much beloved Ink Spots. Anyway he is here. And strangely, and contrary to the normal house rules, Miss Keisker decides to put the boy on tape.

"Over and over I heard Sam saying: 'If I could find a white man who had the Negro sound and the Negro feel, I could make a million dollars.' This is what I heard in Elvis, this . . . what I guess they now call 'soul', this Negro sound. So I taped it. I wanted Sam to know."

The kid finishes and takes his platter home to his mother; his good deed for this day is done. When Sam Phillips hears the tape, he is impressed, but says the boy needs some work. Miss Keisker keeps his address and the phone number of a friend, after which life cruises on in its mellow way. A few months later, on the first Friday of January 1954, the kid returns to cut another private record. He sings "Casual Love" and "I'll Never Stand in Your Way," then he shuffles out of the studio. He starts learning to be a spark, secretly yearns to be a singer, and family struggles continue.

About eight months after he has first visited the Memphis Recording Service, they call him up and invite him back to the studio; they have something to try him with.

Sam Phillips has come across a song called "Without You" and Miss Keisker thinks the kid might be right for it. He isn't. He is awful. He just can't get it right. They try it once more, then give up in despair, have a coffee break. Sam Phillips asks the kid just what he *can* do, and the kid replies: "I can do anything." And by way of demonstration he does western, gospel, Dean Martin, Billy Eckstine—you name it, he tries it, he does it. And Sam Phillips falls for it.

What Phillips then does is arrange a meeting between the kid and a skinny guitarist known to all as Scotty Moore. They meet at Scotty's house and when the kid walks through the door he is dressed all in pink but for his white shoes. They horse around for a while and are joined by Bill Black, who isn't at all impressed by this freaky boy. But Bill Black is a bass player, and when they get into the Sun studios, there is just him and Scotty backing Elvis: they will make some extraordinary sounds.

This test session extends into months of hard labor as they work to develop a style. They don't know what they're looking for, and the kid's voice is weird, but for some reason Sam keeps them at it. A couple of times the kid appears with Scotty's band in a local club, but not too many people think it sounds right. They work on. They are not amused. The kid has wild clothes and he's a bit of a looker, but he sure in hell ain't no great singer. Then, after months, out of some intuition, in the hollows of the studio, in that air of desolation, Sam says: "Okay, this is the session." And they turn on the tapes.

The first thing they try is "I Love You Because," a real country weeper so doleful it is more like a dirge. They do four takes of the song and the kid's voice is freaky, pure country but with something else again. He sings high and sings low, sometimes misses a note, and the trembling on occasion seems deliberate. Also, on the first take, he tries a spoken bridge, during which he drawls his words with all the slimy innuendo of a hoodlum inching into the alley. "Honey," he drawls, breaking down any sentiment, "every time I'm walkin' by your side. . ." And the contrast is stunning. But it doesn't make a great song. It is pure country and western, an undefiled corn-cob weeper, and it has all the shameless sentimentality of that particular genre. Still, they keep trying. On the second take they cut the spoken bridge and instead add a whistled introduction. The kid sings it much deeper, guitar and bass are more assured, and it is certainly the best of the batch. They try it twice more, but one take is not completed and the fourth version will never be released.

He has cut his first disc.

After this, they turn off the tapes and try some of "those country-orientated things." Apparently none of them come to much—most certainly they aren't taped—and they settle for having a break. Sam is back in the control room, the boys are slugging Coke, and the kid takes his guitar in his hands and tries one of his favorites. The song is Arthur Crudup's "That's All Right Mama," a jumping blues number, and when the kid cuts into it, singing high and mean, his guitarist and bassist follow suit. The hair of Sam Phillips stands up on his neck: it's electric. He turns on the tapes, makes them run through it again, and that's it. Finally, and almost by accident, he has found what he wants.

The vocal on "That's All Right Mama" is high, urgent, desolate, and decidedly sensual. It's pure gutter blues with a pounding bass rhythm, but Scotty Moore's guitar retains a country flavor. It is exactly, to the very last note, what Sam Phillips wants. "On one side we had a country and western ballad with a rhythm and blues feel, and on the other side we had a strictly rhythm and blues song with a slight country feel to it." The latter is "That's All Right Mama"; the former is "Blue Moon of Kentucky." When they cut "That's All Right Mama" they need something to back it, and finally, four days later, they find something. The first take of "Blue Moon" is a brief, medium-tempo, country rocker with a strong and assured vocal treatment. At the end of it,

Scotty runs humorously down the chords, that kid takes a nervous breath, and Sam Phillips, with a laugh, says, "Fine, man! Hell, that's *different!* That's a *pop* song!" But they tape another version and this one is much faster, with an extraordinarily driving and eccentric vocal that turns the whole thing inside out. This track it is that will back "That's All Right Mama," and both tracks form a remarkable debut: black music and white music at long last have joined at the crossroads.

It is the Year of our Lord in America in 1954.

Pride, Charley

Born: March 18, 1938, Sledge, Mississippi
Married: Rozene
Children: s. Kraig, Dion; d. Angela

As an insight to Pride's talents, one need only ponder some of his achievements. He has been chosen Artist of the Year and Best Male Country Vocalist of the Year by the Country Music Association; Entertainer of the Year, by the Music Operators of America; Top Country Artist on albums, Top Male Vocalist on singles, and Top Male Vocalist on albums by *Billboard* and Top Male Vocalist in *Cash Box*'s Country Music Award List. In addition, he has won Grammies for Best Sacred Performance for his RCA album *Did You Think to Pray,* for Best Gospel Performance for his single, "Let Me Love," and for Best Country Performance, Male, for his album, *Songs of Love by Charley Pride.*

With his first appearance with the Grand Ole Opry in January 1967, Charley Pride assumed a permanent place in the field of country music and became the first black performer to be recognized as a major country talent.

An RCA recording artist since Chet Atkins signed him in 1965, Charley has developed into a true hit-maker through his many singles, which have been near or at the top of the Country and Western best-selling charts, and the albums he has made, beginning with *Country Charley Pride. The Best of Charley Pride* became his first gold album.

As a stage performer, he draws sellout houses on completely booked-up tours and in the top

Charley Pride

country music rooms in the nation, like the Longhorn in Dallas (now his hometown), Panther Hall in Fort Worth, Randy's Rodeo in San Antonio, and the Playroom and the Domino in Atlanta. His gold album, *Charley Pride—in Person,* was recorded live in Panther Hall.

He became a country-music star after sampling the world of big-league baseball and is now recognized in his new field both in this country and throughout Western Europe. Network TV exposure has

ranged from the "Lawrence Welk Show" and the "Kraft Music Hall" to "Hee Haw" and the "Johnny Cash Show."

Like many other country singers, including Eddy Arnold, Johnny Cash, and Glen Campbell, Charley was raised close to the earth. He spent his youth in the Mississippi cotton fields working beside his parents and his ten brothers and sisters. By the time he was five, he knew farming was not going to be his career. Charley had heard about Jackie Robinson, the great baseball player.

He left his hometown of Sledge at seventeen and started playing ball in the Negro American League, with Detroit and with the Memphis Red Sox. He interrupted this portion of his career for a two-year military stint, during which time he married his wife, Rozene. Returning to baseball, he made it to the majors in 1961 for a brief period, playing outfield and pitching for the Los Angeles Angels.

During this time he was living in Montana, and between baseball seasons, Pride worked as a smelter for Anaconda Mining's zinc complex in Great Falls by day and as a nightclub entertainer evenings.

Late in 1963, one of the great country stars, Red Sovine, happened in on Charley's club act and suggested that the singing ballplayer seriously consider a music career. Sovine arranged for a recording session in Nashville, where Charley went early the following year. The results of the session so impressed Chet Atkins that Charley was signed to a long-term Victor contract, and he cut his first RCA single, "Snakes Crawl at Night," in 1965. His recording of "Just Between You and Me" won him a Grammy nomination in 1966 for the Best Country and Western Male Vocal Performance.

Other Most Promising Male Artist awards followed from many of the country music publications during that year, and these honors were capped by an invitation to debut at the Grand Ole Opry, where he was introduced by his long-time idol, Ernest Tubb. In 1978, his hits included "Someone Loves You Honey" as a single and LP, and "Burgers and Fries."

Prophet, Ronnie

Born: 1943, Calumet, Quebec, Canada
Married: Jeanne

Ronnie played for square dances in

Ronnie Prophet

RCA Records and Tapes

Canada in his teens, moved south to Fort Lauderdale, Florida, and went to Nashville in 1969. His club act described by Chet Atkins as "the greatest one-man show I've ever seen" has made him a headliner at the Sands, Las Vegas, and other major show spots around the country. In 1977, his first RCA album, *Ronnie Prophet,* included hit singles "Sanctuary," "My Big World," "Shine On," and "It's Enough."

Pruett, Jeanne

Born: Pell City, Alabama
Married: Jack
Children: s. Jack; d. Jael

As an exclusive songwriter for Marty Robbins Enterprises, she wrote many of his hits, including "Count Me Out," "Waiting in Reno," "Lily of the Valley" and "Love Me." Her songs have also been recorded by Tammy Wynette, Nat Stuckey, and Conway Twitty. As a singer, her first performing hit was "Hold to My Unchanging Love" in 1971, followed by the superhit, "Satin Sheets," which won *Billboard*'s Best Country and Best Female album awards for 1973. Since then, her hits include: "I'm Your Woman," "Just Like Your Daddy," "A Poor Man's Woman," and her 1978 Mercury single, "I'm a Woman." Jeanne and her Pure Country Band tour the United States and abroad and appear often at Grand Ole Opry.

Jeanne Pruett

Mercury/Lavender-Blake Agency, Inc.

R

Rabbitt, Eddie
(Edward Thomas)

Born: November 27, 1941,
Brooklyn, New York
Married: Jeannine

The son of an Irish fiddler and accordion player, Eddie grew up in
East Orange, New Jersey, playing
local clubs before moving to Nashville in 1967. His first night in the
James Robertson Hotel was so de-
pressing, he wrote "Working My
Way Up from the Bottom." Recorded some time later by Roy Drusky,
it made thirty-three on the charts
and established him as a writer. Although eager to be a recording artist, his early successes were strictly

Anthony Friedkin

Eddie and his father

Anthony Friedkin

as a writer: Elvis Presley did "Kentucky Rain" and it became his fiftieth million seller. Ronnie Milsap did "Pure Love," which also sold over a million. Finally performing himself on Elektra, his "You Get to Me," "Forgive and Forget," and "I Should Have Married You" made the top twenty charts, a warm-up for his first number-one hit, "Drinking My Baby Off My Mind," followed by "Do You Right Tonight." In 1977, other number-one singles included: "Two Dollars in the Jukebox" and "Rocky Mountain Music" also on an LP of the same name and "We Can't Go on Living Like This" from his LP, *Rabbitt*. His big 1978 releases included the single, "I Just Want to Love You" and the top-twenty LP *Variations*.

Radio Stations Playing Country Music

Alabama

WARI	1480
WAAO	1530
WANA	1490
WRAB	1380
WBCA	1110
WYAM	450
WYDE	850
WZZK-FM	104.7
WRAG	590
WBYE	1370
WBIB	1110
WHOS	800
WAGF	1320
WTVY-FM	95.5
WELB	1350
WIRB	600
WLAY-FM	105.5
WXOR	1340
WZOB	1250
WAAX	570
WTWX-FM	95.9
WHRT	860
WBHP	1230
WKSJ-FM	94.9
WLIQ	1360
WUNI	1410
WBAM	740
WHIY	1530
WAOA	1520
WOAB-FM	104.9
WVSM	1500
WTUN-FM	100.1
WEYY	1580
WNUZ	1230
WTLS	1300
WJRD	1150
WETU	1250
WEZQ	1300

5 Hours Daily

WATM	1590
WCRL	1570
WELR-FM	95.3
WJDB-FM	95.3
WYLS	1350

Alaska

KYAK	650
KIAK	970
KNEY-FM	100.1

16 Hours Daily

KNOM	780

12 Hours Daily

KOTZ	720

9 Hours Daily

KTKN	930
KJNP	1170

Arizona

Country Exclusively

KPIN	1260
KCKY	1150
KAPR	930
KAFF	930
KIKO-FM	100.3
KJJJ	910
KNIX	1580
KNIX-FM	102.5
KCUB	1290
KHOS	940
KHIL	1250

Arkansas

Country Exclusively

KPCA	1580
KENA	1450
KBIB	1560
KVOM	800
KOKR-FM	105.5
KDXE	1380
KADL	1270
KYDE	1590
KUOA	1290
KSPR	1590
KTMN	1530
KRLW	1320

California

Country Exclusively

KFVY	1280
KUZZ	970
KROP	1300
KRED	1480
KARM	1430
KEAP	980
KMAK	1340
KFAT-FM	94.5
KNGS	620
KLAC	570
KKZZ	1380
KFOX	1280
KKOK	1410

KGBS-FM	97.1
KHOT	1250
KWIP	1580
KDOL	1340
KDOL-FM	97.7
KNEW	910
KPRA-FM	94.3
KCLM	1330
KZIQ	1360
KGUD	1490
KRAK	1140
KTOM	1380
KCKC	1350
KOZN-FM	103.7
KSON	1240
KSON-FM	97.3
KEEN	1370
KGUD	880
KKIO	1290
KVRE	1460
KVRE-FM	107.1
KGEN	1370
KBBQ	1590
KHAY-FM	100.7
KCIN	1590
KUBA	1600
KHEX-FM	103.9

Colorado

Country Exclusively

KSTX-FM	103.9
KPIK	1580
KPIK-FM	93.9
KSSS	740

Kris Kristofferson

KERE	710
KBRU-FM	101.7
KQUL	1340
KSTR	620
KYOU	1450
KLAK	1600
KLAK-FM	107.5
KPUB	1480
KUAD	1170

Connecticut

Country Exclusively

WCTY-FM	97.7
WEXT	1550
WIOF-FM	104.1

Florida

Country Exclusively

WPUL	1130
WKMK	1000
WBRD	1420
WBGC	1240
WAAZ-FM	104.9
WGTO	540
WDCF	1350
WELE-FM	105.9
WKKX	1310
WCAI	1350
WHEW-FM	101.9
WFTP	1330
WDVH	980
WGMA	1320
WQDI	1430
WKEM	1490

WYSE	1560
WQIK-FM	99.1
WCMG	1090
WVOJ	1320
WFIV	1080
WDSR	1340
WZST	1410
WTOT	980
WTYS	1340
WTAI	1560
WYRL-FM	102.3
WWOK	1260
WCKC	1490
WXBM-FM	102.7
WCCZ	1550
WMOP	900
WLMC-FM	103.1
WOKC	1570
WHOO	990
WPAP-FM	92.5
WSCM	1290
WNVY	1230
WPFA	790
WPLA	910
WJOE	1080
WCCF	1580
WAOC	1420
WELE	1590
WQYK-FM	99.5
WSUN	620
WOMA-FM	94.9
WHBO	1050
WQYK	1110
WFSH	1340
WEAT	850
WIRK-FM	107.9
WPCV-FM	97.5

8 Hours Daily

WGTX	1280
WQUH-FM	103.1
WKWF	1600

7 Hours Daily

WSWN	900

6 Hours Daily

WRYO-FM	98.5
WMUM-FM	94.3
WQSR-FM	102.5

5 Hours Daily

WJSB	1050
WFFG	1300
WAUC	1310

195

Georgia

Country Exclusively

WJAZ	960
WWCW-FM	101.7
WISK	1390
WDOL	1470
WNGC-FM	95.5
WPLO	590
WFNL	1600
WGUS	1380
WMGR	930
WBBK	1260
WYNR	790
WYNR-FM	101.5
WDYX	1460
WGRA	790
WCHK	1290
WCHK-FM	105.5
WLBB	1100
WVMG	1440
WPNX	1460
WFAV-FM	98.3
WCUG	850
WOKA	1310
WOKA-FM	106.7
WXLI	1230
WXLI-FM	92.7
WNRJ	1130
WNMT	1520
WKOG	1560
WKOG-FM	107.1
WGRI	1410
WCEH-FM	103.9
WYYZ	1580
WLOP	1370
WDEN	1500
WDEN-FM	105.3
WBIE-FM	101.5
WMAC	1360
WGSR	1570
WSFB	1490
WLAQ	1410
WBLW	810
WTOC-FM	94.1
WQQT	1450
WLOR	730
WTIF	1340
WLET	1420
WGOV-FM	92.9
WJEM	1150
WVOP	970
WQCK	1600

WLTE-FM	102.5

8 Hours Daily

WGCO-FM	102.3
WSNE	1170
WRCD	1430
WDWD	990
WDAX	1410

7 Hours Daily

WWCC	1440
WRWH	1350
WNGA	1600
WPLK	1220
WZOT-FM	107.1

6 Hours Daily

WULF	1400
WCLA	1470
WCLA-FM	107.1
WJJC	1270
WLFA	1590
WMTM	1300

Eddie Rabbitt

5 Hours Daily

WUFE	1260
WSBG	1350
WLAG	1240
WYTH	1250
WJAT	800
WJAT-FM	98.3
WTGA	1590

Hawaii

Country Exclusively

KAHU	940

Idaho

Country Exclusively

KBRJ	950
KGEM	1140
KMFE-FM	101.7
KUPI	980
KUPI-FM	99.1
KART	1400
KWIK	1240
KPST	1340
KAYT	970
KIGO	1400
KLIX	1310

Illinois

Country Exclusively

WFVR	1580
WRUL-FM	97.3
WKZI	800
WRXX-FM	95.3
WCCR	1580
WAMQ	670
WJJD	1160
WJEZ-FM	104.3
WHOW	1520
WIAI-FM	99.1
WDZ-FM	95.3
WCRA-FM	95.7
WFRL-FM	98.5
WAAG-FM	94.9
WGEN	1500

WJIL	1550
WSMI-FM	106.1
WKAI	1510
WDDD-FM	107.3
WMCL	1060
WAKC	1440
WRKX-FM	95.3
WACF-FM	98.5
WKKN	1150
WLUV	1520
WLUV-FM	96.7
WHBF	1270
WSHY	1560
WSHY-FM	104.9
WFMB-FM	104.5
WLAX-FM	97.7
WPMB	1500

Indiana

Country Exclusively

WIFF	1570
WSCH-FM	99.3
WGTC-FM	92.3
WWCM	1130
WWCM-FM	97.7
WCNB	1580
WROZ	1400
WLYV	1450
WFMS-FM	95.5
WIRE	1430
WKMO-FM	93.5
WWKI-FM	100.5
WASK-FM	105.3
WLBC	1340
WVAK	1560
WVAK-FM	95.3
WART-FM	98.3
WSVL-FM	97.1
WJVA	1580
WNDI	1550
WTHI	1480
WLJE-FM	105.5
WOCH	1460
WOCH-FM	106.1
WPDF	1550
WFML-FM	106.5
WBNL	1540
WBNL-FM	107.1
WFDT-FM	106.3
WAOV	1450
WWHC-FM	104.9
WNON-FM	100.9
WSLM	1220

WSLM-FM	98.9
WAMW	1580

Iowa

Country Exclusively

KKUZ	1150
KHAK	1360
KHAK-FM	98.1
KITR-FM	101.7
KWNT	1580
KSO	1460
KWMT	540
KOUR	1220
KSMN	1010
KWPC	860
KOEL-FM	92.3
KBCM-FM	95.5
KXEL	1540
KNEI	1140

Kansas

Country Exclusively

KKOY-FM	105.5
KOYY-FM	99.3
KWBW-FM	103.9
KCKN	1340
KCKN-FM	94.1
KLIB	1470
KNDY	1570
KOAM	860
KTOP-FM	100.3
KBUL	900
KFDI	1070
KFDI-FM	101.3
KFRM	550
KICT-FM	95.1

Kentucky

Country Exclusively

WCMI	1340
WYWY	950
WCBL	1290
WLBJ	1410
WMMG-FM	93.5
WCAK-FM	92.7
WTCR	1420
WMGE-FM	107.1
WSTL	1600
WKYW-FM	104.9
WGGC-FM	95.1
WKCM	1140
WSGS-FM	101.1
WSON	860

WLCB	1430
WHOP-FM	98.7
WJRS-FM	103.1
WIXI	1280
WAXU	1580
WINN	1240
WTMT	620
WFMW	730
WNGO	1320
WMIK	560
WFLW	1360
WBKR-FM	92.5
WKYQ-FM	93.3
WDHR-FM	92.1
WLSI	900
WRVK	1460
WCBR	1110
WJKY	1060
WSEK-FM	96.7
WRSL	1520
WRSL-FM	95.9
WTKY	1370
WKKS	1570
WEQO	1220
WEZJ	1440
WKDJ-FM	100.1

9 Hours Daily

WGRK	1550
WGRK-FM	103.1
WLLS	1600
WLLS-FM	106.3
WKCB	1540
WKCB-FM	107.1
WMST	1150
WCND	940
WSKV-FM	104.9

8 hours Daily

WKIC	1390
WDOC-FM	95.5
WTCW-FM	103.9

7 Hours Daily

WVKY	1270
WDOC	1310

6 Hours Daily

WMTA	1380
WYGO-FM	99.3
WGOH	1370
WGOH-FM	102.3
WAVE	970
WANO	1230

5 Hours Daily

WCPM	1280
WFKN	1220

WHIC	1520
WHIC-FM	94.3
WHBN	1420
WHBN-FM	99.3
WLBN	1590
WVJS	1420

Louisiana

Country Exclusively

WABL	1570
KTRY	730
KVOB	1340
WYNK	1380
WBOX	920
WLBI	1220
KLEB	1600
WSLG	1090
WFPR	1400
KCIL-FM	107.1
KJEF-FM	92.7
KTOC	920
KXKW	1520
KLCL	1470
KLIC	1230
KDBH-FM	97.7
WSHO	800
KREH	900
KWCL	1280
KPAL	1110
KAGY	1510
KRIH	990
KFLO	1300
KRMD	1340
KRMD-FM	101.1
KZEM	1310
KTIB	630
KMAR	1570
KMAR-FM	95.9
KUZN	1313

7 Hours Daily

KBSF	1460
KTKC-FM	92.7

6 Hours Daily

KALB	580
KCKW	1480
KSMB-FM	94.5
KLLA	1570
KNCB	1600

5 Hours Daily

KEUN	1490
WCKW-FM	92.3
WTGL-FM	103.3
KDXI	1360

Bobby Wright

United Artists Records/Bob Schanz Studio

Maine

Country Exclusively

WFAU	1340
WFAU-FM	101.3
WBGW-FM	97.1
WFST	600
WFST-FM	97.7
WCOU	1240
WCOU-FM	93.9
WXIV	1450
WPOR	1490
WPOR-FM	101.9

Maryland

Country Exclusively

WISZ	1590
WPOC-FM	93.1
WTRI	1520
WZYQ	1370
WFRB	560
WFRB-FM	105.3
WSMD	1560
WXTR-FM	104.1
WMSG	1050
WMSG-FM	92.1
WICO	1320
WICO-FM	94.3
WTHU	1450
WTTR	1470
WYII-FM	95.9

Massachusetts

Country Exclusively

WCOP	1150

WTTK-FM	100.7
WTYM	1600
WFMP-FM	104.5
WNEB	1230

Michigan

Country Exclusively

WNRS	1290
WWKQ	1500
WXOX	1250
WANG-FM	98.5
WKMF	1470
WJEB	1350
WCUZ	1230
WGRY-FM	100.1
WPLB-FM	107.3
WKKM-FM	92.1
WJCO	1510
WBUK	1560
WITL	1010
WITL-FM	100.7
WMUS	1090
WMUS-FM	106.9
WNBY-FM	93.5
WAOP	980
WMBN	1340
WMBN-FM	96.7
WIRX-FM	107.1
WDEE	1500
WSDS	1480
WZND-FM	99.3

Minnesota

Country Exclusively

KKIN	930
KCMT-FM	100.7
KLIZ	1380
KAOH	1390
KAOH-FM	94.9
KRAD	1590
KRAD-FM	103.9
KRSI	950
KDHL	920
KDHL-FM	95.9
KEHG	1480
KEHG-FM	107.1
WKKQ	1060
KRBI	1310
KTCR	690
KTCR-FM	97.1
WLOL	1330
KMRS	1230
KDAN	1370
KPRM	1240
KLOH	1050
KFIL	1060
KFIL-FM	103.1
WKPM	1300
WQPM-FM	106.3
KOLM	1520
KRWB	1410
WVAL	800
WWJO-FM	98.1
KRBI	1310
KRBI-FM	105.5
KLLR	1600
KWOA	730

10 Hours Daily

KBRF	1250

8 Hours Daily

KLGR	1490
KQDE-FM	92.1

6 Hours Daily

WKLK	1230
WKLK-FM	100.9
KLFD	1410
KLFD-FM	95.3

5 Hours Daily

KSUM	1370
KTMF	1350
KOWO	1170

Mississippi

Country Exclusively

WHAY-FM	105.5
WAMY	1580
WVMI	570

197

WRKN	970	KTMO-FM	98.9	
WJBI-FM	101.7	KLEX	1570	
WDSK	1410	KLTI	1560	
WCJU	1450	KMMO	1300	
WMBC	1400	KWOC	930	
WADI-FM	95.3	KMIS	1050	
WCMA	1230	KYRO	1280	
WWTX-FM	95.3	KCLU	1590	
WBSJ-FM	99.5	KZNN-FM	105.3	
WMAG	850	WIL	1430	
WFTO	1330	WIL-FM	92.3	
WGVM	1260	KFEQ	680	
WDMS-FM	100.7	KUSN	1270	
WABG	960	KSMO	1340	
WRIL-FM	100.1	KETU-FM	95.9	
WGUF	1130	KDRO	1490	
WBKH	950	KSTG-FM	97.7	
WVOM	1270	KCTE	1140	
WJQS	1400	KTTS	1400	
WLAU	1430	KTTS-FM	94.7	
WLSM	1270	KWTO	560	
WOKK	910	KALM	1290	
WNAV-FM	103.5	KAMI-FM	95.1	
WBKN	1410	KLPW-FM	101.7	
WGOT-FM	106.3	KWRE	730	
WRJW	1320	KJPW	1390	
WCSA	1260	KYSD-FM	102.3	
WELO	580			
WJLJ	1060			
WJNS-FM	92.1			

5 Hours Daily

WCCA-FM	94.1
WIGG	1420

Missouri

Country Exclusively

KSOA	1430
KBLR	1130
KWRT	1370
KWRT-FM	99.3
KPCR	1530
KPCR-FM	100.9
KQCA-FM	102.3
WZYM	1220
KEXS	1090
KFTW	1450
WRFB	560
WRFB-FM	105.3
KHMO	1070
WMBH	1450
KAYQ	1190
KBIL	1140
KBXM	1540

Montana

Country Exclusively

KANA	580
KFLN	960
KBMY	1240
KOYN	910
KIKC	1250
KMON	560
KHDN	1230
KGEZ	600
KYSS	930

Nebraska

Country Exclusively

KWBE-FM	92.9
KGMT	1310
KRGI-FM	96.5
KRVN	880
KECK	1530
WJAG	780
KOOO	1420
KOOO-FM	104.5
KEYR	690

Nevada

Country Exclusively

KPTL	1300
KVLN	980
KRAM	1340
KVEG	970
KTRI-FM	92.3
KBET	1340
KONE	1450

New Hampshire

Country Exclusively

WDNH-FM	97.5
WOTW	900
WOTW-FM	106.3

New Mexico

Country Exclusively

KALG	1230
KRZY	1450

Woody Guthrie

KHAP	1340
KNFT	950
KCCC	930
KMTY-FM	99.1
KWKA	680
KRZE	1280
KGLP-FM	94.5
KCIA	1110
KGRT	570
KRSY	1230
KAFE	810
KTNM	1400

New York

Country Exclusively

WGNA-FM	107.7
WOKO	1460
WKOL	1570
WSEN	1050
WSEN-FM	92.1
WKOP	1360
WWOL	1120
WWOL-FM	104.1
WFLC-FM	102.3
WBZA-FM	107.1
WQUX-FM	100.9
WXRL	1300
WHN	1050
WKDR	1070
WADR	1480
WNYR	680
WTLB-FM	107.3

6 Hours Daily

WGLI	1290

5 Hours Daily

WBRV	900
WELV	1370
WELM	1410
WIGS	1230
WIGS-FM	92.7
WLFH	1230

North Carolina

Country Exclusively

WWNC	570

WBHN	1590		
WVBS	1470		
WPTL	920		

North Carolina

WAME	1480
WSOC-FM	103.7
WEGO	1410
WDCG-FM	105.1
WTIK	1310
WBXB-FM	100.1
WFAG	1250
WFAI	1230
WFNC	940
WAGY	1320
WBBO-FM	93.3
WFSC	1050
WSFC-FM	96.7
WAKS	1460
WAKS-FM	103.9
WFMC	730
WSML	1190
WKJK	900
WGBG	1400
WNCT	1070
WKDX	1250
WKIT-FM	102.5
WXNC-FM	92.5
WXRC-FM	95.7
WRCM-FM	92.1
WLAS	910
WKTE	1090
WKMT	1220
WRNS-FM	95.1
WJSK-FM	102.3
WIXE	1190
WKRK	1320
WKBC	810
WKBQ	1000
WYNA	1550
WREV	1220
WFMA-FM	100.7
WEGG	710
WKRX-FM	96.7
WBZB	1090
WNCA	1570
WCOK	1060
WFMX-FM	105.7
WKTC-FM	104.3
WETC	540
WKLM	980
WLLY	1350
WBTE	990

WTQR-FM 104.1
9 Hours Daily
WKYK 1540
WELS 1010
WKGX 1080
WSTH 860
8 Hours Daily
WRRZ-FM 107.1
7 Hours Daily
WRGC 680
6 Hours Daily
WATA 1450
WCCE-FM 90.1
WBT 1110
WIFM-FM 100.9
WADE 1210
WKSK 580
5 Hours Daily
WPNF 1240
WMFR-FM 99.5
WSMY 1400
WTLK 1570
WLSE 1400
WLSE-FM 94.3

North Dakota

Country Exclusively
KBMR 1130
KFGO 790
KNDK 1080
KMAV 1520
KMAV-FM 101.7
KTYN 1430
KTGO 1090
KEYZ 1360

Ohio

Country Exclusively
WSLR 1350
WNCO-FM 101.3
WNYN 900
WCLU 1320
WUBE 1230
WUBE-FM 105.1
WHK 1420
WMNI 920
WWOW 1360
WFIZ-FM 105.5
WONE 980
WCNW 1560
WHMQ-FM 100.5
WURD-FM 97.7
WITO-FM 107.1

WLMJ 1280
WHOK-FM 95.5
WIMA-FM 102.1
WBRS 910
WMPO-FM 92.1
WNIO 1540
WOBL 1320
WPAY 1400
WOHO 1470
WTOD 1560
8 Hours Daily
WMGS 730
7 Hours Daily
WPKO 1380
6 Hours Daily
WBCO 1540
WBCO-FM 92.7
WLW 700
WTNS-FM 99.3
WGOR 1520
5 Hours Daily
WMVO-FM 93.7
WLEC 1450
WLEC-FM 102.7

Oklahoma

Country Exclusively
KRPT 850
KEOR 1110
KLTR 1580
KXXK-FM 105.5
KRHD 1350
KRHD-FM 102.3
KCES-FM 102.3
KOKC 1490
KGYN 1210
KCCO 1050
KNED 1150
KMAD 1550
KMUS 1380
WNAD 640
KEBC-FM 94.7
KLPR 1140
KOKL 1240
KVLH 1470
KINB-FM 107.3
KOLS 1570
KKMA-FM 104.5
KTOW 1340
KTLQ 1350
KGOW-FM 92.1
KVOO 1170
KJEM 1530

Oregon

Country Exclusively
KRKT 990
KXIQ-FM 94.1
KEED 1450
KRDR 1230

Oregon

KLAD 960
KMCM 1260
KSHA 860
KBBR 1340
KWJJ 1080
KPRB 1240
KRNR 1490
KOHI 1600
KGAY 1430
KTDO 1230
6 Hours Daily
KBND 1110
KAGI 930
KUMA 1290
KODL 1440
5 Hours Daily
KQIK 1230

Pennsylvania

Country Exclusively
WHOL 1600
WVAM-FM 100.1
WASP 1130
WHYL-FM 102.3
WFEM-FM 92.1
WIOV-FM 105.1
WWGO 1450
WSKE 1050
WIYQ-FM 99.1
WIXZ 1360
WGCR-FM 104.5
WWIZ-FM 103.9
WMLP-FM 100.9
WHYP 1530
WHYP-FM 100.9
WRCP 1540
WRCP-FM 104.5
WEEP 1080
WEEP-FM 107.9
WKBI-FM 94.3
WKMC 1370
WGBI 910
WGMR-FM 101.1
WAYZ 1380

Jerry Wallace

WAYZ-FM 101.5
WWBR 1350
WNOW 1250
WVCC-FM 101.7

Rhode Island

Country Exclusively
WHIM 1110
WHIM-FM 94.1

South Carolina

Country Exclusively
WBEU 960
WBEU-FM 98.7
WHPB 1390
WPUB 1130
WCAY 620
WEZL-FM 103.5
WQSN 1450
WCOS-FM 97.9
WDAR 1350
WDAR-FM 105.5
WELP-FM 103.9
WSHG-FM 106.3
WESC 660
WESC-FM 92.5
WMTY 1090
WDKD 1310
WVAP 1510
WBER 950
WKMG 1520
WHCE-FM 103.9
WAZS 980
WFIG 1290
WGOG 1000
WSJW 1510

South Dakota

Country Exclusively
KKAA 1560
KIJV 1340
KIJV-FM 92.1
KBJM 1400
KMSD 1510
KGFX 1060
KIMM 1150
KTOQ 1340
KXRB 1000
KIOV-FM 104.7
KBHB 810
KIXX-FM 96.1
WNAX 570

Tennessee

Country Exclusively
WSLV 1110
WYXI 1390
WBOL 1560
WUST-FM 96.7
WDOD 1310
WDOD-FM 96.5
WDXN 540
WCLE 1570
WYSH 1380
WYSH-FM 104.9
WKOM-FM 101.7
WDNT 1280
WASL-FM 100.1
WIDD 1520
WIDD-FM 99.3
WIXC 1140
WIZO 1380

WAMG 1130
WOFM-FM 94.9
WSMG 1450
WHBT 1600
WHHM 1580
WHMT 1190
WIRJ-FM 102.3
WJPJ 1530
WJCW 910
WGOC 1090
WBIR-FM 103.5
WIVK 850
WIVK-FM 107.7
WDXL 1490
WGAP 1400
WHDM 1440
WKTA-FM 106.9
WMC 790
WZXR-FM 102.7
WKBJ 1600
WMTN 1300
WMTS 810
WENO 1430
WKDA 1240
WLIK 1270
WTPR-FM 105.5
WUAT 1110
WTRB 1570
WRGS 1370
WORM 1010
WDTM 1130
WLIJ 1580
WJLE 1480
WJLE-FM 101.7
WEDG 1240
WNTT 1250
WECO 940
WPHC 1060
WBRY 1540

8 Hours Daily
WRKM-FM 102.3
WAGG 950
WTJS 1390
WBMC 960
WSMT 1050
WSMT-FM 105.5
WHLP 1570
WIKA-FM 96.7

Tennessee

7 Hours Daily
WLSB 1400
WMLR 1230

Merle Travis

WTNE 1500
6 Hours Daily
WOPI 1490
WBHT 1520
WTBG-FM 95.3
WAEW 1330
WDKN 1260
WDKN-FM 102.3
WYTM-FM 105.5
WATO 1290
WBNT 1310
WBNT-FM 105.5
WPJD 1550
WAAN 1480

5 Hours Daily
WRKM 1350
WHUB 1400
WMCH 1260
WGRV 1340
WMSR 1340
WCMT 1410
WMQM 1480
WSIX 980
WSEV 930

Texas

Country Exclusively
KWKC 1340

KOPY 1070
KDJW 1010
KZIP 1310
KACT 1360
KBUD 1410
KOKE 1370
KOKE-FM 95.5
KVET 1300
KWCB-FM 103.1
KBUK 1360
KLVI 560
KTRM 990
KHEM 1270
KBBB 1600
KSTB 1430
KTTX 1280
KOXE-FM 101.5
KORA-FM 98.3
WTAW 1150
KHLB 1340
KMIL 1330
KDET 930
KCLE 1120
KJCH 1410
KSTA 1000
KVMC 1320
KIKR 900
KIKN 1590

KOUL-FM 103.3
KCIR-FM 107.9
KEWS 1600
KBOX 1480
KWMC 1490
KDNT 1440
KDHN 1470
KDDD 800
KHEY 690
KISO 1150
KLOZ-FM 102.1
KJIM 870
KXOW 1360
WBAP 820
KSCS-FM 96.3
KNAF 910
KBRZ 1460
KGTN 1530
KSWA 1330
KELT-FM 94.5
KGRI 1000
KHBR 1560
KHBR-FM 102.5
KRME 1460
KENR 1070
KNUZ 1230
KTXJ 1350
KERB 600
KPFM-FM 94.3
KOCA 1240
KVLG 1570
KCYL 1450
KPXE 1050
KCLT 1060
KEES 1430
KYKX-FM 105.7
KDAV 580
KLLL 1460
KLLL-FM 96.3
KKYR 1410
KWFA 1500
KBAT-FM 93.3
KJBC 1150
KMOO 1510
KORC 1140
KVKM 1330
KJCS-FM 103.3
KSFA 860
KOYL 1310
KOYL-FM 97.9
KOGT 1600
KRCT-FM 94.3
KPRE 1250

KIKK 650
KIKK-FM 95.7
KKYN 1090
KSOX 1240
KPEP 1420
KTEO 1340
KBUC 1310
KBUC-FM 107.5
KKYX 680
KBAL 1410
KIKZ 1250
KBYP 1580
KTXO 1500
KDWT 1400
KSST 1230
KXOX 1240
KADO 940
KCMC 740
KTLW 920
KROZ-FM 92.1
KZAK 1330
KNAL 1410
KTXN-FM 98.7
KHOO-FM 99.9
KZEE 1220
KLUR-FM 99.9

9 Hours Daily
KULP 1390
KGAF-FM 94.5
KBUS 1590
KRAN 1280

8 Hours Daily
KIVY 1290
KXIT 1410
KXIT-FM 95.9
KPSO 1260
KBGH 1130
KIMP 960
KWFT 620

7 Hours Daily
KIBL 1490
KERC 1590
KMBL 1450
KVLG-FM 104.9
KVWG 1280
KKAS 1300

6 Hours Daily
KWHI-FM 106.3
KGAF 1580
KAML 990
KINE 1330
KVOZ 1490
KTLU 1580

KBMF-FM	98.3	
KTAE	1260	
KTFS	1400	
KVLL	1220	

5 Hours Daily

KVLF	1240
KGAS	1590
KMUL	1380
KGRO	1230
KTUE	1260

Utah

Country Exclusively

KSUB-FM	92.5
KDLT	540
KFTN	1400
KRGO	1550
KSOP	1370
KSOP-FM	104.3
KONI-FM	106.3
KSUN	730

Vermont

Country Exclusively

WHWB-FM	98.1

Virginia

Country Exclusively

WBBI	1230
WPIK	730
WXRA-FM	105.9
WKDE	1000
WKDE-FM	105.5
WODY	900
WBDY	106.3
WBDY-FM	690
WZAP	1080
WKBY	810
WSVS-FM	104.7
WDVA	1250
WFLS	1350
WFLS-FM	93.3
WBOB-FM	98.1
WRAA	1330
WWOD	1390
WSIG	790
WTID	1270
WCMS	1050
WCMS-FM	100.5
WZAM	1110
WPVA	1290
WPVA-FM	95.3
WBLB	1510

WPWC	1530
WEET	1320
WTVR	1380
WXGI	950
WJLM-FM	93.5
WSLC	610
WNLB	1290
WKDW	900
WKCW	1420
WNNT	690
WNNT-FM	100.9
WRFL-FM	92.5

Washington

Country Exclusively

KBKW	1450
KBFW	930
KPUG	1170
KERI-FM	104.3
KELA-FM	102.9
KWYZ	1230
KOTY	1340
KBAM	1270
KAPS	1470
KARY	1310
KAYO	1150
KETO-FM	101.5
KMPS	1300
KQIN	800
KMAS	1280
KGA	1510
KSPO	1230
KMO	1360
KUEN	900
KUTI	980
KUTI-FM	104.1

14 Hours Daily

KENE	1490

5 Hours Daily

KCVL	1270
KFDR	1360

West Virginia

Country Exclusively

WCST	1010
WCST-FM	93.5
WCAW	680
WZFM-FM	98.3
WPDX	750
WPDX-FM	104.9
WWHY	1470
WNST	1600
WAJR	1440

WKYG	1230
WKYG-FM	103.1
WAEY	1490
WAEY-FM	95.9
WMOV	1360
WKLC	105.1
WKLC-FM	1170
WWVA	1170

Wisconsin

Country Exclusively

WAPL	1570
WXRO-FM	95.3
WAXX	1150
WDMP	810
WDMP-FM	99.3
WRDN	1430
WRDN-FM	95.9
WEAU-FM	104.5
WGEE	1360
WLXR-FM	104.9
WMAD-FM	106.3
WTSO	1070
WCUB	980
WBCS-FM	102.9
WEMP	1250
WWMH-FM	95.9
WYTL	1490
WPLY	1420
WGLB	1560
WGLB-FM	100.1
WDOR-FM	93.9
WGBM-FM	102.3
WLKE	1170
WXCO	1230

Wyoming

Country Exclusively

KVOC	1230

Canada

Alberta

Country Exclusively

CKBR	1340
CFAC	960
CFCW	790
CJDV	910
CKGY	1170
CKTA	1570

British Columbia

Country Exclusively

CKAY	1500
CFFM-FM	98.3
CKOO	1240
CKSP	1450
CKWX	1130
CJVI	900

7 Hours Daily

CKOV	630

6 Hours Daily

CJCI	620

5 Hours Daily

CKEK	570

Manitoba

Country Exclusively

CFRY	920
CHMM-FM	97.5

Newfoundland

Country Exclusively

CJCR	1350

CJNW	670

Ontario

Country Exclusively

CKGL-FM	96.7
CKBY-FM	105.3
CFGM	1320
CKFH	1430
CHOW	1470

Saskatchewan

Country Exclusively

CKRM	980
CKKR	1330

14 Hours Daily

CJNB	1050

8 Hours Daily

CKSW	1400

6 Hours Daily

CKCK	620
CJGX	940

5 Hours Daily

CKBI	900

PBS

Johnny Rodriguez

Rakes, Pal
(Palmer Crawford III)

Born: Tampa, Florida

His first Warner's single, "That's When the Lyin' Stops" earned him an ASCAP Award and went top twenty in the national charts. Following it came "Till I Can't Take It Anymore" and in 1978, "If I Ever Come Back."

Raye, Susan

Born: October 8, 1944, Eugene, Oregon

A regular on "Hee Haw" and "Buck Owens All-American Show," Susan has recorded duets with Buck: "Togetherness" and "We're Gonna Get Together." Her solo, "L.A. International Airport," won her two gold records in Australia. Other hits include "Pitty Pitter Patter," "Happy Heart," and "Willy Jones."

Pal Rakes

Susan Raye

Recording Session: Song Idea to Performance Reality

What happens during a recording session? More than fifteen thousand recording sessions were held in Nashville in 1977. Not all of these were country sessions, but each was a focal point for the talents of many businesses and individuals involved in the business of music. The recording session is but one link in a chain of activities that links song idea with the record consumer.

A record begins with a song idea. The country songwriter, when his song is completed, enters into a contractual agreement with a song publisher. The publisher protects the ownership of the song for the writer, collects certain payments connected with the use of the song, and assists the songwriter in getting his material recorded. The songwriter also protects his right to his composition through a contract with a music licensing organization (such as

ASCAP, BMI, and SESAC). These organizations collect fees for performances of compositions and pass payment along to songwriters.

Once a song becomes part of a publisher's catalog, the staff of the publishing company begins to promote the composition in order to have the song issued on record. Song pluggers are publishers' representatives to the record industry—contact A & R (artist and repertory) staff of a record company. The "A & R Director" has the responsibility of finding quality material for recording artists and sometimes has the dual responsibility of supervising the actual recording of a song.

When the A & R man has found a song which he feels will suit the talents of a particular recording artist, plans are made to conduct a recording session. The A & R man (when he actually supervises a session he is called a producer) works with the vocalist in rehearsing the song and contacts the studio musicians needed to perform the selection in the manner most likely to appeal to a wide audience.

A recording session lasts for three hours, and from three to five songs can be recorded during a single session. In Nashville, all sessions are held at the same times—in three-hour segments beginning at 10:00 AM. Sessions are thus held at ten, two, six, and again at ten in the evening. The vacant hour between sessions enables studio musicians—who often work as many as four sessions each day—to pack up equipment and travel from one studio to the next.

The producer enters the recording studio with a firm idea of the sound he wants on a final record. The musicians are assembled, the studio engineer places microphones and adjusts the volume and tone of each instrument by manipulating components of the control-room console, and the session is ready to begin. The producer and engineer sit in a soundproof control room and supervise the recording process. The song is usually performed several times before recording is begun, and

each time the performance improves as the vocalist, sidemen, and engineer work to improve their portion of the recording process. When the producer is satisfied that all concerned are at ease with their parts, he will call for the first "take." The recording process will continue—take after take—until the producer is satisfied with the overall performance.

Even when a quality take is obtained, the recording process need not end. The technology of modern tape recording enables the producer to re-enter the studio to "re-mix" the master tape. A re-mix involves the readjustment of relative tone and volume of instruments and voices recorded in a session. The producer also has the option of recording additional instruments and voices onto a tape after the original session has been completed. This process—called "over-dubbing"—can add a multitude of new sounds to those obtained during the recording session itself.

When the recording session, over-dubbing session, and re-mix are completed, the resulting performance remains as several hundred feet of magnetic tape. The tape is then mastered onto a lacquer disc, and metal stamping parts are prepared to press the final record. Label copy is written, advertising materials are prepared, art work is completed, and the record is pressed, packaged, and released to the public.

Even at this stage in the production of a recording, the manufacturer possesses no guarantee that the recording will become a hit. The record must be made available to radio stations in the hope that it will be played, and it must be advertised and distributed to record wholesalers and retailers around the country.

The process of converting a song idea into a country record involves many separate stages and many individual talents. A hit recording demands quality at every stage. The country recording session stands at the heart of the process, for it is in

the studio that the talents of songwriter, performer, and sideman are brought together in the creation of a unique recorded performance.

Reed, Jerry (Hubbard)

Born: March 20, 1937, Atlanta, Georgia.
Married: Priscilla Mitchell
Children: d. Sedina, Charlotte Lottie

Jerry's career started in his hometown of Atlanta, where he worked days in cotton mills and performed nights in gin mills. At sixteen he was introduced by a policeman friend to Atlanta promoter-publisher Bill Lowery who, in turn, landed Jerry a contract with Capitol Records in 1955. Pretty soon artists like Brenda Lee began recording some of his songs. Uncle Sam became Jerry's employer between 1959 and 1961, and Nashville has had him ever smce. Known as the Guitar Man (after one of his songs with which Elvis Presley had a smash hit) and as the Alabama Wild Man (after another song that he personally has had TWO hit releases on, several years apart), Jerry Reed is constantly on the forward move in his career as "a singer, picker, and writer, in that order."

In 1970, his RCA single "Amos Moses," which he wrote, became a number one country record and crossed over into the Pop charts. It also attracted national recognition for Jerry, won him a Grammy nomination for the Best Country Male Performer of 1970 and landed him a "regular" spot on the "Glen Campbell Goodtime Hour" TV show.

His "When You're Hot, You're Hot," "Lord, Mr. Ford" and "Crude Oil Blues" followed and were national hits.

Some of Jerry's LPs include: *Jerry Reed Explores Guitar Country, Smell the Flowers, Me and Chet, Best of Jerry Reed, Lord, Mr. Ford* and *A Good Woman's Love.*

In 1973 he hosted the "Music Country USA" TV show several times and in 1974 he got his first chance at acting in *W.W. and the Dixie Dance Kings,* which was filmed around Tennessee and Georgia. About Burt Reynolds who's also in the movie, Reed quips: "I had to have a co-star."

Reeves, Del (Franklin Delano)

Born: July 14, 1934, Sparta, North Carolina
Married: Ellen Schiell
Children: d. Ann, Kari, Bethany

The first country artist to sign with Frank Sinatra's Reprise label (in 1958), he and Ellen wrote songs for other artists apart from himself. In 1961, his first was "Be Quiet Mind"; in 1965, his first No. 1 hit, "Girl On The Billboard" followed by other top-charters such as "A Dime At A Time," "Good-Time Charles," "Two Dollars in the Jukebox," and "The Philadelphia Fillies." In 1976, one of his several duets with Billie Jo Spears made the Top 20. Film appearances include: "Forty Acre Feud"; albums, United Artists' *Live At The Palomino* and *By Request* with Billie Jo Spears; 1978 single, "When My Angel Turns Into a Devil."

Rich, Charlie

Born: December 14, 1933, Colt, Arkansas.
Married: Margaret Ann
Children: d. Renee, Laurie, s. Allen, Jack

"The Silver Fox" grew up with three distinctly different types of music, the white gospel of his missionary Baptist parents, the blues of the Black field hands and the country sounds of the Grand Ole Opry. While serving with the Air Force in Enid, Oklahoma, he played with a local jazz band on base and doubled with a small combo in town whose vocalist was—Margaret Ann! The idea of supporting his family with music seemed remote. On discharge, he became a farmer in West Mem-

phis, Tenn. "It rained and rained," Charlie remembers. Margaret Ann got him to do some tapes. Sun Records—which had launched Elvis, Johnny Cash and Jerry Lee Lewis—took him on. In 1959, Jerry Lee's single of his "Lonely Weekends" became a smash hit. Unfortunately, Sun Records was on the decline. Charlie switched over to RCA, had a minor flurry with "Big Boss Man" and kept plugging away until 1965 before his next big hit, "Mohair Sam." Again, the follow-up recordings failed to succeed commercially and it wasn't until 1972—after two decades of struggle—that Charlie Rich truly hit his stride. His version of Kenny O'Dell's "I Take It On Home" hit the Top Twenty followed by another O'Dell song, "Behind Closed Doors" which topped the country charts and crossed over to the Top Ten of the pops, selling more than a million copies. Gathering speed, his follow-up "The Most Beautiful Girl" attained platinum status with more than two million sold. His early work has been re-released. His foreign tours have been a wild success. He scored the films, *Benji* and *For The Love of Benji.* In 1977, his "Rolling With The Flow" made Number One. In 1978, he signed with United Artists, his first album, *I Still Believe In Love* produced by longtime friend, Larry Butler. His first single, "Puttin' In Overtime At Home" moved up high on the charts. In 1978, his hits included "On My Knees" in duet with Janie Fricke, and the LP *Classic Rich.*

Riley, Jeannie C. (Jeannie Carolyn Stephenson)

Born: October 19, 1945, Stamford, Texas
Married: Mitchell Riley, div. and remarried January 26, 1975
Children: d. Kim Michelle

An overnight star with her 1968 recording of "Harper Valley PTA" which sold over four million in the United States and earned three for-

Jimmie Rodgers with humorist Will Rogers

eign gold records, she won the 1968 Grammy for Best Female Country Vocalist. Other hits include: "The Girl Most Likely," "There Never Was A Time," "Things Go Better With Love," "Country Girl," "Oh Singer" and "Good Enough To Be Your Wife."

Rodgers, Jimmie

Born: September 8, 1897, Meridian, Mississippi

Courtesy of Country Music Foundation Library and Media Center, Nashville, Tennessee

brakeman, and baggagemaster, playing his guitar and banjo and singing songs for informal entertainment. His travels exposed him to the songs of average people: hobo songs, blues, mountain ballads, and cowboy laments. At the age of twenty-eight, a lung hemorrhage forced him to quit railroading. Ralph Peer, a representative of the Victor Talking Machine Company discovered him during a talent search in the South when Jimmie auditioned along with a group called the Carter Family. His health began to fail rapidly in 1930 and he made a last recording trip to New York in 1933 before surrendering to his final

bout with tuberculosis. Beloved as the "Blue Yodeler," his "T For Texas" and "Brakeman's Blues" sold over a million copies each. A short film, *The Singing Brakeman,* can be seen at the Country Music Hall of Fame in Nashville. His songs have been assembled by RCA in five LPs, including *Best of The Legendary Jimmie Rodgers* and *This Is Jimmie Rodgers.* On May 24, 1978, a U.S. postage stamp was issued in his honor, the first in the new performing arts and artists series. His hometown holds an annual Jimmie Rodgers Festival in May. For information, write: Jimmie Rodgers Festival, Meridian Mississippi.

Died: May 26, 1933, in New York City

The "Singing Brakeman," also known as the "Father of Country Music," was the son of a railroad man whose mother died when he was four. Raised in the freight yards and switch shanties of the South, he got his first paying job at 14, as brakeman on the New Orleans and Meridian run. From 1911 to 1925, he worked as callboy, flagman,

Jimmie Rodgers

Courtesy of Country Music Foundation Library and Media Center, Nashville, Tennessee

United Artists/Management Three

Rogers, Kenny

Born: April 21, 1941, Houston, Texas

Married: Marianne Gordon

In 1960, a regional hit, "Crazy Feeling," which ultimately sold a million copies nationwide, took Kenny away from Texas and onto Dick Clark's "American Bandstand."

From there, ne joined the New Christy Minstrels and later (with fellow minstrels Mike Settle, Terry Williams, and Thelma Camacho) formed The First Edition. When high school buddy Mickey Newberry brought Kenny "Just Dropped in to See What Condition My Condition Is In," The First Edition took it and made their first ma-

jor hit along with "Ruby (Don't Take Your Love to Town)," "Reuben James" and Mac Davis's "Somethin's Burnin'." Later, as a soloist, Kenny signed with United Artists, leading to three albums and several major hits: "Love Gifted Me," "Homemade Love," "Laura," "While the Feeling's Good." What made him a superstar was "Lucille," which in 1977 hit the top ten in both country and pop charts, was number one in five foreign countries, and was still going strong in 1978. Kenny plays guitar, bass, and "enough piano to get me into trouble." An accomplished photographer, he is proud that his picture of Glen Campbell appears on Glen's *Southern Nights*. Nineteen seventy-eight

was a big Kenny Rogers year. He and Dottie West hosted various country TV specials and won the CMA Vocal Duo of the Year award. Their "Anyone Who Isn't Me Tonight" and "Everytime Two Fools Collide" dominated the charts while Kenny's solos "Love or Something Like It" and "Ten Years of Gold" were top hits.

Ronstadt, Linda

Born: July 15, 1946, Tucson, Arizona

Linda knew she wanted to be a singer from earliest childhood. At eighteen, she went to Los Angeles and formed the Stone Poneys, a group that combined folk, rock, and country. Among the band members

Kenny Rogers

Linda Ronstadt   Jim Shea

was Kenny Edwards who is still Linda's bass player and longtime musical collaborator. In 1967 and 1968, the Poneys made several LPs for Capitol. In 1969, Linda left the Stone Poneys and cut her first solo LP. *Hand Sown, Home Grown,* followed the next year by *Silk Purse,* which included her first hit single, "Long, Long Time" and earned her first Grammy nomination. By 1971, she had formed a new band which included Glenn Frey and Don Henley (who later formed their own group, the Eagles). Their collaboration resulted in her third solo LP, *Linda Ronstadt.* By this time, she was touring widely and moving up the charts. In 1973, she switched to Asylum Records with *Don't Cry Now.* Ironically, the last LP she did for Capitol—one she owed them by contract—was *Heart Like a Wheel,* produced by her new manager, Peter Asher. It hit number one, went

platinum on the LP charts and also contained a hit single, "You're No Good." Now there was no stopping Linda Ronstadt. *Prisoner in Disguise* went platinum in 1975 with "Heat Wave" the big single, and Linda also won the Grammy for Best Female Country Vocal for "I Can't Help It if I'm Still in Love with You." The next year, *Hasten Down the Wind* topped the charts and the single "That'll Be the Day" is credited with starting the Buddy Holly revival. "Lose Again" and "Someone to Lay Down Beside Me" also made the singles charts. In December 1976, her *Linda Ronstadt's Greatest Hits* was released, she won a Grammy for Best Female Pop Vocal Performance for *Hasten Down the Wind*—and for the first time, the Playboy Poll named the same artist as Top Female Singer in both Pop and Country categories—Linda Rostadt. Many peo-

ple call 1977 "The Year of Linda Ronstadt." She was on the covers of *Rolling Stone, Time, People,* and other magazines. Her *Simple Dreams* LP was released to the highest critical acclaim—and produced five hit singles, "Blue Bayou," "It's So Easy," "Poor Poor Pitiful Me," "Tumbling Dice." and "I Never Will Marry." "Blue Bayou" went gold while the LP itself solf three and a half million copies in the U.S. alone. In 1978, she made Asylum history with an initial shipment of over two million copies of *Living in the U.S.A.*

Roundup Records

One of the world's largest catalogs of acoustic music, jazz, traditional, and progressive bluegrass and folk.

The catalog is free. Write to: Box 474, Somerville, ME. 02140.

Jim Shea

S

Sessions, Ronnie

Born: Henrietta, Oklahoma
Birthday: December 7

When he was six, his family moved to Bakersfield, California, the West Coast mecca of country music. Two years later, he became a regular on the "Herb Henson Trading Post TV Show," which led, at age nine, to a contract with Pike Records. "My Last Night in Town" and "Keep a Knockin' " were cut with Little Richard's original band. A stint with Gene Autrey's Republic Records and he was off to Nashville where he lived with Jeannie Seely and her songwriter husband, Hank Cochran. By 1975, he had a number of chart records for MGM, including Hoyt Axton's composition, "Never Been to Spain." Among his more recent hits are "Wiggle, Wiggle" and in 1978 "Me and Millie."

Ronnie Sessions

Shepard, Jean

Born: November 21, 1933, Pauls Valley, Oklahoma
Married: Hawkshaw Hawkins (died 1963); Benny Birchfield
Children: s. Don, Harold, Corey

One of eleven children, Jean learned to sing listening to old Jimmie Rodgers records on a wind-up Victrola. When the family moved to Visalia, California, she formed an all-girl western swing band, The Melody Ranch Girls. Hank Thompson heard her sing, introduced her to Capitol Records, and in 1953, she and Ferlin Husky hit number one with their duet, "Dear John Letter." "Forgive Me John" came next, followed by "Beautiful Lies." That year, she appeared with Red Foley on "Ozark Jubilee." In 1955, the Grand Ole Opry beckoned. Tragedy struck in 1963 when a plane crash killed her husband, Hawkshaw

Jean Shephard

Hawkins, but there was some comfort the following year when she recorded "Second Fiddle to an Old Guitar." More recent hits are: "I'm a Believer," "Poor Sweet Baby," "If Teardrops Were Silver," "Mercy, Ain't Love Good," "My Name Is Woman," and others.

Sheppard, T. G. "The Good" (Bill Browder)

Born: Humboldt, Tennessee
Birthday: July 20
Married: Diane

In his mid-teens, he joined the Travis Womack Band in Memphis as singer/guitarist. Later, as a record promoter, he found a song by an unknown, Bobby David, and tried to sell it. Rejected eight times, he decided to record it himself—and "Devil in the Bottle" became a number-one hit for him. His next,

"Tryin' to Beat the Morning Home," also hit number one, followed by "Another Woman" and "Motels and Memories." In 1976, his albums included *Solitary Man* and a string of hit singles, including "Show Me a Man." Switching to Warner/Curb, his 1977 single, "Mr. D.J.," was a hit. His album, *T.G.,* bowed in 1978 along with the hit single "Daylight."

Smith, Sammi

Born: August 5, 1943, Orange, California

Not an "Outlaw" exactly but professionally as well as personally attuned to Waylon and Willie, she made her first mark as a recording star in 1971 with Kris Kristofferson's "Help Me Make It Through the Night," which was named the CMA Single of that year and sold over two million copies. A rambler from childhood, Sammi grew up in Oklahoma, Texas, Arizona, and Colorado, singing in clubs from the age of eleven. She sang rock'n'roll most of the time until she rediscovered Southern songs. As a songwriter, her "When Michael Calls" was the flip side of the Kristofferson hit. Some of her other compositions include: "Sanders Ferry Lane," "Sand Covered Angels" (recorded by Conway Twitty), and "Cedartown, Georgia" (re-

Sammi Smith

corded by Waylon Jennings). In 1973, Sammi Smith moved to Texas and became part of the musical community centered in Austin. Her affection for Texas is as much musical as personal. Together with Waylon and Willie, she is among the major Southern artists to bring her music to the young Texas audience attending country and rock festivals. In 1975, she signed with Elektra/Asylum, her first album, *As Long As There's a Sunday*. In 1978, she hit the charts with a single, "It Just Won't Feel Like Cheating (With You)."

T.G. Sheppard

Sammi Smith

Burt Reynolds

© Universal City Studios, Inc.

Smokey and the Bandit

(Courtesy of Universal Pictures)

Wild and wooly, the biggest trucker movie ever, it stars Burt Reynolds as "Bandit," Jerry Reed as his trucker buddy, Cledus "Snowman" Snow, and three top country songs, "East Bound and Down," "Bandit," and "The Legend"—all sung by Jerry Reed. Paul Williams is sassy "Little Enos" with six-foot-six Pat McCormick as his belligerent father, Big Enos. The story is a Citizens' Band symphony of envy, greed, lust, and competition in a hair-raising truck race against time and the forces of law and order.

Smokey and the Bandit

The Cast

Bandit...Burt Reynolds
Carrie..Sally Field
Cledus..Jerry Reed
Junior..Mike Henry
Little Enos.....................................Paul Williams
Big Enos.......................................Pat McCormick
Patrolman—Traffic Jam.......................Alfie Wise
Branford..................................George Reynolds
Mr. B.......................................Macon McCalman
Waynette....................................Linda McClure
Hot Pants.....................................Susan McIver
Branford's Deputy........................Michael Mann
Sugar Bear....................................Lamar Jackson
Georgia Trooper..............................Ronnie Gay
Alabama Trooper...................Quinnon Sheffield
Sheriff Buford T. Justice...............Jackie Gleason

The Credits

Executive Producer......................Robert L. Levy
Produced by...............................Mort Engelberg
Directed by....................................Hal Needham
Screenplay by...................James Lee Barrett and
Charles Shyer and
Alan Mandel
Story by..................................Hal Needham and
Robert L. Levy
Director of Photography..................Bobby Byrne
Art Director..........................Mark Mansbridge
Music by.......................................Bill Justis and
Jerry Reed
"East Bound and Down" by Dick Feller and Jerry Reed
Sung by Jerry Reed

Snow, Hank
(Clarence Eugene)

Born: May 9, 1914, Liverpool, Nova Scotia
Married: Minnie Blanche
Children: Reverend Jimmie Rodgers Snow

In 1977, it was Hank's 42nd year in country music with his 104th record, "Still Movin' on #104," his smooth voice and artful picking still movin' on, as well. He started moving early. At fourteen, his stepfather kicked him out. He then joined a fishing schooner as a deckhand and spent the next four years at sea, where he entertained his shipmates by singing and playing the mouth organ. He bought his first guitar for $5.95 and discovered the records of the legendary Jimmie Rodgers at about the same time. The Singing Brakeman became and remains his idol and inspiration (he named his son for him). By the mid-1940s, Hank was performing professionally as The Singing Ranger. His first records, including "Lonesome Blue Yodel" and "Brand New Heart," led finally to the Grand Ole Opry, where he became a regular in 1950. His blockbuster "I'm Moving On" first hit the charts later that year. It still holds the all-time *Billboard* record of occupying the number-one spot in all charts for twenty-six consecutive weeks and staying in the top ten for fourteen months in 1950–1951. His 1977 update proves the timelessness of both the song and the singer remaining on the charts through 1978. Among his major hits are: *I Don't Hurt Anymore, Hello Love,* and a special twin-disc commemorative LP, *This Is My Story.*

Song Sharks

That's what the Country Music Association calls those who prey on the hopes and dreams of inexperienced songwriters. The following is an extract from a booklet, *What Every Songwriter Should Know,* prepared by the Country Music Association.

To get your free copy, send a stamped self-addressed envelope to: CMA, 7 Music Circle North, Nashville, TN 37203.

What Every Songwriter Should Know

Songwriting is a difficult and highly skilled profession. Only those with genuine talent and originality can ever hope to succeed.

If you are a writer of lyrics only, you are a limited songwriter. Similarly a melody without words is only a melody. Both lyrics and music are necessary before you have a completed song.

Few indeed are they who can successfully write both lyrics and melodies. Poor lyrics, or an inferior tune, may each destroy the value of the other. Many successful songs have been written by experienced lyricists in collaboration with able composers.

Explore the possibility of teaming with someone in your home town if you feel weak as a lyricist or melody writer. Be reluctant to buy the ser-

Hank Snow

213

vices of a company which offers to put your poems to music.

The "Song Shark"

It is not the function or the purpose of the CMA to recommend publishing firms. Neither can the CMA take songs from its member writers and place them with publishing firms or recording artists. This is entirely out of the realm of CMA's services.

However, CMA does feel that new writers should be told and warned about a "racket" which has recently grown to phenomenal proportions in the United States and Canada and which, according to U.S. postal authorities, takes millions of dollars annually out of the pockets of the new and inexperienced writers of songs.

Johnny Paycheck

Advertisements appear regularly in certain publications under the headings of "Song Poems Wanted," "Writers Win Fame and Fortune," "Your Song Poems Set to Music," etc. Such advertisers are known by the unsavory title of Song Shark. They thrive on the inexperience of the new and unskilled writer of songs.

Regardless of the merit of the lyrics, they will "accept" them, send you glowing reports, and agree to set them to music for a fee ranging all the way from twenty dollars to several hundred dollars.

These so-called publishers will send you impressive and enforceable contracts. However, no sane person would sign those contracts if he or she actually understood them.

Of the thousands of such songs printed every month, we know of none ever becoming a hit or even earning the cost of the original investment of the writer.

Where both lyrics and music have been written, the Shark is saved what little time or money it costs him to have a tune ground out, but the cost to the writer remains the same.

No matter how poor the lyric or the music, these song sharks will accept it—for a fee (which may even be paid in installments).

The U.S. Postal Department, the Better Business Bureaus, and many reputable publishers constantly warn the public about this racket, but it would almost seem that P. T. Barnum was right.

Examination for a Fee

Another angle, known as the "come on," is the offer of agreeing to have the manuscript examined for a few dollars as to its fitness for "acceptance."

This only means a few additional dollars for the Shark and again, regardless of merit, the composition will be accepted and further fees will be demanded following a glowing report.

These individuals or companies are not publishers. They are simply operators who provide a printing service at exorbitant prices. In every instance, the cost to the songwriter through the song-shark method is far more than he would normally pay to any legitimate printer.

The Music Publisher

The first rule for the inexperienced writer should be: Never Pay Any Money to Any Publisher for Publishing a Song. Nor should payment be made for setting lyrics to music, music to lyrics, examining of manuscripts, or promising to publish and promote.

The publishing business, like any other business, requires experience, skill, and capital, combined with a keen sense of what the public will accept and purchase.

A publisher must have songs to publish and exploit if he intends to stay in business. If a publisher rejects your song, it is because, based on his experience, he does not believe he can "make money" on your material; it may also be that he has so many songs in his office that he cannot afford to take on any more.

Further, and this is most important, it costs a great deal of money to exploit successfully a popular song; many promotions have cost thousands of dollars.

Just publishing a song does not guarantee its success, for that is determined only through acceptance by the general public—and no one else.

Publishers are receiving collectively thousands of manuscripts per year, out of which they must select the songs that result in the very limited number of successes.

A successful publisher, therefore, must be a good businessman. Remember, it is his money he is spending—not the writer's. Every honest and reputable publisher assumes all costs for publication, including professional copies, counter copies, orchestrations, national distribution, and all promotion.

We repeat—do not pay any publisher any money for the publication of your manuscript.

The reputable publisher's chances of success are far greater if he can publish a song by recognized writers or one that is being featured in a motion picture or a successful musical comedy. That is one reason he is reluctant to consider the works of unknown writers.

The Recording Company

Beware of the "operator" who goes by the legitimate name of a recording company or record producer and advertises that for a specified sum of money he will take your music (and your money), have it recorded in the finest studios by the finest professional musicians using top background singers, provide the best in A&R service, and contact the booking agencies; but does not give you proof of what he will do before he gets your money.

These services are offered by all the most responsible and reputable firms. And the respectable firms you want to deal with will furnish you on request a copy of their contract

Steve, Larry, and Rudy Gatlin

before asking you to sign. They will provide you on request an itemized list of the estimated cost of production. They will give you on request a list of the booking agencies which they will contact for you; they will also provide you evidence that they can handle distribution properly.

The unscrupulous ones will promise you everything to get your money, and you will wait a long time before you see a copy of the contract for your attorney to evaluate. Usually that contract will not spell out the specific details of their commitment to you. The contract you may finally get is enforceable and legal when you sign it. You are then bound and you may not get what you thought you bought. Never send a company any money until your lawyer has seen the contract. Once your money is on the way without a contract, it is lost if the firm is disreputable.

Only after you have had an attorney look over the contract, and

only after you have evidence of the firm's determination to provide you with what they have advertised, should you enter into a contract which will cost you money. Even then before you commit yourself to the deal, check by mail with the U. S. Postmaster in the city where the firm is located, check with the Better Business Bureau of that city and check with the Chamber of Commerce, too. Ask them if the reputation of the firm is such that you can trust your money with them. If there is any question in your mind, do not sign, no matter how eager you are to have your music on records. If there is any question, seek out another firm and go through the process of checking up again. It is your money—get value for it.

What the New Songwriter Can Do

First, do not be discouraged. But you must face the facts. It is not sufficient to want to write—you must have the know-how. A great artist, in addition to his natural ability, must spend years in study to attain success. So it is in songwriting.

We repeat, songwriting is a highly skilled profession, requiring—like all the arts—genuine talent, originality, knowledge, and experience.

If you write lyrics only, we remind you that Gilbert's great lyrics would never have been sung without the

masterful music of Sullivan, or someone his equal.

If you have written both lyrics and music yourself, then seek the honest advice and help of an experienced arranger in your city or town. Perhaps someone in the local orchestra or theater can help you. Do not be afraid of criticism.

How to Submit Your Songs

Send your best songs, no more than four at a time, on 7½ IPS tape recorded on one side only. It is best to use a monaural tape machine since most publishers have simple office equipment, and tape recorded on the newer stereo models is often impossible to play.

Do this as professionally as possible. If you have access to a recording studio or a radio studio with an engineer, singer, and musicians, then this will be of great assistance.

Enclose a typewritten copy of the lyrics of each song along with return postage in the event your songs are not accepted. Be sure your name and address are on the tape box and each lyric sheet. Under no circumstances should you send the only copy you have of your songs. The cost of making copies is too reasonable to risk losing an expensive master of your demonstration recording.

When you write to a publisher, ask his permission to send a tape or music. If the letter is not addressed to an individual at the office, your material may be refused and returned unopened. Submit a copy of your music to as many reputable publishing companies as you wish.

Where to Send Your Songs

The three important performing rights' societies which license publishers and pay writers for radio and television performance of their tunes are a good source of lists of reputable publishers. They are: BMI, ASCAP, and SESAC. You might also visit your public library and find telephone books for Nashville, New York, Los Angeles, Atlanta, Memphis, and Detroit. Turn to the yellow pages and look under *music publishers.* Do not overlook local publishers in your own area who are usually more willing to listen to new or unsolicited material and who usually also have an affiliation with a small local record company.

While nationwide success is not likely with these small publishers, many territorial hits are recorded from material from these publishers which often becomes the springboard to greater things for a new writer. Amateur writers will find it extremely hard to get major publishing companies to listen to their efforts. But be persistent.

The road to success is quite as rugged in the field of songwriting as in all others. Paying out your own money will not smooth the path.

How to File a Copyright

There are two ways to get a legal copyright for your music: (1) register it in the Copyright Office in the unpublished form, or (2) publish the work with the legal notice of copyright on each copy.

To register unpublished music, send the following material, together, to Copyright Office, Library of Congress, Washington, D. C. 20540: (1) Application Form E which is provided by that office and will be sent you free on request. Fill it out and sign it. (2) One complete copy of the music (not your only copy). (3) There will be a registration fee of six dollars. Make checks or money orders payable to the Register of Copyrights. Song lyrics (words) without music cannot be registered in unpublished form.

Published music must be copyrighted even if already registered for copyright in unpublished form (usually your publishing company does this). The procedure is as follows:
1) Produce copies by printing or other means, making sure that every copy has legal notice—correct form and position as follows:
  (a) the word "copyright" or abbreviation "copr.," or symbol " c ";
  (b) the year date of publication;
  (c) name of copyright owner or

owners. Example; c John Doe, 1970.

This notice must appear on the title page or the first page of the music. If it is not there, the copyright is lost and cannot be restored.
2) Publishing the music by placing copies on sale, sell them, or publicly distribute them.
(3) Register the copyright immediately after publication by sending the following material, together, to Copyright Office, Library of Congress, Washington, D. C. 20540:
  (a) Application Form E,
  (b) Two complete copies as first published with copyright notice on them, and
  (c) A $6 registration fee.

Conclusion

In summary, the following points are offered as a helpful guide:
1) To begin with, strive for originality in your songs. Try to make your song different in idea, in lyric and in melody, from any song that has ever been written. Remember, all of today's successful, professional writers were once unheard-of amateurs. They became successful by offering something no one had offered before. Keep your approach to songwriting as new and fresh as possible.
2) Deal only with a firm whose reliability can be established by intelligent inquiry.
3) Always read and thoroughly understand any contract or agreement *before* signing to make certain the provisions contained therein meet with your approval. If terms of the agreement are not clear to you, seek the advice of a competent attorney *before you sign.* Keep a copy of all contracts for future reference.
4) Remember that any words can be set to music, from the cheapest jingle to the most beautiful poem. A proficient writer can grind out thousands of tunes each year to order, but such music is rarely, if ever, actually published.
5) The offer by a company to *print* several so-called professional copies

of a song does not mean that the song is being published in the usual sense of the word. The amateur may desire several of them for his own enjoyment, but such copies are generally of no value to music publishers, since they prepare their own copies if they are interested in a song.
6) Although literally thousands of songs are copyrighted each year in Washington, genuine "hits" which are financially successful ventures number only a few hundred songs annually. Of this relatively small number, the overwhelming majority are copyrighted, promoted, recorded, and published by music publishing firms who assume all financial responsibility and do not charge the songwriter for their services.
7) Keep trying! Nobody ever knows where the next hit is coming from.

Elvis Presley

Songwriter Magazine

This is a monthly magazine featuring interviews and features with famous songwriters, producers, publishers, and record executives; there are also how-to articles by successful songwriters, music attorneys, recording engineers, and publishers, and departments like "Songwriter News," the nation's top single charts, album reviews, questions and answers.

Rates are for:
  3 years, 36 issues—$30
  2 years, 24 issues—$22
  1 year, 12 issues—$12
Outside USA, add $2 per year.
Write to *Songwriter Magazine,* P.O. Box 3510, Hollywood, CA 90028.

Spears, Billy Jo

Born: January 14, 1937, Beaumont, Texas

Her first single at age thirteen was "Too Old for Toys, Too Young for Boys," followed a few years later by "Toys, Boys" sung first on "Louisiana Hayride." Her first big country hit was "He's Got More Love in His Little Finger" in 1968, followed by "Mr. Walker It's All Over," in 1969, which brought her to the attention of urban fans of country music. In 1975, she made the charts with "Blanket on the Ground" and later hits: "Stay Away from the Apple Tree," "Silver Wings and Golden Rings," and "What I've Got in Mind." In 1977, her LP *If You Want Me* included ten tunes by top country composers such as Kenny Rogers's "Sweet Music Man," Kris Kristofferson's "Loving Him Was Easier," and Ben Peters's title song. Her "'57 Chevrolet" hit the top fifty in late 1978.

United Artists Records

United Artists Records

Billie Jo Spears

Stampley, Joe

Born: 1944, Springhill, Louisiana
Married: Jo Ann

Joe has had as many as ten hit records in a row: "Soul Song," "If You Would Touch Me," "Billy, Go Get Me a Woman," and one of the biggest truck drivers' songs going, "Roll On, Big Mama." In 1978, his LP *Red Wire and Blue Memories* hit big.

Statler Brothers

Lee De Witt
Born: March 8, 1938, Roanoke County, Virginia

Philip Balsley
Born: August 8, 1939, Augusta County, Virginia

Harold W. Reid
Born: August 21, 1939, Augusta County, Virginia

Don Reid
Born: June 5, 1945, Staunton, Virginia

Friends since childhood, this top vo-

Mercury

cal group started singing together in 1955 and got their first big break in 1963 when they joined the "Johnny Cash Show." Their 1965 recording, "Flowers on the Wall," written by DeWitt, was the first in a long line of hits, including "Bed of Roses," "The Class of '57," "I'll Go To My Grave Loving You," "Thank God, I've Got You," and "I Was There." Their *Best of the Statler Brothers* album went gold with over a half-million sales and was still in the top twenty at the end of 1978 along with *Entertainers . . . . On and Off the Record.* In 1977–78, they released five albums, including two gospels and *Short Stories.* They are winners for six consecutive years (1972-77) of the CMA Vocal Group of the Year award. Since 1971, they have held a July Fourth Country Music Festival in Staunton, Virginia, in the beautiful Shenandoah Valley, with such guest performers as Ronnie Milsap in 1977. Less flamboyant than Willie Nelson's Dripping Springs extravaganza, it attracts over 50,000 fans annually and all profits go to local charities. In 1978, their top-chart singles included "Some I Wrote" and "Do You Know You Are My Sunshine."

Tillis, Mel

Born: August 8, 1932, Pahokee, Florida
Married: Doris
Children: s. Mel, Jr.; d. Pam, Connie, Cindy, Carey April

More than five hundred of his songs have been recorded, including "Detroit City," which went gold for Bobby Bare and has been cut by over a hundred other performers, including Tom Jones and Dean Martin. His "Ruby, Don't Take Your Love to Town" sold a million for Kenny Rogers and The First Edition. Mel makes over two hundred concert dates a year with his traveling band, The Statesiders, named for an early hit, "I Wanna Go Stateside," which he wrote while with the Air Force in Japan. A TV regular on shows including "Tonight," "Merv Griffin," "Dinah Shore," and "Hee Haw," he appeared in the 1977 "Salute to the Beatles" special and as a movie star in *W. W. & the Dixie Dance Kings.* Named Entertainer of the Year by the Country Music Association in 1976, Mel gives himself another title, "Guru of the Stutterers." He turns a speech impediment into a comedy advantage and an inspiration to thousands with the same affliction. Example: "If I wanted to ask my wife to the Saturday night dance, I'd start asking on Monday." His top-ten hits include: "Who's Julie?" "Old Faithful," "Arms of a Fool," "Commercial Affection," "Heaven Every Day," "Honky-Tonk," "One More Time," "Memory Maker," and "Woman in the Back of My Mind." His big 1978 hits were, "What Did I Promise Her Last Night?" and "Ain't No California" and the LP *I Believe in You.*

Tucker, Tanya (Denise)

Born: October 10, 1958, Seminole, Texas

Tanya grew up in Wilcox and later Phoenix, Arizona, where her father, Beau, took her to see such touring artists as Mel Tillis, Ernest Tubb, and LeRoy Van Dyke. Later the family moved to St. George, Utah, where Robert Redford was filming *Jeremiah Johnson.* The producer was more interested in Tanya's horse than the future country music star, but she firmly refused to let her horse appear without her. They both appeared in a cameo role. By 1972, Beau was convinced of his daughter's talent and scraped up enough money for her to make a demo. They sent copies of the tape to everyone in the music industry—and all they got were rejections. Finally, songwriter Dolores Fuller heard Tanya sing and introduced her to famed producer Billy Sherrill. Her very first record was "Delta Dawn," an instant runaway hit that catapulted the fourteen year old to national stardom. Not only was the song captivating, but the adolescent singer sounded like a mature woman of considerable experience. This compelling combination grew even more fascinating with "What's Your Mama's Name?" and "Blood Red and Going Down" in 1973, and "Would You Lay with Me (in a Field of Stone)," which became a major hit in Europe and Australia, too. Later hit singles include: "Lizzie and the Rainman," "Here's Some Love," and "Riding Rainbows."

Turner, Mary Lou "Lulu"

Born: Hazard, Kentucky
Birthday: June 13
Married: David Byrd

While in high school, she sang with a bluegrass band at the Wheeling Jamboree in West Virginia, where she first met Bill Anderson. It wasn't until several years later that the early acquaintance became a pro-

Tanya Tucker

fessional association. In 1974, Mary Lou joined "The Bill Anderson Show." Her first recording with Bill, "Sometimes," hit the number-one spot on all the charts.

Twitty, Conway (Harold Jenkins)

Born: September 1, 1933, Friars Point, Mississippi
Married: Mickey
Children: s. Conway, Jr.; d. Cathy

Conway Twitty's father was a riverboat captain on the Mississippi, and it was his grandfather who gave him his first guitar at age four. At ten, he organized his first band, The Phillips County Rambler, and promoted his own radio show on station KFFA in Helena, Arkansas. After a stint in the army, he decided to change his professional name: "I wasn't shooting any stars out of the sky as Harold Jenkins," he recalls. On a map of Texas, he found the name of a small town, Twitty. In his home state of Arkansas, he found Conway. Putting them together led

MCA Records

Conway Twitty

Mary Lou Turner

MCA Records
United Talent Inc.

eventually to his first success, "It's Only Make Believe," which sold over a million copies in 1958. In 1960, he wrote "Walk Me to the Door" for Ray Price. By 1966, he was recording his own songs, with such hits as "Next in Line," "To See My Angel Cry," "You've Never Been This Far Before," "The Games that Daddies Play," and "She Needs Someone to Hold Her." His "Hello, Darling" hit big in 1970 and bigger still in 1975 when Apollo commander, Tom Stafford, played the song for the Russian Soyuz crew during the joint U.S.-Soviet space venture. (Conway taped a special Russian-language version for the historic link-up.) Another historic link-up was Conway and Loretta Lynn as one of the most celebrated duet teams in country music. Their hit albums include: *Louisiana Woman, Mississippi Man, Feelin's, Never Ending Song of Love* and their big single, "I Can't Love You Enough." Described by Robert Palmer in the *New York Times* as "contributing to a new country candor," Twitty's 1977 singles included "I've Already Loved You in My Mind." Two LPs on the 1978 charts were *The Very Best of Conway Twitty* and *Honky Tonk Heroes* with Loretta Lynn, which includes the hit single "Lovin' from Seven to Ten." Films made in the sixties include *Sex Kittens Go to College* and *College Confidential.*

Wagoner, Porter

Born: August 12, 1932, West Plains, Missouri
Married: Denise Mayree
Children: s. Richard; d. Denise, Debra

The "Thin Man from West Plains," as he is called, got his start in his hometown when as a butcher-store clerk his boss put him on the local radio station to sing a few songs and announce the day's bargains. In the fall of 1951, he moved to a weekly spot on KWTO, Springfield, where, in 1952, the "Ozark Jubilee" was created by the late Red Foley. In 1955, RCA Records signed Porter, his first song, "A Satisfied Mind," hitting the number-one spot. Other hits included "Company's Comin'," "Your Old Love Letters," "The Green, Green Grass of Home," "Sorrow on the Rocks," "I'll Go Down Swinging," and "Skid Row Joe." By 1957, he was a regular on the Opry; by the early sixties, he had his own syndicated TV show. It was in 1967 that singing partner Norma Jean retired to get married—that's when he found Dolly Parton! Their partnership produced the 1969 Grammy Award for "Just Someone I Used to Know" and the CMA Duet Award for 1971. Other duets with Dolly are "Burning the Midnight Oil" and "Please Don't Stop Loving Me." The partnership lasted until 1974 when Dolly formed her own band and began recording as a soloist. Among Porter's top LPs are: *Carroll County Incident, Highway Heading South,* and *Sing Some Love Songs, Porter Wagoner;* duets with Dolly Parton are: *Best of Porter Wagoner and Dolly Parton, Love and Music, Two of a Kind,* and *Just the Two of Us.*

Walker, Jerry Jeff

Born: March 16, 1942, Oneonta, New York
Married: Susan

At sixteen, he left the Catskill Mountains for the streets of New Orleans, where he played the guitar and sang wherever folks would listen—until hitting the road again for Texas where he started a rock group, Circus Maximus. By 1968, he decided to go it alone, recorded his first hit composition, "Mr. Bojangles," and an album for Vanguard, *Drifting Way of Life.* Shortly thereafter, he switched over to MCA for his album *Jerry Jeff Walker,* and in 1973, he spent two sultry summer weeks in Luckenbach, Texas, recording "Viva Terlingua." Finding his musical home in Austin, Jerry Jeff formed the Lost Gonzo Band and recorded "Collectibles," live at Castle Creek and Odyssey Sound. On the move again, "Ridin' High" was recorded in five different cities across the country, including San Francisco, Woodstock (New York) and Nashville. His most recent albums are *It's a Good Night for Singing* and *Contrary to the Ordinary.*

Walker, Jo

Born: February 16, 1944, Orlinda, Tennessee
Children: d. Michelle

Jo Walker is the executive director of the Country Music Association, which she has served since 1958 when she began as office manager. One of country music's outstanding leaders, she ranks high on the list of those responsible for bringing country music to the world. (*See* Country Music Association)

Causey Photography

Jo Walker

MCA Records

Jerry Jeff Walker

Wallace, Jerry
("Mr. Smooth")

Born: December 15, 1945, Guilford, Missouri
Children: s. John Wallace, Wally

Jerry started as a rock'n'roll singer in the late fifties and made many appearances on Dick Clark's "American Bandstand," switched to country, his "Primrose Lane," which sold 1.6 million. Other hits include: "My Wife's House," "Georgia Rain," "Do You Know What It's Like to Be Lonesome?", "I Wonder Whose Baby (You Are Now)," "Wanted Man," "Misty Moonlight," and "If You Leave Me Tonight, I'll Cry." His "I Wanna Go to Heaven" hit the *Billboard* charts in late 1978.

Ward, Jacky

Born: November 18, 1946, Groveton, Texas
Married: Tanya

Children: s. Darrin; d. Vaness, Kay

Born to a musical family, Jacky at one point held down three jobs: a salesman in the morning, a disc jockey in the afternoon, and an entertainer at night at local Texas clubs. With a friend's backing, he cut his first single, "Big Blue Diamonds," in 1970. A local hit in Houston, it soon caught on nationwide. Since then, his Mercury hits have included "Stealin'," "Dance Her By Me (One More Time)," "I Never Said It Would Be Easy," and his 1977 release, "Why Not Tonight," all included in his debut album, *Jacky Ward*. An electrifying stage performer, Jacky astounds audiences with his impressions of personalities, including Elvis, the Platters, Gabby Hayes, the Diamonds, Walter Brennan, John Wayne, and Johnny Cash. He made his acting debut in the CBS-TV series, "Nashville 99." His 1978 hit, "A Lover's Question," went to the top of the charts as both a single and an album. His duet with Reba McEntire, "Three Sheets in the

Jacky Ward

Jerry Wallace

Wind," first appeared on the charts in May 1978. His outside interests are helping to raise funds for the Arthritis Foundation and The March of Dimes. He appears regularly on telethons.

Wells, Kitty
(Muriel Deason)

Born: August 30, 1919, Nashville, Tennessee
Married: Johnny Wright
Children: s. Bobby; d. Ruby, Carol Sue

The undisputed Queen of Country Music has the distinction of being the first female artist to reach number one on the country music charts with her 1952 million-selling Decca recording of "It Wasn't God Who Made Honky-Tonk Angels."

Since then, she has had over twenty-three top-slot songs. Her duet with Red Foley, "One by One," was on the charts for fifty-two weeks and number one for twenty-six. She was voted Number One Female Country Artist for twelve years straight (1952–1964). Since 1969, she and her husband have starred in their own syndicated TV show. In 1976, she was elected to the Country Music Hall of Fame. Her LPs include: *The Kitty Wells Story, Dust on the Bible, Golden Favorites, Guilty Street,* and *Forever Young.*

Wembley Festival

Also known as the International Festival of Country Music, held each Easter since 1968 at the Wembley Empire Pool, England. Founded by British entrepreneur Mervyn Conn, "Wembley" introduced country music to British audiences. Now hundreds of thousands of fans flock to see and hear such superstars as Kenny Rogers, Dottie West, Waylon & Willie, Dolly Parton, Johnny Cash, Skeeter Davis, Larry Gatlin, Donna Fargo, Merle Haggard, and many more. If you're going to be in England at Easter, write for information: Mervyn Conn Ltd., 45-46 Chandos Place, London, WC 2, England.

West, Dottie (Dorothy Marie)

Born: October 11, 1932, McMinnville, Tennessee
Married: Bill West (div.), Byron Metcalf
Children: s. Morris, Kerry, Dale; d. Shelly

The oldest of ten children, Dottie majored in music at Tennessee Tech, played in nightclubs, and cut her first record for Starday in 1959. A contract with Atlantic Records followed, but on the recommendation of Jim Reeves, Chet Atkins signed her with RCA in 1962. Jim Reeves's recording of "Is This Me?" won Dottie the 1961 BMI Writer's Award. Probably her best-recog-

Dottie West

nized songs are "Here Comes My Baby," which won the 1964 Grammy, and her trademark, "Country Sunshine," which started out as a Coca-Cola commercial in 1971, won

the advertising world's Cleo Award, and eventually two Grammy nominations! A member of the Opry since 1964, Dottie travels with her band more than 200 days a year, logging up to 125,000 miles. She has made two vastly successful European tours and is a summer fairgrounds favorite in the U.S. In 1973, she opened the Memphis Symphony Orchestra's season and performed for a week with the Kansas City Symphony. In 1977, her United Artists LP *When It's Just You and Me* featured eleven great country songs, including the title song, "The Lovin' Kind," and "Tiny Fingers." Teamed with Kenny Rogers, she has achieved superstardom in such duet releases as "Anyone Who Isn't Me Tonight" and "Every Time Two Fools Collide," also sharing with Kenny the Vocal Duo award for 1978.

Williams, Don

Born: June 18, 1947, Floydada, Texas

He is known as the gentle giant—lean, laid-back, with a husky warmth that is as at home in New York's Carnegie Hall as the Wembley Festival outside London. In Corpus Christi, Texas, in 1964, Don formed the Pozo Seco Singers, a trio that sang a variety of popular music

Dottie West and Kenny Rogers

United Artists Records

from folk to pop to country. Their first single, "Time," climbed to the top ten, followed by "I'll Be Gone," "I Can Make It with You," "Look What You've Done," "I Believed It All" and "Louisiana Man." Pozo Seco disbanded in 1971. In 1972, Don made his first single, "Don't You Believe," followed by "The Shelter of Your Eyes," which gave him his first appearance on the country charts. Among the over five hundred songs he's written are "Some Broken Hearts Never Mend," the 1978 top of the charts "I've Got A Winner in You," and many of the songs on his hit album, *Country Boy* which made the top fifty LP charts along with a later release, *Expressions*. As a movie personality, he costarred with Burt Reynolds in *W.W. and the Dixie Dance Kings* and would like to make more—"but only," he says, "if it's strictly family fare."

Don Williams

Williams, Hank, Jr.

Oedipus Rocks
The Fall and Rise of Hank Williams, Jr.
by John Eskow

The following article appeared in New Times *magazine in 1977.*

Like his father before him, Hank is a singer, and even his speaking voice borders on song. He commands a range of Southern vocal tricks, from a playful falsetto crack to a sagelike *basso profundo,* with separate controls for drawl, speed, and irony: Each story becomes an aural roller-coaster ride. The one he tells now is especially bumpy.

It was August 8, 1975. He'd just recorded a landmark country-rock album, *Hank Williams Jr. & Friends,* that signaled his emergence from his father's shadow. Climbing a Montana mountain with a guide and his son, he stood at the Continental Divide and looked out.

"It takes a while to get up to 9,000 feet. We were lookin' over at Salmon, Idaho, right by a brass stake that marks the Divide. We were on Ajax Peak, which is like a knife edge—you've really got to climb around to get there.

"We're lookin' for mountain goats, way up past the tree line. And finally we started back down, crossin' some pretty rough terrain. And I stepped in the guide's footprint, but it had loosened and I got caught in a snow slide.

"It was just like fallin' out an airplane—straight down. So down I went, slidin' headfirst on my back. Emotionally, I just froze inside. No feelin'. Just shock. And I thought: *You're dead. You're just gonna splatter on the rocks.*

Then, after that thought got out of the way—all this is goin' on within seconds—I flipped over so I was slidin' headfirst on my stomach, and I tried to get that .44 out of my shoulder holster, tried to dig that long barrel into the snow, to try and break the fall. 'Course that was a joke.

"Then I swung my feet down under me as I felt the first little rocks hittin' me, and I decided that the first boulder I hit, I'd just kick out with all my might. Bump, bump, bump, I felt the rocks gettin' bigger, I was bouncin' across 'em. So I drew up my legs and kicked out.

"Dick [the guide] was watchin'; he said it looked like a guy comin' off a ski jump. Then it was a free fall, with me flippin' over. As I'm fallin', I see this huge mountain lake, and I said 'I'm gonna try and land in that lake.' 'Course that would've killed me right away.

"Finally, I hit that snow like a swan dive. There was a boulder stickin' up through there, and I just hit it straight on, headfirst. It just literally split my face in half. It started right at the top of the hairline, split me right exactly between the eyes, down the left side of the

Universal Management

nose—stopped at the chin, although that was broken too . . .

"Came to a rest slumped over in a sittin' position. First thing I done was to look at my hands—you always look at your hands, for some reason—and I couldn't see anything wrong! I thought, hell, I've made it! And I started gettin' my hands up into my head, and I don't have any nose, any teeth—I don't feel any *head.* It's just all a hole, and I'm puttin' my fingers up in it. Just a hole from the lip all the way up, and I'm puttin' my hands inside it . . . grabbin' hold of my brains and all this gobbledygook.

"And Dick gets down there—course there was a lot of snow, retardin' the bleedin'—he starts tearin' my hands away. I'm sayin', 'What is it, what is it?' And he says, 'It's your *nose,* it's your *nose.'* He said it was all he could do to keep from throwin' up. And I saw that he was cryin', and he's a pretty tough old boy.

"Then I jumped up, with this big surge, and I said, 'I'm walkin' out of here, let's get to the Jeep.' Then, of course, the blood came out in torrents, just like turnin' on a water hose, pumpin' out with every heartbeat. And my right eye's hangin' out. And Dick keeps sayin', 'It's your nose . . .' Then I just made two or three steps and piled up. So Dick grabbed all this stuff hangin' out and just shoved it back into place, and it made a terrible sound—all this flesh and bone crunchin' up. Then he tore his shirt off, ripped it up, and wrapped the stuff in place as best he could. No tellin', no way to describe what he seen.

"Now I'm gettin' cold—real cold—so he made a rock

enclosure around my head. Now the little boy gets down there, and 'course he's cryin', 'cause he's seen this terrible fall, and he wants to go for help. But Dick just grabs him and shakes him and tells him to just keep me talkin', kick me in the back now and then to get that junk out of my mouth. And Dick goes lookin' for help.

"Now I'm alone with this boy, and he's stunned. That's when the bad period set in, the give-up period, when I just knew that I was dyin'. And I'm lyin' there, lookin' out with one eye at this great scenario, these beautiful snowy mountains—very peaceful, if you weren't in my situation . . . And I thought: This is death.

"And I said to the Lord: I've wanted to die a lot of times. But I wanted it to be *onstage,* or an overdose in a car—you know, some nice *musical* death. Not like this, alone in the snow with a little boy chatterin' on beside me.

"By now he's talkin' a blue streak—his coon dog's the best coon dog in the world, and he's gonna win a prize at the fair, and he loves to go fishin' . . . And I'm thinkin' about my own little boy, and about Becky, and the guys in the band, the bus, my mother, my grandfather—the whole thing . . .

"But then all that's gone, and it's just *here comes death, whatever it is.*

"Now for some reason my eye—the one still in my head—caught sight of these two rings on my hand, the H and W, my initials. And for some reason, seein' those rings made me think I could live. And I started poundin' my hand in the snow, poundin' with every heartbeat. When they finally got to me, I'd dug a crater two feet deep in that snow. Two and a half hours went by that way.

"But now the boy's still ravin' on, and I'm tryin' to answer him—couldn't understand me 'cause of the gook in my throat, but I said, *'I'm not givin' up here, I'm gonna fight this thing.'*

"Now his daddy's at the foot of the mountain. And he yells up to the boy, 'Is he still talkin'?' And I wanted to jump up and holler, 'Hell yes, get up here!' I could see him down there, and he looked like a giant—some muscles in my brain had been strained, affectin' my sight in the eye that was workin', and everybody looked like a giant to me. Dick looked like he could just reach up the mountain and carry me away himself.

"He hollered up, 'The helicopter's coming!' Now he'd found a forest ranger, by pure luck. Otherwise he'd have had to drive to the ranger station, which was twenty-seven miles away.

"Then the medics came, and it was in with the Demerol, in with this and that. Wrapped my head in bandages. And these rescue guys had this cocoon-like stretcher, and they had to carry me.

"And it's hurtin' now. Bad. And then I realize I'm goin' on the *outside* of the chopper, it's a one-man machine. And my cocoon is clamped to the outside. Up goes the helicopter, and I'm right out there in the wind, on the struts. And I'm wonderin' if I'm gonna die in this

cocoon hangin' off a helicopter.

"But it didn't take long before we set down on a ranch. They got me right into this Cessna, did some more work on me there, and off we go. We've still got this 100-mile trip to make.

"We land in Missoula, and it's right into another helicopter. This is nearly five hours after the fall. They've got bottles and needles hangin' over me. And we set down on the helicopter pad and we're inside the hospital.

"I never lost consciousness the whole time. The doctors said that had a lot to do with me livin'.

"And they started cuttin' off my clothes, my shoulder holster, and they went to cut off the cross I wear around my neck. I started yellin', 'No! Don't cut that cross!' And that's the last thing I remember before I went under. And later I had all that stuff—clothes, holster and cross—sewed back together.

"Four doctors operated on me for 7½ hours. And as soon as I woke up in that hospital bed, I thought: *The hard part's over. Now the healin' can begin.*

"I woke up the next evenin' in intensive care, and my jaws were wired shut. 'Course there were no teeth. I'm runnin' my tongue around, feelin' nothin' but brass wires. Tubes down the throat, the whole bit. I rolled my eye around and looked around: Everything was so lilywhite in the room, and I saw the mountains out the window covered with snow, and then I was out again.

"They said, 'If he makes it eight days, he'll live.' But they didn't expect me to. They figured my brain had to be infected, from me touchin' it and the wind cuttin' through it.

"And my head's a basketball, all shaved too, with stitches and wires all over it. But I couldn't see myself.

"Next mornin' I asked the nurse, 'Is this my nose?' And she said yes. I said, 'Are you sure it's not a plastic nose?' And she said no. See, it was just flapped over there, like you took a flap of cloth and peeled it away, and they just hooked it back in there. So it was my nose.

"Then I started noticin' the sounds—everything was too loud! The blips on the oscilloscope were like hammer blows! They were soothin', for what they meant, but too loud.

"But now I'm gettin' better, better, takin' liquid through a straw, but the pain is gettin' worse, so I'm takin' a lot of Demerol, too.

"Then I caught myself callin' for Demerol when I didn't need it. Johnny Cash was in my room, and he'd been through his pill thing, and he said: 'Hoss, don't let me catch you buzzin' for that Demerol when you don't need it—'cause it's *real good,* ain't it?' And I said, *'Uh huh!'* But I remembered that, and I caught myself.

"On the eighth day they gave me a whirlpool bath, and that was the most fantastic sensation you can imagine. By now I could take little steps on my own, and I had to go to the bathroom, so they let me go myself.

"Well, they'd forgotten there was a mirror in that bathroom. I looked in that mirror and it was . . . *bad.*

Much worse than I'd expected. Just this tremendous, swollen head, a monster's head—one eye screwed way off to the side, like an involuntary thing, the other eye black, jaws wired together, no teeth—it's got a grotesque look to it. There's a hole in my forehead where the bone's sunken in, and you can see the heartbeat pulsin' in my forehead. Terrible green and blue colors, stitches down the middle of the face, unbelievable weight loss, bony limbs, ribs stickin' through flesh. Muscles gone. That was a downer. I figured I'd get some Frankenstein roles. Or some leftover Jack Elam parts.

"That's when I resolved myself that music was over. I thought, hell, there's no way to get past this stuff! And I'd told God many times I didn't want to sing, so this looked like the deal goin' down that way. I went into a rejection period.

"Next day they brought a guitar down there, into the rehabilitation unit. I knew I could move my hands, but . . . it was a pretty quiet moment. Then I started, real slow at first, and soon I was rollin' along! Then it almost turned into Request Time. Cash was there, and he'd sing a song and I'd tinkle along. And that was a rush.

"Better and better and better. So I asked 'em if I could hunt in October, which was two months later. They said, 'No, you'll be here at least six weeks.' Fifteen days later I left.

"Dick's wife, Betty, said, 'You've been left here for some purpose.' It seemed that way. Shuffled outta that hospital and up to Dick's house. Stayed there for a month, readin' every Indian book I could find. Bought a guitar and started playin'. Bought a big hat to cover the hole in my skull, sunglasses to cover my eyes. And blue jeans—Gawd, that felt good, to wear blue jeans!

"I'm still wired together. Couldn't see too good, but I'd watch the Yosemite Sam cartoons at 3:30. Progressin' along.

"Then I had to go back to Missoula to get the wires out. Doctor sat me down in a chair and said, 'Hold on, this is gonna hurt a little bit.' By now they'd given me so much pain killer they couldn't give me any more, so it had to be done without it. And he said, 'This wire is coming from just behind your eyeball,' and he got hold of it and just yanked it clean out through my jaw. And it hurt, all right. 'Cause it was wire through bone.

"Then he took the other one out. Well, my jaws have been wired for a month. So when we got back to Dick's house I had Betty make me up the most beautiful tuna fish sandwich. And I took this big bite, so excited to be eatin' again—and there was nothin' but a wet circle on the bread where I'd bitten. See, all the muscles were gone. Freaky. So I threw the damn sandwich and bounced it off the wall.

"Well, I could eat, but not that stuff. So Betty started makin' spaghetti, casseroles, stuff like that. Man, I was *really* doin' good then! I eat a lot anyway, and I thought: This is great!

"Also, I could start to sing now. Plus I took my .45, to see if I could sight with one eye, and I hit the damn bull's-eye first time. That really turned me on.

"Left Montana in October with my big Alabama hat pulled down low. Got home, started drivin' the pickup, shootin', feelin' good. Then the doctor told me the jaw was healin' wrong. Swung over to the left. This was two weeks after I'd started eatin', and he said they'd have to wire the whole thing over.

"Now this was a bummer.

"Back to the hospital, back on the table, pop, pop, break the jaws again. Take a knife and cut the gum away. Bring it over there, line it up right. I'm wired up again. And they worked on the nose—the nose is headin' east, lookin' pretty bad.

"Come back to Cullman, wired up. Went huntin' that season, like they said I wouldn't do, killed a deer. Go back to Nashville and they yank the wires out again. Nose is better, eyes a little better.

"Mother died right about then, and at the funeral I guess I looked a little weird. The papers said, 'Williams looks like death himself.' Big funeral—George Wallace came down, a bunch of other folks. All the black people linin' the streets, and white people, heads bowed. It was a rough time.

"Then oral surgery, takin' metal out of the roof of my mouth. Then we need a forehead plate to get the brain covered better, 'cause it's just skin still, no bone. This was March. April we started playin' shows again.

"Got this funny toupee on my head, along with the hat and glasses.

"Then we had to go to this eye doctor, get the orbit of this eye built up. We get it done, leave the hospital, the eye looks a little bit funny.

"We go down to Becky's folks' house for Thanksgiving. And we're sittin' around the table and everybody's givin' me some mighty strange looks. So I go into the bathroom—somethin's come loose, and this whole implant has rotated up, and this eyeball is stickin' out—it's red, it's blue, it's terrible, it's runnin'. Had to go back for another implant.

"See, all these operations—you're lookin' forward to each one. Each one's a step. Each one moves you forward. . . ."

To be born Hank Williams, Jr., in 1949 was to be the namesake of a god. His father was—and still is—adored with fervor throughout America. His first hit, "Lovesick Blues," established him as the greatest draw the Grand Ole Opry ever had. Through his songs—"Your Cheatin' Heart," "Jambalaya," "I'm So Lonesome I Could Cry" —he became the down-home poet of hell-raising and grief. Add a death at twenty-nine from speed and alcohol, and you have all the ingredients for an instant myth.

The last few years of his life were a boozy fog, marked by a divorce from his wife, Audrey. Although still idolized, he was increasingly tormented by the forces that shaped his lyrics. His one sustaining joy was Hank Jr., who was three years old the night his father died in the back seat of a new '52 Cadillac.

When asked what he remembers of Hank Sr., the son

at first responds with a brusque "Nothing." Then he ponders the question for 30 seconds. "Wait—just a snapshot image in an airplane, once. And backstage at the Opry—I knocked something over . . ."

But if his memories are vague, there were always thousands of people to fill him in. The Hank Williams legacy was his, whether he wanted it or not.

He was raised on the belief that loneliness was in his bloodline, along with music and alcohol. As if the "lovesick blues," like black lung, was a disease linking the generations.

When he was eight years old, he was thrust into a career as a professional specter, playing his father's songs for crowds of necromantic drunks. Red Foley, the Opry star, would sit backstage with the child and tell him: "You're a ghost, son, nothin' but a ghost of your daddy." His mother would hold him close and say virtually the same thing.

For months at a stretch he would tour the honky-tonk circuit, rooming with legendary wild men like Johnny Cash and Jerry Lee Lewis. He'd watch Cash stuff cherry bombs down motel toilets and rig booby traps for the maids; he'd serve as mascot for troops of stoned musicians; and he'd steal every show because his name was Hank Williams.

Then he'd go home for a while and sit in class with the other third graders.

"It was a *bit* schizophrenic," he says with a wry smile. "At first, I thought bein' Hank's boy was the greatest thing in the world—a ghost of this man that everyone loved. They think I'm daddy—how wonderful. Mother's smilin', she's happy, money's rollin' in, manager's hap-

py—seemed ideal. Then, round about my teens, it all hit me at once."

One can only try to imagine how adolescence hit Hank Williams, Jr. When he was sixteen, he had a number-one record on the C & W charts—"Standing in the Shadows," a recitation set to music. MGM, his record company at the time, had him overdub his voice onto Hank Sr.'s songs, and released two albums that featured a living teenager harmonizing with his dead father.

A heavy drinker since his mid-teens, he embarked on a nonstop bender through his early twenties.

"It was the whole country-music syndrome. I got to where I didn't have any more hangovers—woke up drunk, went to sleep drunk." During this period he also co-starred in a movie, *A Time to Sing,* with Ed Begley, did the sound-tracks for several other films, and married for a second time.

He was rich, sweet-faced and an idol by proxy. But in addition to his Jack Daniel's habit, he'd become addicted to Darvon. He seemed bent on replaying his father's melodrama—live hard, die young and be played by George Hamilton in a cheesy film biography. (The movie, *Your Cheatin' Heart,* has grossed millions over the years; Hank Jr. did the soundtrack.) With a myth for a father, and a classic stage mother, he was caught in a Freudian squeeze play.

In 1973 he snapped. "Booze, sleeplessness, pills, depression, it just got to be too much." Just as his father had done twenty years before, he began missing gigs, acting crazy, inching closer to ruin.

"I was still havin' to do shows as daddy. I'd sit home listenin' to Chuck Berry and Fats Domino, thinkin' of musical concepts myself, but I'd still have to play those lonesome songs of Hank's—and they were hittin' pretty close to home. Marriage bustin' up—I was supposed to be this big success, but where were the friends? Where were the lovers? I guess it all ganged up on me. So I tried the check-out route."

In a 1974 song, "Getting Over You," he describes his attempted suicide. . . . [To get over whom? He says it's addressed to his first wife, but the lyric makes sense as a message to his father, too. In any case, friends got his stomach pumped in time.]

[Then] he sought help from a Nashville psychiatrist, not an easy step for a man trained in macho loneliness.

"Well, I'd been huntin' with him, so I trusted him as a man. And it was pretty much life-or-death at that point."

The psychiatrist diagrammed a deadly triangle that had kept Williams trapped and depressed: his mother, widely described as a hard-drinking, haunted woman who exploited her son; his manager, who resisted Hank's creative impulses; and the city of Nashville. All conspired to keep him a ghost.

"The doctor said, 'You'd best get the hell out of this town. Ain't no good times for you here.' So I did—moved down to Cullman, Alabama. Started havin' some fun. Realizin' that self-pity is bullcrap.

"Pain is somethin' you get to leanin' on. I fell into that trap of thinkin' I had to suffer to create. Finally I realized: Hell, I don't need it *that* bad. No matter how good the songs that might come of it, *nothin's* worth that kind of pain."

Friday night. A redneck civil war rages in the Palomino, L.A.'s country-music venue. Roughly half the patrons are bouffant-and-sagging-jowls types who've come to hear a seance, a slavish evocation of Hank Williams Sr.; the other half are spaced cowboys who want Hank Jr., rock, blues and all. The schism widens as the band moves into a signature tune of Hank Sr.'s, "You're Gonna Change (Or I'm Gonna Leave)."

It's the old lyric, all right—a typically Williams mix of plaint and whimsy—but it's done in a grinding, Chicago blues adaptation that strikes a bouffant next to me as sheer heresy.

"Shoot, he's got it all niggered up," she whispers in disgust to her husband. Meanwhile, the cowboys are stomping and yipping their approval.

Hank's voice is a wonder—it hits a high, keening note and holds it for eight bars, then nose-dives into a cavernous bass without hesitation. As a pure instrument, his voice far surpasses his father's; few white singers can compete with him. (One voice teacher has compared his singing to opera star Luciano Pavarotti's.)

Hank sings with his head tilted back, sunglasses dazzled by the baby spotlights; he looks, and sings, like a blind man. (Since the accident he's worn a Stetson to hide a dented forehead, and shades to hide eyes that don't match.)

Mayday, mayday—there's danger at a table right in front of the bandstand. Two drunken couples are passing their multicolored drinks around like joints, with predictably bad results. They're alternately shaking with the music and slumping in their chairs, fixing Hank with the hopeless fish-eye stare of the truly wasted.

As he finishes "Stoned at the Jukebox," a great outlaw anthem from the *Friends* album, one of the women springs back to life. "Hank!" she screams. "Play 'Cheatin' Heart' for Hank and Audrey!" With this, she digs a crumpled twenty from her purse and flings it onstage. Hank ignores it, but more bills come sailing up from the crowd, many with requests scribbled on them. Napkins inky with requests fly onstage. *People* with requests fly onstage.

"Gawd, I hate that shit," Hank says later. "Sometimes I kick the damn bills off the stage, hopin' to head it off. And sometimes I just stop and lecture 'em. I say, 'Look. At one point in my life I was programmed to be my daddy. But my daddy's career is doin' pretty good, so how 'bout lettin' me work on my own?'"

Hank Williams, also known as Luke the Drifter and Old Lovesick, fathered Hank Williams Jr., aka Luke the Drifter Jr. and Bocephus.

As far as Hank Jr. can remember, "Bocephus" was the name of a hillbilly comedian's puppet in the Grand Ole Opry. In 1951 and 1952, during Williams' greatest stardom, little Hank would sometimes watch the wild shows at Ryman Auditorium. He was entranced by the dummy. So his father, having already named him after himself, renamed him after a puppet.

It's best to cast a wary eye on symbols when you're dealing with real people's lives. Bocephus might also be, Hank Jr. says, "just some silly hillbilly name."

Now the band's warming up the crowd, beginning the second set. Chris Plunkett, the bass player, sings a country-rock call-to-arms, "The South's Gonna Do It." He sings it with deep conviction, and the crowd hoots him on, never suspecting that this drawling Johnny Reb is a jazz composer from Asbury Park, New Jersey.

After three songs they introduce Hank. Back onstage, fighting a high fever and flu, he starts out ferocious. He's got that hell-raising mania that punk bands counterfeit, a roadhouse urgency that precludes slickness.

It's so easy to milk pathos in C&W bars—all it takes is a few songs that Hank describes as the "my-darlin'-left-me-so-I-got-drunk-drove-home-and-ran-over-someone's-little-girl" kind. For the most part, he resists this temptation, going after ecstasy instead. He seems to want to squeeze his whole body through the microphone, into some wilder land. Sometimes his lip, permanently numb from the fall, actually curls around the mike, and he has to pull his face away.

And sometimes he falters. Never scrupulous about tuning his guitar, he's capable of playing an entire song in the key of X, loud. And when his energy sags, the act deflates instantly, as it does now in mid-set. Three or four tunes drone by in a stupor. Hank's major problem as a performer is also his strength: Like all instinctive artists, he leads with his subconscious. But in an era when music is market-tested, shrink-wrapped and sold like deodorant, a few dull stretches and discordant notes seem a small price for authenticity.

By the end of the set, he's got his grin and *elan* back in place, and he's singing with the power of a Ray Charles, rocking through "Jambalaya"—"Son of a gun, we'll have big fun on the bayou." The band rips into the last descending chords, and Hank's already moving through the crowd as the ovation begins. . . .

Welcome to the Motel California: Howard Johnson's in North Hollywood. In a working year, Hank spends 150 to 200 nights in motels like this—a toilet on perpetual flush, Art Drecko lamps with switches hidden in unlikely places, elevators where the air is so denatured that it's like riding in a giant menthol filter.

We meet first on neutral turf, his manager's room. Becky, his wife of a year, and several associates are there to run interference: After twenty-five years of being grilled about his father, he's initially nervous at interviews.

"Say Jawn," says J.R. Smith, his manager, "y'all bein' a writer, y'all must know this Paul Schrader fella?"

Schrader, who wrote *Taxi Driver* and directed *Blue Collar,* has conferred with Hank, Jr., about doing a new film biography of his father.

"That'd be a *real* good lick," says Hank. His enthusiasm is understandable: How would you like to remember your father as played by George Hamilton?

Without seeking it, we're into the father-son question. "See, the record companies tell me I'm writin' too *personal* when I talk about my relation to daddy," he says. "But every town we play at, some young person comes up and says, 'I had the same routine with my father.' So it seems like it's pretty universal."

Outside, the blond canyons look down at the sea. Hank's wearing his gray high-rise Stetson and denim, a cowboy in a long black limo, cruising L.A. The sun glints off the diamond clef above the hat brim, gleams on the ever-present shades.

We're headed for Nudie's, the Paris of redneck couture, the Hollywood shop that's draped rhinestones around everyone from Elvis Presley to Elton John, by way of Dolly Parton. Albert and Becky shift uneasily as we approach—Hank's been known to buy outfits he doesn't need at Nudie's, and they're wondering what new extravagance he's got planned.

(One point about Hank Williams, Sr.: In addition to the long shadow he left for his son, he also left Hank, Jr., a share of his royalties—something like $250,000 a year.)

Nudie himself greets Hank at the door. Nudie, at seventy-five, is American weirdness at its zenith—both larger than life, and smaller. A wizened Brooklyn-born Jew in a Stetson of his own, wearing one black cowboy boot and one yellow one, he clearly revels in the role of Crusty Old Bastard.

He greets Hank like a beloved nephew, which, in a sense, he is. Hank, Sr., was a close friend of Nudie's, and bought all his outfits at the shop; his skeleton now reposes in a Nudie burial suit. Nudie remembers "little Hank" from his crib days.

"I made that boy his first rhinestone suit when he was two," he says, ordering an employee to dig up a photo. "Yes sir . . . they used to send his daddy out to me for drying out. Sometimes we'd just both get wet."

Among the 2,800 photos on Nudie's walls, a somber oil painting of Old Lovesick occupies a prized space. Nudie sits down facing it and takes an ancient mandolin out of its case. Hank sits under his father's lean face and takes the guitar someone offers him.

There's mandolin talk and reminiscing as they tune up. Nudie starts to play an old hill ballad, "Ramona," a haunting air with its Scotch-English roots still audible. Nudie plays his mandolin—two centuries old—with great tenderness and very little skill, and sketches the melody with a timeworn voice. . . .

Hank, who rarely wears anything more gaudy than Levi's, is suddenly enchanted by a jumpsuit—skintight and spangled with purple butterflies—that Elvis Presley ordered just before his death. As Becky and Albert exchange helpless glances, he goes to try it on.

Alone with Nudie in a corner of the store, I ask him about Bocephus.

"I've known that boy all his life. He's a helluva man, a helluva singer, and let me tell you something from the bottom of my heart—I seen him gettin' laid when he was *seven years old!*"

(Later, when I read the quote to Hank, he roars and shakes his head. "Naw," he smiles, "I was eight.")

Hank comes back, decked out in butterflies. He buys the suit for $1,200—only, it seems, because of its connection to Elvis. (Five days later he decides he doesn't really want it, and has it shipped back to Nudie.)

After visiting a few guitar shops, we return to Nudie's for a photo session on the roof. Hank's mood, dampened by flu and medication, has been slowly warming as we drive.

His size and manner and history conspire to make you forget his age. Until now, he's shown no sign of being twenty-eight, but clowning on the roof, with the L.A. skyline behind him, he becomes a young man.

"Hello," he intones, in a perfect imitation of Lorne Greene on "Bonanza," "this is the Ponderosa, and these are my people . . . some of 'em are a little *weird,* but they're all I've got. This here's my horse Fag . . . "

Once he gets started on Wild West shtick he reveals a little-boy side. He's a passionate fan of Yosemite Sam, the Mel Blanc cartoon sheriff. He even got Blanc to record the message on his phone-answering device— "All raht, you ornery varmint, leave yer name 'n' number or ah'll plug ya fulla holes, ya big galoot!"

Hank's sense of humor is a hybrid—sometimes it's backwoods mock-dumb ("They're gonna have another drought in L.A. 'cause all this rain's washed the water away"), and sometimes it's downright black. (At one point at the Palomino, when his amplifier began to squeal, he said, "Sorry, I'm gettin' some feedback from these wires in my head.")

But the humor vanishes as quickly as it appears, as Hank stares down at Los Angeles.

"Gawd," he sighs. "Sometimes it seems I've been on the road forever."

It's Saturday night at the honky-tonk, with all that that implies. A three-hundred-pound behemoth in worsted picks a fight with a scrawny longhair, a tattoo artist covered with his own handiwork chats with a woman in leather, John ("Gentle on My Mind") Hartford is called onstage to play a remarkable solo on his face.

"Git rowdy," someone hoots, as someone always will. This is the Temperament Exchange: For the price of a draft you buy the rights to a stranger's psychosis, or a night's feigned intimacy . . . GIT ROWDY! IT'S SATURDAY NIGHT, GODDAMMIT!

Becky Williams, with her seraphic face and calm intelligence, is probably the least rowdy person in the place. She talks in a Louisiana accent thick as gumbo, with that lilting question mark at the end of each sentence.

"I first met Hank just a week before his fall. Next thing I knew he'd fallen off that mountain, and they told me he'd never look the same again. Only thing that worried me was that, with the plastic surgery, his face might not seem . . . real. But it did. And he seemed like the same person, too."

In C&W circles, of course, the "good-hearted woman" is the traditional R_X for the blues. Becky Williams is certainly that, but she's quite a bit more. She graduated from Louisiana State University with a major in music, and she's one of the few people who can read serious novels in crowded motel rooms.

"I'm damn lucky to have that woman," Hank says when she's out of earshot. "She stood by me and never flinched a bit. Not only that, she's a pretty good hunter. We can share things . . . I looked at her in the hospital one day, and I thought: If it's this good through the bad times, think what the good times will be like. And let me tell you, they've been *good.*"

By now the Palomino crowd is screaming for him. Tonight there are fewer death-cultists in the audience, a few more true fans. It's a war of attrition, but it's slowly being won.

"Ladies and gentlemen, let's hear it for the one and only BOCEPHUS . . . MR. HANK WILLIAMS, JR.!"

Williams' home is 140 miles south of Montgomery, where his father lies buried. A ritual visit to Hank Sr.'s grave is the C & W equivalent of communing with Keats at his graveside in Rome—hundreds of songs have been written about it. Hank, Jr., sings the best of them, "Montgomery in the Rain," written by Steve Young. "I'm gonna go out to Hank's tombstone, and cry up a thunderstorm chain . . ."

Hank adds a chilling line at the end of Young's song: "You all know me well by the songs on the cemetery wind . . ." And he pronounces it *winnnnnd,"* so it whistles through the room. When he sings it, you're not sure if you're hearing a voice from the grave, from a living son, or from some ghastly fusion of the two.

"The pure products of America go crazy," said William Carlos Williams. If that's true, we might be grateful that nothing is pure anymore. Hank Williams's voice mapped out an America of unyielding farms and open skies, bad luck and long railroad trains; and his son was supposed to live in it. But it was a smaller America, without Motown bass lines and Eric Clapton guitar licks, and to keep a child/man there was to freeze him in time. So Hank Jr.'s story has been a long catching-up, a fight to be his own contemporary.

It's been a story rife with purity and craziness. Pain alternates with gross comedy—at his mother's funeral, Bob Harrington, the "Bourbon Street Preacher," stood over the open coffin singing "Hey, Good Lookin' " to the deceased. Blood ties loosened and tightened—a Southern gothic sense of predetermination—and at the center, one human, who somewhere found the sanity to say, "I don't want to be a legend, I just want to be a man. . . ."

Leona Williams

Williams, Leona

Tally/MCA Records

Born: January 7, 1943, Vienna, Missouri
Married: Ron Williams

In 1966, huband and wife joined Loretta Lynn's band, "The Blue Kentuckians" (Leona sang and played bass; Ron played drums). In 1968, after more than a dozen singles and two albums for Hickory, she toured thirteen foreign countries including war-torn Vietnam. In 1970, she joined Merle Haggard's Road Show. As a writer, her biggest hit, "Dallas," was recorded by both Tammy Wynette and Connie Smith. As a performer, her hits include "Country Girl with Hot Pants On."

World's Largest Indoor Country Music Show

On Sunday night, March 5, 1978, the country music phenomenon that has been sweeping the rural areas of America for years finally exploded onto the national scene when more than 65,000 people jammed into the mammoth Silverdome Arena in Pontiac, Michigan, to attend "The World's Largest Indoor Country Music Show." The crowd was the biggest in history to attend a country music jamboree.

The record-breaking audience clapped its hands, stomped its feet, and sang along with great enthusiasm and verve as favorite country and bluegrass performers, including members of The Grand Ole Opry, put on the wildest country music show ever.

Kenny Rogers and Dottie West cohosted the gala event, which was taped as a two-hour prime-time special for the NBC TV, seen on April 5, 1977.

More than one hundred performers and musicians took part in this historic country music event, including: Roy Acuff; Minnie Pearl; Grandpa Jones and his wife,

Ramona; The Oak Ridge Boys; The Kendalls; Bill Monroe; The Osborne Brothers; Larry Gatlin; Red Sovine; Little Jimmy Dickens; Don Williams; The Grandfather Mountain Cloggers; singer-songwriter Jeanne Pruett; harmonica virtuoso Charlie McCoy; and many others.

Three headliners—cohosts Kenny Rogers, The Oak Ridge Boys, and The Kendalls—performed the songs that won them 1978 Grammy Awards, the recording industry's highest honors.

Rogers sang his big hit, "Lucille," as well as some of his past golden record sellers. The Oak Ridge Boys, in their set, offered "Have a Little Talk with Jesus," and The Kendalls, in their section, sang "Heaven's Just a Sin Away."

The show was the first nonsports network television show to originate from the Silverdome (the world's biggest indoor arena and the home of the Detroit Lions professional football team). The special was produced by Jim Fitzgerald and Rudy Callicutt, Vincent Scarza, the director.

Rudy Callicutt Productions set the previous attendance record for an indoor country music concert April 16, 1977, with 27,000 fans at the Capitol Center in Washington, D.C., for "The Grand Ole Opry Stars on Tour." The company also produced two specials for the NBC Television stations, "Country Onstage Backstage, I and II," with Fitzgerald as host.

Wynette, Tammy (Wynette Pugh)

Born: May 5, 1942, Red Bay, Alabama
Married: George Jones (div.), Michael Tomlin (div.), George Ritchey
Children: d. Grier, Jackie, Tina, Georgette.

Success must be very sweet for Tammy, who was rejected by five labels before Billy Sherrill signed her to Epic Records and recorded "Apartment #9" (written by Johnny Pay-

Tammy Wynette

check) in August 1966. Since then, she has been named CMA Female Vocalist of the Year for three years in a row (1968–1970). Her 1970 Grammy Award recording of "Stand by Your Man" is one of the biggest-selling singles by a woman in country-music history. Her major hits mark the emergence of a new breed of country woman: "Your Good Girl's Gonna Go Bad," "I Don't Wanna Play House," "Take Me to Your World," "D-I-V-O-R-C-E," and "Kids Say the Darndest Things." Her *Greatest Hits* LP has earned well over a million dollars. In 1977, her "Southern California" duet with ex-husband George Jones was a top country single. By early 1978, she had released three post-George Jones LPs, including *Let's Get Together,* which also became a hit single and *Womanhood.* Her "I Want to See Jesus on the Midnight

Special" also made the hit singles charts. Her happiness was marred by a bizarre kidnapping in a Nashville shopping plaza in September 1978. Released shaken but unharmed, she hired fifty bodyguards for subsequent tours.

Yankee

The New England monthly magazine from the publishers of *The Old Farmer's Almanac.* Rate is $8 for 1 year. Write to *Yankee,* Dublin, NH 03444.

Zodiac Signs of Country Music Stars

Aquarius the Water Bearer
(January 21–February 19)

Aquarius people are the dreamers, the "absent-minded professors" who look as if they're miles away and generally are! It's hard to get them to make a decision but, once they do, you can count on them to keep their word. Original thinkers and extremely independent, Aquarians don't believe in borrowing or lending. Their powers of concentration are strong, if they like what they're doing. Their motto: Live and let live.

Tony Booth	Doug Kershaw
Jimmy Bush	Claude King
Henson Cargill	Pee Wee King
Mac Davis	Jim McReynolds
Don Everly	Ray Stevens
Tennessee Ernie Ford	Ernest Tubb
Claude Gray	Jo Walker
Norma Jean	Jimmy Waverly

Pisces the Fish
(February 20–March 20)

Pisces people are extremely sensitive and can be easily hurt. They encourage others to depend on them and sometimes crack under the strain of too much responsiblity. Pisceans must work extra hard to overcome shyness and uncertainty. Artistic and imaginative, they can create much out of little, make a barren room seem like a palace, an ordinary meal a feast. Practical jokes, mimicry, and impromptu speeches are second nature, as are music, art, and literature.

Liz Anderson	Jan Howard
Jim Ed Brown	Sonny James
Cliff Carlisle	Loretta Lynn
Martha Lou Carson	Jerry Reed
Johnny Cash	Carl Smith
Tommy Cash	Hank Snow
Roy Clark	Cliffie Stone
Dick Curless	Doc Watson
Johnny Dollar	Bob Wills
Dave Dudley	Faron Young
Don Gibson	

Aries the Ram
(March 21–April 20)

Aries people are friendly, forceful, and generally have a beguiling smile. Both idealistic and down to earth, they

Doc Watson

are outspoken about their feelings and often naive in their expectations. Faithful, honorable, and romantic by nature, they may seem easy to take advantage of—but don't try it; you may be surprised how strong an Aries can be.

Bobby Bare	Judy Lynn
Glen Campbell	Loretta Lynn
Jack Clement	Charlie McCoy
Vernon Dalhart	Moon Mulligan
Al Dexter	Johnny Paycheck
Dean Webb	·Carl Perkins
Lefty Frizzell	David Rogers
Merle Haggard	Cal Smith
Emmylou Harris	Margo Smith
John D. Loudermilk	Mal Wiseman
Bob Luman	Sheb Wooley

Taurus the Bull
(April 21–May 21)

Taurus people are strong, ambitious, and flirty. Also stubborn! So don't push them or they may even turn belligerent. They work hard for what they want to achieve and keep trying until they achieve it. Good friends, loyal lovers, they can be counted on in all situations; love, family, and business.

Duane Allen	Ira Louvin
Jack Anglin	O.B. McClinton
Eddy Arnold	Joe Maphis
Bob Ascher	Willie Nelson
Joe Bonsall	Mickey Newbury
Maybelle Carter	Roy Orbison
Danny Davis	Stella Parton
Rodney Dillard	Richard Sterban
Whitey Ford	Johnny Wright
Johnny Horton	Tammy Wynette

Stella Parton

Harry Langdon

Gemini the Twins
(May 22–June 21)

Gemini people are generally in conflict with the two warring sides of their nature. Quick-witted, versatile, and impatient, they usually have ten things going on at once. Their charm makes them good salesmen, politicians, and performers. Often torn between love and fame, they try to achieve the excitement and tranquillity of both. They want traditional values but thrive on change.

Buddy Alan	Waylon Jennings
Lee Arnold	Kris Kristofferson
Chet Atkins	Leon Payne
Clyde Beavers	Kenny Price
Johnny Bond	Don S. Reid
Billy "Crash" Craddock	Wynn Stewart
Howard Dixon	Stringbean (David Akeman)
Jimmy Driftwood	Mary Lou Turner
Red Foley	T. Texas Tyler
Connie Hall	Vic Willis
Tom T. Hall	Hank Williams, Jr.
Burl Ives	

Cancer the Crab
(June 22–July 22)

Cancer people are night people. They thrive on after-dark activities both personal and professional. A natural commedian, the Cancerian has the ability to entertain others and also to be a good audience and enjoy the antics of others. Naturally quiet and gentle, they are soft-hearted, poetic, and usually musical. Money is very important though more for the security it represents than the actual things it buys.

Rosalie Allen	Charlie Louvin
Elton Britt	Jesse McReynolds
Sara Carter	Ken Marvin
June Carter	J. E. Mainer
Cowboy Copas	George Morgan
Roy Drusky	Marvin Rainwater
Lester Flatt	Del Reeves
Woody Guthrie	Jeannie Seely
George Hamilton IV	Rod Sovine
Doyle Holly	Doyle Wilburn
Bradley Kinkaid	Guy Willis

Leo the Lion
(July 23–August 23)

Leo people are astute, organized, and extremely generous party-givers. They are good, if firm, teachers and excellent executives. Romance is essential to their existence yet they prefer to be "strong" and have others lean on them. Personal habits run to extremes: Leo is either a terrible slob or a meticulous fussbudget. A terrific person to have around in an emergency, Leo takes charge with calm authority.

Rex Allen, Jr.	Harold W. Reid
Philipe Balsley	Jim Reeves
Molly Bee	Connie Smith
Hank Cochran	Sammi Smith
Bobbie Gentry	B. J. Thomas
Bobby Helms	Mel Tillis
Homer & Jethro (both)	Justin Tubb
Merle Kilgore	Porter Wagoner
Buck Owens	Tex Williams
Webb Pierce	

Virgo the Virgin
(August 24–September 23)

Virgo people are dependable, sincere, natural worriers, and devoted to their families. Often hypochondriac with mountains of pills, vitamins, and special foods at hand, they are usually extremely healthy. Punctual, practical, and truthful, they are sometimes shy and rarely reveal inner torment. Cheap sentimentality enrages them as does laziness, stupidity, and false flattery. Virgo plays life straight and expects the same of others.

Roy Acuff
Don Bowman
Patsy Cline
Jimmie Davis
Chuck Glaser
Billy Grammer
Sylvia Fricker
George Jones
Buck Kazee
Bill Monroe

Jimmy C. Newman
Tommy Overstreet
Bill Phillips
Jimmie Rodgers
Hank Thompson
Conway Twitty
Freddy Weller
Kitty Wells
Hank Williams

Libra the Scales
(September 24–October 23)

Libra people are good-natured and pleasant but hate to take orders. Although they may seem balanced and agreeble, they are also restless, stubborn, and impatient. Their most frequent natural role is that of the mediator. They don't take sides in a quarrel. Rather, they bring both sides together. Intelligent and creative, they seek beauty and justice in all phases of life. They love deeply, passionately, and make fierce demands on their partners.

Lynn Anderson
Clarence "Tom" Ashley
Gene Autry
Jerry Clower
Stoney Cooper
Dorsey Dixon
Johnny Duncan
Stuart Hamblen
Wanda Jackson
Grandpa Jones
Jerry Lee Lewis

Harry K. McClintock
Uncle Dave Macon
Melba Montgomery
Bonnie Owens
Susan Raye
Marty Robbins
Tanya Tucker
Ian Tyson
Leroy VanDyke
Dottie West

Scorpio the Scorpion
(October 24–November 22)

Scorpio people often hide behind a cold, expressionless face to keep others from moving in too close. Brave in the face of danger or hardship, intensely loyal, Scorpions never forget a slight or a betrayal. If you ask their opinion, they'll be frank, often brutal in their response. Yet when Scorpions fall in love, there is no passion or gentleness to compare with their feelings.

Bill Anderson
Archie Campbell
A. P. Carter
Lee. T. Clayton
Floyd Cramer
Dale Evans
Barbara Fairchild
Donna Fargo
Dallas Frazier

Kinky Friedman
Stonewall Jackson
Patsy Montana
Sonny Osborne
Minnie Pearl
Roy Rogers
Troy Seals
Jean Shepard
Charlie Walker

Sagittarius the Archer
(November 23–December 21)

Sagittarius people are born optimists though sometimes they back the wrong horse. Lucky in love, delightful flirts, they value their freedom and resent anyone trying to box them in. Good tempered, generous hosts, they enjoy life and want others to be happy-go-lucky, too. Rigid authority annoys them; they like breaking silly rules.

Gracie Ashworth
Bill Carlisle
Johnny Carver
Spade Cooley
Little Jimmy Dickens
Freddie Hart
Jim Glaser
David Houston
Ferlin Husky
Brenda Lee
Rose Maddox
Jody Miller
Bob Osborne
Eddie Rabbitt
Charlie Rich
Johnny Rodriguez
Ronnie Sessions
Nat Stuckey
Merle Travis
Billy Edd Wheeler
Teddy Wilburn
Skeeter Willis

Eddie Rabbitt

Capricorn the Goat
(December 22–January 20)

Capricorn people are strong, quiet types who secretly yearn for praise and admiration. Beneath the quiet facade is often a zany sense of humor and a willingness to take chances. Capricorns usually have a deep sense of tradition yet give themselves wholeheartedly to the most unorthodox goals. They are good at delegating authority. They hate to waste time. They travel when necessary but prefer staying home.

Rex Allen
Skeeter Davis
Phil Everly
William Lee Golden
Jack Greene
Hawkshaw Hawkins
Goldie Hill
Bobby Lord
Lulu Belle
Leon McAuliff

Barbara Mandrell
Rose Lee Mathis
Roger Miller
Dolly Parton
Elvis Presley
Ray Price
Tex Ritter
Earl Scruggs
Billy Waller
Slim Whitman

Index